The Bolsheviks and Britain during the Russian Revolution and Civil War, 1917–24

The Bolsheviks and Britain during the Russian Revolution and Civil War, 1917–24

Evgeny Sergeev

BLOOMSBURY ACADEMIC
LONDON • NEW YORK • OXFORD • NEW DELHI • SYDNEY

BLOOMSBURY ACADEMIC
Bloomsbury Publishing Plc
50 Bedford Square, London, WC1B 3DP, UK
1385 Broadway, New York, NY 10018, USA
29 Earlsfort Terrace, Dublin 2, Ireland

BLOOMSBURY, BLOOMSBURY ACADEMIC and the Diana logo are trademarks of
Bloomsbury Publishing Plc

First published in Great Britain 2022
Paperback edition first published 2024

Copyright © Evgeny Sergeev, 2022

Evgeny Sergeev has asserted his right under the Copyright, Designs and Patents Act, 1988,
to be identified as Author of this work.

The dogs of the Entente: Denikin, Kolchak, Yudenich, 1919. Private Collection.
Deni (Denisov), Viktor Nikolaevich (1893–1946). (© Hulton Archive / Getty Images)

All rights reserved. No part of this publication may be reproduced
or transmitted in any form or by any means, electronic or mechanical,
including photocopying, recording, or any information storage or
retrieval system, without prior permission in writing from the publishers.

Bloomsbury Publishing Plc does not have any control over, or responsibility
for, any third-party websites referred to or in this book. All internet addresses given in
this book were correct at the time of going to press. The author and publisher regret any
inconvenience caused if addresses have changed or sites have ceased to exist, but can
accept no responsibility for any such changes.

A catalogue record for this book is available from the British Library.

A catalog record for this book is available from the Library of Congress.

ISBN:	HB:	978-1-3502-7351-1
	PB:	978-1-3502-7350-4
	ePDF:	978-1-3502-7352-8
	eBook:	978-1-3502-7353-5

Typeset by Integra Software Services Pvt. Ltd.

To find out more about our authors and books visit www.bloomsbury.com
and sign up for our newsletters.

For Irina, Denis and Oleg

Contents

List of Illustrations	viii
List of Maps	ix
Preface	x
Maps	xi
Acknowledgements	xiii
List of Abbreviations	xiv
Select Chronology	xvii
Introduction	1
1 The problem of Brest in Soviet-British relations	5
2 British armed intervention 'by agreement'	23
3 The so-called 'complot of ambassadors'	39
4 Oriental trends of the Soviet-British relations, 1918	53
5 'Stillborn crusade' against Bolsheviks and 'Russian question' at the Paris Peace Conference	71
6 The Baltic problem, Soviet-Polish war and trade negotiations	89
7 From bad to worse: Soviet-British relations in the Middle and Far East, 1919–22	109
8 Soviet Russia and Great Britain at the international conferences, 1922–3	123
9 The 'Curzon ultimatum' of 1923	139
10 The USSR's recognition by Britain and its repercussions	151
Epilogue	167
Notes	171
Select bibliography	231
Index	258

Illustrations

1	Robert Bruce Lockhart, head of diplomatic delegation to Russia, 1918	13
2	Soviet diplomacy front-runners, 1918–24	16
3	Stepan Shaumian, chairman of the Baku Commune, 1918	55
4	General Mayor Lionel Dunsterville with his staff in Baku, 1918	57
5	General Mayor Wilfrid Malleson, 1918	57
6	British delegation at the Paris Peace Conference, 1919	73
7	'Into Russia, Out of Russia', Caricature, *Daily Express*, 8 September 1919	74
8	'Winston's Bag', Caricature, Star, 21 January 1920	88
9	'Russian Jazz', Caricature, *Star*, 31 May 1920	99
10	British delegation at the Cannes Conference, 1922	128
11	Christian Rakovski, Soviet charge d'affaires, 1924	148
12	James Ramsay Macdonald, prime minister, 1924	152
13	Grigory Zinoviev, leader of the Comintern, 1924	160

Maps

1 British military-diplomatic missions to Soviet Turkestan, 1918–20   xi
2 British armed intervention in the former Russian Empire, 1918–20   xii

Preface

Nobody can deny that a long book is best served by a short preface. I began research for this monograph after my study on the history of the Russo-British competition for the mastery over Asia – the so-called *Great Game* – materialized in the monograph dedicated to the period of 1857–1907. Obsessed with the idea of a fresh, unbiased representation of bilateral relations in the twentieth century, I soon realized the paucity of scholarly studies on this subject with some of them full of stereotypes and propaganda clichés. That is why my purpose was to bridge this gap through analysing objectives, methods, achievements and failures of both Russian and British sides in the epoch of global revolutionary turmoil. The sources I researched in archives and libraries comprised declassified documents as well as those memories, diaries and private correspondence which have been recently published in both Russian and English.

In fact, there has been as yet no comprehensive work addressed to the entire span of Russia's contacts with the UK in political, economic and cultural spheres since the Bolshevik revolution up to the collapse of the Soviet Union. Hence, I believe that the present volume opens a series of academic monographs covering the controversial history of ups and downs in the Russo-British intercourse through the age of industrial development. It is also hoped that the contents of this book will help to promote more reflection among historians and policy makers on the questions under consideration while demonstrating that sometimes the study of history can bring insights for present and future predicaments.

Maps

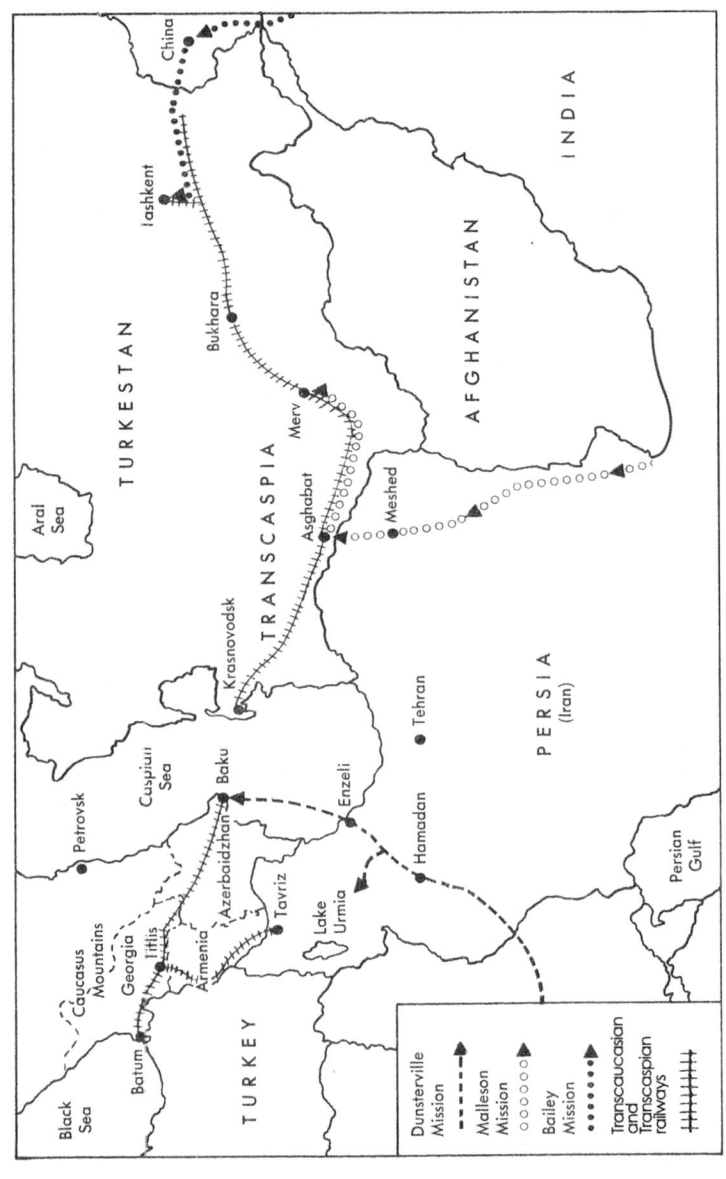

Map 1 British military-diplomatic missions to Soviet Turkestan, 1918–20.

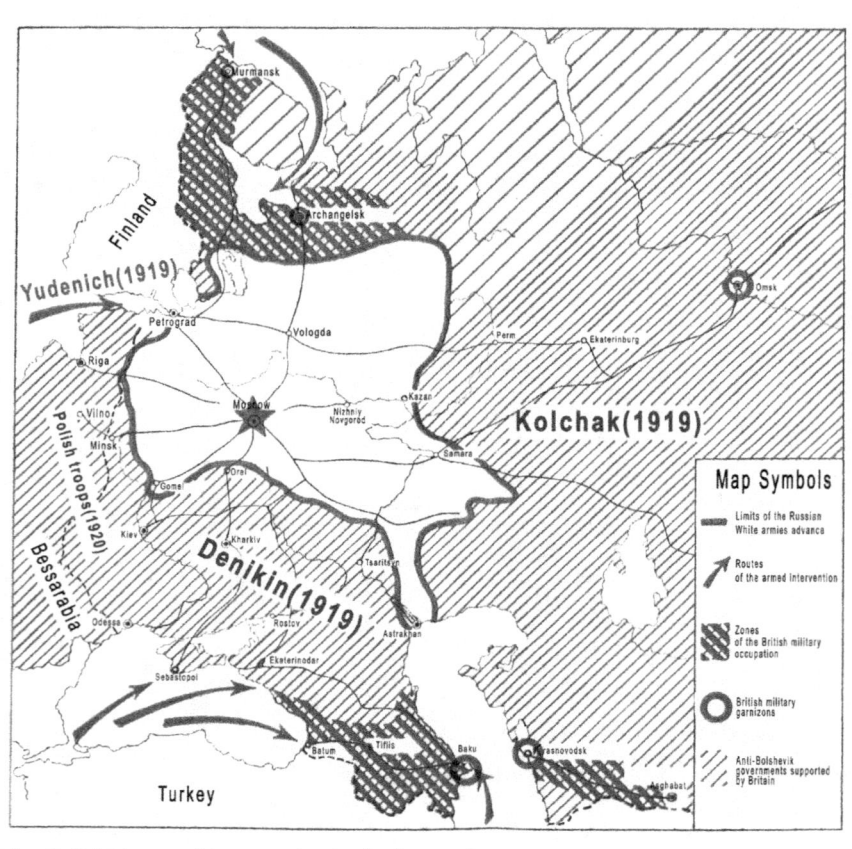

Map 2 British armed intervention in the former Russian Empire, 1918–20.

Acknowledgements

The research has been made easier by the sympathy of many people whose aid was of great importance to me. That is why I have incurred many debts of gratitude, and it is my pleasure to acknowledge them. There are many colleagues from Russian and British academic institutes and universities, archivists and librarians who provided much advice and valuable recommendations in preparing the book for publication. I have to thank my colleagues – the members of the international Study Group on the Russian Revolution, especially James Ryan, with whom I discussed the composition of the manuscript – for debating the results of my research at the seminars in 2017–21. My special gratitude goes also to Mark Posser, who contributed to editing one of the chapters. I trust that other benefactors and copyright owners whom I have failed to trace or thank will accept my gratitude and forgive my shortcomings. In the final stages I have been helped significantly by the editors of Bloomsbury Academic Publishing – Rhodri Mogford and Laura Reeves who skillfully guided me through the publication process.

To the beloved members of my family – Irina, Denis and Oleg, I owe an unrepayable personal debt for their understanding and patience that made it possible for the monograph to see the light of day.

Abbreviations

Text

ARA	American Relief Administration
AFSR	Armed Forces of Southern Russia
ARCOS	All-Russian Cooperative Society
ASWC	Allied Supreme War Council
C-in-C	Commander in Chief
CP	Conservative (Unionist) Party
CPGB	Communist Party of Great Britain
FO PID	Foreign Office Political Intelligence Department
GC&CS	Government Code and Cipher School
ILP	Independent Labour Party
LP	Labour Party
MI5	Security Service (UK) для объяснения большей части сокращений
MI6	Secret Intelligence Service (UK)
MP	Member of Parliament
NKID	Narodnyi Kommissariat inostrannykh del (People's Commissariat for Foreign Affairs) (Russia)
OGPU	Ob'edinennoe glavnoe politicheskoe upravlenie (Special Main Political Department), the heir to the Cheka
Politburo	Politicheskoe Bureau Rossiiskoi Kommunisticheskoi Partii (bol'shevikov) (Political Bureau of the Russian Communist Party (Bolsheviks))
POWs	prisoners of war
SNK	Soviet Narodnykh Komissarov (Council of People's Commissars)
TUC	Trades Union Congress
VCHEKA	Vserossiiskaia Chrezvychainaia komissiia po bor'be s kontrrevoliutsiei i sabotazhem (All-Russian Extraordinary Commission on combatting counter-revolution and sabotage)

VSUR	Vooruzhennye sily yuga Rossii (Supreme Commandment of Southern Russia)
Zentrosouz	Zentral'nyi souz rossiikikh potrebitelskikh obstchestv (Central Union of Russian Consumer Societies)

Notes and bibliography

ADM	Admiralty Papers (UK)
AMEL	Leo Amery Papers
AVPRF	Arkhiv vneshnei politiki Rossiiskoi Federatsii (Russian Federation Archive of Foreign Policy)
BDFA	British Documents on Foreign Affairs
BL	British Library
BLAAS	British Library African and Asian Studies
CAB	Cabinet Office Papers
CO	Colonial Office Papers
CPGB	Communist Party of Great Britain
CU CAC	Cambridge University Churchill Archives Center
CUL	Cambridge University Library
CUP	Cambridge University Press
DBFP	Documents on British Foreign Policy
DS	David Soskice Papers
DVP SSSR	Dokumenty vneshnei politiki SSSR (Documents of the USSR foreign policy)
FO	Foreign Office Papers
FRUS	Papers Relating to the Foreign Relations of the United States
GARF	Gosudarstvennyi Arkhiv Rossiiskoi Federatsii (Russian Federation State Archive)
HO	Home Office Papers
HP	Samuel Hoare (Lord Templewood) Papers
HUP	Harvard University Press
HMSO	His (Her) Majesty Stationary Office
KV	Security Service Personal Files

LG	David Lloyd George Papers
MS. Milner	Alfred Milner Papers
MUN	Ministry of Munitions Papers
MUP	Manchester University Press
OUBL	Oxford University Bodleian Library
OUP	Oxford University Press
PA	Parliamentary Archives (House of Lords)
PD	Parliamentary debates
PRO	Public Record Office
PUP	Princeton University Press
RGAE	Rossiikii gosudarstvennyi arkhiv ekonomiki (Russian State Archive of Economics)
RGASPI	Rossiikii gosudarstvennyi arkhiv sotsial'no-politicheskoi istorii (Russian State Archive of Social-Political History)
RGAVMF	Rossiikii gosudarstvennyi arkhiv Voenno-Morskogo Flota (Russian State Naval Archives)
RGVA	Rossiiskii gosudarstvennyi voennyi arkhiv (Russian State Military Archive)
T	Treasury Papers
TNA	The National Archives
TS	Treasury Solicitor Papers
UB CRLSC	University of Birmingham, Cadbury Research Library, Special collections
UCP	University of California Press
WO	War Office Papers
YUP	Yale University Press

Select Chronology

1917

Dates	Events
8–16 Mar	February stage of the Great Russian revolution
30 Mar	Britain recognized Russian Provisional government
Jun	Arthur Henderson's mission to Russia
3 Jun	Leeds 'Soviet' Convention
7–8 Nov	November stage of the Great Russian revolution – Bolsheviks headed by Lenin took over in Petrograd
8 Nov	Decree on Peace adopted by the Second All-Russian Congress of Soviets
23 Nov	Britain and other major Entente states remonstrated against Lenin's proposal to start peace negotiations with the Quadruple Alliance
25 Nov	All-Russian Constituent Assembly elected
3 Dec	Peace negotiations started in Brest-Litovsk
23 Dec	Cecil – Milner memorandum on the spheres of responsibility in European Russia

1918

Dates	Events
4 Jan	Litvinov appointed Soviet representative in London
5 Jan	Russian expeditionary forces began to withdraw from Eastern Anatolia and Northern Persia
7 Jan	Buchanan left Petrograd for London
13 Jan	Lockhart departed from Britain to Russia
19 Jan	All-Russian Constituent Assembly prorogued
3 Feb	Russian obligations for foreign loans cancelled by the Bolsheviks
10 Feb	Trotsky broke negotiations with the Quadruple Alliance in Brest-Litovsk; Kamenev and Zalkind arrived in Britain for diplomatic consultations
15 Feb	Lockhart's first meeting with Trotsky
18 Feb	German troops resumed their advance on the Eastern front

28 Feb	Foreign diplomatic missions left Petrograd for Vologda
3 Mar	Treaty of Brest-Litovsk signed
6 Mar	First British expeditionary troops landed at Murmansk
5 Apr	Japanese and British troops landed at Vladivostok
22 Apr	Decree on state monopoly of foreign trade adopted by the SNK Bailey left Srinagar for Tashkent on a secret mission
14 May	Czechoslovak legionnaires rebelled in Chelyabinsk
27 Jun	Bicherakhov signed agreement with Dunsterforce
6–7 Jul	Left Socialist Revolutionaries revolted in Moscow
17 July	The tsarist family shot in Ekaterinburg
22 Jul	British economic mission arrived in Moscow
2 Aug	Anti-Bolshevik coup occurred in Arkhangelsk while the Entente expeditionary troops entered the seaport
4 Aug	Dunsterforce arrived in Baku
9 Aug	British Consulate General closed in Moscow
25 Aug	'Complot of ambassadors' set into motion in Moscow and Petrograd
31 Aug	British naval attaché Francis Cromie shot by the Cheka agents in Petrograd
14 Sep	Dunsterforce evacuated from Baku
18–19 Sep	Twenty-six Baku Commissars shot in the Transcaspian desert of Kizyl-Arvat
11 Nov	Armistice in Compiegne ended the First World War
17 Nov	British troops returned to Baku
23–7 Nov	British troops landed at the Russian Black Sea ports of Novorossiysk, Sebastopol and Odessa
25 Nov	State trial for the 'Lockhart (ambassadors') plot' opened in Moscow
25–7 Dec	Two Soviet Baltic Float destroyers bombarded Revel (Tallinn)

1919

4–6 Jan	First skirmishes between Soviet and Polish troops in the Vilna area
18 Jan	International Peace Conference opened in Paris 'Hands off Russia' committees began to emerge in Britain
4–6 Mar	British government decided to completely withdraw from Russia

Select Chronology

9–14 Mar	Bullitt held talks with Soviet leaders in Moscow
15 Mar	Communist International (Comintern) founded in Moscow
3 May	Third Anglo-Afghan War began
21 May	British Caspian Naval Flotilla defeated the Red Caspian Flotilla in the Tuba-Karahan Bay
29 May	British military instructors used poison gas against the Red Army troops to the south of Arkhangelsk
12 Jun	Declaration of Allied support to Admiral Kolchak adopted in Paris
28 Jun	Peace treaty between the Allies and Germany signed in Versailles
4 Jul	The Cabinet recognized unofficial state of war with the Bolsheviks
3 Aug	British troops evacuated from Krasnovodsk
26–7 Sep	Last Entente expeditionary troops withdrew from Arkhangelsk
12 Oct	Last Entente expeditionary troops evacuated from Murmansk
8 Nov	Lloyd George made speech on peace with the Bolsheviks
18 Dec	Bailey left Bukhara for Mashhad

1920

16 Jan	Entente Supreme Council decided to lift the blockade of Soviet Russia
12 Feb	Anglo-Soviet agreement (Litvinov–O'Grady) on the exchange of POWs signed in Stockholm
24 Apr	The first TUC delegation left Britain for Soviet Russia
25 Apr	Polish troops launched a general offensive against the Red Army
18 May	Red marines landed at the Persian seaport of Enzeli
31 May	Soviet trade delegation opened talks with Lloyd George in London
9 Jun	Soviet trading company ARCOS established in London
8–10 Jul	The Entente's conference held in Spa (Belgium)
10 Jul	British troops evacuated from Batum
31 Jul	Councils of action established in Britain to oppose new armed intervention against Soviet Russia
14–17 Aug	Defeat of the Bolshevik troops on the Vistula
23–4 Aug	National minority movement established in London

8 Sep	The First congress of the peoples of the Orient opened in Baku
11 Sep	Kamenev left London for Moscow
12 Oct	Armistice between Soviet Russia and Poland concluded in Riga

1921

16 Mar	Anglo-Soviet trade agreement signed in London
18 Mar	Peace treaty between Soviet Russia and Poland signed in Riga
1 Apr	Royal Navy suspended hostilities against the Bolshevik battleships and submarines

1922

10 Jan	Entente Supreme Council invited Soviet official delegation to participate in the Genoa conference
17 Mar	The Baltic League proclaimed in Warsaw with Britain's support
10 Apr	International economic conference opened in Genova
16 Apr	Soviet-German treaty signed in Rapallo
15 Jun	International economic conference opened in The Hague
5 Oct	Krassin–Urquhart contract annulled by the Kremlin
20 Nov	International conference on the Turkish question opened in Lausanne
30 Dec	Soviet Union established

1923

22 Mar	Demonstrative anti-clerical trial opened in Moscow
28 Mar	Two British trawlers detained by the Soviet coastal guards near Murmansk
31 Mar	Offensive diplomatic note sent to British mission in Moscow
7 May	One more British trawler arrested in the Soviet territorial waters
8 May	Curzon declared 'ultimatum' to the Soviet government
4 Jun	Soviet government acceded to principal British claims
30 Aug	British government's accord with Rakovsky's appointment as the charge d'affaires
15 Oct	Soviet-British Society for refunding grain export set up in London

1924

21 Jan	Death of Vladimir Lenin
22 Jan	First Labour government established
1 Feb	British *de jure* recognition of the Soviet Union
14 Apr	Anglo-Soviet conference opened in London
10 Jul	Society for cultural reproachment between Britain and the USSR founded in London
5 Aug	London Metropolitan Police searched the premises of the *Workers' Weekly* because of the Campbell incident
8 Aug	Anglo-Soviet general and commercial treaties signed in London
25 Oct	Zinoviev (Comintern) letter published in British press
29 Oct	Labour Party defeated in the general election
11 Nov	The second TUC delegation left Britain for the USSR
21 Nov	Conservative Government repudiated Anglo-Soviet Treaties

Introduction

Perhaps it is no exaggeration to say that the relatively short period of 1918–24 holds a special place in the relations between Russia and Great Britain. The formation of the Versailles international order had an impact on both the spirit and dynamics of bilateral contacts in all spheres, when initial hostility, reflected in the Entente's intervention against the Soviet regime, changed first to humanitarian, then to economic and finally to political collaboration, culminating in the USSR's diplomatic recognition by the UK.

Despite the importance of this topic, the scholarship of the Soviet Russia's relations with Britain in the immediate aftermath of the First World War still lacked a comprehensive study based on both Russian and British primary sources. My purpose is therefore to bridge this gap by the reconstruction of the trends which strongly affected the establishment of the Versailles–Washington system of international relations.

For clarity, it is necessary from the very beginning to point to the issues remaining outside the scope of my research. First, I do not intend to discuss the domestic developments in Russia because it was analysed in numerous academic monographs and articles. Second, this study does not suggest any comprehensive consideration of the Allied armed intervention as well as that of the restoring of the Entente states' relations with Moscow after the withdrawal of Western troops from Russia. It was Britain's contribution to this controversial process that I meticulously explore bearing in mind its regional variations and interconnection with the policies of other contemporary geopolitical actors.

In the process of writing this book, I posed and sought to find an adequate answer to the following questions of primary importance, without an understanding of which it is hardly possible to reconstruct the dynamics of Russian-British relations in the twentieth century: How did the revolutionary events of 1917 affect the military alliance between Petrograd and London? What were the origins of a dramatic transition from friendly cooperation to outright animosity in the later years? Why did the British armed intervention fail, and what are the reasons for the recognition of the Bolshevik dictatorship by the UK government?

The monograph approaches these problems by a combination of chronological, typological and comparative narration focusing on diplomatic documents of various origins, declassified intelligence reports, parliamentary debates and private papers, most of which have never been examined by researchers. To achieve the proposed goal, I suggest the detached and balanced interpretation of sources through the cross-verification of seemingly controversial and often debated evidence from Russian and British archives. To verify the bulk of biographical materials, chronological periods and geographical locations, I necessitated a select number of reference editions.[1]

It seems prudent to begin any survey by discussing the scholarship of the selected topic. Soviet historians could work merely with the published volumes of diplomatic correspondence and proceedings of international conferences or national periodicals. In addition, their academic studies were carried out under hard ideological pressure while being subjected to severe political censorship. The frequent inaccessibility of archival records as well as the inability to research in the UK national archives deprived Russian explorers of many significant primary sources. To emasculate their studies, Soviet authorities made almost impossible discussions with foreign colleagues at academic conferences which often led to biased and superficial conclusions. The situation changed for the better only after the end of the Cold War epoch, when the pluralism of conceptual approaches took over in the post-Soviet scholarship.[2]

On the other hand, for Western historians delivering their attention to contacts between Moscow and London in the first half of the 1920s, Soviet archives and libraries continued to be inaccessible until the end of the twentieth century. Besides that, the general admission to private collections of papers has been restricted in the UK until the beginning of the 2000s. Suffice it to note that many MI5 files have been declassified only ten years ago. This led to the remarkably limited number of books highlighting the key events in the Soviet-British diplomatic intercourse after the Bolshevik revolution which were published in the previous decades.[3]

The temporal framework of the monograph is justified by the developments which decisively influenced bilateral relations. The starting point is the Great Russian Revolution of 1917. Although it caused a protracted Civil War, the narration covers its aftermath until 1924 when the Soviet-British reproachment occurred. The diplomatic recognition led to the rearrangement of the contacts between Soviet Russia and Great Britain, indicating transition from military, sometimes severe confrontation to reluctant, albeit necessary collaboration.[4] It seems this approach is assuming even more relevance in the modern period when the global comity of nations is forced to confront with the unprecedented challenges of the post-industrial period in various fields – from climate changes and pandemics to the hazards of international terrorism and uncontrolled refugees' invasion in developed countries.

The structure of the book has been adapted to the author's view of the period under description. Its core is organized as ten chapters dealing with various problems of the Soviet-British intercourse during 1918–24, beginning with the period of the Russian revolution and Civil War. Several consequent sections tackle crucial and much debated issues referring to the normalization of bilateral relations in the aftermath of the Entente's armed interference into Russian domestic affairs.

Each chapter is provided with epigraphs and endnotes while the whole contents are also supplied with select chronology and bibliography. The images of politicians, diplomats or military commanders mentioned in the book as well as other placates assist the general reader to perceive the 'spirit of the era'. All dates are rendered according to the Gregorian calendar employed in the West, which is thirteen days ahead of the Julian one in use by the Russians before 1 February 1918. The metric system is usually used unless otherwise stated. A golden rouble was equivalent to one tenth of a pound sterling in 1917. Transliteration from the Cyrillic alphabet adheres to the Library of Congress system without diacritic marks, while common spellings are given to most proper names.

In notes and commentaries for archival materials, the author puts *ob.* for folio's backside, *f.* for *fond* (collection), *op.* for *opis'* (inventory), *pap.* for *papka* (folder), *d.* for *delo* (file), *l. (ll.)* for *list (lists)* (folio, folios) and col. (cols) for column (columns).

1

The problem of Brest in Soviet-British relations

An apparition with countenance different from any yet seen on earth stood in the place of the old ally. We saw a state without a nation, an army without a country, a religion without a God.

Winston Churchill[1]

After the signing of the 1907 Anglo-Russian convention on the delimitation of spheres of influence in Asia, the previous confrontation gave way to reproachment turning into alliance during the First World War. Yet even before the Bolshevik party seized the state power in November 1917, and the new Russian government – Council of People's Commissars (Soviet Narodnykh Komissarov – SNK) chaired by Vladimir Lenin – embarked on peace negotiations with the Quadruple Alliance, the British ruling elites plotted a new political course towards Russia.[2]

The euphoria among left-wing political groups caused by the downfall of the tsarist autocratic rule and the establishment of the democratic Provisional government enthused certain Labour Party front-runners, such as James Ramsay Macdonald and Philip Snowden, to agitate in favour of the Russian revolutionary experience. As one prominent Labour leader put it in the newspaper article, 'the revolution in Russia is the biggest event of the war. If it succeeds in establishing a Social Democratic Republic it will be the most momentous event in the history of our time'.[3] What seemed even more important for British public opinion, the overthrow of the autocratic regime in Russia was inseparable from the hope of a speedy and just ending to the terrible war. Unsurprisingly, the so-called Leeds Convention adopted by 1,200 participants of the pacifist meeting on 3 June advocated holding elections to local workers' and soldiers' councils across Britain.[4] Meanwhile the members of the Imperial War Cabinet under David Lloyd George, the distinguished leader of the Liberal Party, debated two lengthy memoranda regarding Russian foreign and domestic affairs.

The first note by George Nathaniel Curzon, Lord President of the Privy council, was full of scepticism for the prospects of Russia's further participation in the coalition war. The former viceroy of India and the future foreign secretary expected its imminent exit from the Entente due to the fecklessness of administration, collapse of economic infrastructure and general disarray of public order.[5]

Leo Amery, the parliamentary under-secretary of state for foreign affairs, drafted the second memorandum. Representing an influential, albeit informal, cohort of politicians, associated with the *Round Table* – an international journal launched in 1910, he supervised the delivery of weekly reviews to British ministers and military commanders as well as to the leaders of British dominions.[6] Amery was convinced that although Russia was unlikely to completely stop hostilities, it would most certainly confine the war efforts to purely defensive operations.[7]

The ill-fated offensive by the former imperial army on the Eastern front in July 1917 following the capture of Riga and the Monsoon islands by the German troops in September–October added to the obvious inability of the Russian Naval General Staff to carry out even a limited amphibious operation against the Ottoman forces in the Straits of Bosporus. The disastrous experiences only intensified the British annoyance of their eastern ally's aspirations for a separate peace with the Quadruple Alliance. At the regular Cabinet session on 17 September 1917, the ministers discussed the wire from George Buchanan, the ambassador to Petrograd.[8] They were unanimous in the opinion that an extremely prudent policy towards Russia seemed the only possible scenario in these circumstances, given the failed British attempt to mediate between Alexander Kerensky, who chaired the Provisional government, and Infantry General Lavr Kornilov, the Russian C-in-C at the time, allegedly plotting a coup d'état.[9]

Meanwhile the Entente strategic position continued to deteriorate. Apart from heavy war casualties and the food shortage caused by merciless attacks of German submarines, widespread tiredness of the wartime restrictions was running rampant in civil population. Despite the United States' siding with the Entente since April 1917, victory still seemed to many contemporary observers a remote achievement. This is evidenced by Charles Scott, the editor of the liberal *Manchester Guardian* and an intimate of Lloyd George. Scott's conversation with Winston Churchill, then the minister of munitions, mentioned a possible compromise with Germany by offering it Poland and Lithuania. Although Churchill eventually abandoned this idea, Lloyd George and the American President Woodrow Wilson did not rule out analogous projects.[10]

In a letter to King George V on 18 October 1917, the prime minister pointed out to the challenges which the Cabinet met in the foreign policy. These were a possible withdrawal of Russia and Italy from the war, the French reluctance to intensify war efforts and the delay in the American troops' arrival at the Western front. All these motivations made it inevitable for Britain to carry on fighting virtually alone, sacrificing the 'colour of the nation' on the altar of victory. Hence, concluded Lloyd George, the British would have to strictly adhere to defensive strategy in several months to come while escalating their naval blockade of Germany in the war of attrition.[11]

Doubtlessly, the British desire was that Russia remain in the war and the Eastern front be maintained, and if this required changes in war aims, then the British were willing to do so.[12] However, even among the Unionist (Conservative) leaders, the partisans of a 'compromise with the Second Reich at any price' like Henry Lansdowne, the former head of the Foreign and War Offices, were rapidly gaining support. His proposal to Arthur James Balfour, the foreign secretary, on 16 November 1917, included five major points which provided for the immediate termination of hostilities and the return of the warring states to the situation *ante bellum*. Two weeks later, Lansdowne published an open letter of the same content in the *Daily Telegraph*.[13]

It should be stressed that Kerensky and Mikhail Teretschenko, the last foreign minister of the Provisional government, vacillated between the assurances of the British Cabinet in the Russian capability to go on fighting and the bitter reproaches to Whitehall on the British naval inactivity in the Baltic theatre of war. As if to add to London's frustration, the two Russian statesmen sent greetings to the conference of Sinn Fein, the National Irish Party.[14] Kerensky's modern biographer wrote that he always expressed an ambivalent attitude towards the Entente: while advocating the urgency to fight side by side with allies, he bestowed on them a high moral obligation to provide an unlimited assistance to a newborn Russian democratic republic.[15]

A private message to Lloyd George became Kerensky's last desperate diplomatic move. It was William Somerset Maugham, later a brilliant novelist and dramatist, whom Kerensky asked to consign it to Lloyd George on the very eve of the Bolsheviks' coup in Petrograd. Maugham, dispatched by the MI6 to collect intelligence on the current developments in Russia, agreed to act as a courier between the prime ministers.[16] In Kerensky's opinion, Lloyd George ought to request Berlin to commence preliminary peace negotiations, but under such conditions that Germany would hardly accept. The Kaiser's rejection, in turn, would have helped the Provisional government to reshuffle the war mechanism and attest to the Central powers' disregard to seek for equitable armistice.[17]

Against this international background, the sensational news began to come from Petrograd, where the Maximalists, as European periodicals called the Bolsheviks, arrested the members of the Provisional government on 7-8 November, only Kerensky escaping from the capital at the last moment. Yet the initial information about a new surge of turmoil in Russia met a feeble reaction from either the UK officials or the public at large. Suffice it to say that the Entente leaders and diplomats had sent an invitation to Teretschenko to attend a regular Allied conference early in November. The Russian foreign minister was expected to arrive in Paris 'escorted' by ambassador Buchanan.[18] While ignoring abstruse pieces of intelligence, the Cabinet debated the question of Russia's representation in the inter-allied council on the very day of the Bolsheviks' seizure of the state power. Ironically, the ministers appeared far more concerned with the collapse of the Italian army at Caporetto on the Austrian front than with the anti-democratic putsch in Petrograd.[19]

However, the British mass-media commented on the Russian situation as early as on 8 November, when the conservative *Morning Post* came out with the headline 'Revolution Made by Germany'. The author maintained that Lenin together with his associates, no matter how long their grip on power would be, had already proved to act as the bitter enemies of Britain and clear friends of Germany.[20] Yet whatever puzzling the Russian 'jig-saw' might seem to European press, the Foreign Office almost immediately terminated the diplomatic accreditation of Konstantin Nabokov, the acting charge d'affaires of the former government.[21]

Meanwhile the Allied diplomatic corps conferred at the premises of the British mission in Petrograd at the initiative of Joseph Noulens, the French ambassador to

Russia.²² The meeting led to further consultations between Buchanan and Noulens on 9 November, when both diplomats did not exclude the occupation of the Russian capital by the Entente military contingents, should Kerensky regain control over it.²³ Yet the insurgency of the Petrograd military cadets along with the ineffectual attempt by the Committee for the Salvation of Motherland and Revolution to fight back against the Maximalists ended in a complete debacle. The coup in Petrograd triggered the pro-Bolshevik Red guards taking over their opponents in Moscow following a week of intense street skirmishes. The apparent void of administration in Central Russia and the demagogic decree of peace proclaimed by the Second All-Russian Congress of Soviets on 8 November spurred Buchanan to set up at least temporary contacts with the Bolshevik administration. According to the intelligence, merely three active Russian armies out of five had submitted to the Bolshevik rule by mid-November 1917.²⁴ As some observers recalled, the notions akin to the 'peace without annexations and contributions' seemed a novelty to many Russian soldiers who considered them to be simply the 'nicknames of the former Tsar and Tsarina'.²⁵

In Buchanan's opinion, what the Entente powers needed was at least to demonstrate preparedness to contemplate the Bolshevik terms of the armistice to keep the eastern ally at war and thwart Germany's access to Russia's rich natural resources. On 20 November, the ambassador reported to London: 'Personally, I believe we need to set with it [the Bolshevik Government] at least some kind of contact for running current affairs'.²⁶ The transformation of his attitude to the Bolsheviks might be also explained by allegations of the prearranged selling the Baltic Fleet battleships to the Germans. These rumours even encouraged the Admiralty to scheme a torpedo attack against the Russian men-of-war by seven submarines stationed at the naval base proxy to the Finnish seaport of Helsingfors (Helsinki). On the other hand, the War Office instructed the Captain of the First Rank (later Commodore) Francis Cromie, the acting naval attaché in Petrograd, to persuade the Baltic Fleet chief officers either to boycott the transfer of Russian dreadnoughts to the enemy or to arrange for sinking them by themselves.²⁷ What was more important, by the end of November, opinion was firm in London that 'Russia should not be considered in future Allied military plans and that no shipping should be allocated to her'.²⁸

The insufficient and conflicting pieces of intelligence from various sources led Whitehall to opt for a 'wait-and-see' political course. Another lamentable rationale for this alternative might be the deficient knowledge of new Russian political frontrunners. As one diplomatic historian truly remarked, 'the titular government of Russia was composed of the unknown personalities of unpredictable quality, mouthing phrases of unmeasurable menace'.²⁹

London's initial restraint was also fueled by Russian domestic affairs. In the first place, the authority of Kerensky's last administration inside the country declined to such an extent by the end of October 1917 that the possibility of the Bolshevik coup merely worried foreign diplomats. According to their forecasts, if Lenin overthrew Kerensky, the road to a 'new more vigorous government' would be opened in a few weeks.³⁰ Secondly, the British ruling circles anticipated the election of the All-Russian Constituent Assembly which, according to the repeated statements by the Provisional government, was bound to legitimize a democratic regime.³¹

Yet it took not so much time for these expectations to have given way to the overall anxiety. On 9 November, the readers of several newspapers became aware of the bloody events in Petrograd. For example, The *Times*' editorial proclaimed 'Russia's critical hour'.[32] In the following days, other journals speculated on the objectives of Lenin's government, especially, upon those concerning the Eastern front. Newspaper columnists almost unanimously juxtaposed the March anti-monarchy people's revolution with the November usurpation of state power by a handful of the Maximalists, allegedly subsidized by Berlin. However, the European press agencies expected the Russian Germanophiles' failure to stop the country's disintegration, had the First World War continued to go on, whereas a minor number of left-wing and pacifist periodicals did not rule out an armistice in short time.[33]

The MI5 personal files relating to Lenin and other Bolshevik front-runners shed light on what information the Cabinet disposed to assess Russia's prospects to sign a separate peace treaty with Germany and its satellites. Some intelligence experts argued that the Bolsheviks' concept of international relations consisted of three points. Firstly, since Soviet Russia and Germany allegedly remained the latent allies despite a temporal confrontation, they took little interest in the creation of the world order modelled according to a democratic pattern. This was allegedly evidenced by Lenin's content to receive financial allocations from Berlin to a value of 4 million roubles. Secondly, the Bolshevik and German political goals in Europe corresponded tactically, but not strategically, because the former sought the communist revolution to gain sway on the sub-continent while the latter hankered for Germany to establish hegemony in Europe. Finally, Lenin was convinced that the Bolshevik administration ought to copy certain German state, industrial and financial structures to improve domestic governance.[34]

Since 1915 the MI5 agents had been making up the personal dossiers of the leading Maximalists such as Lev Trotsky, Grigory Zinoviev, Leonid Krassin and others.[35] They seemed to be first to analyse the Bolshevik programme as a polemical document challenging the British foreign policy's goals. Hence, the MI5 drew the Cabinet's attention to the activities of Maximalists. A special instruction to the MI5 agents reads, 'Remember that the Bolsheviks loath Britain and its well-organized democratic regime more than any other country.'[36]

Apart from MI5 files, the weekly reports about Russia by the Foreign Office indicated that 'Bolshevism is essentially a Russian disease; it is Tolstoism distorted and carried to extreme limits. But in the present case it has been fastened on and poisoned by the Germans for their own purposes.'[37]

Captain George Hill, one of the most informed and effective MI6 officers, who visited the Smolny Institute – the Bolshevik headquarters in Petrograd – shortly after the November coup, was deeply impressed by how the new regime 'looked certain to cut all its ties with the Entente governments'. He portrayed Bolsheviks as 'ruthless, ignorant, pig-headed' persons, 'seeking to conduct affairs on a strict adherence to a few second-hand phrases'.[38]

While the armed clashes between the Red guards and their opponents were in full swing in Petrograd and Moscow, Trotsky notified the Entente diplomats about the establishment of the Peoples' Commissariat for foreign affairs (Narodnyi Komissariat inostrannykh del – NKID).[39] Contrary to his own dislike for this kind of bureaucratic activity, Lenin persuaded his lieutenant to head this body. On 10 November 1917, Trotsky announced to the astonished Entente representatives in Petrograd that the Bolshevik leadership strongly believed in the prominence of world revolution and, consequently, in the irrelevance of traditional diplomacy *per se*. As the NKID chief further claimed, the UK status at that crucial moment was second only to that of Germany because the triumph of Communism on the British Isles – in 'the citadel of capitalism' – would have made irrevocable the victory of world proletarians.[40] Ten days later, Trotsky wired to London, Paris and Washington about the Bolsheviks' intention to deliberate the conditions of a preliminary peace treaty with the appointed Central powers' representatives.[41]

Numerous periodicals mirrored the lack of unanimous opinion on the Russian policy inside the British government, while the common reader was prompted to scoop controversial information from Petrograd or Moscow. For example, a remark by the world famous novelist and playwright Maxim Gorky, who called the Bolsheviks 'visionless fanatics, dishonest adventurers, plotters and anarchists', verged upon a notice about the anticipated arrival of the British official delegation, chaired by Churchill, in Petrograd.[42] Although this idea appeared too bizarre to be brought to life, certain British ministers put forward a project of the so-called South-Eastern Union of Russia – a quasi-independent republic in the regions inhabited mainly by the Don and Kuban Cossacks.[43]

It should be noted that the former minister of social charity, Prince Dmitry Shakhovskoi, drew Buchanan's attention to the idea of fund-raising by the Russian banks in Ukraine and Poland in order to financially back up the anti-Bolshevik resistance.[44] As one British historian argued, Colonel Terence Keyes employed by Buchanan to collect political intelligence on the Russian domestic affairs played a crucial part in channelling money to the Don chieftain (ataman), Cavalry General Alexei Kaledin. In November–December 1917, Keyes made several trips between the Russian headquarters in the Romanian town of Lasi and Novocherkassk – the informal capital of the projected South-Eastern Union.[45]

In the absence of any lucid and coherent coalition strategy, the Allied diplomats in Petrograd opted for the boycott of Lenin's government.[46] Robert Cecil, the minister of blockade, admitted to the British press on 23 November that there existed a number of reasons which might excuse the vagueness of the Cabinet's stance. They were, in the first place, Bolshevik's vociferous statements on the immediate conclusion of separate peace; secondly, the inability of Kerensky and his followers – the so-called 'Russian revolutionary democrats' – to regain state power with the help of the Petrograd garrison; thirdly, the poor chances to legitimize the All-Russian Constituent Assembly as a counterbalance to the SNK.[47]

Despite the lack of a consolidated approach to the Russian problem, Cecil pretended to avow a kind of the joint view of the Russian developments to evidently mollify the British audience's critical view of the government's political inconsistency. As he put it, almost all the initial actions by the Bolshevik leaders proved ill-conceived, provocative and treacherous, while their appeals to the Allies aimed primarily at driving a wedge between them. Cecil further mentioned the abortive attempts by the SNK to effectively govern Russian regions, for example, that of the Don region, where chieftain Kaledin had already outlawed local Soviets. In the current situation, concluded Cecil, it would be excessively reckless to expect any kind of the official or semi-official diplomatic recognition of the Bolshevik regime by London.[48]

The Entente's decision to carry on the 'wait and see policy' was followed by the Foreign Office imitative to stop the receipt, publication and transmittance of all the wires and radiograms from Russia. At the same time, ambassador Buchanan declined Trotsky's proposal to join the preliminary peace talks with the representatives of the Quadruple Alliance in a small border town of Brest-Litovsk. Moreover, the People's Commissar threatened to arrest the British ambassador should he continue to surreptitiously interact with Kaledin's emissaries or the leaders of the forces offering anti-Bolshevik resistance.[49]

On 3 December 1917, the Cabinet's meeting resolved to provide 'effective military assistance to any representatives of the Russian people who wish to resist German armed intervention'.[50] This decision was supported by Paris joining in the diplomatic blockade of Soviet Russia. The publication of secret diplomatic papers by the SNK along with the Bolshevick's demagogic appeal to Asian nations 'to start up struggle for the liberation from the British yoke' only added 'fuel to the fire' of the flaring conflict.[51]

Consequently, another Cabinet meeting on 6 December had the Russian issues on the agenda, including the German menace to the northern seaports of Murmansk and Arkhangelsk, the situation on the strategic Trans-Siberian railroad, and the fate of the Russian Baltic and Black Sea Fleets. The debates led to the prohibition of military and technical assistance to Russia until the state of affairs became clearer.[52]

Two days later, Buchanan convoked a press-conference, which was held at the premises of the British diplomatic mission in Petrograd. After a few platitudes about his great sympathy with the Russian people, the diplomat blamed the Bolsheviks for the violation of previous agreements and emphasized the preparedness of the Entente and the United States to recognize the only legal body – the All-Russian Constitutional Assembly. He strongly condemned inflammatory appeals to the subjugated nations of the Orient as well as the unfriendly attitude to more than 7,000 British nationals engaged in the Russian industry, trade and education.[53]

By the end of 1917, the war situation became so aggravated that the Entente military strategists did not anticipate the collapse of the Quadruple Alliance before 1920. According to their calculations, the armistice on the Eastern front would mean a transfer of German infantry divisions, from thirty to sixty, to France and Italy, the repatriation of 1,600,000 Central powers' POWs from Russia to Europe and the capture by the Bolsheviks of the stockpiled munitions, delivered to Russia by the Entente in 1914–16.[54]

Pessimistic sentiments prevailed not only among the UK statesmen, but also in public opinion. As Beatrice Webb, one of the co-founders of the English socialist movement, penned in the diary on 10 January 1918, 'the New Year opens in gloom. Germany is stronger and more successful relatively to the Allies than she has ever been since the first rush to Paris. The governing class of Great Britain is no longer certain of ultimate victory – all the prophecies of failure of manpower or financial inability on the part of Germany have been falsified.'[55]

Distrust of the Entente's capability to take the upper hand in the global military conflict affected the views inside the British ruling circles on any adequate response to the Bolshevik challenge. Many top politicians together with Generals Alfred Knox and Charles Barter, accredited at the Russian army supreme headquarters during the war, dismissed any political contacts with the Bolshevik 'usurpers'. Considering their coup d'état as a 'personal humiliation', Churchill claimed at the public meeting in Bedford on 11 December 1917: 'Russia has been thoroughly beaten by the Germans. Her great heart has been broken, not only by German might but by German intrigue, not only by German steel, but by German gold.' It was the Bolsheviks, in Churchill's opinion, who deprived the Allies of their honoured victory while making them suffer undesirable hardships.[56]

There were considerably fewer politicians who favoured, if not diplomatic recognition, but at least, the maintenance of contacts with Soviet Russia. Aside from certain left-wing Labour activists, like George Lansbury, some influential statesmen as Alfred Milner, the war secretary, shared this view. They were supported by the prominent South African governor, Lieutenant General, later Field Marshal, Jan Smuts, and Lloyd George himself, who was even wittily nick-named by his assistants as 'Kerensky of the West' because of his populist statements and open sympathy with Trotsky.[57] The *New York Times* editorial manifested the arguments of those who argued for the reconciliation with the Soviet regime: 'If the world is to be made safe for democracy, a self-governing Russia must emerge from this Bolshevik welter, and that can come only with the help and encouragement of Great Britain, France, and the USA.'[58]

An intermediary standpoint between the above-mentioned political groups was occupied by the people insisting on conducting a cautious, albeit vigilant policy towards Russia. Far less sure of the Bolsheviks' capability to hold on for a considerable period, the conservative *Daily Telegraph* maintained: 'There is no sane who would give them as much as a month to survive.'[59] Supported by certain Foreign Office analysts, later the renowned diplomatic historians like Arnold Toynbee, Robert Seton-Watson and James Headlam-Morley, Balfour substantiated this approach in a memorandum for the Cabinet on 9 December 1917. The foreign secretary stressed that neither policy would be more fatal than the one giving Russia an excuse to invite the German military in the guise of saviours and friends. At the same time, he persuaded his colleagues to make use of the peace negotiations in Brest to demonstrate to the Allies and neutrals what a heavy burden Europe might take on itself in case of Germany's military triumph.[60]

The attitude of 'aloofness' towards Soviet Russia by the British political elite in the critical situation can also be illustrated by Francis Bertie, the ambassador to France, who wrote in the diary on 14 December 1917: 'As for Russia, let them fight each other until the Bolsheviks harden the majority and are killed. Meanwhile here [in France] there are people, and serious ones, succumbing to the belief that we shall receive armed assistance from Russia next summer. By then, that country will possibly cease to exist as a whole.'[61] In fact, the necessity of Russia's dissuasion from signing a separate peace with the Central empires continued to dominate the UK official and public discourse through the early period of the Soviet rule.[62]

Almost simultaneously, on 4 December 1917, the Cabinet drafted a programme of measures to be carried on in accordance with France to divide the 'spheres of responsibility' in European Russia meaning Bessarabia, the Crimea, Southern Ukraine and the Caucasus. According to Soviet diplomatic historians, the Allied governments plotted 'to capture and dissect Russia for the subsequent destruction of the Bolshevik system'.[63] But in reality, they sought to evade the occupation of these areas by German, Austrian and Ottoman military contingents. Implicitly, the Anglo-French convention acknowledged the rights of all the nations, populated the cited areas, to self-determination while opposing the pan-German projects of *Mittel Europa* and pan-Turkish plans of *Great Turan* in the Middle East.[64]

Approved by George Clemenceau, the French prime minister, the agreement gave way, albeit circuitously, to the Entente's armed interference in Russia's domestic affairs. That is why London and Paris immediately notified Rome and Washington about the so-called Cecil–Milner memorandum signed on 23 December 1917. As the latter statesman, perhaps with a modicum of sarcasm, commented the event to Lloyd George: 'Civil war or even the mere continuation of chaos and disorder [in Russia] would be an advantage to us [the British].'[65]

Almost simultaneously, the Cabinet decided to dispatch Robert Bruce Lockhart to Petrograd on a special mission. He was a thirty-year-old diplomat who had been

Figure 1 Robert Bruce Lockhart, head of diplomatic delegation to Russia, 1918. Photo courtesy of Wikimedia Commons (public domain).

serving as the British vice-consul and later acting general consul in Moscow for several years before the Russian revolution. Scottish by birth, Lockhart was chosen at Milner's recommendation.[66] Condemned by the British press for inactivity in tackling the Russian problem, Buchanan had to resign and left Petrograd on 6 January 1918. His deputy, Francis Lindley, became the chargé d'affaires *ad interim*.[67]

It is appropriate here to dwell on the organization of Lockhart's mission, since diplomatic historians still debate its aims and consequences.[68] This appointment was precipitated by the intensive consultations between the Cabinet members, military experts and diplomatic pundits in the period from 18 to 21 December 1917. The Foreign Office invited Lockhart to share his vision on the current events in Russia with such statesmen as Milner, Curzon, Smuts, Cecil and Edward Carson, the minister without portfolio. The prime minister had a final lengthy conversation with the nominee, instructing him on dealing with Lenin and Trotsky.[69]

Yet the interdepartmental disputes doubtlessly influenced the mission's tangible results. While Lloyd George ordered Lockhart to probe the Bolsheviks' position on the strain of the Russian military efforts, Milner recommended his protégé 'to put a spoke in the wheels' of the separate peace talks and 'by any means strengthen the Russian resistance to German demands'.[70] To get a full impression of controversies inside the British political elite, one has to mention Lindley's report to the Foreign Office about the planned trip. The acting chargé d'affaires maintained that Lockhart's special mission should be presented to the Bolsheviks merely as the visit of a commercial representative. Otherwise, in Lindley's opinion, it would diminish the status of the regular diplomatic mission. Thus, Lockhart's credentials should be restricted to the mediation in the disputes between the British diplomats and the NKID's top clerks.[71]

On 31 December 1917, the Cabinet finally announced Britain's aims in the First World War. This was done in response to the Soviet and Austrian statements specifying principal approaches to peace negotiations. Lloyd George hastened to avow his government's objectives to the trade-union bosses in London Caxton-Hall on 5 January 1918, three days before Woodrow Wilson announced his famous 'Declaration of Fourteen Points'. As one modern Russian historian correctly remarked, the prime minister reflected a compromise that could not be relegated to the 'back burner' by the British ruling elite's various cohorts.[72] Lloyd George described the relations to the Bolshevik regime in the streamlined phrases:

> We shall be proud to fight to the end side by side with the new democracy of Russia. But, if her present rulers act in a way, which is independent of the Allies, we have no means of intervening to arrest the catastrophe which is assuredly befalling their country. Russia can only be saved by her own people.[73]

Now just a word or two about the Bolshevik interpretation of the Soviet – British relations by the end of 1917. As is well known, the perception of Britain by Russian officials and common people varied in historic periods, though it had been far from positive, sometimes even reaching to the degree of outright Anglophobia. Yet the communist revolution added a new connotation of 'the oldest bastion of capitalism and a bulwark of anti-Bolshevik forces' to the substantially negative image of Britain.[74] In the very existence of the British Empire did Lenin and his followers see the main hindrance for the global anti-bourgeoise revolution. To eliminate this obstacle, Bolshevik theorists suggested a spectrum of political means. Their dominant group, including Lenin himself, and the left socialist revolutionaries, acting temporarily as the Bolshevik political partners, anticipated the forthcoming workers' revolts across the Central empires that would converge the world war into a class armed struggle for the establishment of the 'global republic of Soviets'.[75]

However, such Bolshevik mandarins as Trotsky and many others believed that any further interaction with the Entente, and, foremost, Britain, was not only desirable, but also profitable to the Soviet regime. One former tsarist diplomat recounted that Trotsky, as the head of the Soviet delegation at the second stage of the Brest-Litovsk negotiations with Germany and its satellite-states, threatened to immediately revive the Eastern front in concord with London and Paris.[76]

The armistice that the Bolsheviks signed with the enemy states on 15 December 1917 spurred the British government to set up, first, The Russian Information Committee, chaired by Milner, and later – the Russia Committee headed by Cecil. These institutions comprised the Foreign Office pundits along with military strategists from the War Office and the Admiralty. Their activities were evidenced by the fact that the latter committee held fifty-six meetings during January – mid-July 1918. Typically, the initial points on the agenda were the demobilization of the Russian active troops and the prevention of grain supply from Ukraine and Belarus to Germany and Austria-Hungary suffering the Entente blockade.[77]

The principal issue remained, however, the Russo-German talks in Brest-Litovsk. As one British high-ranking employee put it in the diary:

> The time now is to publish a declaration on war aims as a counter-offensive to the offer of the Central powers to the Bolsheviks. The prime minister, Smuts and Lord Robert Cecil are drafting such a declaration. Their idea is to make it ultra-democratic, to go to the farthest points of concession so as to produce maximum effect in Turkey and Austria, and not less to support the war spirit at home, which has seriously weakened, partly through weariness, through the atmosphere caused by soldiers returning, through the increasing difficulties in obtaining food and through the distrust of the Cabinet's war aims.[78]

Lloyd George nevertheless sought on one hand to secretly support anti-Bolshevik insurgencies inside Russia while on the other to deal with the Soviet regime via Lockhart. It is small wonder that Trotsky compared the Entente leaders to the casino players who prudently 'put chips on each number during the roulette game'.[79]

Lockhart's commitment as a new British extraordinary emissary to Soviet Russia could not be left without retaliation. On 4 January 1918, the SNK appointed Maxim Litvinov the provisional plenipotentiary in the UK compelling the Home Office to

Figure 2 Soviet diplomacy front-runners, 1918–24. (left to right: Maxim Litvinov, Georgy Chicherin, Lev Karakhan). Photo courtesy of Wikimedia Commons (public domain).

release him and Georgy Chicherin – another prominent political émigré – from jail, wherein they were detained for pacifist actions during the war.[80]

The preference for Litvinov as the diplomatic representative in Britain may be explained by his tarrying there as a political refugee since 1909. Having changed occupations – from the personal tutor of the Russian language to the private secretary of the Moscow People Bank's director – Litvinov married Ivy Low, a niece of *The Times* correspondent in Washington.[81] To many contemporaries, the future head of the Soviet diplomacy resembled a 'somewhat sinister Teddy-bear' or Mr. Pickwick, the famous character from one of Charles Dickens' novel. Fully aware of the proverbial 'English way of life', Litvinov might be portrayed as an utter pragmatist whose temperament left no place for 'revolutionary romanticism'. Moreover, the rationality of thinking enabled him to easily establish the links with those politicians, diplomats or public figures who might be personally useful for him. As an American journalist remarked, Litvinov's expectations of the world revolution vanished with the last volleys of cannons on 11 November 1918.[82] It is also worth citing Beatrice Webb's opinion on Litvinov's *credo*. Following lunch with the new Soviet representative, she put it as follows: 'He believes in a government of proletariat, and he does not believe the English race capable of it. He is pessimistic about the Russian revolution. Unless capitalism is overthrown in other countries, the Russian revolution will not survive.'[83]

Litvinov embarked on the diplomatic activity in the atmosphere of the Brest-Litovsk negotiations, which Lenin used not only to achieve peace but also to politically blackmail the Entente powers. To make the matter even worse, the Bolsheviks ruthlessly dissolved the All-Russian Constitutional Assembly on 19 January 1918 and, as a 'cherry on cake's top', decreed the annulation of Russian state foreign debts on 3 February.[84] Objections by the Entente diplomats in Petrograd followed the Foreign Office repudiation to accredit Litvinov as a new Russian delegate at the court of St James. He was forced therefore to informally deal with Whitehall through Reginald Leeper, Australian by birth, serving in the Foreign Office political intelligence department (PID).[85]

In defiance of these obstacles, Litvinov's initial weeks in the office were marked with the tempestuous activity that developed along several lines. Above all, he took over the staff of the former Russian diplomatic mission in London. Having launched the putative Soviet embassy, or as he called it Russian People's mission, at his own apartment rooms, Litvinov did his best to make Nabokov consign to him the keys of the Chesham House – the former residence of the tsarist ambassador. At the time, Litvinov's personnel consisted of five employees, including Litvinov's spouse, a secretary and three assistants who were either political emigrants or the members of the Russian military procurement commission in the UK. Besides that, he assumed consular functions, including visa support to repatriates trying to accumulate the financial resources of all other Russian representative offices which put an end to the monthly allocations by the British Treasury to the former embassy and consulates on the British Isles.[86] On 12 January 1918, Litvinov addressed a proclamation to British workers in the *Daily Herald*, the leading left-wing Labour periodical,[87] and a month later he circulated a note of protest to Balfour, referring to the conscription of the Russian citizens staying on the UK territory.[88]

Despite this feverish public activity, he was repeatedly mentioned in the personal files of the Scotland Yard Special Branch concerning the subversive activity of pacifists in Britain. For example, George Cave, the Home Secretary, even defined the distribution by Litvinov of the pacifist pamphlets in London as a breach of the diplomatic code. Supporting these accusations, Cecil also mentioned Litvinov abetting the citizens of the Jewish origin to propagate pacifism in the army and navy.[89]

Litvinov's lecture at a public meeting in London on 22 January 1918 along with his oration at the Labour Party's annual conference in Nottingham on 23–25 of the same month caused anxieties in Whitehall.[90] Basil Thomson, the assistant commissioner of the Scotland Yard Special Branch, later the director of the Home Office intelligence department, reported to Lord Cave that Litvinov 'set up the Red guards detachments with the help of 23,000 political refugees from Russia of the Jewish origin who had temporal registration in the London East End'.[91] As if on demand, some right-wing Unionists and Liberals launched a newspaper campaign to discredit Litvinov as a person allegedly subsided by the Germans through secret channels.[92]

Russian emigrants also contributed to the demonization of the Bolshevik diplomacy. On 28 January 1918, Bertie noted in the diary: 'Maklakov [a prominent member of the Russian Constitutional Democratic Party] came to me to dissuade from any engagement with the Bolshevik government. Lenin and Trotsky would attribute this kind of position to our fear and intensify their propaganda in England'[93]

In attempt to bolster up Litvinov's efforts and respond to Lockhart's mission, Trotsky sent his brother- and the son-in-law Lev Kamenev, the chairman of the

All-Russian central executive committee, and Ivan Zalkind, the deputy commissar for foreign affairs, to London on a special mission.[94] On reaching Aberdeen, Kamenev and Zalkind were thoroughly checked by the local police, administrating the confiscation of the bank cheques to a value of £5,000 and £10,000, respectively. In addition, thirty secret blueprints of the Russian warships and the maps of the British submarines' routes in the Baltic Sea were also discovered in their personal belongings.[95]

Both Soviet emissaries were nevertheless given permission to proceed to London by train. Although there is no concrete information of their conference with Cabinet members, it is highly likely that they met Leeper and other Foreign Office leading officials.[96] Remarkably, Beatrice Webb penned in the diary after her meeting with Kamenev and Zalkind:

> I asked them whether the Bolsheviks Government wished us to accept the terms of their peace with Germany as a settled fact. They both replied that we [the Bolsheviks] should be compelled to do so because we could not beat Germany. They did not seem to care for the lost provinces – nor did the Russian proletariat, they said. All they wanted was to be let alone to complete the social transformation they had begun.[97]

While Lockhart was establishing confident connections with the Bolshevik front-runners after his arrival in Petrograd on 27 January 1918, the ministers resumed urgent consultations on the situation in Russia. These led to a resolution on 7 February, which reaffirmed the initial directives for Lockhart's mission: 'We agree that there is currently no way to go for absolute recognition, however, it is highly undesirable to bring the case to a complete rupture.'[98] The following day, Lloyd George informed his colleagues about the British proxy's suggestion to recognize the Soviet regime and even accept Chicherin as a negotiator in the British capital.[99] The prime minister was inclined to agree with Lockhart's recommendation, referring to the Bolsheviks' anticipation of a mass uprising among German and Austrian workers if Berlin and Vienna disregarded the terms of a 'just peace' that the Bolsheviks suggested to the Central powers in Brest-Litovsk. But Lloyd George's intention met the reservations by Cecil, Churchill and Curzon. As the latter sarcastically remarked in a private letter to Balfour on 10 February 1918: 'The trouble with the prime minister is that he is a bit of a Bolshevik himself. One feels that he sees Trotsky as the only congenial figure on the international scene.'[100]

Lloyd George's antagonists claimed that Soviet Russia's official recognition looked untimely, considering the Bolshevik separate diplomatic contacts with the Central empires. Eventually, the Cabinet agreed on the lengthy resolution of fifty-one points. Offered by Balfour and amended by Cecil and Philip Kerr, the prime minister's private secretary, it envisaged the restoration of the Russian front as well as the settlement of the Polish and Romanian issues before the recognition of Lenin's administration.[101]

However, some formidable obstacles laid ahead: the occupation of Bessarabia by Romanian troops, the uncontrolled demobilization of the tsarist army which amounted to merely 20 per cent in the spring of 1918 and the shortage of munition at the disposal of the Red guards for the military defence of the capital. The menace was exacerbated by the announcement of the Ukrainian sovereignty in Kiev on 24 January 1918.[102]

The economic situation in Russia which rapidly deteriorated in the winter of 1917–18 seemed far from optimistic too. The fears of the Allies increased by the alleged reorganization of Russian military plants under the surveillance of German supervisors, which probably meant the redistribution of their production in favour of the enemy states.[103] A British engineer at the Moscow factory recalled how the workers demanded the entrepreneurs 'to payout lavish bonuses that were earned by them in the course of the First World War'. Responding to these calls, the Soviet government raised the wages of industrial workers to 26 per cent for the period of November 1917–January 1918. This decree led to nearly all small-sized and a great number of bigger enterprises' lockdown, causing mass indignation.[104]

Confronted with three alternatives – either to recognize the Soviets, support the anti-Bolshevik movement in South-Eastern Russia or anticipate the diplomatic collapse in Brest, the Cabinet ministers considered rapprochement with the Bolsheviks to be too risky.[105] At the same time, deprived of instructions and disturbed with the British diplomatic staff's unfriendliness in Petrograd, Lockhart had to proceed with any contacts with the Bolshevik leadership at his own risk.[106]

Some biographers wrote of spontaneity or even carelessness that dominated his nature. According to Nina Berberova, a well-known Russian political emigrant, 'he was a cheerful, sociable and intelligent man with no primness, but mannered with the warm sense of camaraderie, a light touch of frivolity, irony and open, inoffensive ambition'. Yet the periods of riotous activity and deep apathy interlaced in his behavior.[107] Other observers emphasized Lockhart's selfishness as a preponderant manner of character.[108] A third group of contemporaries described him as a kind of an Epicurean, keen on 'easy living', but without enough portion of self-discipline in the fulfilment of whims.[109] Some eyewitnesses argued that he had Russian qualities and spoke the language of Alexander Pushkin almost 'without English accent'.[110]

On 15 February 1918, the British emissary briefly met Trotsky for the first time, following the latter's return to Petrograd from Brest-Litovsk. The People's commissar assured Lockhart that the Germans were unlikely to restart their offensive. In case they would, Trotsky promised the resumption of armed resistance, especially with the Entente's military support.[111]

At first it seemed that Lockhart's telegrams to London were welcomed by Balfour and, more importantly, by Lloyd George himself. On 21 February, the foreign secretary informed the young diplomat that even though any British action in conjugation with the Bolsheviks was predicated on purely pragmatic calculations, so far as they were opposing common enemies or at least not allying with them, the Bolshevik's policy might correspond with Britain's interests.[112]

Unfortunately, Lockhart's recurrent appeals to the Foreign Office met no favourable response from Whitehall top officials. Moreover, there were politicians and generals who regarded his 'flirtation' with the Bolsheviks as immoral, conducting by 'a fool or a traitor deserving of gallows'.[113] It is small wonder that Lindley complained to London that Lockhart treated Trotsky 'as if he were a Bismarck or a Talleyrand', while another official urged Balfour 'to recall this impudent young man'.[114]

Meanwhile, Lenin's apprehension of the situation became more pragmatic. Right after the Germans resumed their march to Petrograd on 18 February, he welcomed the Allied support in case of a 'revolutionary war'. Forty French staff-officers, who might be commissioned to form a core of the new Russian voluntary army, initially seemed a robust defence force against enemy encroachments. But on 23 February, Lenin strongly advocated a peace treaty with the Germans at any price, though Trotsky agreed with the members of the French military mission on a plan of laying mines in the roads and bridges around Petrograd in case of the Kaiser troops eventual offensive.[115]

The Cabinet's hesitation could explain Trotsky accusing Lockhart of the anti-Bolshevik intrigues at their next meeting, even though he promised to the British emissary that if a peace treaty were concluded, it would mean just a tactical manoeuvre by the Bolsheviks.[116] Nonetheless, three days later, the Allied diplomatic missions totalling 130 personnel began to evacuate from Petrograd. After the failure to safely pass via Finland, all the foreign diplomats, except a few lucky British officials, made their way to Vologda, a small provincial town on the Volga-river, where they had been staying until the end of July 1918 (see Chapter 2).[117]

Only after the Soviet delegation headed by Grigory Sokol'nikov left Petrograd for the final round of diplomatic talks in Brest-Litovsk, Lockhart was given a chance to see Lenin on 1 March 1918. The latter assured the diplomat of the Soviet passive resistance to the German aggression, which, in his opinion, would not allow the enemy to make use of Russian food reserves and natural resources. Lenin also mentioned the expediency for the German military commanders to position substantial military contingents on the occupied Russian territory. 'As long as there is a German menace, maintained the Bolshevik leader, I am eager to risk the cooperation with the Allies, so far as it will temporarily be beneficial to both sides.'[118]

Following the signing of the Brest-Litovsk treaty on 3 March, the SNK set up the Higher Military Council under Trotsky who immediately proposed to conscript 1.5 million people. Consequently, Lockhart met him on the third occasion. The diplomat reported to London:

> I had a long conversation with Trotsky today. He informed me that the Fourth Extraordinary Congress of Soviets would probably declare a Holy War to Germany on 12 March or act in a way that would make it inevitable for Germany to violate the armistice. However, to succeed in this policy, it is important to refer [at the Congress] to the reality of the Allies' support.[119]

The explanation of the government's course towards Russia can be found in Amery's diary. According to the record on 6 April 1918, 'we [the British] should offer to recognize the Bolsheviks at the end of a definite period of weeks or months if meanwhile they accepted Japanese help, allowed us to get through to Transcaucasia, and showed signs of really creating a proper army'.[120] That is why, concluded Amery, the foreign secretary recommended to persuade the Bolshevik leadership of 'the Japanese coming to Russia as friends and not as hostile occupants'.[121]

However, all the efforts by the Soviet government to obtain the guarantees of military assistance from the Allies through diplomatic channels by delaying the ratification of the separate peace treaty came to nothing. In response to the desperate cables that Lockhart wired to London on the urgent need to restore the alliance with Russia, the ministers averted from any concrete promise of aid. Owing partly to the negative reaction by the British officials and public to Russia's treason, but even more due to the hesitance of the Cabinet members, London was losing time in the hopeless attempts to find a compromise.[122]

On 7 March 1918, the Russia Committee proceeded to debate measures to be taken for the protection of the military depots in Arkhangelsk as well as the scenarios the Entente troops' dispatching to Siberia.[123] Meanwhile the Cabinet was deliberating Trotsky's request of a possible military assistance in case of the German and Austrian armed invasion of Ukraine.[124] Yet Balfour and Cecil continued to obstruct any positive step while on the other hand favouring the landing of the Japanese troops in Vladivostok under the plausible excuse of the probable military counteraction against the German intrigues in the region.[125]

The last chance to draw Lenin and his colleagues to the side of the Allies evaporated on 15 March 1918 when the Fourth Congress of Soviets ratified the treaty of Brest.[126] On receiving this news, the Allied governments reckoned the direct armed interference in Russia's domestic affairs as inevitable. Three days later, they jointly condemned the separate peace as illegal.[127]

The correspondence between Litvinov and Chicherin, who succeeded Trotsky as the acting commissar for foreign affairs on 13 March, contains a printed review by an anonymous expert, probably, Litvinov himself, of the Soviet-British relations in the period between November 1917 and March 1918. The author noted that before the signing of the 'bawdy', as Lenin himself called it, treaty of Brest, there were voices in the British press for another envoy, presumably, of the left-wing political orientation, to be seconded to Petrograd in order to assist Lockhart in his negotiations with the Bolsheviks. According to the document, several British sea cargoes visited Russian ports as 'a goodwill gesture' in February – early March 1918 but the conservative politicians and press launched a campaign of deceptions and accusations on the part of the Bolsheviks.[128]

Since a detailed analysis of the Brest treaty is beyond the scope of this study, the author merely gives a general view of the losses that Russia suffered in March 1918.[129] According to the People's commissariat of foreign trade, the country lost 1 million square kilometres of its territory, 50 million of population, 26 per cent of railroads, 27 per cent of farmland, 33 per cent of industrial enterprises, 75 per cent of coalfields, 76 per cent of mines and 100 per cent of oil fields. Additionally, the Bolshevik government was obliged to allocate to Germany a sum of 1 billion gold roubles.[130] Only 39 per cent of the local Soviets approved the terms of the separate treaty despite the overall moral and economic exhaustion from the war, leading to anti-Bolshevik riots in both big cities and municipalities of Russia's European part.[131]

The Bolsheviks' withdrawal from the war meant an improvement of a general strategic situation for the Central empires, accompanied by a breakthrough of their economic blockade. Furthermore, a menace to the British overseas possessions in Asia, most of all to India, assumed a new reality.[132] Perhaps the opinion of the British historians who paralleled the conclusion of the treaty of Brest with the signing of the

Molotov–Ribbentrop Pact in 1939 might be regarded as a hyperbole, but thenceforward European public began to consider Bolshevik leaders the 'self-seeking fanatics who would not hesitate to cut their dearest friends' throats if it suited their purposes'.[133]

For the fear of the Germans' unexpected capture of the Russian northern capital, the transfer of the Soviet government to Moscow had been surreptitiously carried out in the period from 8 to 12 March 1918.[134] Interestingly, Trotsky arrived in Moscow by a special train as a newly appointed People's commissar for military and naval affairs, accompanied by Lockhart.[135] Although the British diplomatic agent along with three other auxiliary members of his mission occupied a separate coach, he received an invitation to lunch with Trotsky in the dining-car. As Lockhart recalled later, they continued to debate consequences of the Brest treaty and the establishment of a new conscription army in Russia.[136]

The removal of the Russian capital from Petrograd to Moscow terminated the period in the Soviet-British relations which is noticeable for a series of futile attempts to revive their military alliance. If the UK failed to return its former ally to the war trenches, Soviet Russia under the Bolshevik rule dropped out not only from the Entente member states but also the ranks of great powers.

2

British armed intervention 'by agreement'

> *The Allies cannot regard with indifference the German encroachments in Russia and Siberia. To guard against this menace, they might be led to intervene without inferring in the domestic affairs of Russia and with no concealed purpose of annexing territory.*
>
> Joseph Noulens, French Ambassador to Russia, April 1918[1]

Despite their significance, the Soviet-British relations in the tempestuous period between the conclusion of the treaty of Brest in March and the announcement of the Compiegne armistice in November 1918 remain understudied. Though it seems incorrect to write off the scholarship of the Soviet epoch as 'having no value at all',[2] a distorted, tendentious interpretation of the British policy towards Soviet Russia became commonplace for the Stalinist concept of London offering 'to reinstate the regime of large bourgeoisie and landlords' in the USSR.[3] Only during the recent three decades did the Russian historians begin to reconsider the period of the revolution and the Civil war in this country on an impartial basis.[4]

At the same time, the most part of non-Soviet historiography could hardly be recognized as a profound contribution, given the fact that it was grounded upon a limited number of primary sources in Russian. Besides that, the cold war mythology, prevailing in public conscience, distorted the impartial depiction of Soviet-British interactions.[5]

Aside from Socialist publicists traditionally blaming the 'international imperialism' for all mortal sins, the idea of the urgent need to stop the virus of Bolshevism spreading into Europe seemingly dominated the studies published in the West.[6] Yet certain diplomatic historians suggested their own, often contradictory views of the British military interference in Russian affairs. For instance, there were authors who explained the armed intervention by the need to prevent the defeat of the Reds from the White Russians.[7] Others drew attention to the Entente's desire to invade the territory of the former ally to avoid the American influence in Eastern Europe.[8] A third cohort of historians believed that 'there was no coordinated interference at all, while each of the Entente member-states acted on their own will'.[9] One more group of writers regarded the foreign invasion as a justified step 'from a moral point of view', since the Bolshevik regime might be considered a forerunner of all the totalitarian systems.[10] There were also publications speculating on the Russian Civil war through the lens of the 'global military conflict in continuation'.[11] Finally, the book about an active involvement of the British military intelligence in actions carried out by the Allied task forces in the north and south of European Russia deserves special attention.[12]

This controversy stems from the lack of comprehensive studies on the phenomenon of intervention including Britain's role in the process. The problem cannot be tackled by a simple statement that the British prime minister's ideas on Russia were 'as confused as the situation itself', or by an argument that 'anti-Bolshevism, and anti-Germanism frequently overlapped'.[13] One can describe persisting gaps in the scholarship by three notions regarding the Cabinet's reasons for the armed interference, the forces which the British officialdom supported during intervention and the impact it had upon bilateral relations in the immediate aftermath as well as over a longer time scale. At the risk of coming across as reductionist, the present author remains merely within the scope of the British contribution to the Western 'crusade' against the Bolsheviks, leaving aside other Entente members' participation in the affair.

For the starting point, one should review the UK statesmen contentions at the time. In fact, Alfred Milner, the war secretary until February 1919, expressed the most popular justification for the armed intervention against Soviet Russia. This was an open betrayal of the allies by the Bolsheviks at the First World War's crucial stage. One Milner's biographer maintained that to him 'the immediate purpose of intervention, ranking higher than denying Allied munitions and Russia's resources to the Germans, was to stop the German relocation of troops to the West'.[14] As the study strongly suggests, there were three consequent periods of the Entente intervention: from the spring to the autumn of 1918, the winter of 1918–19 and the spring–autumn of 1919.[15]

Traditionally, the first period was defined by historians as 'intervention at invitation'.[16] Morton Price, a correspondent to the *Manchester Guardian*, pioneered the usage of this catchword in his edited memoirs. Sympathetic to the 'Communist experiment' in Russia, he noted that the Bolsheviks initially put up with the Murmansk and Arkhangelsk Soviets in the welcome of the Entente expeditionary troops protecting Northern Russia from the German invasion early in 1918. According to Price, the Kremlin leaders, most of all Lenin and Trotsky, regarded this military support as a counterbalance with the pro-German government established in Kiev under the former tsarist Lieutenant-General Petr Skoropadsky who proclaimed himself the Chieftain, or Hetman of Ukraine.[17]

Nevertheless, the present author argues that it is more correct to describe the early stage of the Allied military invasion as 'intervention by agreement'. To corroborate this concept, it is necessary to review the situation in the northern Olonetsk and Arkhangelsk provinces, where the administrative authorities still adhered to regulations by the former Provisional government. It was Captain of the second rank Georgy Veselago, the executive chairman of the Murmansk Soviet People's collegium, who encouraged political contacts with the Entente powers' consulates and military missions in the period of the Brest negotiations.[18] At the same time strategists in the Foreign and War Offices drew up various projects of the so-called Russian Northern Federation or the Belomor-Onega Republic on the vast territories to the north of Vologda.[19] The diplomatic correspondence demonstrates that as early as in December

1917, after the consultations with the British charge d'affaires Francis Lindley and the French ambassador Joseph Noulens, a special liaison officer was sent from Murmansk to Novocherkassk to solicit Generals Alexeev and Kornilov's backing for the anti-Bolshevik armed resistance in the north of Russia.[20]

In the interim vacuum of state power, there also emerged a movement for the creation of the Russian Karelian Federation supported by Douglas Young, the British consul in Arkhangelsk. Acting initially at his own risk, he favoured a conference of the delegates representing eight provinces, willing to announce its cessation from Russia. Although the Foreign Office instructed Young to subsidize this meeting, he was advised to tackle the matter as informally and cautiously as he could. On the eve of his departure from Petrograd to Britain, Buchanan also wired to Balfour about the possible 'emergence of a new Northern Republic with Arkhangelsk as its capital'.[21] On 10 January 1918, the news hit *The Times* headline as 'Sterling Currency for Northern Russia'. The publication exposed the British plans to devise a special currency for the provinces in view.[22] A fortnight later, Major General Frederick Poole, the head of the British supply mission, later the Allied troops' C-in-C in the region, reported to the War Office on the reasons for the creation of the federation. Moreover, he attempted to reaffirm the military tops in London that a single battleship would be enough to capture Murmansk or Arkhangelsk where the British would acquire for the profitable wood and railroad concessions.[23]

As has been noted above, the Bolshevik annulment of the foreign debt along with the signing of the Brest treaty led to a wave of vehement protests in the Allied countries. Characteristically, the Entente diplomatic note warned Trotsky on 4 March 1918, the member-states became willing to abstain from any further munition supply to Russia as well as from the transfer of weapons, stockpiled at the seaports, to inland the country.[24] Yet, as early as in January, the SNK established an extraordinary commission on unloading the seaport of Arkhangelsk which consequently took the military depots under its jurisdiction. Contrary to the appeal from the British and French representatives, it accelerated the evacuation of these supplies by trains at the average pace of 3,000 tons per week from Arkhangelsk and Murmansk to Vologda and Kotlas.[25]

The danger of the Finnish encroachments of Karelia in the coalition with German troops became evident to London at the turn of 1918. The sedative assurances of Karl Mannerheim, the C-in-C of the newly conscripted national army of Finland which gained independence in December 1917, contradicted the invitation of the Germans by the government, allegedly to fight pro-Bolshevik Red guards on its territory.[26] The declaration of Mannerheim's willingness to swipe the Reds off the country precipitated the conclusion of the peace treaty between Berlin and Helsinki which was followed by the Germans landing on the Baltic coast in early March 1918. These events demonstrated the urgent necessity of collaboration between local Soviets and the Entente commanders 'on the spot' to repulse an expected coherent Finno-German attack on the Russian military garrisons in Karelia.

Under these extreme circumstances, the Murmansk Soviet notified Lenin and Trotsky of the initiative by Counter-Admiral Thomas Kemp, the commander of the British North Atlantic Squadron which consisted of a dreadnought, two cruisers and more than thirty auxiliary vessels. Kemp proposed collective Russo-British measures to defense the Murmansk railroad. On 1 March 1918, Trotsky informed Alexei Yuriev, the chairman of the Murmansk Soviet, of the SNK's consent with 'any kind of assistance, though unofficial, by the Allied military missions in the struggle against the German and White Finnish troops'.[27] Fully aware of the need 'to save time', Yuriev reached on the following day a 'verbal agreement' with the commanders about the coherence of efforts to shield Murmansk and Russian Karelia from the German invasion. The local Soviet authorities and the Entente commanders even set up a collaborative military council which comprised Russian, British and French emissaries.[28]

Taking into consideration the accord with the Murmansk Soviet, Kemp ordered on 6 March 1918 the landing of 130 British marines from the battleship *Glory* anchored in the water area of Murmansk.[29] The procedure had taken five days to be completed without any protest from the local Soviet. On 14 March, another detachment of 500 marines, this time from the HMS *Cochran*, joined their brothers-in-arms on the shore, while four days later, in turn, the French marines disembarked at the distance of 12 kilometres from the seaport of Murmansk.[30]

Ten days later, General Poole submitted to the Cabinet a detailed scheme of the Entente troops' deployment in the northern region of Russia and the plan for their combined operations with the military formations and vessels, disposed by the Murmansk Soviet against both German submarines and land troops threatening to capture a town of Kem – the important railway hub to the south of Murmansk. Chaired by Cecil, the members of the interdepartmental Russia Committee deliberated this plan at the meetings that were held on 4 and 10 April. They recommended to the Cabinet to send Poole to Arkhangelsk on a special military mission. It was planned that he would join Lockhart, mentioned in the previous chapter, as a political counsellor, albeit this idea had never been brought to life.[31]

Thus, the advance to Murmansk by the German-Finnish troops numbered 2,500–3,000 infantrymen was repulsed by the joint Anglo-Franko-Soviet counter-offensive in early April 1918, which validated the urgency of protective measures carried out on Poole's recommendations.[32] As Chicherin cynically claimed, 'we [the Bolshevik authorities], not having sufficient armed forces at the moment, could accept the help of the devil and its granny, had it been beneficial to us'.[33]

By the beginning of April, 600 British marines and infantrymen were stationed in Murmansk. Yet this garrison still seemed insufficient for effective rebuff, considering the surplus German divisions' arrival in Finland. That is why it was bolstered by supplementary Allied contingents.[34] Their reinforcement continued through April and May 1918, when the amount of the task forces increased to 400 French infantrymen and 1,200 Serbian military. In the beginning of August, the total strength of the armed interventionists, stationed in the north of Russia, reached 8,000 men in comparison with two North Karelian regiments controlled by the Murmansk regional Soviet (one of them consisting of volunteers under the British command).[35]

This seemed to be the first demonstration of Britain's successful collaboration with local Soviet authorities since they managed to arrest the German and Finnish attacks against Karelia. Additionally, their involvement in the military operations under consideration reduced the German General Staff's capability to transfer large amounts of troops to the Western front at the pace of six divisions a month that had been typical for the previous winter months.[36] More importantly, there emerged a real prospect of a bilateral rapprochement, predicated upon British offer, albeit seemingly too vague, to contribute to the organization of a new Russian national army.[37]

The role of Lockhart's diplomatic mission, on the one hand, and Trotsky as the People's commissar for war and navy, on the other, might be considered significant for the restoration of the Russo-British alliance. The fact was that after the old army's demobilization, the Bolshevik regime could only rely upon the following categories of armed forces: poorly drilled Red guards; the units of the ex-POWs volunteers (primarily the Austria-Hungarians); and several thousands of those Chinese ex-contracted workers (*kuli*) who had been transferred from the north of Russia to the central provinces following the construction of the Murmansk railroad in 1916.[38] These detachments should be supplemented with eight (not six as some historians mistakenly wrote[39]) Latvian riflemen regiments who sided with the Bolsheviks and on 13 April 1918 were unified in a division under Joachim Vacetis, a former tsarist Colonel. That is why an urgent need of a conscripted army made Trotsky to call for the Entente's immediate aid.[40]

Meanwhile the so-called Russian bureau, a section created by the MI6 in accordance with the Russian General Staff as early as in September 1914, continued to function in Petrograd during the winter of 1917–18.[41] From the very beginning, the bureau sought to collect intelligence on the German divisions' transfer from the Russian to the Western fronts as well as on the German naval routes in the Baltic and Black Seas. By the end of 1917, its military personnel increased to eighteen persons under Major Samuel Hoare, later to become the UK foreign secretary.[42] Captain George Hill, one of the Bureau staff, recalled that his colleagues 'deciphered German codes, opened their letters and read most of their correspondence without even being suspected', aiding the Russians in 1917 to reset their military intelligence on modern principles.[43]

Following the period of the power vacuum in Russia, the Bolsheviks restarted the collaboration with some British intelligence officers in February–March 1918. Under these circumstances, Trotsky deliberated the formation of the Red Army and the navy with the British and French military missions in Russia. He proposed that the modernized Russian officer corps should be recruited from the war veterans and ex-POWs. The Entente representatives, in turn, suggested that a special group of primarily French officers under the aegis of Division General Henri Berthelot could help in forging a core of the new Russian army's commanding personnel.[44]

Regarding a possible British participation, Lockhart saw it in the reshuffle of the Russian military, especially naval, intelligence as well as in the restart of domestic railway cargo traffic. Even some strongest opponents to the Soviet regime, such as Milner and Churchill, seemed in favour of getting in touch with Lenin and Trotsky, albeit for merely tactical reasons. As Churchill argued in the memorandum for the Cabinet:

> If the Bolsheviks could be 'induced' to make common cause with Romania and jointly attack Germany, that would be the moment to send to Moscow representatives of the Allies of sufficient weight, to give the Bolshevik government

a new element of stability and a means of reaching a working arrangement with other classes of Russian society.[45]

Surprisingly, according to Churchill, former US President Theodore Roosevelt and the French war minister Albert Thomas could equally claim to serve as a mediator between the Entente members and the Soviets. And 'safeguarding the permanent fruits of revolution' in response to the increasing German pressure might be considered as a somewhat universal justification for Russia's continuation of the First World War. Churchill concluded, perhaps, far too optimistically, that 'the intellect of Russia, including the Bolsheviks, must, whatever happens in the long run, be hostile to Prussian militarism and therefore drawn towards the Allied parliamentary democracies'.[46]

Having received a cold shoulder in London and Paris, these projects were however doomed to fail, also because Lockhart along with his consiglieres proved incapable to persuade both the Soviet mandarins and the Cabinet ministers to decide on their realization.[47] Moreover, many MPs became annoyed at the recruitment of German and Austrian POWs in the Red Army, taking into consideration their total amount of 1,600,000 in Russian camps by mid-1918. To diminish this frustration, the Foreign Office even required the exact statistics from Lockhart, who, in turn, consigned his assistants to set off for a six-week inspection trip across Siberia where the POWs' camps were located.[48]

Towards May 1918, Captain Hill together with another intelligence officer, Colonel George Boil from Canada, oversaw an ample network of agents and saboteurs in the south of Russia. If the former collected information about enemy troops' displacement between the theatres of war, the latter arranged for the destruction of the machinery and equipment at the Donbass coal and iron mines. The large extent of this activity attested to the fact that German military authorities were prompted to relocate four active army corps from the Western front to suppress Ukrainian guerrillas, though the requests by Lockhart for the time delivery of munitions to them fell on the deaf ear in the War Office.[49]

Only the general spring offensive by the German troops in France enforced the Cabinet to temporarily abstain from aloofness. It was in April and May when the collaboration between Trotsky and Lockhart resumed at the intensity equal to that in February 1918. On 6 April the French, Italian and American representatives also joined the negotiations. After intense debates, the Cabinet approved Lloyd George's proposal to station British battleships in major Russian seaports to get ready for landing operations in case of emergency.[50]

In mid-April Lockhart held one more meeting with Trotsky. The latter requested assistance in the reorganization of the Black Sea Fleet along with the recovery of railway traffic and the reanimation of the Arkhangelsk cargo port.[51] Responding to Lockhart's application for further instructions, Balfour informed him of British terms to be discussed with Soviet leaders:

> The Bolshevik administration should try to raise an efficient national army, organise guerilla warfare against the Germans and prevent supplies from reaching them; they should invite Allied military and naval assistance at Murmansk if the

railway was threatened and, in any case, through Vladivostok; the Allies should bind themselves to evacuate all Russian territory at the end of the war and, while in Russia, should take no part in political or economic controversy.[52]

Meanwhile Trotsky additionally questioned Lockhart on restarting coherent military struggle against the Ottoman troops in Transcaucasia.[53] That is why the Entente military attachés convened to adopt a programme of collaboration with the Bolsheviks. Following their conference at the premises of the French mission in Moscow, Lockhart sent the document to London on 15 April anticipating the Cabinet's prompt decision.[54] Characteristically, Milner informed Bertie, the ambassador to France, about the desirability to deal with the Bolshevik government because of the German's advance,[55] while Cecil revealed to Balfour that the only way to win the war was 'to restore Russia and re-establish the Eastern front'.[56]

Apart from the military sphere, there were observers who referred to the glimmer of economic contact between Soviet Russia and the UK. One should bear in mind that the British industry had been fulfilling Russian war contracts until March 1918. Their cancellation by the Bolsheviks would lead to inevitable bankruptcy of many British companies.[57] The contracts were carried on through the inter-departmental Russia trade committee whereto the Treasury delegated John Keynes, later a renowned economist.[58]

Meanwhile Leslie Urquhart, a business tycoon and public figure, evaluated the chances of postwar economic reconversion at the next session of the Russia Committee. Having personal commercial interests in the resumption of economic relations with Russia, Urquhart dug in the heels to be reimbursed for his property, most of all – the gold mines of the Lena and Kyshtym area in Siberia. Covering his personal ambitions with the need to protect national interests, he wrote: 'The British government must appreciate that a friendly Russia, industrially developed, as well as economically and financially strong, is a source of strength to the British empire', because it 'will provide Great Britain with a large and valuable exchange of trade'.[59]

Probably, the only result of these tumultuous activities was the UK commercial delegation to have arrived in Moscow in the mid-summer of 1918. According to the diplomatic note to the NKID by the Board of Trade:

> It is thought that this mission should go to Russia ostensibly as representing British traders and not the British government; but that the Bolshevik government should be given to understand, unofficially, that the British government is really at the back of the mission and that its members are at the disposal of the *de facto* Russian government to advise and help them, so far as they may desire it, with regard to reconstruction of the economic side of administration.[60]

Despite the Bolshevik demagogy, there existed champions of the Soviet-British reconciliation amid the Kremlin officialdom, including Trotsky, Sokol'nikov and Krassin, to mention but a few.[61] As the national daily *Izvestiya* wrote on 17 May, 'the Allies ought to make amendments for Soviet Russia, and first, to officially recognize the Soviet regime because any further deference would lead to the triumph of the German imperialism'.[62]

The British delegation led by William Clarke, inspector general of the Board of Trade overseas department, consisted of Urquhart as the chairman of the newly constituted non-governmental committee of Russia private creditors and two other renowned industrialists. Accompanied by Brigade General William Ironside who was attached to the Allied expeditionary troops in Northern Russia, the delegates reached Murmansk by sea on 21 June.[63] Following their arrival, Clarke set off to Vologda where the Entente diplomatic missions were waiting for him. On 7 July, he received a note by Chicherin on the Bolshevik government's concord to confer with the British in the Soviet capital.[64]

Yet the anti-Bolshevik revolts in several northern towns slowed down the delegation's coming to Moscow no sooner than on 22 July. Their first meeting with Mikhail Bronsky, chairing a department of the Commissariat of trade and industry, took place in the atmosphere of increasing tension between London and Moscow. Consequently, both negotiating sides were doomed to fruitless discussions without any definite result. The emissaries demanded state guarantees for British capital investors who had already allocated more than 500 million gold roubles in Russian industries. Enthusiastic about mining concessions, the Bolshevik leaders needed the resumption of the equipment's delivery by British manufacturing companies, previously contracted and already paid for in advance by the Provisional government, such as locomotives, lathes and agricultural machines.[65] In addition, the Kremlin was also concerned at the internment and subsequent requisition by the UK authorities of Russian cargo ships in British ports.[66]

Obviously, these consultations had little chance for success, given the determination of the Allied diplomatic missions to depart from Vologda on receiving intelligence about their troops' advance along the Murmansk and Arkhangelsk railroads to the Russian central regions. The withdrawal from Soviet Russia on 25 July 1918 put an end to commercial negotiations which had been frozen until May 1920.[67]

Some front-line statesmen, in both London and Moscow, detested even a flicker of the Anglo-Bolshevik dialogue. On the British side, they endorsed the Japanese armed intervention in the Russian Far East as well as the uprising of the Czechoslovak legionaries who were eager to fight the Red guards along the Trans-Siberian railroad from Samara on the Volga to the seaport of Vladivostok (see below in the chapter).[68] The Soviet side, in turn, rejected a compromise with the Entente for the fear of the German political pressure upon Moscow similar to that in Ukraine that led to the downfall of the Central Rada government in Kiev late in April 1918.[69] According to Lockhart's diary, this event was regarded by the Bolsheviks as the emergence of a counter-revolutionary stronghold in the European part of the former tsarist empire, threatening to their rule.[70] A similar tune was heard in the reports by Price, the aforementioned *Manchester Guardian* correspondent, who bogeyed the European public opinion with the prospect of restoring a Germanophile regime in Russia.[71]

The Cabinet's approach to the Japanese involvement in the Russian Civil War should also be taken into consideration. As Lloyd George wrote in the memoirs, his colleagues did not seek to completely oust the Soviet government from Moscow but intended to prevent it from overwhelming those anti-Bolshevik movements which were eager to fight the Germans.[72] It is known that the Central executive committee of

Siberian Soviets was elected at the congress in Irkutsk on 6 November 1917, but three months later, a parallel administrative organ – the so-called Provisional government of autonomous Siberia – emerged in Tomsk. In the summer of 1918, the latter relocated first to Harbin, then – to Vladivostok where the ministers heralded their willingness 'to separate from Russia and join the USA as a member-state'.[73] Aside from this audacious project, the Transbaikal Chieftain (Ataman) Grigory Semenov, a former Cossack officer, announced the restoration of monarchy with Mikhail Romanov, the younger brother of Nicolas II, as a new emperor.

Bearing in mind that the American state secretary Robert Lansing debated the replacement of Russian troops for the Japanese manpower on the Eastern front as early as in the summer of 1917,[74] it is worth citing the diary of Charles Scott, mentioned in the previous chapter. Following the conclusion of the treaty of Brest, the prime minister told Scott that he himself 'did not like intervention of Japan', and that 'the only thing to be said for it was that it might cut off the food supplies from Siberia'. 'This could only be done, admitted Lloyd George, if the advance of Japan were pushed a very long way'.[75]

The prime minister's position seemed to decisively affect the Cabinet's endorsement of the Japanese armed involvement.[76] As the assistant British military attaché in Peking wrote in 1918, 'if Japan is not given a free hand in some part of the Far East, there is a danger that she might actually go over to the enemy. With Russia a prostrate neutral between them, Japan and Germany would form an extremely strong combination, which would threaten the whole of the Allies' possessions in Asia and even in Australia'.[77]

It is after this decision that Balfour wired to Lockhart about the desirability of the Kremlin achieving accord with both Japan and Romania to rebuff all potential German encroachments of the Russian territory. It was expected that it would be done by Moscow similarly to how the expeditionary commanders had concluded the provisional agreements with the Murmansk regional Soviet.[78] However, Moscow and Tokyo failed to achieve it. The divergence of opinions among Bolshevik top officials attested to the fact that Trotsky himself did not mind Japan stationing troops in the Far East, while Lenin, Felix Dzerzhinsky, the chairman of the Cheka, and Joseph Stalin, then the People's commissar for nationalities, became frustrated at this prospect. They reminded to the SNK members that the Japanese light cruiser *Ivami* had anchored at the bay of Vladivostok as early as on 12 January 1918 without permission of the local Soviets. Shortly afterwards, *Asachi*, another Japanese battleship, joined *Ivami*. By mid-April, several Entente men-of-war were stationed in the water area of Vladivostok despite the NKID's strong deprecations.[79]

On receiving the ill-judged approval of the Japanese intervention from President Wilson who nevertheless remained sceptical about the whole expedition, the Entente conference, held in London on 16–17 March, also voted for it.[80] To be fair, some Cabinet members, for example, Smuts, warned that 'the consequences were incalculable and might be tremendous'. In fact, Smut's annoyance equalled his concerns about unpredicted consequences of the Japan's military invasion of Siberia.[81]

Although the Japanese expeditionary forces that landed in Vladivostok on 5 April to putatively secure the lives of their compatriots did not exceed 500 marines, the Cabinet decided to symbolically support the Asian ally with a squad of 50 sailors from the HMS

Suffolk.[82] Commenting on this violation of the Russian territorial integrity, the SNK declared on 6 April that England was going hand in hand with Japan in disarming Russia.[83]

Even after the landing troops had been called back on board the Allied transports in late April, the British engagement in the matter, doubtlessly, complicated Lockhart's efforts to revive at least a phantom partnership with Russia. His disappointment was evidenced by the change in tactics proposed at the regular seminar of the Entente delegates which took place at the premises of the French diplomatic mission in Moscow on 14 April 1918. Instead of further offers to restore the Eastern front with the help of the Soviet regime, Lockhart and Noulens set about drafting effective measures to overthrow it.[84]

The situation became even worse because of the anti-Bolshevik rebellion of the Czechoslovak legion which in accordance with the SNK was bound to leave the Russian territory for Western Europe via Siberia and Vladivostok.[85] Owing to the German offensive on the Western front and the Bolsheviks' abstention from re-entering the First World War, this agreement had been modified by Anglo-French strategists in such a way as to allow 45,000 Czechoslovak war veterans to replace demobilized Russian troops on the Eastern front. Basically, the idea to use Czechoslovak legionnaires as a strike force against the Central powers emerged as early as in the summer of 1917 during Somerset Maugham's unofficial trip to Russia. Later the Cabinet considered the establishment of an autonomous republic in the south of Russia with the military assistance of former POWs including the Czechs and the Slovaks.[86] When their vanguard units reached Vladivostok on 4 April, other train echelons allocated for six operative groups were still moving at slow pace along the Trans-Siberian railway. On 27 April, the Allied Supreme War Council (ASWC) circulated a memorandum on their advisable engagement in the defensive fights against German troops in Northern Russia.[87]

Accordingly, the Central committee of the Bolshevik party met on two occasions to discuss the ASWC collective note concerning the redirection of the legionnaires from the Far East to the north of European Russia. Taking place on 6 and 10 May, these sittings revealed a crucial discord amid the Kremlin leadership regarding Russia's political orientation either to the Entente or to the Quadruple Alliance. Like the left Socialist revolutionaries, who adopted a similar resolution at the conference in May, a cohort of the top party functionaries headed by Trotsky and Sokol'nikov advocated the continuation of the anti-German war. Put it another way, they favoured the admittance of Japanese troops and Czechoslovak legionnaires to the Eastern front as supplementary military contingents to constrain the Germans creeping occupation of the Russian territory until a new Russian national army would be set up.[88]

This contention, however, challenged a tenable position of Dzerzhinsky and Yakov Sverdlov, the chairman of the All-Russian Central Executive Committee. Also supported by Chicherin, this policy aimed to rely upon the Central empires in the confrontation with the Allies. Lenin himself drafted the text of a secret motion in favour of a closer association with Berlin instead of recovering collaboration with the Entente powers.[89]

Exposing the arguments of those people who pointed out to the downfall of the socialist government in Kiev because of the military coup arranged by the Germans,

Lenin opposed adherence to a particular strategy in dealing with 'two groups of the imperialistic powers'. Furthermore, a proponent of diplomatic flexibility, he claimed at the Moscow municipal conference of the Bolshevik party:

> While remaining far from the repulsion to the military alliance with any belligerent coalition in principle, on condition it would help to strengthen the Soviet rule without violating its foundations and arrest the onslaught on it by any imperialist power, we [the Bolsheviks] cannot at this time reach an agreement with the Anglo-French group, because the divergence of the German troops from the West is of the genuine importance to the latter.[90]

The Bolsheviks needed this diplomatic step for the lack of a conscripted army, economic collapse and failures of foreign policy which Lenin acknowledged at his first meeting with the German ambassador Wilhelm von Mirbach-Harff on 16 May 1918.[91] By that time, contrary to the treaty of Brest and the disregard of the NKID's almost weekly protests, the troops of the Central empires were moving eastward to the major industrial centres of Russia seizing creepily one Russian province after another. They occupied Crimea on 3 May, Rostov-on-the Don on 5 May and Odessa on 16 May. As a member of the German diplomatic mission recorded, 'the longer the peaceful respite lasted, the more Lenin's miscalculations became obvious, while the peace of Brest remained a paper declaration, and neither side regarded it as practical, workable and final'.[92] Typically of the Bolshevik front-runners, they were so pessimistic that did not exclude the German capture of Petrograd with their further retreat to the Urals where it was supposed to create the Ural-Kuznetsk Republic, and in case of emergency – even the Kamchatka Republic in the Far East.[93]

Another noticeable feature of the Soviet regime's fecklessness was the anti-Bolshevik riots that swept across some towns – such as Rybinsk, Pskov and Novgorod as well as in some minor district towns of European Russia in the spring of 1918, all of them ruthlessly suppressed by Latvian riflemen and the Red guards.[94]

Even though the British submarines, attached to the Russian Baltic Fleet, were destructed by the acting naval attaché Francis Cromie in the water area of Helsingfors on 3–5 April 1918, the Bolshevik putative intention to consign the Russian men-of-war to Germany remained a problem to the Cabinet.[95] This is why the Admiralty designated Cromie to scuttle four Russian dreadnoughts and fourteen destroyers in the Finnish gulf of the Baltic Sea. On 16 May, he reported to London about the well-conceived measures to be taken in a week, should German troops occupy Petrograd and capture Kronstadt – the principal sea-fortress guarding the 'cradle of revolution'.[96] Meanwhile Lord Cecil received a piece of intelligence about the Soviet government's resolution to disarm the battleships stationed mostly in Odessa and Sevastopol in return to Germany's official recognition of the Bolshevik diplomatic missions in neutral countries.[97]

Returning to the Czechoslovak legionnaires' role in the armed intervention 'by agreement', it should be noted that many Soviet historians traditionally pinned responsibility for the anti-Bolshevik rebellion upon the British and French secret services which putatively abetted the former Czechoslovak POWs to disobey to

Bolsheviks' regulations.⁹⁸ Yet the factual motive for their insubordination seemed different: although these rules required the legionnaires to retain no more than ten rifles and a machine-gun per a hundred servicemen as a necessary means of self-protection, every legionnaire unit concealed substantially more munition.⁹⁹ Sparked by the national animosity between the Hungarians and the Czechs, a minor incident at the railway station of Chelyabinsk resulted in a large-scale armed clash and subsequent skirmishes. To cope with them, Trotsky ordered the local Soviets to arrest the representatives of the Czechoslovak national committee and to isolate the legionnaires designated for the armed protection of Murmansk and Arkhangelsk.

The Bolsheviks' repression infuriated the legionnaires, expanding the revolt along the Trans-Siberian railway from Penza to Omsk.¹⁰⁰ On 28 May, Chicherin appealed to Lockhart for the British assistance in the suppression of the mutiny. But Trotsky's order to shoot down any armed legionnaire for disobedience following the SNK's decree to confiscate their light weapons caused a surge of vehement protests by the Entente diplomatic missions.¹⁰¹

The mutiny coincided with Poole's arrival in Murmansk as a nominee to the position of the supreme commander of the Allied force. Almost simultaneously, Sergei Natsarenus, the extraordinary commissar of the Belomor region, came to Murmansk on 24 May.¹⁰² Judging by the correspondence between the NKID and the Entente diplomatic missions, the steady increase of the Western forces in the Russian north irritated Lenin and Trotsky. The Kremlin's indignation attested to Chicherin's enquiry on 2 April to Lockhart about the UK long-term objectives in the Arkhangelsk province.¹⁰³ Referring to Noulens' interview on 25 April, Chicherin repeated the Bolsheviks' call for the Entente states to make clear their policy towards Soviet Russia.¹⁰⁴ In mid-May, the NKID warned the Murmansk Soviet that the Allies were sending counter-revolutionaries to the territory of Soviet Russia. Ten days later, Chicherin echoed this warning by claiming that 'no local Soviet organization should seek the aid of one imperial coalition against the other'.¹⁰⁵

Following the Bolsheviks' refusal to abide by the terms of the agreement with the Czechoslovak national committee, the Soviet rapprochement to Germany assumed real outlines. Hence, the ASWC drafted a special memorandum on the transition to the second stage of intervention, this time without agreement. The document suggested 'to send sufficient British, French or American troops to Arkhangelsk and Murmansk to hold these entries into Russia against any reasonably probable attack, and to act as the rallying points for Russian and Czechoslovak anti-German forces'. As the document further claimed, the Entente military contingents should be sent to the Far East 'to give the Siberian expedition a manifestly Allied character'. In the final phrase, the memorandum welcomed 'the landing by the Japanese government of whatever force may be necessary to occupy the Trans-Siberian railway as far as Chelyabinsk'.¹⁰⁶

Referring to a possible invasion of Karelia and Kola Peninsula, the ASWC decided to station the task forces under Poole as the C-in-C at the Russian northern seaports, even without permission of local Soviets. Meanwhile Natsarenus held meetings, first, with Kemp, then with Poole, which however only increased the Kremlin pessimistic premonitions.¹⁰⁷ Responding to the Soviet diplomatic note which condemned any kind of a foreign armed intervention, Lockhart called for a verbal agreement between

Trotsky and the Allied military attachés which they concluded on 4–5 May. It provided for the 'unloading of the Arkhangelsk port' in strict accordance to the scheme that the Soviet government and the Entente military missions had successfully agreed upon. As the British diplomat pointed out to Chicherin, while the regional military commissar Feodor Ogorodnikov was obliged to control the depots of munition at the Russian northern seaports, the SNK committed Mikhail Kedrov, the extraordinary commissar, notorious for the ruthless crackdowns of anti-Bolshevik agitators, to Arkhangelsk. Following his arrival in the city, the 'unloading procedure' continued even at a higher pace without contacts to the local Entente representatives. Symptomatically, Kedrov initiated the conscription of workers and peasants to the local Red guards detachments in late May, which immediately prompted mass protest.[108]

Recurrent Chicherin's appeals to the Foreign Office to stop the landing of the Entente troops on the Russian territory fell on the deaf ear in London.[109] As one observer remarked, the local military authorities got in touch with the Allied commanders to defuse commissar Kedrov's activities in the region. Against this background, the bombardment of the Revel seaport carried out by five British destroyers on 12 May further worsened the Anglo-Soviet relations.[110]

Diplomatic consultations, held by Adolf Ioffe, the Soviet diplomatic representative in Berlin, with Richard von Kuehlmann, the German state secretary for foreign affairs, reflected the Kremlin's growing concerns. As the former reported to Moscow on 20 May, the Germans guaranteed to stop military advance to the inner Russian provinces in case the Bolsheviks abstained from reviving the alliance with Britain and France. Moreover, Ioffe informed Chicherin about Germany's 'sincere desire to economic collaboration', expressed by Kuehlmann.[111] Three days later, Lockhart, for his part, let the Foreign Office know about the Bolshevik willingness to build up tight economic connections with Germany.[112]

Meanwhile Major General Poole ordered the formation of the so-called Slavo-British Legion. This decision compelled Natsarenus to declare an ultimatum to the Allies urging the immediate recognition of the Soviet regime threatening to 'drop off the Entente's expeditionary forces into the sea'. When Poole and Kemp rejected these demands, the Bolshevik emissary demanded their instant departure from Murmansk and Arkhangelsk.[113]

While Chicherin never stopped to reassure the British diplomats that 'the Bolsheviks would keep friendly relationship with any belligerent coalition that is least hostile to them', the German Emperor William II secretly ordered on 23 June 1918 to abstain from any further penetration of the German troops into the Russian territory. The same day Kuehlmann wired to Chicherin that the Kremlin officials should not anticipate any surprise attack on Petrograd by German or Finnish forces.[114]

There remained nonetheless enough room for undertaking a diplomatic manoeuvre. Not surprisingly, Churchill submitted a memorandum to the Cabinet underscoring the importance of Russian troops returning to the trenches. He claimed: 'If we cannot rebuild the fighting front against Germany in the East, the war will never end.'[115]

Alexander Kerensky, who had escaped from Russia with the aid of Lockhart, also favoured the armed intervention without agreement. Shortly after his arrival in London, he was first received by Lloyd George at Downing Street and then by Milner and Kerr. As the latter recorded, the visitor sought to persuade Lloyd George that the Russians were not generally against foreign military presence in the country but would never agree to the intervention of the Japanese troops.[116]

The disruption of the telegraphic communication between Moscow and London compelled Lockhart to deliver a note of protest to Chicherin. In response, the latter pointed out to the British marines' continuous landing at the Murmansk port.[117] During a telegraphic dialogue with Yuriev, the chairman of the Murmansk Soviet, Lenin gave him the last warning on 26 June: 'If you still do not feel like understanding the core of Soviet foreign policy, equally hostile to the British and the Germans, then blame yourself.'[118]

This crucial period was marked by the Cabinet's preference for the open armed intervention without agreement. This decision on 28 June apparently led to the ASWC resolution of 3 July to strengthen the task force in Northern Russia with six more battalions of the British, French and Italian marines.[119] At the same time, most members of the Murmansk Soviet spoke in favour of further collaboration with the allies, dismissing the Kremlin's instructions. On receiving this information, Trotsky initiated a decree on the armed resistance to the interventionist troops including those of the British empire. Natsarenus, in turn, directed the Arkhangelsk Soviet to arrange for the military protection of the city from the 'anti-Bolshevik invaders'. Contrary to any instructions from Moscow, the Murmansk Soviet endorsed a provisional agreement with the Allied military commanders in a written form, which was bound to come in force immediately after the signing.[120]

To Russian political emigres' regret, the speculations about anti-Bolshevik circles sponsoring mass revolts in the big cities controlled by the Soviets remained a kind of wishful thinking. The assassination of the German ambassador, Count Wilhelm von Mirbach, and the rebellion in the capital raised by some influential left Socialist revolutionaries on 6–7 July 1918 were easily suppressed by the Latvian riflemen, nevertheless instigating Berlin's offer to Lenin to expulse the Entente military missions from Russia.[121] On the other hand, the Allied expeditionary forces were advancing along the Murmansk railroad in the southward direction, albeit at a slow pace, causing the liquidation of local Soviets and the wave of repressions against their members, as it, for example, occurred in the town of Kem' (see Chapter 3).[122]

Karl Radek, then the chair of the NKID department of European countries, was assigned to commit the last attempt to avoid Bolsheviks' full-scale confrontation with Britain and the other Entente member-states. It was carried out against the background of the United States joining the intervention on 6 July, when Wilson countenanced the landing of 7,000 marines in Vladivostok.[123] Commissioned by Lenin and Chicherin, Radek arrived in Vologda, where the Western diplomats were residing since their evacuation from Petrograd in late February 1918. Escorted by a British journalist Arthur Ransome as a voluntary interpreter, the Kremlin's emissary sought to persuade Lindley, Noulens, Pietro de la Torretta (the Italian representative) and David Francis (the American ambassador) to cease their voluntary exile in Vologda and move to Moscow.[124] Having failed to fulfil this task, Radek had nothing to do but to leave Vologda on 17 July. Following a week after his departure, the foreign personnel of diplomatic missions set off from Vologda to Arkhangelsk on the back route to their motherlands.[125]

However, the situation became even worse after the murder of the Austrian-Hungarian C-in-C in Ukraine, Field Marshal Hermann von Eichhorn, on 30 July. Alike Mirbach's assassination, this top military commander was murdered by the member of the left Socialist Revolutionary party. Sentenced to death, the killer confessed to the German investigators that he kept in touch with the Entente secret services.[126]

In the meantime the SNK demagogically appealed on 1 August 1918 to the 'workers of France, Britain, America, Italy and Japan' with the following motion: 'Not only did the Allies help us to recreate our defensive ability, but ... they endeavored to destroy it by all means, amplifying the inner devastation and cutting us off from the remained reserves of bread.'[127] Stirring up the Anglophobe hysteria, the Kremlin also offered to Karl Helfferich, the German charge d'affaires *ad interim* in Moscow, to start a 'parallel' counter-offensive of the Bolshevik and German troops against the expeditionary forces in the north of Russia while reassuring Lockhart and Joseph Fernand Grenard, the French General Consul in Moscow, that the Soviet government was not going to declare war on the Allies and was merely taking defensive measures.[128]

While both sides – the Bolsheviks and the Entente – reciprocally heralded their good-will, the Entente troops entered Onega, the port on the Belyi Sea. This event was followed by the landing of the Entente joint task force amounting to 13,182 servicemen at the mouth of the Northern Dvina River in the suburbs of Arkhangelsk.[129] But even before this intrusion, the anti-Bolshevik faction of the city administration took over in the city. On 26 July, Bolshevik commissar Kedrov escaped from Arkhangelsk escorted by the officers of the Belomor military district. As some contemporary observers put it, most residents, exhausted with the Bolsheviks' tyranny, warmly welcomed the Allied troops.[130] Yet Major General Poole, who became the actual administrator of the city, almost instantly established court martials, introduced death penalty and abolished Bolsheviks' decrees. The amount of the landing forces in Murmansk had increased to 10,334 marines towards the end of September 1918, which stressed the importance of holding this strategic point in the British hands.[131]

Consequently, anti-Bolshevik political parties founded the so-called Supreme government of northern provinces, headed by Nikolai Chaikovsky, a prominent representative of the People's Socialist Revolutionary party. Significantly, it was decided to form the local voluntary military contingents under the command of the Major General Charles Maynard who later described this episode in the book of memoirs.[132]

In early August 1918, the British expeditionary troops reappeared in the port of Vladivostok, bolstered by a battalion of the Middlesex Royal regiment that was transferred from Hong Kong, and also by other minor military contingents.[133] According to the US defence minister, Newton Baker, who spoke at the Senate military committee on 15 September 1918, the British interventionist troops in Russia to the east of the Urals consisted of the battalions from the New Hampshire and Middlesex Royal regiments, and several artillery brigades, totalling 1,500 servicemen compared to 9,000 American and 70,000 Japanese soldiers occupying the Russian territories from Vladivostok to Irkutsk.[134]

Apart from Siberia and the Far East, British troops also entered Baku to repulse the Turkey offensive in the strategically important Transcaucasian region, rich with oil fields. A special military force of volunteers under Major General Lionel

Dunsterville was committed to take control over the Azerbaijan capital while another military contingent, consisted of the Anglo-Indian riflemen under Major General Wilfrid Malleson, was instructed by the War Office to rebuff the Bolsheviks' advance towards Ashgabat – the administrative centre of the Transcaspian province (see Chapter 4).[135]

However, the Cabinet members addressed the peoples of Russia with a special statement, drafted by Buchanan and adopted by the Russia Committee. The declaration disapproved of any Britain's aggressive intentions, reaffirming the Russian population of the Allied intention to appease to their country.[136]

Under these circumstances, the Soviet authorities had nothing to do but to search the premises of foreign embassies following by the arrests of Russian and foreign employees regardless of their diplomatic immunity. The number of people jailed by the Cheka agents in Moscow and Petrograd by 4 August reached 200.[137] Additionally, several thousand former tsarist military officers and administrative officials were imprisoned on the charge of cooperation with the Allies. The surge of detentions seemed so high that Cromie, the acting naval attaché, petitioned to the Admiralty to issue an ultimatum, threatening the Bolsheviks with a 'punitive Entente military expedition'.[138] On 8 August, the SNK cancelled the Russo-British convention of 1917 which allowed for all Russian citizens to join the active military service in the Allied armies or navies.[139] The following day, Chicherin proposed to London to reciprocally evacuate British and Soviet diplomats from London and Moscow, respectively.[140]

The aggravation of tension was intensified by Lenin's public statement in Moscow that Soviet Russia was in a state of war against the Allies, albeit no official declaration had been made by both sides.[141] According to Lockhart's diary, on receiving this news, the Czechoslovak legionnaires joined right-wing Socialist revolutionaries in Kazan to overthrow the local pro-Bolshevik Soviet on 8 August. In response Trotsky announced the establishment of the North-Eastern front to counteract both the rebelled Czechoslovaks and the Western expeditionary troops.[142]

On 6 August, Lockhart allegedly visited the NKID to consign to the People's commissar a diplomatic note about the breakup of the Anglo-Soviet diplomatic contacts.[143] However, the British Commissioner seemed to deliberately distort the real course of events. As a matter of fact, on 8 August, the Foreign Office instructed him to 'maintain the existing relations with the Bolsheviks as long as possible, and in the event of an imminent rupture, to hold them fully responsible'.[144] Significantly, the Cabinet continued to uphold the appearance of the intervention 'by agreement', which one modern writer depicted as 'stalled', even after the Allied flags had been dropped down on their consulate buildings in Moscow on 9 August.[145]

In the meantime, the conclusion of a supplementary economic agreement to the treaty of Brest marked a new stage of the Soviet-German rapprochement, which led to Russia's transformation into the 'economic satellite' of the Central empires. When it was signed on 27 August 1918, the British government forfeited even the minor chances to prevent the collapse of the bilateral relations.[146] The so-called 'complot of ambassadors', or as the Soviet historians defined it the 'Lockhart plot', became a final, albeit adventurous, attempt to prevent Russia's alienation from the Entente in the period of the decisive battles on the Great War fronts.

3

The so-called 'complot of ambassadors'

By the autumn of 1918, the counter-revolutionary wave reached its highest level. In Moscow, it felt like before a thunderstorm.
　　　　　　　　　　　　　　　Martin Latsis, the deputy chairman of the Cheka[1]

It seems unlikely to find a more dramatic period in the history of the Russo-British relations than that of the few weeks in August–September 1918 when according to the Bolshevik leaders themselves, the regime was balancing on the verge of collapse. The commencement of an open military interference by the Entente powers, the abolition of local Soviets in many regions (except several central provinces), recurrent anti-Bolshevik rebellions in big cities against the background of economic disarray, widespread famine and epidemics – all these developments threatened to bury the hopes of Lenin and his associates to hold power in Russia and expand the Communist revolution to Europe.

In late August 1918, the Cheka agents exposed an anti-Bolshevik conspiracy called the 'Lockhart plot' by the Soviet press. As the editorials in the *Pravda* and *Izvestiya* signalled to 'all the workers and peasants of the first proletarian state': it was the Allied diplomatic missions in Moscow and Petrograd along with the Western intelligence services who had concocted the fruitless coup d'état. On the other hand, London and Paris continually refuted any accusations of their official representatives' involvement in the case. It is critically important, therefore, to reconstruct the course of events as well as their impact on Soviet-British relations in short- and long-term perspectives.

The initial plans of some leading Entente statesmen to overthrow the Bolshevik commissars dated back to March 1918. As has been noted in previous chapter, the Brest treaty turned Soviet Russia into a neutral state which enabled the Bolshevik government to embark on diplomatic manoeuvring between the Entente powers and the Central empires. Lacking comprehensive information about the Kremlin's intentions and considering the Germans' new offensive on the Western front, the Cabinet commissioned Sidney George Reilly, one of the most qualified MI6 officers, to examine the Russian situation during a kind of inspection trip. Apparently, this choice was not accidental because Reilly (originally Sigmund, or Sigismund Rosenblum) was born somewhere in the province of Odessa and spent his childhood in the Russian empire. After emigrating to Europe, he volunteered for the British secret intelligence service under the surname of his second wife. In the course of the Russo-Japanese War, Reilly contacted various tsarist politicians, public figures, industrialists and aristocrats until the Russian revolution broke out in March 1917.[2]

Captain Mansfield George Smith-Cumming (also known as C.), the director of MI6 at the time, awarded with two Russian military orders of St Stanislav and St Vladimir for the rapport in the sphere of military intelligence, recommended Reilly to Lloyd George as a liaison officer to be sent to Bolshevik Russia.[3] This preference might be explained by Smith-Cumming having information about Reilly's excellent knowledge of Russian political situation as well as of his good command of foreign languages. Besides that, Reilly's capability to obtain top secret documents, such as the German naval code in 1916, predetermined Reilly's appointment as well.

On 15 March 1918, C. briefed the MI6 officer in the aims of his secret mission providing Reilly with the cash to the value of £500 in banknotes and £750 in diamonds. Strange as it may seem, the Soviet 'diplomatic representative' Litvinov also contributed to the preparations when he handed to the MI6 agent a letter of recommendation.[4] As one writer explained, Litvinov obviously mistook Reilly as a British businessman sympathizing with the economic reconstruction of the former empire.[5]

Ten days later, Cromie received a wire about Reilly's prospective coming to Russia. Some modern historians suggested that the Cabinet sought to prevent the Bolshevik government from rapprochement with Germany following the conclusion of the Brest treaty.[6] At the same time, there is no reason to suppose that Reilly's reports played a decisive role in prompting Whitehall to launch an armed intervention in Russia. By all odds, it was Lockhart's adjustment of his originally positive attitude towards the Bolshevik authorities that could have influenced the British government's position. In fact, the young diplomat was motivated by the key events such as the SNK's deliberation in favour of further reconciliation with Germany and the growing internal social resistance towards the Soviet regime.[7]

Lockhart's hesitation to maintain close contacts with the Bolshevik rulers may be also evidenced by Balfour sarcastically notifying the diplomat:

> You have at different times advised against Allied intervention in any form: against it by the Japanese assistance; against it at Vladivostok; in favour of it at Murmansk; in favour of it with an invitation; in favour of it without an invitation, since it was really desired by the Bolsheviks; in favour of it without invitation whether the Bolsheviks desired it or not.[8]

Anyway, the German supreme commandment's decision to halt the further eastward advance into Russian territory on 23 May 1918 encouraged Lockhart to leave Moscow for Vologda where the reduced personnel of the foreign diplomatic missions had been staying since the end of February. The British emissary aimed to sound out Noulance and Francis, the French and American ambassadors, respectively, on their vision of the Bolshevik policy towards the Central powers. Following a lively discussion, the Western diplomats decided to embark on preparations for a large-scale armed intervention in Russia, retaining minimal necessary contacts with the Kremlin in order to safeguard their interests against German increasing political pressure.[9]

For his part, Dzerzhinsky offered a way to make the allies' seditious activities benefit the interests of the Soviet regime. Predicated upon his subversive revolutionary tactics, these ideas underpinned the Bolsheviks' further manoeuvres between the warring coalitions. That is why the 'complot of ambassadors' may arguably be also identified as 'Dzerzhinsky plot', since the head of the Cheka oversaw not only any domestic turmoil but also destabilizing activities by Western intelligence agencies.[10]

The Soviet interpretation of the conspiracy originated in the statements of the All-Russian central executive committee which informed the shocked Russian people of an overthrow of the Bolshevik government planned by the Entente diplomats and spies under their supervision. Commenting on the failed plot, the Kremlin appealed to soldiers and workers in the Entente states, exposing the conspirators' goals, including the arrest of top Bolshevik administrators and the encouragement of 'famine in the big cities of European Russia by performing acts of sabotage at railway stations and depots to cut them off from food supplies'. Intending to cohere the revolt of the Moscow garrison with the anti-Bolshevik military units' advance towards the Soviet capital, they ostensibly planned to introduce a military dictatorship in Russia and resume hostilities against the Central empires to prevent the country being transformed into Germany's vassal-state.[11]

Some further pieces of information might be extracted from an open letter by Réne Marchand, the French correspondent to the *Figaro* – one of the leading Paris journals. Addressing his message to Raymond Poincaré, the president of the Third republic, Marchand wrote how Allied diplomats and military representatives concocted various scenarios of the anti-Bolshevik coup at the premises of the American consulate in Moscow on 25 August 1918.[12]

Martin Latsis, the Cheka collegium member, who had contributed to the creation of the Red guards, avowed that the total amount of 10 million roubles were spent on the organization of the plot. As he argued in his memoirs, the British and French secret agents set up an extensive network of espionage inside central Soviet administrative bodies. Their activities, therefore, led to the 'counter-revolutionary surge raising to the highest level' by the autumn of 1918 when everybody in Moscow 'felt the coming storm'.[13]

Another eminent Cheka official, Yakov Peters, who temporarily acted as its head (albeit only for a few weeks in July and August the same year), narrated the acts of sabotage that the 'Entente spies' contrived to carry out before the coup. These included blowing up both highway bridges and the railway overpasses in the suburbs of Petrograd. Peters assessed the Red terror as a spontaneous, although inevitable reaction to the assassination of Moses Uritsky, the chairman of the Petrograd Cheka section, as well as to the abortive attempt to Lenin's life on 30 August in Moscow.[14]

After a few books dedicated to the 'Lockhart plot' came out in the 1920s, this episode faded from the professional discourse for decades, being revisited only by Petr Mal'kov, a former Baltic Fleet seaman, who acted as an interim chief administrator of the Smolny in 1917, later to become a new commandant of the Kremlin.[15] Another period of attention to the plot coincided with the fiftieth anniversary of the Bolshevik revolution when a stream of publications flooded Soviet periodicals. Based on certain declassified documents and interviews with surviving participants, the belletristic versions of the 'Lockhart plot' made the real picture wholly obscure.[16] The situation changed only in recent years, when Russian historians moved away from the Communist propaganda truisms by reconsidering available primary sources.[17]

From the very beginning, their Western colleagues refuted any anti-Bolshevik conspiracy devised by the British or any other diplomatic missions, blaming only individual adventurers such as Reilly. Amusingly, there were authors who accused Trotsky of being involved in the preparatory activities for the coup.[18] Since the late 1960s the non-Soviet historians have written about the complete falsification of the anti-Bolshevik conspiracy by the so-called double-agents, or agent-provocateurs, who were implemented in the counter-revolutionary 'underground' by Dzerzhinsky's order.[19] In the late 1990s–early 2000s, Western authors admitted that the failed coup d'état was undertaken by secret intelligence agencies under the vigilant surveillance of the Bolshevik leaders.[20] The recent studies merely reiterated traditional approaches, nuancing only episodes of this 'true British' intrigue, as one writer coined the case.[21]

That is why the present author's priority has been to suggest an objective version of events. First of all, one should bear in mind that Reilly and other MI6 officers involved in the matter had two alternatives: either to openly recover the British alliance with Russia by coercing the Bolshevik leaders to ignore the clauses of the Brest treaty, or to surreptitiously arrange the overthrow of the Soviet regime with the help of various domestic counter-revolutionary forces.

With Litvinov's letter of recommendation and an identity card of the Petrograd Cheka criminal department that Reilly had managed to obtain through an old acquaintance of his, the 'master-spy' met Vladimir Bonch-Bruevich, the SNK chief administrator, on five occasions during April–May 1918. Their extensive conversations resulted in Lenin and Trotsky's consent to provide Reilly with information about the redeployment of German and Austria-Hungarian troops on the Russian, Belorussian and Ukrainian territories.[22] Moreover, Reilly negotiated with certain Kremlin top officials an assistance in the organization of an anti-German uprising in the occupiers' rear.[23] As the documentary records evidenced, Reilly together with the above-mentioned Captain Hill actively cooperated with the staff of the so-called Military control office of the People's Commissariat for war and naval affairs. Besides, they contacted a new-born counter-intelligence service for combatting espionage activity inside the Cheka.[24] Some historians perhaps excessively wrote of Reilly's decisive influence which he exercised upon the Bolshevik officialdom in the spring of 1918. Apart from other ideas harboured by C., the head of MI6 envisaged a new configuration of Russian intelligence under the British guidance to better interact with the Allies.[25]

Meanwhile Reilly contacted the members of the anti-Bolshevik Union for Protection of Motherland and Freedom chaired by Boris Savinkov – the notorious Socialist Revolutionary and Kerensky's closest assistant in 1917. Commodore Cromie arranged Reilly's meeting with the members of the Union to prevent the Bolsheviks' consignment of Russian battleships to the Germans. He designed to enrol former Russian naval officers into the British military service by appealing to their patriotic sentiments and promising that they would be lavishly paid by the Admiralty if neglecting the Bolshevik commands.[26]

It is worth keeping in mind that up to 50,000 demobilized Russian army and navy officers had assembled in Petrograd by the spring of 1918.[27] Scarcely one or two out of ten could survive on their miserable retirement pensions. The register list of Russian volunteers opting for British military service that was found at the premises of the Petrograd diplomatic mission during the Cheka search on 31 August 1918 attested to this estimation (see the end of the chapter).[28] According to the secret reports by the Main Staff registration office, since the beginning of 1918, 'the British, French and American missions, especially the consulates [of these states], have been intensively visited by Russian officers'. They applied for enlistment in the Allied troops or marine crews, imploring Western diplomats for reimbursement of travel costs to Britain, France or the United States. On receiving subsidies in cash, however, many Russian officers preferred to vanish without trace, making it difficult to uncover the networks of espionage.[29] At the same time, Aleksander Fride, the former Lieutenant-Colonel of the Russian army, agreed to be appointed the head of a section at the Moscow military district's headquarters. On getting access to classified intelligence files, he became an MI6 informant while his sister acted as a courier between Fride and Reilly who managed to recruit the Latvian-born officer.[30]

As it was stated in the previous chapter, a significant proportion of those servicemen who backed the Bolsheviks in November 1917 were native Latvians differing in their perception of the Soviet rule. Most of them became the Bolsheviks' striking military force in anticipation of their homeland being granted independence. Others refused to acquiesce to the Soviet regime considering Lenin and his lieutenants as the Germans' marionettes who kept on oppressing Latvia. But by mid-1918 a large section of Latvian servicemen in Russia had not yet taken a side. The ambiguous attitude to the Bolsheviks along with their position as a kind of communist 'praetorian guards' prompted competition between the Bolsheviks, Germans and allies for the control over this armed force.[31]

The reasons for the anti-Bolshevik sentiments varied among Latvian war veterans, though they had been subjected to political purges like other Soviet regiments. Most rank-and-file were displeased with the Bolsheviks' failure to live up to their initial promises as well as with Moscow closing eyes to the Germans occupying the Baltic provinces. In July 1918, the Latvian servicemen even went so far as to separately negotiate with certain German high commanders to be given an opportunity to return home, although their repatriation was not allowed.[32]

The overall economic and social instability made the Latvian servicemen dislike the Soviets, fearing their homeland would never become independent.[33] In the opinion of Karl Helfferich who succeeded Count Mirbach as the German ambassador in Moscow, some Latvian riflemen units were ready to betray the Bolsheviks in favour of Central powers, given the guarantee to restore peasants' land ownership in the Baltic provinces.[34] The Bolsheviks' confiscation of grain surplus in rural households on the territory under their control as well as the abolition of military commanders' electability together with the restoration of death penalty in the armed forces also destabilized the situation while the Kremlin kept on using the Latvian regiments in punitive operations against anti-Bolshevik insurgents.[35]

Not surprisingly, the so-called Latvian Club – an informal association of war veterans in Petrograd – had attracted Cromie's attention since late December 1917. On his recommendation, Reilly focused on the Latvian officers who regularly attended the club. It was there some of them were recruited to become saboteurs and informants of the Entente's intelligence agencies, including MI6.

These activities could not escape surveillance by the Petrograd Chekists, especially in the circumstances of civil unrest coupled with various external threats to the Soviet rule. That is why Dzerzhinsky and Peters initiated the establishment of a fictitious National Latvian committee consisting of the delegates elected by their military units.[36] The Cheka bosses' original purpose was merely to eliminate counter-revolutionary organizations which embraced a wide range of their political opponents – from monarchists to anarchists. In late May–early June 1918, the Cheka agents captured dozens of Savinkov's agents, though he again escaped the arrest. Following the suppression of the left Socialist revolutionaries' revolt in Moscow on 6–7 July, Dzerzhinsky's intentions seemed to have undergone changes spurred by two major events – the execution of the tsarist family in Ekaterinburg on 17 July and the Entente refocusing on the arrangement for a broader-scale armed intervention in Russia without agreement with local Soviets.[37]

Presumably, it was in mid-July when the Cheka became aware of Reilly, Cromie and Lockhart concocting an anti-Bolshevik coup d'état to be performed by Latvian riflemen in Moscow and Petrograd. To discredit the Bolshevik central authorities and divert their attention from the capitals, the MI6 officers meant to synchronize social unrest with the Entente expeditionary troops' onslaught upon the positions of the Red Army to the south of Murmansk and Arkhangelsk. The wide purge of the Cheka personnel in the aftermath of the failed July mutiny seemed to facilitate the realization of the aims in view.[38]

By implementing the two Latvians – Sprogis and Engelgardt under the sobriquets Shmidkhen and Bredis, respectively, into Cromie's inner circle of proxies, and through him – into the cohort of Reilly's and Lockhart's consiglieres, the Cheka had achieved their goal of fabricating false impression of all the Latvian riflemen being fully sympathetic with the anti-Bolshevik movement. During their conversations with Cromie and Reilly on several occasions in the second half of July–mid-August 1918, Shmidkhen and Bredis persuaded the British of their compatriots' willingness to put an end to the Soviet regime.

Edward Berzin, a commander of the First Latvian light artillery battalion, played a crucial part in the imitation of the plot by the Chekists. Shmidkhen introduced Berzin to Reilly while the latter consigned to the Latvian officer the substantial sums of 700,000, 200,000 and 300,000 roubles on 19, 21 and 28 August, respectively. Berzin was bound to distribute the cash among Berzin's fellow commanders who were supposed to betray the Bolsheviks in favour of the Entente.[39]

It should be mentioned that Lockhart and other eyewitnesses deliberately concealed an important detail regarding the preparation of the fake conspiracy. In the present author's opinion, it was Maria (Mura) Zakrevskaia who had acted as the guarantor of Shmidkhen and Bredis in their communication with Cromie. She had perfect command of at least three European languages, working as an interpreter for the staff of the British diplomatic mission in Petrograd, a position she had got supposedly at the recommendation of Meriel Buchanan, the daughter of the former ambassador. To all appearances, while carrying out the Cheka chefs' personal assignments, Zakrevskaia combined spying with personal affection to Lockhart.[40]

It remains unclear which of the Entente military missions – British or French – posed the question of the Latvian rifle division opening the front for the Allied task force advance from the north and east.[41] Anyhow, since the armed intervention assumed a coalition character from the very beginning, Lockhart needed his colleagues' strong support. They were Robert Wardrope, the British general consul in Moscow; Fernand Grenard, the French general consul; Dewitt Clinton Poole, the US general consul; and Xenophon Kalamatiano, the head of the American information bureau who had been running a clandestine espionage network in the Russian empire since 1914.[42]

Eager to preserve their capital till the downfall of the Bolsheviks, some Moscow industrialists and bankers sponsored the anti-Bolshevik conspiracy by giving money to Lockhart and Reilly in return for special bills valued in pounds – the debt receipts with guarantees of repayment issued by the Treasury or the War Office. Reimbursement would be accessible only after the Bolsheviks' collapse. Should it fail, Lockhart promised assistance in his creditors' escape from Russia. Fully aware of this practice, the Chekists, on their side, let these diplomatic representatives collect money hoping to lull them temporarily into a false sense of security in order to confiscate the accumulated sum after the plot was exposed.[43]

Having returned to London from Soviet Russia, Lockhart drafted a top-secret report for the Cabinet on 5 November 1918. He absolved himself of responsibility not only for any illegal activity but also for the indirect endorsement of the extended scheme of the plot allegedly proposed by Reilly together with Cromie. As Lockhart tried to prove, he abstained from any secret dealings with Reilly or other intelligence agents, being however informed of their contacts with the anti-Bolshevik dissidents. Regarding the proposal to abet the Latvian riflemen in the riot against the Soviet rule, Lockhart persuaded the Foreign Office that it was a collective decision. The cool reception by high-ranking Whitehall officials who informally denounced him as 'an intrigant and hysteric schoolboy' demonstrated their frustration of his mission's results. Yet the audience given to Lockhart by King George V became a moral compensation to a hapless diplomat awarded with the order of St Michael and St George.[44]

In fact, Lockhart obviously misled Balfour and other Cabinet members. While working in the archives, the present author succeeded to find a contemporary account by Henry Armour, the US diplomatic secretary in Moscow at the time. On 7 September 1918, he informed the British envoy to Stockholm of Lockhart's plan to consign large sums of cash to the Latvian 'praetorian guards' in order to inspire their anti-Bolshevik sentiments and trigger the military coup three days later.[45] To all appearances, Reilly and Cromie motivated Lockhart to amend the original scenario of the complot, focusing on the simultaneous grab of state power in Moscow and Petrograd following the fiasco of the Entente advance against the Soviet troops in the first half of August.[46] Three arguments attest to the plotters' disappointment with the armed intervention 'by agreement', assumption of total corruption among Latvian commanders as well as expectations of the mass revolt against the harsh regulations introduced by the

Bolsheviks. There is every reason to believe that, similarly to other Entente diplomats, Lockhart merely 'washed his hands' of the coup, handing over 'dirty work' to Reilly, Cromie, Hill and other intelligence personnel.[47]

Already in his first confidential conversation with Berzin on 17 August 1918, Reilly revealed the stages of the coup: after the Bolshevik leaders assemble an Extraordinary All-Russian central executive committee at the Moscow Bolshoi theatre to ratify the economic treaty with Germany, the Latvian rifle division designated to safeguard the central Soviet administrative bodies was bound to prompt other military garrisons to side with the Bolshevik opponents. Put another way, the Soviet 'praetorian guards' ought to have sparked a series of mutinies leading to the arrest of the People's commissars and the establishment of the directorate chaired by Berzin and comprising three persons. Following this stage of the coup, the plotters should form two new national armies in the Moscow and Petrograd military districts.[48] To fulfil this task, the Latvian commanders needed to delay a regular monthly payment to lower ranks. It was also intended that they would capture several freight cars loaded with the Bolshevik state gold reserves at the railway station in the north-western suburbs of Moscow.[49]

Soviet authors traditionally pointed out to the planned arrest and execution of Lenin and his closest supporters by the conspirators, linking the 'Lockhart plot' to the attack on the Bolshevik leaders by the left Socialist revolutionaries when Uritsky was killed, and Lenin gravely wounded. It is also necessary to bear in mind that the Petrograd Cheka agents arrested Leonid Kanegisser – the murderer of Uritsky – at the premises of the English club on the Neva embankment, which enabled them to accuse the British diplomats and intelligence officers of involvement in the crime.[50] However, the available correspondence shows that the conspirators were aiming not to kill the People's commissars but to discredit their rule. What corroborates this conclusion is the plotters' intention to enlist the support of the Russian Orthodox church hierarches. According to documentary records at our disposal, they consigned 5 million roubles to Tikhon, the newly elected Patriarch, to organize thanksgiving prayers after the overthrow of the Bolshevik regime, though Hill denounced the bribe in the report to C.[51]

The Allied representatives who gathered at the building of the US general consulate in Moscow on 25 August rejected Reilly's adventurous plan to remove the Bolsheviks from power. Yet he only postponed its implementation to 6 and later to 10 September when a joint session of the All-Russian executive committee and the Moscow Soviet was expected to be held. As Hill's report evidenced, Reilly left for Petrograd in the aftermath of the mentioned conference to inspect local Latvian units which were planned to involve in the mutiny.[52]

The tragic events of 30 August compelled the Cheka bosses to cease a 'cat and mouse' game with the conspirators, though the Red terror's starting point remains a disputed issue in the scholarship. Some historians argue that it was initiated by the suppression of the Petrograd military cadets' uprising as early as in November 1917, or by the shooting of citizens deprecating the All-Russian Constituent Assembly's crackdown in January 1918. The reasons are given that the assassination of Vladimir Volodarsky, the editor-in-chief of the Petrograd daily *Krasnaia Gazeta*, on 20 June as well as the execution by the Entente expeditionary forces of the Kem' commissars in mid-July triggered another waive of the Red terror.⁵³ According to the representative of the German supreme military commandment in Moscow, the suppression of the July anti-Bolshevik mutiny led to mass execution of the left Socialist revolutionaries by the Chinese military volunteers on the Bolshevik service. Obviously, the massacre of the tsar family on 17 July approved by the Kremlin was another highlight of the Bolshevik atrocities.⁵⁴

In the author's view, the Red terror as an officially proclaimed domestic policy began in late August–early September 1918, when Trotsky and Dzerzhinsky launched mass repressions across Soviet Russia.⁵⁵ The execution of several hundred former tsarist civil administrators and military commanders carried out by the Chekists in the autumn of 1918 without the slightest hint of fair trial attested to this conclusion. Additionally, one should bear in mind numerous arrests of foreign citizens (in Petrograd alone, twenty-eight British and eleven Frenchmen were jailed) along with confiscation of their property.⁵⁶ The detention of Lockhart by the Chekists on 1 September followed by his second arrest five days later was a reaction to Litvinov's imprisonment in London early in the month.⁵⁷

The situation became even more aggravated on 31 August when a group of Cheka agents rushed into the premises of the British mission in Petrograd which remained under the auspices of the Netherlands since the early days of the month. The attack led to the death of Cromie who defended the first-floor office rooms. Whereas the arrest of Lockhart met an unexpectedly mild reaction from the Foreign Office, the assassination of the UK acting naval attaché and the detention of dozens of British citizens gave the Cabinet a plausible excuse to immediately dispatch to Moscow a note of strong remonstration against these actions.⁵⁸ One may agree with the argument that 'Cromie's death in defence of the embassy did more than any other single act to convince the British that the Bolsheviks were indeed barbarians'.⁵⁹ For example, Churchill circulated a special memorandum to the Cabinet, inviting colleagues, 'despite the strong employment of many other issues', to draw up a list of those responsible for the murder of Cromie and announce inevitable retribution against the Bolsheviks, no matter how long it would take.⁶⁰

The Foreign Office appeals to stop repression and punish the guilty persons found support amongst the Allies and associated states. Moreover, as Austen Chamberlain, then the minister without portfolio, wrote to his sister Hilda, 'even Germans and Austrians joined with the neutrals and Allied representatives in protest against indiscriminate murder and the blind fury of terrorism'.⁶¹ The widespread negative reaction by European statesmen and public opinion compelled Chicherin to dispatch two circular notes to London, Paris, Rome and Washington on 7 and 12 September in order to justify the Cheka's internment of numerous foreign nationals. Naturally, he pinned the blame for Cromie's assassination on the commodore himself.⁶²

It is crucially important, therefore, to reconstruct the scene of the tragic accident which occurred in Petrograd on 31 August, given the fact that this episode attained different explanations. The official British interpretation ran as follows: at about 7 pm (according to other sources – 4 pm), Cromie, armed with two revolvers, bravely defended the grand staircase leading to the first floor of the premises where he kept secret files, presumably, the lists of those Russian officers and civil servants who had been recruited to join the anti-Bolshevik mutiny. In fact, Cromie's action towards the unexpected guests infringing on the embassy's diplomatic immunity was an attempt to buy time for the elimination of compromising catalogues and records. Some American historians even supplemented this version with a claim that Dzerzhinsky had deliberately ordered the assassination of the British officer, so that the latter could not refute the Bolshevik interpretation of the 'Lockhart plot'.[63]

Accordingly, Soviet diplomatic historians created a different picture. It not only originated from the publications by the *Pravda* and *Izvestiya* but was also rooted in Zinoviev's speech at the meeting of the Petrograd Soviet on 1 November 1918.[64] The Bolshevik leader blamed the British who allegedly exploited the embassy building to surreptitiously confer with Russian counter-revolutionaries. The operation was portrayed as a polite request by the Chekists to allow the search of the premises, in response to which Cromie opened gunfire, killing the group's senior officer who had asked him in English to cease fire, and wounding three other rank-and-file before he was fatally shot in the head.[65]

However, this study demonstrates that certain former Russian senior administrators used to confer at the premises of the British Petrograd mission, secretly overseen by the Cheka agents. On 31 August, Cromie with another MI6 officer was holding a confidential discussion with two double agents nicknamed as Shtekel'man (or Shtegel'man) and Sabir enlisted by the Petrograd Cheka as early as in the spring of 1918. Apart from these individuals, more than a dozen of the auxiliary personnel were staying in the building on that night. But it was Savinkov whom the Chekists most wanted to arrest. If the senior officer of the group knew him by appearance, other servicemen had no idea of how Russia's supreme political terrorist looked like in reality.

According to the by-stander's account, when Cromie confronted the attackers at the top of the front staircase, he started shooting at the Chekists climbing the stairs.[66] A rash shooting, which lasted several minutes, led to tragic results: a Cheka agent was killed by 'friendly fire', while two others were gravely wounded by Cromie who received two bullets to the back of the head. There could be reason to conclude that Shtekel'man or Sabir shot Cromie to cover the tracks of their rapport with MI6.[67]

Yet there are certain gaps in the understanding of the motives. In particular, the following questions remain: Did the Petrograd Chekists act on their own will or on the instructions from Moscow central office? Was Sidney Reilly associated with the Cheka invasion of the mission? Could the German military intelligence be somehow involved in the murder of Cromie to vindicate Count Mirbach's demise?[68]

As the embassy personnel later recalled, the Chekists turned the entire building upside down in the search of Savinkov. They confiscated the documents which Cromie did not manage to destroy and appropriated most of the fur overcoats, silverware, books, works of art, and even pieces of furniture. Only the intervention of the Danish and Dutch envoys saved the premises from complete looting. As for the Commodore's dead body, it was buried with all necessary rituals in the Petrograd's Smolensk cemetery on 6 September 1918, albeit the local authorities failed to preserve his grave until today.[69]

Meanwhile, the Bolsheviks launched an unprecedented xenophobic campaign in the press even before the official announcement of the complot. Some newspapers published Zinoviev's appeal, who was putatively also attacked by a killer at the *Astoria* hotel in Petrograd, 'to grant the right to workers to lynch any intellectual right on the streets'.[70] Lockhart depicted some well-known political figures such as Trotsky, Kamenev and Radek, all of them urging the immediate execution of the detained British and French citizens.[71] Soviet punitive organs on all levels enthusiastically supported the campaign of unrestricted terror. 'We need neither courts, nor tribunals! Let the vengeance of the workers raise, let the blood of Socialist revolutionaries and White Guards pour out! Destroy out the enemies physically!' – demanded the *Petrograd Pravda* on 1 September 1918.[72] Another public statement by Zinoviev signalled an apotheosis of mass hysteria when he called for the elimination of 10 per cent of the Russian citizens who were dissatisfied with the Bolshevik regime.[73]

The result was the persecution and killing of British subjects in the provinces under the Bolsheviks' rule, as it happened to certain Mr A. Smith, who was executed without investigation and trial by the Chekists in the small Siberian town of Verkhoturie on 13 October 1918.[74] Kalamatiano became the last victim of the terror to have been arrested on 18 September in front of the American consulate following his return to Moscow from the trip to Ufa. Unable to withstand ruthless interrogations, Kalamatiano betrayed to the tormentors a network of secret informants which the Americans set up in Russia during the First World War.[75]

The bloody repressions against anti-Bolshevik groups aimed at controlling the Russian population and may also be explained by low personal culture of many rank-and-file Chekists, combined with messianic vision of their chiefs who believed their sacred duty was to exterminate all 'bourgeoise exploiters'. Like French Jacobins in the late eighteenth century, some of them stated that they were guided by 'new morality' predicated upon 'glorious ideals of destruction of all violence and oppression in the world'.[76]

Following the complot's fiasco, the witch-hunting in the Red Army and navy led to a massive purge of all displeased with the existing regime. Those people suspected of contacting the British or French missions were immediately sacked, arrested and in many cases executed. As the head of the Naval General Staff reported to Trotsky and Peters in October 1918, the Chekists exposed and eliminated sixteen 'Anglo-Americano-French spies', including the chief of the Red Army's Main Staff registration service, his assistant and the director of the Red naval military intelligence.[77]

Lockhart's interrogations by Peters and Lev Karakhan, the deputy People's commissar for foreign affairs, took place on several occasions in the period from 6 to 15 September at the Lubyanka central prison, wherefrom the diplomat was later transferred to a secure apartment within the Kremlin wall. For obvious reasons, the British and Soviet versions of these interviews differed. If Lockhart downplayed his role in the plot to evade harsh sentence, the interrogators corroborated British diplomat's involvement in the conspiracy, expostulating him on going to the Bolsheviks' service.[78]

By 20 September, the Foreign Office and the NKID had finally settled Lockhart–Litvinov exchange together with the reciprocal deportation of their assistants. Five days later, the Soviet representative left Aberdeen via Norwegian seaport of Bergen for Petrograd. In his absence, one of Litvinov's closest associates – Theodor Rothstein – assumed the duties of the Bolshevik government's representative in the UK. Accordingly, thirty-one British and twenty-five Frenchmen, including Lockhart and Grenard, released from prison, managed to cross the Finnish border by train to reach Stockholm on 9 October.[79] Some authors credited either Peters or Zakrevskaia with Lockhart getting permission to quit Soviet Russia. Yet their personal motives should be viewed as secondary consideration while the primary motivation was the Bolsheviks' objective 'not to burn all bridges' between Russia and Britain in case their relations returned to normality someday.[80]

The Supreme revolutionary tribunal put an end to the 'Lockhart plot'. Whereas Western newspapers ignored it, the Bolshevik press highlighted the trial on a regular basis. It took the court a week in the interim from 25 November to 3 December 1918 to sentence six persons to death (including four people – in absence) and ten – to prison. Eight supposed plotters, apparently the Cheka double-agents, were exonerated by the court. Sidney Reilly managed to bypass the traps and escaped from Russia, though the Bolshevik put a price of 100,000 roubles on his head. In fact, merely one death sentence was carried out – that of Aleksander Fride on 17 December 1918, while the same punishment to Kalamatiano was later changed for a lengthy prison sentence. He was however released on 21 August 1921 at the request of the American Relief Administration (ARA) and deported to the United States, where he died two years later.[81] Strange as it may seem, none of Latvian officers were brought to court. As Reilly confessed to the Chekists who interrogated him after he was finally arrested in 1925, 'I presume that Lockhart's trial involved people who had nothing to do with me, or on some occasions only the remotest connection with the case, for the persons standing close to me set off to Ukraine immediately after the conspiracy had been disclosed.'[82]

The 'complot of ambassadors' was featured in several novels and movies both in the USSR and abroad. Instantly, Lockhart was the lead character of the Hollywood cinema blockbuster *British Agent* in 1934, whereas the Soviet film, entitled *Whirlwinds Hostile (Vikhri vrazhdebnye)*, commemorated the complot's thirty-fifth anniversary in 1953. On 7 March 2006, the Supreme court of the Russian Federation refused rehabilitation of all the accused persons.[83]

Summing up, it is necessary to answer the following questions: How should one evaluate the activities of British diplomatic representatives in Soviet Russia during the summer months of 1918, and was there a real chance for the plot to be brought to life by the foreign missions?

This research strongly suggests that the failure of the 'intervention by agreement' was mainly due to the Bolshevik leaders' unscrupulous diplomatic manoeuvres between the warring coalitions. At the same time, the activation of domestic counter-revolutionaries prompted the British government, as it had often happened before, to resort to alternative means. The combined operation to replace the Bolshevik rule by military dictatorship could provide the re-establishment of the Eastern front until the allies' victory was gained. On the other hand, remaining feckless enough to conduct an independent foreign policy, Moscow would inevitably become a satellite of Western powers. However, owing to a deficit of appropriate financial resources as well as the munitions required by the UK for the final offensive in the summer – autumn of 1918, most British statesmen considered a large-scale armed intervention in Russia as a very risky and therefore useless enterprise. That is why London and

Paris made a bet on a coup d'état by internal Bolsheviks' opponents backed by the British and French missions.

Given the general pattern of the coup, the plotters relied upon the assistance of Latvian rifle units whom they intended to convince into rebellion. Despite Lockhart's inexperience in producing anti-governmental plots and Reilly's adventurism, the conspirators should have concentrated them either to the north of Moscow or in the Volga region, instead of spreading forces thinly between different fronts. At the same time, one may conclude that the plan to rely on the Latvians in the anti-Bolshevik uprising was difficult to carry out for its impudent nature, exacerbated by the constant hesitance of national servicemen, and, what seems even most important, the preventive actions undertaken by the Cheka. In fact, Dzerzhinsky and Peters steered the plotters down the wrong path with the help of double agents through the disinformation that the conspirators received from Lubyanka central office through various channels.[84]

Some historians maintain that Marchand came to Lubyanka to share the intelligence of the complot right after the meeting of the Entente diplomatic and military representatives on 25 August. Then the correspondent of the *Figaro* was recommended by Lenin and Dzerzhinsky to reveal the 'insidious intentions' of Western representatives in the open letter message which had the effect of an exploding bomb.[85] It is also clear that two other factors played a crucial part. First, Lockhart, Reilly and Cromie seriously underestimated the long-time experience of the Cheka's bosses as former 'professional revolutionaries'. Second, the British diplomats and intelligence officers nourished a sense of arrogance about their limitless organizational and financial capacity. It was this false impression that allowed historians to define the conspiracy as a 'true British plot'.[86] In any case, one could be led to believe that Reilly's desire to disrupt local authorities by conducting sabotage at numerous factories, warehouses and railway communications could not be brought to life.[87] This author is not willing to demonize the 'master spy' whom some specialists almost went as far as to call almost the main culprit of the Red terror in the autumn of 1918.[88]

Because of some MI6 officers, the idea to undermine the Bolshevik rule had been converted in the full-scale plan of a military coup d'état by the end of August 1918. Available evidence indicates that Lockhart provided diplomatic cover and partial financing for the coup, while Reilly together with Cromie acted as its general managers – the former in Moscow and the latter in Petrograd. As for other British diplomats, they kept away from the conspiracy, informing London of current developments in Russia and running only occasional errands for Lockhart, Reilly or Cromie.[89]

This chapter demonstrates that it is more correct to term the failed attempt to overthrow the Bolshevik regime as the 'general consuls' plot'. The British MI6 agents along with some diplomatic employees made a decisive contribution to its organization. Yet Dzerzhinsky and Peters succeeded in catching Lockhart, Cromie and Reilly in the trap. The failed coup d'état led to launching the mass Red terror inside Russia as well as to the beginning of the Entente full-scale armed intervention against it in the end of 1918. The ill-famous conspiracy ruined the Soviet-British relations, expelling in this way any possible steps towards rapprochement until the spring of 1920, when the new political and economic developments made it again possible.

Meanwhile the NKID repeatedly informed the Allied governments on the Bolsheviks' readiness for negotiations. On 24 October 1918, Chicherin addressed Wilson and on 3 November, the People's commissar sent a similar request to the Entente political front-runners via neutral Sweden. Three days later, the delegates of the Sixth All-Russian Congress of Soviets announced their peace offer to foreign peoples and governments.[90]

Referring to Cecil's memorandum of the Russian situation for the Cabinet, Buchanan described the situation in the following manner:

> So long as Trotsky, Lenin and their associates retain power, we shall never have an effective guarantee that German activities will cease. We must, however, make it clear that our sole object is to free Russia from those who have betrayed her to Germany and to prepare the way for the holding of a Constitutional Assembly with a mandate to form a stable central government, and to organize an armed force for the maintenance of order.[91]

Having failed to forcibly change the Bolshevik regime, the Entente elite circles confronted the so-called 'Russian problem' – one of the most complicated international issues in the world war's aftermath. As the next chapter will show, it assumed even more importance in Asia, where the traditional geopolitical competition between Russia and Britain aggravated on a new ideological basis.

4

Oriental trends of the Soviet-British relations, 1918

British India
Is sending their officers.
They need oil,
They need cotton,
While whip and military campaign,
Are their passion.
But the English boot wants most of all
To crush the Soviet rule.

Nikolai Aseev, the Soviet poet, 1928[1]

For the last two centuries, the peoples inhabiting the vast areas of West, Central and East Asia played a prominent role in the development of Russo-British relations. It was in these regions the so-called Great Game which combined the two empires' rivalry and collaboration lasted for decades in the second half of the nineteenth century. In 1907 St Petersburg and London formally ended this competition by signing a special convention on the demarcation of their 'spheres of influence' in disputable territories of Afghanistan, Persia and Tibet. Yet some key issues remained unsettled, while Germany, Japan and the United States took the stage of world politics on the eve of the First World War.[2]

The Great Russian revolution deeply transformed the general situation in Asia. It led to developing Bolshevism among non-European, primarily non-Christian nations and ethnic groups. On 3 December 1917, the SNK appeal *To All the Labouring Class Moslems of Russia and the Orient* was followed by the publication of the Entente secret agreements on the partition of the Ottoman empire. The armistice on the Caucasus front between Russian and Turkish troops in mid-December 1917 put an end to the earlier Russo-British cooperation in the Near and Middle East.[3] The Soviet government's decision to withdraw the Russian expeditionary force from Eastern Anatolia and Northern Persia became a final point leading to the abrogation of the Russo-British convention.[4]

Yet further steps, taken by the Bolshevik policymakers before the signature of the Brest treaty, for example their calls to London for granting independence to Egypt and

India, attested to the resumed geopolitical rivalry between Soviet Russia and the UK in Asia, albeit this time on ideological ground. The German-Turkish threat to Britain's interests became just another reason for the Entente invasion of Transcaucasia and Central Asia – the spheres of traditional Russian influence.[5]

Before considering these oriental trends, it is worth bearing in mind that George Curzon, repeatedly mentioned in the previous chapters, may be called the engineer of the UK oriental policy in the aftermath of the Great War. Acting as the foreign secretary during the 1919–20 Paris peace conference, he hammered out nearly every Cabinet decision on relations with Asian countries.[6] Not surprisingly, Curzon also directed the interdepartmental Eastern Committee – the only consultative government body in the Lloyd George government to deal exclusively with the Middle East.[7]

It is well known that the predecessors of the Eastern Committee were several other configurations with a narrower range of functions.[8] Towards the beginning of 1918, Curzon felt dissatisfied with the coalition government's strategy in Asia. He was deeply concerned with the Foreign and India Office pursuing the eastern policy on their own, without rapport with the War Office, Admiralty or Board of Trade. Curzon suggested, therefore, the Eastern Committee's recommendations on key issues of the Asian political agenda to elaborate a coherent view of the situation.[9]

At its first session on 28 March 1918, the committee outlined the framework of an international order to be set up in the Middle East. Delivering a lengthy lecture to the audience, Curzon, who chaired the meeting, indicated certain principal trends of the UK principal political course. They included the expulsion of the Turkish sultan from Constantinople, the revision of the 1916 Sykes–Picot agreement on the Ottoman possessions, the establishment of Britain's protectorate in Persia and the territories inhabited by the Arabs as well as the elimination of Russia's malicious influence in Central Asia.[10] As Cecil claimed at the committee's session on 2 December 1918, 'Russia was to be feared not so much because she was Bolshevik as because she was a great power whose interests placed her astride the lifelines of the British empire'.[11]

According to Curzon, the British policy in Asia should be predicated on counteraction to the 'Red expansion', especially against India. For the preservation and even reinforcement of Britain's position, Curzon proposed taking the Arab territories, Persia and Afghanistan under the UK aegis by setting up a cluster of independent 'buffer states', such as Kurdistan, khanates of Bukhara and Khiva, Eastern Turkestan and Tibet.[12]

In the Kremlin, no experts of Curzon's caliber could be named among the Bolshevik front-runners, for neither Lenin, Trotsky or Chicherin, not even Stalin, who was in charge of the People's commissariat for nationalities, possessed knowledge and practical experience, suffice to formulate an adequate policy in Russia's southern 'soft underbelly'.[13] In fact, dealing with the Ottoman empire, Iran, Afghanistan, China and Japan fell in the competence of Lev Karakhan mentioned in the previous chapter. He became Chicherin's deputy in the spring of 1918 supporting him against Litvinov during their constant personal clashes.[14]

Already the initial Bolshevik statements regarding their attitude to oriental countries revealed the objective to diminish the negative consequences of the Brest treaty in Transcaucasia and Turkestan, where Moscow sought to rely first on the pan-Islamic and then on nationalist movements balancing between both the German-Turkish and

Anglo-French alliances.[15] The Kremlin tried, therefore, to prevent Britain along with other great powers from the creation of 'buffer states' on the fringes of the Ottoman empire, searching, at the same time, to bolshevize Russia's neighbouring countries.[16]

In the meantime, the political struggle between Lenin's supporters and the opponents of the Brest treaty as well as the demobilization of the Russian active troops in the Caucasus triggered the announcement of the Transcaucasian Democratic Federation in Tiflis on 22 April 1918. Almost simultaneously, the Commune regime was proclaimed in Baku, the capital of Azerbaijan. Stepan Shaumian, a member of the Bolshevik party Central Committee, chaired the Baku SNK and concurrently procured the post of the regional commissar for foreign affairs.[17]

In the UK, the Cabinet reviewed the situation on the former Russian empire's southern outskirts as highly unfavourable to Britain. London and Delhi kept on receiving intelligence about German expeditionary corps on the way to Transcaucasia. At the same time, Ottoman infantry units resumed offensive in the direction of Batum, an important Black Sea transport hub equipped with an oil terminal, as well as towards Tiflis, the political centre of Transcaucasia. Having captured Batum in mid-April, the Turkish troops were as close as 20–25 kilometres to Tiflis by the end of the month.[18]

Figure 3 Stepan Shaumian, chairman of the Baku Commune, 1918. Photo courtesy of Wikimedia Commons (public domain).

Moreover, secret agents of the sultan government continued to recruit volunteers in Afghanistan for a *jihad* (sacred war) against the British. To aggravate this situation, about 180,000–190,000 German, Austrian and Hungarian ex-POWs, held in the camps on the territory of Russian Turkestan, became a potential threat to the Entente. Under the influence of German propaganda, they intended to pass to Europe through the Middle East or, had their attempt failed, to strike in the rear of the British troops in Persia and Mesopotamia.[19]

The seizure of Poti, another important Black Sea port, by German expeditionary forces on 25 May 1918, along with independent Georgia's immediate exit from the Transcaucasian Democratic Federation and the signing of six unfair treaties with Berlin were followed by the establishment of the informal German protectorate over Western Transcaucasia, whereas the remaining territory became the Ottoman sphere of influence.

These events coincided with Moscow contacting Mirza Kuchik Khan, an insurgency leader fighting for Gillian, a northern Persian province. On 23–24 May 1918, Feodor Raskol'nikov, then the deputy People's commissar for military and naval affairs, together with Georgy Ordzhonikidze, the chairman of the Bolshevik North Caucasian defence council, met Kuchik Khan in the Caspian Sea coastal town of Rasht to encourage the declaration of the Persian Soviet Socialist Republic. Obviously, any alliance between the Baku Commune paramilitary contingents and the detachments of separatists, bolstered up by the Germans and Turks, undermined stability in the region.[20]

There was however one more economic motive for the British to increase activity in the Muslim Orient, namely, the fact that 432,000 tons of raw cotton were stockpiled in numerous depots across the Ferghana valley in Central Asia. The break in the railway connection between it and European Russia could make this substantial resource an easy prey by the Turks and Germans.[21] Under the considered circumstances, the Cabinet developed operations in rapport with the Anglo-Indian troops controlled by Frederick Chelmsford, the viceroy of India. The Cabinet aimed to avert the intrusion of German-Turkish expeditionary troops into Transcaucasia, Persia and Russian South Turkestan. Another objective was to oust local nationalists sympathizing with the Bolsheviks from these territories. To attain both goals, two special military missions under the orders of Major Generals Lionel Dunsterville and Wilfrid Malleson were designated to set off to Persia in the spring of 1918.[22]

Although both Dunsterville and Malleson originated from the British specific 'caste' of colonial administrators, there was a noticeable difference between them. While the first officer studied in the army college together with Rudyard Kipling and appeared to his subordinates as a 'father-commander to the fingertips',[23] the second military official made his career in secret intelligence agencies after graduating from an artillery school. Shortly afterwards, he was appointed the head of the Indian Army Main Staff reconnaissance department, and later took various commanding positions in the British colonial administration in both East and Central Africa. Compared to his colleague, Malleson was an introvert, demonstrating on every possible occasion excessive rigidity in communicating with his subordinates.[24]

On 30 January 1918, the British Imperial Staff instituted a section of military intelligence which, in turn, formed the expeditionary task force under Dunstrerville's

Figure 4 General Mayor Lionel Dunsterville (extreme left) with his staff in Baku, 1918. Photo courtesy of Wikimedia Commons (public domain).

Figure 5 General Mayor Wilfrid Malleson, 1918. Photo courtesy of Wikimedia Commons (public domain).

command.²⁵ Its officially proclaimed objective became the reanimation of anti-Turkish front by inviting the Armenians, Kurds and Aysors into the volunteer military service on the side of the Entente. Dozens of British war veterans together with servicemen from dominions agreed to join the expedition. Significantly, the essential criteria were a good command of Russian and a benevolent attitude to the former Romanovs' empire. Twelve ex-tsarist officers were also enrolled in Dunsterforce, or the Hush-Hush brigade, as it was dubbed by some War Office strategists. This unofficial epithet masked another secret purpose of the mission – to surreptitiously counteract the spread of Bolshevism in the Middle East.²⁶

At the Eastern Committee's regular conference on 8 February 1918, the experts claimed that the British policy should aim at the protection for the Armenians, building an alliance with the Arab people and inhibiting pan-Islamic as well as pan-Turkic propaganda to frustrate anti-British nationalistic uprisings in Persia, Afghanistan and Northern India.²⁷ It is hardly possible to share the opinion of those historians who denied either any anti-Russian geopolitical or, in a narrower sense, anti-Bolshevik focus of Dunsterville's mission.²⁸ A convincing rebuttal of this view was his wire to the War Office on 5 May 1918: 'Bolshevism is far from being firmly rooted in the Caucasus, but its malevolent tendencies have permeated the bloods of all the races in their part of the world: the present ultra-democratic movement in Persia is really the same spirit as Bolshevism.'²⁹

Even before the concentration of the whole manpower, the front team of Dunsterville's brigade (fifty-five persons in four jeeps and forty trucks escorted by the armoured vehicle) left Baghdad in the direction of Tiflis on 29 January 1918. There the head office was planned to be stationed along with 67 officers and 204 rank-and-file.³⁰ The route of the expedition passed through Enzeli, a Persian port in the Caspian region, wherein it arrived on 17 February. Yet a few days later the expedition was forced to return to Hamadan, a small provincial town southeast of Tehran, because the Bolshevik Soviet of Enzeli, backed by the military garrison of 3,000 apprised Dunsterville of the forthcoming signature of the Brest treaty with the Quadruple Alliance. Besides, local Persian authorities distrusted the British and were unwilling to cooperate with them against the Ottoman troops. The Hush-Hush brigade was compelled therefore to tarry in Hamadan for another three months, either constructing or mending roads, bridges and lines of communication.³¹

This delay led to the negotiations between Dunsterville and Cavalry General Nikolai Baratov whose mounted corps had interacted with the British expeditionary troops on the Mesopotamian front as early as in 1916–17.³² Hamadan was to become a meeting point for volunteers demobilizing from the Russian Caucasian army in the period from January to May 1918. Yet both Dunsterville and Baratov admitted the failure of the efforts 'to pour new wine in old bottles', for most of the Don, Kuban and Terek Cossacks refused to continue military service, even being subsidized by the British. Regarding Baratov himself, he craved a permission to leave for India, whereas about 1,000 war veterans, personally devoted to Colonel Lasar Bicherakhov, one of the best officers of the Caucasian mounted corps, joined a rearguard detachment of volunteers under the latter's command. Subordinated to the British until the conclusion of the treaty of Brest, it ensured the evacuation of the Russian manpower from Mesopotamia and Persia.³³

For his part, Bicherakhov believed in empire's restoration and denounced the 'scornful' Breast peace treaty which put an end to the Russian armed struggle against Ottoman troops.³⁴ Despite certain tactical divergence between Dunsterville and Bicherakhov in organizing military campaign, the former suggested to the latter to revive a united Russo-British front against the Turks, preventing them from allying with Kuchik Khan To guarantee the Colonel's loyalty, Dunsterville offered him ammunition and money subsidies averaging 10 million Persian krans (the equivalent of £200,000).³⁵

Bicherakhov's interaction with Dunsterforce in north-western Persia proceeded from May to mid-August 1918, although a formal agreement was signed only on 27 June after the Hush-Hush brigade had removed from Hamadan to Enzeli and then further to Tabriz.³⁶ Towards the end of June, the armed forces under Bicherakhov totalled 1,200–1,500 infantry and cavalry men, equipped with a portable radio-station, a few machine-guns and light artillery cannons as well as with eight armoured vehicles and four airplanes. Attached to the contingent, five British officers acted as liaison personnel in dealing with both Dunsterville and native chieftains.³⁷

Some historians portrayed the relatively short-term existence of the Baku Commune as the most striking episode of the Soviet-British relations in Transcaucasia. The story received a contradictory explanation in Anglo-American scholarship, depending on available sources.³⁸ It is important therefore to reconstruct the final events of the Baku Commune together with the ill fate of the twenty-six commissars who headed it during the period in question.

The secret negotiations between the Baku rulers and Bicherakhov on the collaborative defence of the city began as early as in April 1918, following the Ottoman troops' first offensive against it. Yet they came to nothing for several reasons. In the first place, the Baku Soviet cherished hopes to stop the Turkish advance with the help of the new recruited Red Caucasian army. Secondly, the commissars counted on a massive aid from Moscow, but, unfortunately for them, Lenin and Trotsky were able to send the reinforcements of merely 780 armed marines from the Caspian port of Astrakhan. Finally, the assistance of Dunsterforce might be also of use, taking into consideration their war experience and appropriate equipment.³⁹

Following the pattern of the 'intervention by agreement', described in the previous chapters, the Baku Soviet intensified the contacts with Bicherakhov towards the summer of 1918.⁴⁰ For the commissars, the situation seemed alarming because of the Red Caucasian army's constant retreat on the Turkish front. At the same time, the detachment under Bicherakhov defeated Kuchik Khan's guerrillas, making possible to redislocate the Hush-Hush brigade from Hamadan to Kazvin.⁴¹

On 19 June, the Baku Commune's representative in Enzeli defined Bicherakhov in a telegram to Shaumian as a patriot of Great Russia, albeit imbued with 'Napoleonic ambitions'.⁴² Thus, making a bet on the alliance with Bicherakhov allowed the Baku commissars to save the regime, should 'intervention by agreement' go for naught. The Baku SNK even convinced him to formally incorporate his brigade into the Red Caucasian army. On 7 July, Bicherakhov was ordered to defend the western sector at the approaches of the Azerbaijan capital. However, he agreed on two conditions: the Baku Soviet was bound to supply the detachment with necessary reinforcements of manpower and munitions while Bicherakhov should be nominated the supreme commander of all anti-Turkish military contingents defending the city.[43]

On 16 July, the Baku Soviet again considered the invitation of Dunsterforce to protect Baku, although the British Major General adhered to expectant tactics, bearing in mind a vast numerical superiority of the Turkish infantry divisions over the defenders.[44] The discussions between the local Soviet bureaucrats proceeded until the end of July. Initially inclined to accept the assistance of Dunsterforce, Shaumian was later compelled to reject the British aid under the Kremlin's pressure. Lenin and Stalin demagogically urged him 'to implement independent international policy as well as to decisively combat the agents of foreign capital'.[45] Suspecting Dunsterville and the British consul Ronald Macdonell in concocting a coup d'état, Shaumian argued that they ought to submit to the Baku SNK regulations, including an absurd obligation to consign to the commissars all their correspondence with London in declassified form.[46]

Apparently, Bicherakhov's sudden decision to transfer his detachment from the front-line trenches to Derbent, a town far north of Baku, became a cold shower to the Baku Soviet.[47] It accepted the resignation of the Commissars with a slight majority of twenty-three votes, handing power to the so-called government of the Central Caspian Dictatorship on 31 July 1918. The new city administrators were elected from the delegates of the Provisional executive committee and the members of the Caspian Military Flotilla central commission. Yet when Shaumian and other commissars were escaping Baku on board a steamer following by sixteen transport vessels loaded with the Commune's assets, the local anti-Bolshevik marines prohibited this evacuation in the moment of the Turkish second general assault.[48]

After the overthrow of the commissars, nothing prevented Dunsterforce from entering Baku by the agreement with the Central Caspian government on 4 August.[49] While paying tribute to the experience and personal bravery of the war veterans commanded by Dunsterville, some observers, including Macdonell, remarked that 'none of these men had seen a town or the bright light' for a very long time, and 'when they arrived in Baku the spirit of "wine, women and music" was at its height and of far greater importance than killing the Turks'.[50]

In fact, Baku's garrison comprised various military contingents of all races, nationalities and confessions – from the Armenians to the South Africans as well as from anarchists to monarchists, mostly opposing the British presence in Transcaucasia. Animosity to the Hush-Hush brigade assumed even more strength after Dunsterville ignoring the Central Caspian government's prohibition, determined to requisition oil products for his needs in the seaports of Enzeli and Krasnovodsk.[51]

While the Soviet propaganda created an Anglophobic myth of the 'sneaky' British who 'massacred all the Bolsheviks and their sympathisers in Baku', abandoning front-line trenches at the first cannon volleys by the Turks,[52] even a simple comparison of attackers and defenders – 28,000 versus 13,000 – attested to the inability of Dunsterforce as well as of the whole city garrison to endlessly rebuff the enemy's onslaught.[53]

Meanwhile Shaumian's second bid to escape from Baku, this time on board three steamships in the night of 13 August, also failed due to the stormy weather and a new counteraction by the Caspian Flotilla battleships.[54] Accused of treachery and embezzlement of public funds, the commissars were arrested on 26 August by the Central Caspian government that established the Emergency investigation commission to bring them to court.⁵⁵ Two weeks later, it charged Shaumian and his colleagues with negligence in undertaking preparations for the defence, mismanagement of defenders' rear, disregard to military experts and repeated attempts to desert the besieged city. Only the hasty evacuation of the Central Caspian government from Baku during the Turkish third attack prevented the hearings in court being held in due course.⁵⁶

On 14 September 1918, the Hush-Hush brigade which counteracted the main strike of the advancing Turks and lost up to 180 (according to other data – 125) volunteers killed, wounded and missing, sailed off from Baku to Enzeli. Two days later, notwithstanding the tenacious resistance, the enemy troops rushed into the city central districts where the massacre of the Christians by the Muslims was already in full swing. Following this event, the War Office ordered a dissolution of the brigade with the transfer of its functions to the so-called North Persian Force under the command of Lieutenant General William Thomson, later the Baku Military governor.⁵⁷

Before presenting the present author's concept of the Baku commissars' tragedy, it is necessary to review the second British military-political mission to the Middle East led by Major General Malleson. On 2 February 1918, Lord Chelmsford petitioned the India Office for sending a small reconnaissance group to Mashhad – the administrative centre of the Khorasan province in Persia, used by the British as a regional observation point, wherein the East Persian barrier squad had been staying since 1915.⁵⁸

The German occupation of the Black Sea ports as well as the Turkish offensive in Transcaucasia compelled the British General Staff to accelerate Malleson's departure to Mashhad, arriving there by early July 1918. A month later, the personnel of his mission averaged 500 servicemen and technicians. Like in the case of Dunsterforce, it aimed to thwart the German-Turkish eventual breakthrough to Central Asia which could occur in rapport with the Bolsheviks' penetration in the region. Mallesons's another task was to neutralize the activity of Muslim extremists who planned to recruit the so-called Army of Islam from 30,000 German and Austrian ex-POWs. He was also instructed to take control over the Russian Central Asian railroad and navigation routes in the Caspian Sea.⁵⁹ Contradictory to the opinion of some historians who argue that there is no evidence that London 'ever seriously contemplated bringing down' the Soviet regime in Turkestan,⁶⁰ the War Office authorized Malleson to promote the establishment of pro-British puppet states in Transcaspia, bound to shield India and other British territorial possessions in Asia from the Bolshevik aggression.⁶¹

While Malleson was making all the necessary arrangements in Mashhad, the workers and peasants of the Turkestan Soviet Republic resisted the conscription to the Red guards which led to mass riots resulting in the overthrow of the Bolshevik rule and the establishment of the Executive committee of Transcaspia, relying mainly on those railway employees and workers who disliked the Communist regime. On 12 July 1918, the ministers of a new provisional government were appointed, mostly from the right-wing Socialist revolutionaries, with certain Feodor Funtikov, a former locomotive driver, as their chairman.⁶²

Threatened from the east by the advancing Red guards in the anticipation of the Turkish offensive from the west as well as of overall Muslims' revolt, the Ashgabat government seemed unable to wield power without foreign military aid. On 29 July, they adopted a special resolution on the urgent need 'to accept the British support in the struggle against the German-Bolsheviks'.[63] Shortly afterwards two emissaries set off from Ashgabat to Mashhad to confer with Malleson on military and financial assistance. On 8 August, the latter got instructions from Simla, where the Anglo-Indian administration traditionally sojourned in summertime, to back up Funtikov and his associates. The debates led to the signing of an agreement on 19 August 1918 which provided the deployment of British garrisons in the Transcaspian strategic strongholds and the freedom of the Allied navigation in the Caspian Sea. For its part, the Ashgabat government guaranteed the UK to uphold British exceptional economic interests in the region, including the right to requisition raw cotton stockpiles. The new administrators were ready to consign the warships and merchant vessels in the Caspian Sea as well as the capital assets of the Krasnovodsk port and the equipment of the Central Asian railroad to the British military administration.[64]

Towards mid-August 1918, from 1,200 to 1,700 people of the Nineteenth Punjab, Yorkshire and Hampshire infantry regiments along with the Twenty-eighth Light cavalry regiment and an artillery platoon were stationed in Transcaspia. Several bloody skirmishes between them and the Turkestan Red Army occurred with changing success from August to October 1918. Although the British failed to seize Khiva, Bukhara and Tashkent, they occupied Merv and Krasnovodsk, rebuffing the Red Army's attacks as well as the German and Austrian POWs' penetration into Persia to join the Ottoman troops.[65]

Captain (later Major) Reginald Teague-Jones performed key liaison functions in the triangle between Mashhad, Baku and Ashgabat. As it will be shown below, he played a crucial role in the tragic fate of the Baku commissars. Peter Hopkirk was the first modern author who had thoroughly studied Teague-Jones' personality, expressing a sincere admiration of this man in the introduction to the diaries published after the latter's demise: 'Captain Reginald Teague-Jones, who possessed exceptional credentials for undertaking this difficult and dangerous task, was fluent in Russian, German, French, Persian and Hindustani. Having educated in St Petersburg, he was also well versed in the ways of political extremists.'[66]

In fact, Teague-Jones prevented the selling of huge raw cotton stockpiles to German agents. He also reconnoitered bridges and drainage pillars along the Central Asian railway between Krasnovodsk and Ashgabat to select suitable places for laying mines in the event of British retreat.[67] Late in August, Teague-Jones took part in the battle against the Red guards that occurred near Kaakhka, a small railway station 150 kilometres east of Ashgabat. Wounded in the leg and transported to the city's hospital, he soon became aware of Dunsterforce's retreat from Baku and the arrival in Krasnovodsk of the steamship with twenty-six ex-Commissars on board.[68]

Subsequent events received different interpretations by historians. The mythologized version that prevailed among Soviet authors represented the misfortune of the Baku commissars in the most favourable light for Moscow. Yet it seemed so far from reality that the actual developments still need to be traced in accordance with primary sources now available to researchers.

For this reason, the present author takes a step back to the earlier situation in Baku in mid-September when the former commissars were released from detention owing to lavish bribes and the chaotic situation. They hastily boarded the steamship *Turkman* to leave Baku shortly before the advancing Ottoman troops captured the city. Stepan Shaumian and his lieutenants even managed to take on board one or two machine-guns, dozens of rifles, foodstuffs and a safe with the cash totalling 1,500,000 roubles. The casual by-standers evidenced the refugees on board averaging 600 persons, including the ex-commissars with their families.[69]

However, Shaumian failed to threaten or bribe the captain and his crew encouraging them to sail to Astrakhan in the Volga estuary under the Bolsheviks' control. The *Turkman* continued its route to Krasnovodsk administered by the anti-Soviet Transcaspian government.[70] Recognized among other refugees by the sea-port authorities, the commissars were immediately arrested on the *Turkman* reaching the harbour, and taken to the city prison.[71] Despite the protest which Shaumian forwarded to Bicherakhov as a nominal supreme military commander of the Central Caspian dictatorship, twenty-six commissars were accused of capitulation to the Ottoman troops in Baku. The local press in turn regarded the arrested Bolsheviks as the 'hostages' of the local administration threatening them with death penalty.[72]

The role of Teague-Jones in the case remained obscure. As he insisted in his explanatory note to the India Office on 7 June 1922, he had left the meeting of the Ashgabat government before a final decision was taken on the execution of Shaumian and his colleagues.[73] Yet only two people could have proposed the death sentence – Sergei Druzhkin, a former law student who hated Bolshevism and was possibly mentally unstable, and Semion Gaudiz, a railway worker who commanded the Ashgabat police. Both were the left-wing Socialist revolutionaries involved in the execution of the Ashgabat Bolshevik leaders during the anti-Soviet rebellion in July 1918. Significantly, one eyewitness later referred to the statement by Gaudiz that 'twenty-six commissars from Baku were killed by a squad of the Socialist revolutionary militants'.[74] One more argument can be found in the collection of private papers belonging to Major T. Jarvis – an officer from Mallesons's staff. In September 1918, he reported to the higher commandment that 'the shooting of the commissars took place at the initiative of extremists among railway workers who had their own motives – fear and revenge, so as not to leave alive the former Baku rulers'.[75]

Five years later, Teague-Jones resolutely denied his presence at the place of execution because of the wound in the leg that prevented him from a trip on the special train to Krasnovodsk. Yet there is an obvious discrepancy between his explanatory statement to the India Office and the request to the Foreign Office for protection from the persecution by Bolshevik secret assassins. Whereas Teague-Jones initially mentioned Malleson's reluctance to take responsibility for the Baku commissars' transportation from Krasnovodsk to Mashhad, later he revealed Malleson's determination to ensure their safety on the way to British India.[76] The early version seems to be closer to truth, since Teague-Jones wrote in the diary about Funtikov's account of Malleson's refusal to accept the arrested commissars in Mashhad, leaving their fate to the mercy of the Ashgabat governors.[77]

In the present author's opinion, Teague-Jones left the extraordinary sitting of the Ashgabat government because of his poor health, on the one hand, and the impression that the local authorities would carry on the execution on their own. Hence it was unreasonable to keep on staying till the session was over without getting involved in the decision that would compromise the British military mission. Thus, Teague-Jones became aware of the departure to Krasnovodsk of the special train with twenty-six commissars no sooner than in the evening of 19 September when he could at last apprise Malleson of the Ashgabat governors' fatal decision to shoot the Baku leaders in the sands of the Agdzhagum desert near Kizyl-Arvat, 202 kilometres eastward of Ashgabat.[78]

Some misinterpretations of this event survive until today. For instance, the senior train conductor who witnessed the execution, confessed to the investigators of the OGPU, as the VCheka was renamed in 1923, that he had noticed a British officer among the commissars' custodians. Besides, there are grounds to believe that Teague-Jones was fully aware of the planned execution, sending an anonymous confidant who might be taken for the mentioned military.[79]

It took the Bolshevik policymakers a few months to verify Teague-Jones' bogus statement. The radiograms with an offer to exchange the Baku ex-rulers for the British citizens detained in Soviet Russia were repeatedly sent to London on 24 January, 13 February and 23 March 1919. Apart from this, Chicherin demanded Balfour to prove to the non-participation of British military representatives in the execution.[80] The doubts about the fate of the commissars vanished in the spring of 1919 after Vadim Chaikin, a well-known lawyer and member of the Socialist Revolutionary party central committee, published the results of his investigation in a series of reports which were later put together as a book.[81]

As the present author's study reveals, the planned shooting simply could not get an official approval since it was beyond Malleson's competence. Yet the British general realized that the arrival in Krasnovodsk of the Baku commissars, some of whom had a good command of English, could potentially affect the morality of the Anglo-Indian troops leading to their refusal to fight the Bolsheviks. One could also be led to believe that Malleson's personal attitude to Shaumian and other commissars remained negative. As the retired Major General claimed in his memories, the Bolsheviks deserved execution for copious hostilities against their opponents. Malleson constantly emphasized the British concerns about their eventual 'infiltration of the Caspian region to launch there a propaganda campaign in favour of Communism'. At the same time, he wrote that he personally opposed the execution because he needed the twenty-six commissars alive as a kind of potential hostages to bargain with the Kremlin for the release of interned British citizens.[82] According to Malleson, when the two messengers of the Ashgabat government arrived in Mashhad on 20 September 1918 to inform him on the execution, they explained it by the fears of a pro-Bolshevik uprising in Ashgabat, had the commissars been released.[83]

Strange as it may seem, but Malleson allegedly requested Teague-Jones 'if it was not late, to hand over the commissars alive' to the escort sent from Mashhad. Although this record is not found in the India Office files, being seemingly extracted from the file by later censors, it provided an alibi to both Malleson and Teague-Jones. Even so, another Malleson's wire to Simla on 23 September shed a new light on the situation:

It is reported that twenty-six Bolshevik leaders ex Baku have been shot, and 5 or 6 unimportant ones spared. I can express no opinion as to the question of justice, but apart from this, the alleged execution is politically advantageous as it means Ashgabat government have burnt their boats as regards Bolsheviks.[84]

In response, Malleson was ordered 'to take over the Bolshevik prisoners and hold them as hostages without acquainting the Ashgabat government of the reason for so doing'.[85] The tactics of Chelmsford's administration assumed clear interpretation in the telegram to Malleson from Hamilton Grant, the foreign secretary of the government of India. He requested the Major General to request the leadership of the Turkestan Soviet Republic to guarantee the safety of the British officers accredited in Tashkent (their story is narrated in the end of the chapter). This wire indicated that the Baku commissars, albeit dead, kept on being used as a bargain chip in the diplomatic duel between Moscow and London.[86] A week later, Malleson was authorized by the viceroy's administration to warn the Transcaspian government against further abominable steps since 'they might delay support and pose it outside any laws of civilized society'.[87]

Following the investigation conducted by Chaikin, Chicherin informed to Balfour by radiogram that 'the British military mission together with the Russian Transcaspian counter-revolutionaries concocted the assassination of the Baku commissars'.[88] Two days later, Stalin published an article in the *Izvestiya* likening 'civilized and human' British with 'imperialist cannibals, deeply rotten and deprived of all moral power'.[89]

The Bolsheviks proceeded to play this trump card, proclaiming the executed Baku leaders the 'heroes of revolution'. After the British expeditionary troops had been evacuated and the Soviet rule restored in Transcaspia, the Soviet authorities reburied their remains at one of the Ashgabat squares. Later they were transported to a specially built memorial in the centre of Baku. The opening ceremony took place on 8 September 1920 to celebrate the First congress of the peoples of the Orient conferring in the city.[90]

When several leading Russian Socialist revolutionaries were brought to a grand trial organized by the Kremlin in 1922, the British participation in the execution of the twenty-six commissars was not mentioned at all. In response to Chaikin's suggestion to invite Malleson and Teague-Jones as witnesses at the trial, the India Office denied any records of the case.[91] To convince the Bolshevik government that the charges against the considered persons were unsubstantial, Robert Hodgson, the British acting diplomatic agent in Moscow, held a lengthy interview with Karakhan on 4 August 1922.[92] But his efforts went for naught. Subsequently, various UK government bodies kept on rejecting British citizens' participation in the execution. It is noteworthy that the members of the TUC, on a visit to Baku in the fall of 1924, became astonished when they were brought to the mausoleum of the twenty-six commissars to listen to a lecturer accusing the British military mission of the crime.[93] Because of the aggravation of the armed conflict between Armenia and Azerbaijan for the territory of Nagorno-Karabakh in 1990, the mausoleum was dismantled by hooligans, and the remains of twenty-three persons (three identification tags had not been found at all) were again reburied in one of the city cemeteries. Anyway, the tragic saga of the Baku Commune added certain negative moments to the perception of Britain in Russia, making an additional scar on the collective memory of the Azerbaijanis and Armenians.[94]

The survey of the Eastern trends in the policy of both Moscow and London would be incomplete without mentioning the secret expedition by Lieutenant-Colonel Frederick Bailey to Russian Turkestan in 1918–19. His activity as an entomologist who gathered one of the best private collections of butterflies and concurrently as an intelligence officer became known to British public when the *Journal of the Central Asian Society* heralded it in 1921. Bailey was awarded the gold medals of the Royal and Scottish Geographical Societies for his achievements in the exploration of Asian territories and inhabitants before the outburst of the First World War. After being wounded in the battles of Gallipoli and Flanders, he joined the Secret Intelligence Service to oversee operations in the Middle East. Finally, the government of India dispatched him on a secret mission to Tashkent.[95]

The proposal originated with Commander Josiah Wedgwood, a Liberal MP who communicated it to John Shuckburgh, the secretary of the India Office political department. Wedgwood's idea was to 'send a number of energetic and determined officers ... from India, and to give them a kind of roving commission to work for British interests in Central Asia'. As he pointed out, they would travel under whatever 'cover' might be thought best, but, of course, without any official rank.[96]

Bailey and his associates faced several serious tasks: first, to collect intelligence about the situation in Turkestan, especially on the Indian frontier; secondly, to counteract German and Turkish influence there; thirdly, to disrupt the escape of former POWs from the territory of Russian Central Asia through Persia and Afghanistan to Europe; fourthly, to counteract the Bolsheviks' subversive activities as well as their anti-British propaganda in Oriental countries. It was also essential to obtain some financial compensation for the property of the Indian entrepreneurs confiscated by Soviet authorities. Finally, the select intelligence officers were instructed to find out the ways to support the Emirate of Bukhara and the Khanate of Khiva in their preservation of sovereign status.[97] Although certain Soviet historians mentioned the 'coordination of anti-Bolshevik efforts to topple the Soviet regime in Russian Turkestan' as the main objective of Bailey's mission, this study argues that these plans were of a far less scale.[98]

On 22 April 1918, Bailey left Srinagar, a rear base of British expeditions to Central Asia, for Tashkent via Kashgar. He was accompanied by Major Latham Blacker, a former military aviator, who, disguised as a trader, had made a trip to the capital of Russian Turkestan before the world war. Apart from this officer, Percy Etherton, a commissioner by the Foreign Office, also escorted Bailey on the route to Kashgar. He was bound to replace George Macartney who had occupied the position of the General consul in Kashgar ever since 1890. The mission convoy included ten volunteers from the British troops in India as well as fifty Orenburg Cossacks safeguarding Bailey until the Russian border, wherefrom a detachment of the Red guards consisted of the former POWs – the Czechs and Austrians – took the baton to Tashkent.[99]

On 7 June, Bailey's group arrived in Kashgar, where Etherton was destined to serve for the next few years. Instead, Macartney joined the mission together with the Russian dragoman Georgy Stefanovich and his spouse. Following a few weeks of relaxation at the British consulate's premises, they set off to Tashkent, reaching it on 14 August. It was the day when the first skirmish between the British expeditionary troops in Transcaspia and the Red guards occurred at the settlements of Bairam-Ali and Mary.[100]

Strange as it may seem, but the leaders of the Turkestan Soviet Republic initially welcomed the British emissaries' arrival, since they naively believed that the UK 'revolutionary House of Commons' was struggling with 'the reactionary House of Lords'. That is why, not wishing to interfere with this 'fair battle for freedom' which might facilitate the diplomatic recognition of the Bolshevik government, local policymakers perceived Bailey's arrival in Tashkent as a sort of the official diplomatic mission.[101]

Nonetheless, Bailey and Blacker were thoroughly examined by the local Chekists.[102] On obtaining a permission to stay on the territory of the Turkestan Soviet Republic, the visitors focused on disrupting the recruitment of former POWs. They also aimed to agree with the Soviet authorities on the transfer of raw cotton stockpiles to India as well as on the joint counteraction against Islamic propaganda. Bailey regularly dispatched reports to Delhi and London on current events in Turkestan, keeping in touch with Malleson in Mashhad and Etherton in Kashgar. Although for a short term, he became an official MI6 resident in the whole Central Asian region.[103]

On 14 September 1918, Macartney and Blacker headed to India leaving Bailey alone in Tashkent. While remaining under permanent surveillance of the Tashkent Cheka, Bailey managed to fool them, using interdepartmental rivalry and personal intrigues. He moreover succeeded in preventing the Germans and Turks' interference in the affairs of Soviet Turkestan, keeping in touch with the anti-Soviet underground circles in Tashkent and with Major General Aleksander Dutov, the Chieftain (Ataman) of the Orenburg Cossacks, whom he promised British financial subsidies and munitions.[104] This clandestine activity led to Bailey's arrest on 15 October 1918 by the Chekists, though he was miraculously released after a lengthy conversation with the Tashkent government's senior officials. Five days later, however, the Kremlin countenanced Bailey's new arrest, but this time he found shelter in the nearby mountain area, changed appearance and fabricated a new passport on the name of an Albanian POW.[105]

In the autumn of 1919, Bailey managed to get an identification card of the inspector serving in the Turkestan military district's counter-intelligence department. This incredible appointment was evidently caused by the chaos and disarray that wielded in the local administration. Yet both Malleson and Etherton cast doubt on the effectiveness of Bailey's activities in Central Asia after discovering numerous contradictions in his reports.[106] Amusingly, the Cheka bosses finally sent him to the Emir of Bukhara to discover the location of a fugitive British spy, Lieutenant Colonel Bailey.

One of the results he had achieved in Tashkent was gathering intelligence about the Bolsheviks' project to establish a training centre for 'Indian revolutionaries' with the assistance of certain Mohammed Barkatullah, the former 'minister for foreign affairs' of the so-called Committee of India independence founded in Berlin during the war and later reorganized into the 'Provisional government of India'.[107]

According to Bailey's reports, the propaganda centre in Tashkent was engaged in printing anti-British pamphlets in several languages for the subsequent circulation to Persia, Afghanistan and India. Bailey also apprised Simla of the Soviet plenipotentiaries in Tehran – Nikolai Bravin from January to June 1918 and Ivan Kolomiitsev – from July to November of the same year, sponsoring nomad tribes in the North-West Frontier Province of India.[108] On 18 December 1919, Bailey surreptitiously left Bukhara in the company of the closest assistants. They reached the Tejend-river, bordering the Iranian territory. Lucky enough to safely cross it, Bailey's group arrived in Mashhad on 14 January 1920. Although the Bolsheviks announced that he was shot in a boundary skirmish, Bailey returned to London to deliver a lecture on the situation in Soviet Turkestan at the Royal Central Asian Society's special seminar.[109]

For obvious reasons, the Cabinet aimed to defend India as the 'pearl of the English crown'. Hence Dunsterville, Malleson and Bailey were commissioned to fulfil this task. On the other hand, as early as in late December 1917, the SNK allocated 2 million gold roubles to stir up a revolutionary surge abroad, including India. However, the Kremlin leaders were plainly short of power to fully support nationalist movements in Hindustan, bearing also in mind their poor knowledge of the current ethnic and confessional situation. For example, Lenin erroneously believed that the Indian population were mostly the Muslims.[110]

Nevertheless, from the very beginning of their rule, the Bolsheviks proclaimed that 'until India was not liberated, Russia would not get rid of the British threat'.[111] As Hopkirk correctly remarked, 'for them a Soviet India remained the ultimate prize in Asia, and Moscow had no intention of abandoning its hopes of achieving this, however long it took'.[112] This opinion is evidenced by Konstantin Troianovsky who headed the NKID's Indian section in a leaflet. Published in the spring of 1918 as a 'new political programme' for oriental countries, it demonstrated the inevitability of the Western countries' social collapse until they ceased to exploit the East. Moreover, Troianovsky maintained, 'the Russian revolutionaries and international socialists, must not only welcome the revolution in India, but also directly and indirectly support it with all strength'.[113]

His programme consisted of fifteen points type-written on four pages. It envisaged an 'intimate and strong Indo-Russian rapprochement on the grounds of the common struggle against the Western European imperialism, oppressing India at present and directly threatening Russia'. Among the main initiatives to destabilize the domestic situation in India, Troianovsky defined the support for an armed uprising of the native tribes by the allocation of 500,000 roubles to the Muslim volunteers who were designated to act as an armed convoy for the Soviet trade delegation that would be dispatched to Delhi. Yet this mission was planned to be merely a stalking horse for a future revolt.[114] For all its fantastic nature, the project in view could be called the first scenario of the revolution's export to an Asian country, fully attesting to the Bolsheviks' intention to strike a blow upon Britain's 'colonial backyard'.[115]

Consequently, many UK statesmen considered the rebuff of the 'Bolshevik threat' to India as the next round of the traditional geopolitical competition in Asia. According to Manabendra Roy, a well-known figure of the Indian national movement, its leaders pinned hopes upon the support of Japan, the United States and even Mexico in this struggle. Since the world war demanded Indian manpower on a large scale, a tangible diminution of the military contingents capable of suppressing the social unrest within the British Raj became evident towards 1918, when the government of India disposed of merely eight battalions of troops scattered over the vast peninsula.[116] To thwart the nationalists' machinations and reduce the fight for 'home rule' by Mahatma Gandhi's followers, Chelmsford undertook the administrative reform in 1918 which was approved by the Cabinet at the initiative of Edwin Montagu, the head of the India Office. It proved to be the first major step in granting autonomy to India with the hindsight of the Russian revolution.[117] As the former governor of Bombay, the president of the Indo-British association, Lord Sydenham, commented in the *Morning Post*, 'Russia gave us an amazing illustration of what happens when the rule is destroyed, and 80 per cent of people are illiterate. The results [of revolution] would be even more catastrophic to India.'[118]

Despite the Chelmsford–Montagu reforms, the situation in India continued to be explosive. The main challenges to the British rule were the Bengal and Punjab national movements coupled with the attempts by Indian left-wing revolutionaries to relocate their 'provisional government' from Berlin to Kabul. As has been noted above, the projects to enlist volunteers to join the Army of God on the territory of the Ottoman empire also contributed to both London and Delhi's annoyance. In addition, the Bolsheviks stimulated the Indian extremists to exploit the Tashkent training centre as a bridgehead for instigating anti-British unrest.[119] The report for 1918 delivered to London by the viceroy's administration stated that 'the German machinations intensified by the disintegration of Russia posed a danger to the very approaches to India'. At the last stage of the world war, the Indian internal stability seemed so fragile that, using Malleson's metaphor, 'the government of India could hardly sleep at night'.[120]

As for the Far East, its occupation by the Entente troops, and above all, Japan's expeditionary forces domination in the area from Vladivostok to Chita, as well as the establishment of the regional anti-Bolshevik administrations in several Siberian cities, deprived the development of the Soviet-British relations of any auspicious prospect.[121]

Meanwhile the signing of the Compiegne armistice led to the Entente powers facing a new dilemma regarding attitude to Soviet Russia: which way to choose – a full-scale armed intervention, a resolute political and economic blockade or a gradual transition to the peaceful coexistence with the Bolsheviks?

The next chapter will demonstrate what solution Whitehall had opted for and how it affected the bilateral relations in the aftermath.

5

'Stillborn crusade' against Bolsheviks and 'Russian question' at the Paris Peace Conference

Worker, be strong!
The Entente is trembling,
Proletariat of the West
Is coming to your aid.

Soviet propaganda poster, 1919.[1]

In a book of memoirs, the left-wing journalist Morton Price, mentioned in the previous chapters, referred to his pamphlet *The Truth about the Russian Revolution*. It was published to make his compatriots aware of at least one British 'who did not keep silence' during the Entente intervention in Russia when a minor group of Western citizens in Moscow joined Price in offering support to the Bolshevik regime confronting other European states.[2] As Henry Wilson, the chief of the General Staff, indicated in the diary after the British police strike late in August 1918, 'now the real threat to us is not the Boshi, but the Bolshevism'.[3] Basil Thomson, one of the high-ranking police administrators, shared this opinion denouncing Bolshevism as 'a type of infectious disease that spreads quickly but secretly until, like a cancerous tumour, it eats without a trace the tissue of society'.[4]

The Entente overall offensive in the second half of the year necessitated further clarification of the British stance towards Russia because there were obvious contradictions between the Entente members' positions and disagreements within the Cabinet ministers. However, most politicians and generals preferred to rescind the Soviet-German separate treaty, give assistance to anti-Bolshevik forces and promote the survival of the sovereign states which emerged on the ruins of the Romanovs' empire.[5]

The Compiegne armistice on 11 November and the annulment of the Brest treaty by the Soviet government two days later prompted Whitehall to recognize those new-born nations which had announced their independent status prior to the armistice. Additionally, Lloyd George and his colleagues decided, albeit reluctantly, to maintain a large British military contingent in Russian northern provinces as well as to hold on the Batum – Baku strategic railway in Transcaucasia. It was also deemed important to counteract Bolshevik propaganda in the British Isles.[6]

Thus, without formally declaring war on Soviet Russia and explaining its objectives to public, the Cabinet authorized an open wide-scale military intervention in Eastern Europe. Only in December 1918 did Cecil specify Britain's intentions accusing the Bolsheviks of Cromie's murder and repressions against Western citizens including nationalization of their property in Russia.[7] For the next few months, Britain refunded the White armies and trained their commanding staff, keeping in touch with anti-Soviet subversive organizations inside the country.[8]

By April 1919, British military formations on the Russian territory amounted to 23,000–27,000 servicemen under the order of seven generals. They fought the Bolshevik troops in the northern and southern provinces of the European part (approximately 10,700 and 4,800 soldiers, respectively), in Siberia and the Far East (1,000 and 4,500 people), in Transcaucasia and Turkestan (1,000 and 4,800 volunteers).[9] On 31 October 1918, the War Office ordered the occupation of the Caspian oil fields, taking under control the mentioned railroad from Baku to Batum. On 23 November, the Entente flotilla, led by the British men-of-war, entered the harbour of Novorossiysk; three days later other Entente battleships anchored at the bay of Sevastopol while the headquarters of the British expeditionary forces moved to Tiflis towards mid-December 1918.[10]

But the ongoing discussions between Lloyd George, Balfour, Curzon, Churchill, Milner, Cecil and A. Chamberlain impeded the elaboration of a consistent political course towards Russia. Whereas Churchill openly favoured the restoration of Russia as 'united and indivised' country, except for Poland and Finland,[11] his colleagues regarded indirect financial and material support to the new nations corresponding with Britain's strategic goals. They believed that Russia should be split up into minor quasi-state entities, dependent on Britain, France or the United States, to effectively protect Europe and Asia from the proliferation of Bolshevism.[12]

On the other hand, some left-wing Labour politicians called for the unconditional recognition of the Soviet regime. Lloyd George and his closest consiglieres were inclined to make such a decision because weak Russia, even under the Bolsheviks' rule, seemed far better meeting Britain's interests in the postwar world.[13] Numerous cases of dissent by servicemen in the anticipation of demobilization and the establishment of the self-appointed workers' council in Glasgow in the spring of 1918 fully attested to the Bolshevik ideas threatening the UK social stability.[14] It was also important for the government to militate against the 'Hands off Russia' national movement initiated by the public committee of London shop-stewards on 18 January 1919.[15]

The opening of the international peace conference in the French capital on the same day led to the 'Russian question' assuming a prominent place on its 'hidden' agenda. While preparing for debates, the Cabinet members deliberated the situation in Russia on several occasions – on 31 December 1918; 10, 13 January; and 12–13 February 1919. As a result, most government ministers regarded it useless to further expand the British military presence there claiming that the 'army was prepared to go anywhere for liberty, but it could not be convinced that the suppression of the Bolshevism was a war for liberty'.[16] As the *Daily Express* wrote on 3 January, paraphrasing Otto von Bismarck's famous mantra, the 'frozen plains of Eastern Europe are not worthy of the bones of a British grenadier'.[17]

Figure 6 British delegation at the Paris Peace Conference, 1919. (left to right: Arthur Balfour, Edward Montagu, David Lloyd George, Austen Chamberlain, William Hughes, Lord Birkenhead, Lord Cecil, Winston Churchill, Maurice Hankey, Henry Wilson). Photo courtesy of Wikimedia Commons (public domain).

All Churchill's attempts, supported by Cecil, Henry Wilson and Lieutenant General George Macdonough, the director of military intelligence, to persuade Lloyd George to use Polish troops, the German units in Eastern Baltic or Swedish volunteers to defeat the Bolsheviks scored no success.[18] On 10 January 1919, General Wilson penned in his diary: 'The more I think about Russia, the more convinced I am that we should

Figure 7 'Into Russia, Out of Russia', Caricature, *Daily Express*, 8 September 1919. Photo courtesy of Wikimedia Commons (public domain).

keep out of the scrum. If the Americans and French like to go in let them. At the same time, we should order the Boches to hold up Bolshevism.'[19] Nonetheless, on 17 January, Churchill suggested to Lloyd George to extend the military service of those volunteers who participated in the intervention, as well as to create a special armed task force of 1 million. But this scenario was rejected by the prime minister.[20]

At the Cabinet meeting held on 12 February 1919, Austen Chamberlain criticized the prolongation of intervention, referring to President Wilson's decision to evacuate

American troops from Russia in the nearest prospect. The chancellor of the exchequer agreed with Lloyd George to withdraw British military contingents from Eastern Europe, Central Asia and the Far East, expressing his opposition to Churchill's project to actively supply Admiral Aleksandr Kolchak with munitions.[21]

Even some staunch opponents of Soviet Russia, such as Edwin Montagu, wrote to the prime minister that it was hardly necessary to take any partial measures against the Bolsheviks, except for a full-scale war which Britain could not afford for many reasons. Lloyd George, for his part, publicly stated on 17 February that 'if we are committed to a war against a continent like Russia, it is the road to bankruptcy and Bolshevism in these islands'.[22] Additionally, the prolongation of the armed intervention by Britain met opposition from the dominions which revealed their intense disagreement with Canadians, Australians or South Africans to be sent to Russia as fresh manpower.[23]

Early in February 1919, the Canadian General Staff informed Churchill, who had been appointed the state secretary for war, that the dominion's public opinion strongly disapproved of the involvement in military operations against the Bolsheviks. Following this statement, Robert Borden, the Canadian prime minister, notified Lloyd George about Ottawa's firm intention to evacuate Borden's compatriots from Russia in April. Meanwhile, on 5 March, William Hughes, the head of the Australian government, rebuked Lloyd George for the unacceptably slow demobilization of Australian servicemen. A month later, Louis Botha, the president of the South African Union, joined these protests too.[24]

It is important to note that the Bolshevik leadership strived for the normalization of Soviet-British relations on the eve of the Quadruple Alliance's terminal defeat. However, the 1918 November revolution in Germany revived the Bolsheviks' rosy hopes for the eventual success of the anti-capitalist pan-European revolution. Taking the floor at the Sixth All-Russian congress of Soviets, Lenin announced that 'British troops are about to invade Russia from the south and the Dardanelles, or through Bulgaria and Romania', while secretly ordering to spare no expense in support to left-wing social groups in the UK.[25]

Significantly, the Bolsheviks' perception of Britain combined an admiration for the achievements in various fields of science, technology and culture with a condemnation of the 'capitalist' political system and the 'unbridled exploitation of colonial territories'. But behind the veil of propaganda campaigns, the NKID applied strenuous efforts to restore connections with the former ally. On the eve of the Paris conference, Moscow sent two emissaries to London. Unfortunately, no documents manifesting this trip have been found in the archives so far, except for a reference in Kerensky's memoirs. As he noted, they had arrived in London early in December 1918 to convince Lloyd George that 'a good relationship' with the Bolsheviks was possible through Britain's assistance to the Russian economy staying in complete disarray.[26]

Meanwhile, Chicherin kept on dispatching proposals to the Entente Supreme military council and to the American administration at the preparatory stage of the Paris conference and after its opening. A survey of the Bolshevik foreign policy undertaken by the British General Staff's analysts enumerated the Soviet peaceful initiatives only for the last quarter of year:

On the 24th of October [1918], they [the Bolsheviks] proposed an armistice to President Wilson; on the 3rd of November, Litvinov arrived in Stockholm; later he moved to Copenhagen, where he is avowedly attempting to enter negotiations. It was stated on the 4th of December that his object is to prevent intervention and to obtain some form of recognition for the Soviet government, in return for which the Bolsheviks would make great concessions.[27]

On 14 and 17 January, 4 and 18 February, 19 March and 7 May, Moscow recurrently appealed to the participants of the Paris forum. The sources attested to at least eleven attempts of this kind since the Compiegne armistice.[28] Although a decisive breakthrough could not be achieved, they triggered a joint Anglo-American suggestion to convoke a conference of Russian delegates representing local governments in various parts of the former empire. It was Borden who suggested to assemble them somewhere in Europe despite other British dominions turning a cold shoulder to this intention. Lloyd George's justifications of the presence of Russian delegates at the conference by its huge manpower losses in the war, vast territory and the status of great power were also rejected by other Entente states. Under these circumstances, both Lloyd George and Wilson opted for the Prince (Prinkipo) Archipelago in the Sea of Marmara between the European and Asian coasts of the Ottoman Empire as a venue for the projected conference.[29]

On 20 December 1918, the last foreign diplomat – the Swiss envoy – left Soviet Russia for Europe and a week later, the government of the Weimar republic repudiated any official relations with Moscow.[30] In June 1919, the representative of the Dutch Red Cross departed from the Soviet capital completing the isolation of the Bolshevik regime. Henceforward, the task of resuming Russia's involvement in world politics became one of the major international issues.[31]

Even a hypothetic invitation of delegates from Russia to the French capital impelled a series of fierce debates in the Entente political circles, especially among the anti-Bolshevik emigrants. Meanwhile British diplomacy overtured the prospect of pacifying the former tsarist empire via a general discussion with the members of the so-called Russian political council which embraced former tsarist diplomats.[32] The debates proceeded at the preparatory session of the Council of Ten, the Paris conference's informal consulting body, on 12 January 1919. In the aftermath, Lloyd George delivered a keynote lecture to the Entente delegations that assembled to draft the preliminary agenda of the congress, emphasizing poor chance for 'establishing peace on solid foundations, while the civil war is tearing Russia apart'.[33]

On 20–21 January, Lloyd George, the French Prime Minister George Clemenceau, the head of the Italian government Vittorio Orlando, the Japanese Deputy Prime Minister Shionji Kinmochu and Woodrow Wilson agreed on the Entente's address to all 'Russian political groups'. The following day it was sent as a radiogram to Moscow and other big Russian cities – Arkhangelsk, Omsk, Ekaterinodar, etc., where various non-Bolshevik administrations temporarily located. They were invited to confer at the Prinkipo Islands to mould a united delegation for the Paris international congress.[34] Yet the initiative was doomed to failure from the very beginning because the very concept of the Bolsheviks, their opponents and the leaders of new-born national states on the territory of the former empire sitting together at the conference table was utopian. The practical implementation of this project conflicted with desires not only of the anti-Bolshevik forces inside Russia but also those of influential emigrant organizations.[35]

Their February memorandum to the Foreign Office implored the Entente leaders to abstain from dealing with the Kremlin. 'Communicating with them', wrote the authors of the petition, 'means for Western democracies to perceive the "poison" of violence and terror'.[36] Moreover, in order to configure British public against the Soviet rule, certain journalists disseminated in the European mass media fantastic rumours about 'nationalisation of women by the Bolshevik commissariats of free love', 'conversion of Orthodox cathedrals into brothels' and 'the gangs of the Chinese thugs rambling about Russian streets to persecute enemies of regime'.[37]

The fact was that Bolshevik front-runners were similarly split in the view of the necessity to confer with their opponents. Whereas Lenin, Chicherin and Litvinov advocated the Prinkipo project, Trotsky and some high-ranking Red Army commanders denounced it, insisting on the preservation of *status-quo*.[38] Nevertheless, the NKID forwarded a diplomatic note to the Entente and the United States with the far-going proposals: Moscow declared its readiness to acknowledge Russia's financial obligations to Western creditors, pay interest on loans by supplying raw materials to the former allies as well as by granting economic concessions to foreign enterprises. The Bolsheviks also declared their readiness to stop revolutionary propaganda and even cede territories to the new-born national states. Not surprisingly that political observers called their proposals the 'second Brest agreement', but this time with the Entente.[39]

According to the Foreign Office, Grigory Zinoviev, then the chairman of the Petrograd Soviet, revealed the true goals of the Soviet government at the meeting on 27 January 1919 when he declared that imperialist powers pursued two main political courses: one being aggressive and the other – more cautious, albeit perfidious: 'If we send a delegation [to Prinkipo], Zinoviev argued, its objective will be to get these gentlemen to unmask themselves.'[40]

Meanwhile Churchill cabled to Generals Maynard and Ironside commanding the Allied task forces in the north of Russia:

> It would be better to risk a few thousand men (though there would be no risk if the railway could be put right) than to allow the whole fabric of Russo-Siberian resistance to Bolshevism to crumble. What sort of a peace should we have if all Europe and Asia from Warsaw to Vladivostok were under the sway of Lenin?[41]

Lloyd George, for his part, was flooded with the war minister's offers on how to settle the 'Russian problem' by military means, for instance, with the help of numerous volunteers enlisted in European countries and British dominions to fight the Reds.[42] The chair of the Cabinet was fully aware that the ministers would never adopt the scheme of an anti-Bolshevik 'crusade', for they considered deliveries of munitions to the Russian Whites the only real method of Britain's interference in Russian domestic affairs. He moreover persuaded Churchill and other proponents of the 'crusade' that it would only consolidate population around the Bolshevik party.[43]

On 14–15 February 1919, the delegates in Paris debated the 'Russian issue' on the second occasion. Churchill and the French Marshal Ferdinand Foch, the Supreme military commander of the Entente troops in Europe, advocated the armed intervention on a broader scale. The war minister briefed the delegates in the project to recruit punitive military forces, involving German officers, to direct them against the Red Army. In Churchill's opinion, this measure would guarantee free democratic elections in Russia under the control of the Entente member-states.[44] Foch envisaged, in turn, the departure of 2 million American troops to Russia to establish a core of the so-called 'Army of Liberty' with the possible involvement of those Russians, Poles and Romanians who were eager to fight the Bolshevik usurpers.[45]

But all these plans confronted Lloyd George's strong opposition. The 'Welsh wizard' regarded the 'crusade' would not only enable Lenin to stay in power but sow the seeds of Bolshevism in Western Europe. Responding to Churchill's alarmist speeches, the prime minister, temporarily absent from Paris, disavowed the main clauses of his plan in a wire to the Entente leaders.[46] Towards mid-February 1919, their dispute assumed such intensity that some political observers did not rule out either Lloyd George's resignation, if the Unionists could consolidate their ranks, or Churchill's demonstrative exodus from the Cabinet. On 17 February, the latter had to explain his position on the 'Russian question' in a message to Lloyd George. Having assured the prime minister of his personal loyalty, Churchill warned him nonetheless against the eventual military alliance between Germany and Russia with Japan's potential accession. In his view, if certain decisive counteractions were not taken, Berlin could regain its influence upon Russia compensating for the loss of the German overseas dependencies. As Churchill argued, the fruits of victory in war might be wasted in five years.[47]

For his part, Lloyd George stipulated four principles which he thought should underpin Britain's policy towards Russia. In a conversation with Phillip Kerr, his closest associate, the prime minister denounced the sending to Russia of regular troops, except for enrolled volunteers. At the same time, he advocated their evacuation in the shortest time as well as military and financial support to the White governments. Another important diplomatic move should be the admission of new East European independent states to the League of Nations to safeguard their sovereignty.[48]

Having rejected the considered projects of a 'crusade', Lloyd George and Wilson authorized a trip to Moscow of a young American diplomat William Bullitt, accompanied by Captain William Pettit from MI5 and a journalist Louis Steffens.[49] Although Bullitt's informal talks with Lenin, Chicherin and Litvinov which he held in Petrograd and Moscow from 9 to 14 March 1919 ended in the adoption of seven provisions of a future peace treaty between the Entente and Soviet Russia, his efforts went for naught. Obviously, the Western ruling class was not prepared to officially recognize the Bolshevik regime when the White armies headed by Kolchak and Denikin were scoring success in the first half of 1919.[50]

Many European policymakers were scared by the revolutionary surge in Central Europe under the slogan 'All state power to Soviets!' Some Conservative journals, such as the *Daily Mail*, launched a campaign to discredit 'the regime of Commissars' which, among other real sins, was absurdly accused of bribing Western industrialists through granting discounts to Jewish financial agencies in Russia.[51] Almost simultaneously, the *Times* introduced readers with a series of biographical sketches describing certain Kremlin mandarins. One of them, Zinoviev, was depicted as 'a regular Britain's foe' who 'for the past three months has tried to instill in Petrograd workers a fervent hatred of England as a country which Russia will never be able to reconcile with'.[52]

Typically, on returning from Moscow to Paris, while talking to the British prime minister on the second occasion, Bullitt was shown a recent copy of the *Daily Mail* with another shocking anti-Bolshevik article. In doing so Lloyd George exclaimed: 'Until the British press publishes things like this, how can you expect me to be prudent in relation to Russia?'[53] Besides, he could hardly ignore the telegram signed by 200 MPs, demanding the government to abstain from Soviet Russia's official recognition.[54]

On 3 April, a joint conference of the LP and TUC called for the immediate withdrawal of all British troops from Russia.[55] As Reginald Esher, one of the King's entourage, noted in the diary, 'the British people were thoroughly tired of the war, were determined not to embark again on extensive military operations … in Russia, and were showing increasing impatience over the slow progress made with the peace treaty'.[56] Consequently, the Foreign Office drafted a top-secret memorandum for the Cabinet regarding the settlement of the 'Russian problem'. On 16 April, Lloyd George voiced the document in the House of Commons, likening the situation in Russia to 'a volcano that was still in fierce eruption'. The prime minister added that 'the best thing you can do is to provide security for those who are dwelling on its remotest and most accessible slopes, and arrest the devastating flow of lava, so that it shall not scorch other lands'.

He further disavowed Bullet's mission and identified reasons for Britain's refusal to negotiate the Soviet government's recognition. These were the lack of legitimacy, the 'serious crimes' committed by the Bolshevik leadership and the continued 'attacks' by the Red Army against the pro-Entente political groups in Russia. 'Has anyone reckoned up what an army of occupation would cost in Russia?', the head of the Cabinet asked the audience, concluding his oration with a remarkable phrase: 'I would rather leave Russia Bolshevik until she sees her way out of it than see Britain bankrupt.'[57]

This statement meant that the Cabinet bet on the 'indirect' intervention exploiting the White military leaders, like Admiral Kolchak, as stalking-horses for Russia's transformation into a cluster of states dependent on Britain and France. London's option for this strategy might be also expounded by the fact that the Bolsheviks' regime hardly fit the Versailles world order as it was projected by Lloyd George and Wilson.[58]

Naturally, the Paris conference delegates concurred in favour of a rigid diplomatic and economic isolation of Soviet Russia. On 24 May 1919, the Entente leaders deliberated this problem at Wilson's residence in Paris. They arranged for a collective note to Kolchak whose Anglophile position was known in London owing to information received from Major General Knox and some other British military emissaries to Russia.[59] The Allies suggested to the admiral to convoke the National Constitutional Assembly, hold free local elections, shun the restoration of landlords, safeguard the independence of Poland and Finland, cooperate with the League of Nations on the status of the republics in the Baltic, Transcaucasia and Central Asia, organize a special conference on the Bessarabian question and agree with the obligation to refund foreign debts. On receiving albeit evasive, but nevertheless a concord from Kolchak, the Western top statesmen recognized his government *de-facto* on 12 June 1919.[60]

Temporarily, the admiral became the most popular Russian military commander in the British Isles. Suffice it to note that some ladies of the high society wore tokens with his portrait, while politicians preferred to neglect the anti-democratic coup, committed by Kolchak in Omsk on 18 November 1918. This attitude arose partly due to the reports from General Knox staying at the Russian Supreme ruler's headquarters, when he suggested to form a Russo-British brigade of 2,000 servicemen with the UK commanders.[61] This proposal resulted in a cadet training school which was established on the Russkiy Island near Vladivostok in the winter of 1918–19. The British military instructors were engaged in drilling Russian volunteers, which made *The Times* to report on the first 500 graduates joining the Kolchak troops.[62]

The active logistical support to the armies under the admiral's order included seventy-nine cargo vessels with weapons, munitions and uniform sufficient for the army of 100,000.[63] As Knox stated in October 1919, British officers assisted in training more than 1,500 Russian subalterns and the same quantity of non-commissioned officers. He also pointed out that the supply to Kolchak of a few hundred thousand rifles, hundreds million gun-cartridges, a hundred cannons, a thousand machine-guns, several hundred thousand sets of uniforms and other military equipment enabled his troops to continue fighting the Reds for several months. Additionally, London credited Kolchak's government to secure a portion of the Russian state gold reserve retained by some Czechoslovak commanders in Siberia.[64]

Yet like in the case of Lavr Kornilov (see Chapter 1), the public euphoria about Kolchak did not last long. The subsequent defeat of his armies in the summer of 1919 spurred the transfer of the Entente military aid to the troops ordered by another former tsarist General, Anton Denikin, who announced the 'march towards Moscow' in October the same year.[65] The Russian diplomat Evgeny Sablin wrote to the White Armed Forces of Southern Russia (ASFR) department of foreign affairs that the British military, returning from Russia, 'described Denikin, his armies and administration with delight'. Sablin apprised his correspondent of Churchill hanging a map in his study to calculate the distance from the front-line of the White offensive to Moscow. 'He [Churchill] is looking forward to the moment of its [Moscow] capture and worries, as if any unexpected events in the rear would not frustrate the "flight" of the White armies', Sablin remarked, claiming that Denikin's victories made him a new idol of admiration by general British public.[66]

The excitement culminated in the end of September–early October 1919 when Denikin's advanced detachments were approaching Tula, an ancient town at the distance of less than 200 kilometres to the south of the Russian capital. *The Times* expressed surprise 'if a government grounded on terrorism, as in the case of the Bolsheviks, had a determination to stand to the last', while the *Daily Telegraph* convinced the reader that there was 'no way for the Soviets to arrest his [Denikin's] forward movement'.[67] It is also known that Churchill intended to visit Moscow after it was occupied by Denikin's troops to personally welcome the winners. On 24 October, the war minister was promised by the Parliament the allocation of £14 million to maintain the military assistance to the Russian Whites. Yet this loan became the last British expenses of the armed intervention in Russia.⁶⁸

Halford Mackinder, a world-known British geographer, was chosen by the Cabinet for a special trip as the high commissioner for South Russia on the eve of 1920. He visited Ekaterinodar, Rostov-on-the-Don and Novorossiysk, conferring with Denikin and his closest associates. According to the latter's memoirs, Mackinder sought a close coordination to be established between the Whites and Polish troops in order to reanimate the project of the so-called Black Sea (or Crimean-Cossack) Federation including Ukraine, the Don and Kuban regions along with the North Caucasus. Interestingly, the delegates of the Ukrainian People's Republic at the Paris conference did not oppose projects of this sort.⁶⁹

Mackinder's memorandum for the Foreign Office and his replies to questions put to him at the Cabinet meeting on 29 January 1920 are of interest as the account of an eyewitness. While presenting personal qualities of the anti-Bolshevik leaders, Mackinder pointed out to their failure to beat the Red Army due to the inability to suggest a comprehensive programme of Russia's modernization. He wrote about mass repressions committed by the Denikin officers against not only local Soviet officials but also ethnic minorities, such as the Jews and Gypsies. Mackinder also drew attention to the significant strengthening of the Red Army, which, in his view, 'very quickly adopted the German methods of armed fighting'. Among the measures of practical importance proposed by Mackinder was a combination of a diplomatic recognition with the conclusion of temporary military alliances with Poland, Romania and even Bulgaria to bring Soviet Russia to complete isolation.⁷⁰

On discussing this information, the Cabinet members overruled further armed intervention against the Bolshevik regime for the lack of funding, manpower and public support, still refusing to enter negotiations with the Kremlin. Russia's bordering states were advised to restrain from any aggressive steps against their former metropolis in the anticipation of Britain's assistance. Another decision focused on granting humanitarian support to Russian political refugees.⁷¹

In the meantime, the shipment of military equipment and munitions to Denikin's troops reached an unprecedented scale. One historian reported the bulk of strategic materials being sufficient to fully equip with the German trophy assets of twelve infantry divisions.⁷² The AFSR were supplied by the British alone with twelve tanks which constituted the so-called South Russian tank squad. A total of 558 artillery cannons and howitzers, 160,000,000 rifle cartridges, 450,000 greatcoats and 645,000 pairs of military boots were delivered to Denikin as well. One hundred and sixty-eight airplanes were redeployed to South Russia from the military bases on Malta and Lemnos, whereas a few British men-of-war together with several speeding torpedo boats controlled the Azov, Black and Caspian harbours. Towards the end of 1919, the military mission's staff positioned at the AFSR headquarters amounted to 1923 servicemen.⁷³

As some pilots of the so-called squadron Z. recalled, their training airbase was situated near Taganrog – a port on the Azov Sea. A total of 356 officers along with 1,102 rank-and-file were engaged in the air raids against the Bolshevik as well as the Ukrainian nationalistic troops. In the late autumn of 1919, British commanders even planned to drop off twelve twenty-pound bombs on Moscow during a special attack from the aerodrome in the suburbs of Kharkov.[74]

Regarding the situation in the north of Russia, it should be repeated that the War Office's principal goal remained the control of the shortest possible routes to the country's western provinces.[75] On 23 March 1919, the Treasury informed the military ruler of the Northern Province, Lieutenant General Evgeny Miller, on about a monthly subsidy of 5 million roubles to his administration. Calculations made by historians demonstrate that the Cabinet expenses on the armed intervention in North Russia alone exceeded £23 million.[76] It is also important to mention the usage of chemical weapons by the British troops against the Red Army on the Northern front.[77] Churchill became one of the most ardent advocates of poison gas as a means of deterrence. In a message to General Wilson the war minister frankly wrote:

> I do not understand this squeamishness about the use of gas ... I am strongly in favour of using poison gas against uncivilised tribes. The moral effect should be so good that the loss of life should be reduced to a minimum. It is not necessary to use the deadliest gasses: gasses can be used which cause great inconvenience and would spread a lively terror and yet would leave no serious permanent effects on most of those affected.[78]

Major General William Silbert, the head of the War Office chemical warfare service, took special interest in testing poisoned gasses against the Bolsheviks. On 11 April 1919, twenty-five military instructors were forwarded to Arkhangelsk, being equipped with 50,000 portable gas generators and 10,000 respirators.[79] The debates by military experts about the better way of application – either with the help of air bombs or 9.45-millimeter trench howitzer shells stuffed with mustard gas – ended in favour of the latter method, adopted by the Cabinet on 12 May 1919. Thus, a special British detachment used mustard gas against the Bolshevik units in the forest to the south of Arkhangelsk on 29 May 1919. It was also applied by Denikin's troops fighting the Red guards in the suburbs of Tsaritsyn (now Volgograd), the city on the Volga, in the summer of 1919. According to Major General Herbert Hollman, the chief of the mission, '120 rounds were fired on the enemy in the trenches in the open steppes'. Regretfully, there is no available evidence of casualties caused by this chemical attack.[80]

Returning to foreign policy issues, one should bear in mind that the Entente leaders were more at odds about how to find an adequate solution of the 'Russian question' through 1919. Denikin remarked in the aftermath of the civil war that 'the British policy was boggling in great dependence on failures or successes on the White fronts, modifying the intentions either of our friends or foes among the public and parliamentary circles of England'.[81] The Bolsheviks, for their part, kept on intimidating the Entente leaders of Russia's eventual disintegration should the Whites take over. In their opinion, this could lead to the prevailing German or Japanese influence.[82] Yet statesmen like Lloyd George promoted the country's confederalization which would cease to pose a threat to the Versailles order. There were also politicians, Curzon as an instance, who offered creating a belt of buffer limitrophes to curtail the Bolshevik menace and make it possible for Britain to oversee Russia's political course.[83] It was this section of British ministers that Lenin referred to when he stated at the conference of the Moscow Province executive committees that 'England wishes to have under its aegis new small states, such as Finland, Estonia, Latvia and Lithuania, having no business and even regarding disadvantageous the restoration of the tsarist or at least bourgeois Russia'.[84]

By virtue of the coalition government, Lloyd George himself had to manoeuvre between different groups of political front-runners, the leaders of British dominions and his Entente partners. Although the 'Russian issue' was discussed at the government meetings at least on six occasions during July 1919 alone, the prime minister's position as well as that of his key colleagues shifted with every new piece of information about the situation in Eastern Europe. On 4 July, the Cabinet members officially recognized the state of war with the Bolsheviks, although they decided to abstain from any public declaration.[85] However, in the end of the month, Balfour compiled a memorandum specifying economic blockade as the most suitable means of pressure upon the Kremlin.[86] On 14 August, Lloyd George avowed the need not only to withdraw expeditionary forces from Russia as soon as possible but also to cease funding as well as delivering munitions to the Whites armies.[87]

Almost simultaneously, Curzon reviewed the European situation. While drawing his colleagues' attention to the *de-facto* recognition by the British government of independent Estonia and Latvia, on the one hand, and Kolchak's administration, on the other, he criticized the Cabinet's policy towards Russia. As he pointed out,

> No further steps have been taken to endeavour to secure the cooperation of the border states of Russia in the policy laid down by the Allied powers, and no communications have been addressed to the representatives of these States in Paris despite their repeated requests to be informed of the intentions of the Allied governments.[88]

On 12 September 1919, Curzon wrote to Lloyd George that the 'restoration of Russia' would lead to the 'revision of Versailles', because the Bolsheviks would reclaim the lost territories, including Finland, the Baltic republics and Poland. Under these circumstances, Germany would be given a chance to restore its predominant position in continental Europe. 'Sazonovs [Sergei Sazonov – the tsarist pro-Entente foreign minister during the world war] denikins and kolchaks have nothing learnt for the last two years', stressed Curzon, 'they are hidden Germanophiles in heart, while on the surface – open Russian imperialists'. But 'feeble Russia' in Curzon's opinion was also capable of producing trouble to Britain, although to a much lesser extent. That is why he recommended Lloyd George to seek support in strong Poland as a 'buffer-state' between revolutionary Russia and defeated, albeit nationalistic, Germany. The best way out of the stalemate, according to Curzon, was the creation of the United States of Russia, for which a special meeting of the Entente member states should be convoked at the Paris conference.[89]

The psychological fatigue of war, causing social unrest and disorder, along with enormous economic difficulties compelled the Entente governments to embark on the evacuation of their forces from the Russian territory in the fall of 1919.[90] It is worth bearing in mind that Paris withdrew its marines from the Black Sea after their unexpected revolt in Odessa as early as in April the same year. And Washington followed the example in June when practically every American military serviceman was withdrawn from Vladivostok. Therefore, Lloyd George appealed to Churchill on 22 September, requesting him to stop dealing exclusively with Russia and pay attention to the issues of national economy's recovery. Three days later, Whitehall suggested to the Baltic states to set up a peaceful dialogue with Moscow.[91] Consequently, in September and November the same year, the British volunteers left the Far East, albeit the railway mission was remaining in Vladivostok until the end of 1920, while the expeditionary forces departed from Arkhangelsk on the night of 26–27 September 1919 and from Murmansk on 12 October.[92] Other Entente interventionists were removed from the Caucasus in the middle of the same month with the exception for Batum where they had been staying until 10 July 1920. Late in November 1919, the British battleships left the eastern sector of the Baltic Sea as well.[93]

As has been mentioned above, the Bolsheviks offered to the leading Entente powers the peaceful settlement of the armed conflict on several occasions. As Krassin, then the minister for foreign trade, wrote to his spouse from Petrograd on 25 October 1919, 'any further protraction of warfare is unlikely to benefit even our real enemies, and if Denikin fails to conquer us before the winter (and he will doubtfully succeed), then perhaps England will understand that it is in its own interest to try to cope with Bolshevism in the economic field on the ground of restricted but peaceful relations'.[94]

On 11 and 14 July 1919, the Paris Council of Ten discussed economic sanctions against Soviet Russia, leading to the Entente leaders split into proponents and opponents of the blockade. The telegram to Wilson (who had already left Paris) motivated it by domestic political instability in European countries as well as by the lack of funding to continue military support to the anti-Bolshevik resistance.[95] The official declaration of Soviet Russia's economic blockade by the allies followed on 10 October 1919. Moscow desired, for its part, to impose peace talks on London through the repatriation of thousands Russian ex-POWs and refugees.[96] Hence, on 24 November 1919, Lloyd George and Francis Pollock, the acting head of the US delegation in Paris, agreed on a diplomatic concordance with the Soviet regime once the Bolsheviks refunded Russia's foreign debts and recognized new sovereign states.[97]

According to Churchill's estimation, the overall British expenditure on the armed intervention amounted to £500 million, although certain economic experts pointed out to a lesser sum of £107 million spent by Britain in Russia from November 1918 to April 1920.[98] But what seems even more important, the Allied military missions proved unable to effectively monitor the use of material aid and cash flows by various anti-Bolshevik leaders whose activities caused deep concerns in London.[99]

The blockade of Soviet Russia by Western countries meant refusal of their governments to issue visas, custom certificates and trade consignments as well as the stoppage of mail correspondence and creation of other legal barriers for private banks intending to cover financial transactions. Meanwhile the lectures delivered by Lloyd George on 8 and 17 November 1919 assumed public's attention. The first oration was made in London's Guildhall and became a sensation, for the prime minister overruled any solution of the 'Russian question' by military means. More than that, he acknowledged the need to seek *modus vivendi* with Moscow. It had startled many political observers because the Entente Supreme military council deliberated in September 1919 the proposal of the Polish Prime Minister Ignatius Paderewski to organize the invasion in Russia of the 500,000 legionaries.[100] Besides, as the reader knows, the Parliament had approved a new financial credit to the White generals only three days before Lloyd George took the floor. General Wilson metaphorically described the episode in his diary: 'Our prime minister seemed to have thrown a Prinkipo fly into the turtle soup of the Entente, causing the fathers of the City nausea from the whole dish.'[101]

However, the prime minister repeated his view, having triggered Denikin's message with reproaches of 'flirtation with the Bolsheviks'.[102] The extremely negative reaction by the White emigrants to the obvious turn in the British attitude to Russia was clearly seen in Nabokov's letter to Nikolai Chaikovsky, the prime minister of the White Russian government in Northern Russia: 'Yesterday [on 17 November 1919] the Bolsheviks were reviled in the House of Commons *dans les grands prix*. But Lloyd George did not promise to talk to them, making it transparently clear that the united Russia acts as a bogey for England.'[103]

The conflict of interest among the allies concerning the 'Russian problem' was manifested at the final stage of the Paris conference. During the meeting of the Entente leaders and the ministers for foreign affairs in London on 11–13 December 1919, Lloyd George told Clemenceau that the Cabinet cancelled refunding the anti-Bolshevik forces in Russia while maintaining its economic blockade as well as transforming the border states into the principal barriers to the bolshevization of Europe.[104]

The repatriation of Russian ex-POWs also affected the British and French position. To accelerate the process, a special Allied subcommittee was set up in the French capital on 25 July 1919. Almost simultaneously, Maxim Litvinov, who became the deputy people's commissar for foreign affairs after returning to Russia, conferred with the British representatives in Copenhagen in the summer and autumn of the same year. Owing to these informal parleys, brokered by the Danish Red Cross delegates, the return of the Russians from Central Europe began as early as in March 1919. Sponsored by the International Red Cross, their routes to the homeland were laid via Romania in the south, Poland in the west and the Baltic states in the north-west.[105] As for the exchange of British subjects for Bolshevik prisoners, it took place at the request of the regional Soviet authorities and local commanders of the Entente troops in the spring of 1919 on the Finnish border, although the official start dated to 16 November when the subsequent group of ex-POWs was exchanged for fifty-five UK subjects in Revel (now Tallinn). Curiously, the Treasury reimbursed the Danish Red Cross with 50,000 roubles for these efforts.[106] On 7 November 1919, Curzon communicated to Chicherin the Cabinet's consent to continue negotiations on POWs' exchange. A week later, James O'Grady, a Labour MP and the Secretary of the National federation of unqualified workers, met Litvinov in Copenhagen.[107] Although O'Grady was instructed on the necessity to shun any political topics, Litvinov managed to involve his vis-à-vis in a dialogue about lifting the Entente's blockade and regulating bilateral relations.[108]

The end of the Paris conference on 21 January 1920 nearly coincided with the last phase of Litvinov–O'Grady consultations when the latter informed Curzon of a draft agreement. On 5 February, the British government adopted the document with a few minor amendments to be signed a week later.[109] While hammering out the consolidated strategy towards Soviet Russia, Lloyd George, as one contemporary observer penned in his diary, 'gave Winston [Churchill] a dressing down about Russia' at the Cabinet meeting on 9 February. 'Our policy, argued the prime minister, was to try to escape the results of the evil policy which Winston had persuaded the Cabinet to adopt', for Churchill 'was not only backing the wrong horse but a jibbing horse, namely Denikin'.[110]

For his part, Litvinov reviewed the negotiations in the following way: 'He [O'Grady] often referred to the modification of English policy in the Russian issue, but I requested proofs. I asked him to strain all efforts upon lifting the blockade as well as stopping to incite the border states to attack us.'[111] This evaluation was evidenced by O'Grady's private message to Litvinov. The British emissary assured his diplomatic partner that he would do everything, both publicly and informally, to end the unfortunate developments between Moscow and the rest of the world. Meanwhile the exchange of prisoners between Moscow and London, regulated by the Litvinov–O'Grady agreement, proceeded from 5 November to 5 December 1920.[112]

At the time, Edward Wise, one of Lloyd George's leading economic consiglieres, apprised him of a possibility to open channels with Moscow through Russian cooperative societies – non-governmental associations that began to emerge in the country since the end of the nineteenth century. Shortly afterwards the British prime minister discussed this issue with the heads of the Entente delegations in Paris. He argued in favour of an arrangement with Russia for the exchange of commodities which would help Western countries to cope with the postwar economic crisis, accompanied by the galloping inflation. 'Prices were going up in France, Italy and Great Britain, and this very fact tended to create Bolshevism', stressed Lloyd George. As he predicted, 'the moment trade was established with Russia, communism would go'.[113]

The assurances given by the top managers of the Central Union of Russian consumer societies which embraced 20,000 affiliated companies, to Wise that the organization acted independently of the Kremlin, enabled the Entente Supreme Council to declare the abolition of Russia's economic blockade on 16 January 1920.[114] The prospect of Europe's industrial and financial recovery began to assume tangible foundations.[115] As George Riddell, the British press-attaché in Paris, recorded in the diary, 'the allies now understand the impossibility of fighting the Bolsheviks in Russia. No nation is prepared to supply troops or money'.[116]

On 23 January, following the closure of the Paris conference, Lloyd George approved the establishment of the inter-departmental committee chaired by Wise who also headed the commission on the restoration of trade relations with Russia in the Entente Supreme economic council.[117] Yet in order 'to save face', the Entente statesmen stipulated in the press communique issued on 16 January that this measure did not cease Russia's political isolation, whereas the Cabinet defiantly neglected another Chicherin's appeal to immediately start peace talks on 24 February 1920.[118]

Nevertheless, the prime minister declared: 'We have failed to restore Russia by force. I believe we can do it and save her by trade. Commerce has a sobering influence in its operations. The simple sums in addition and subtraction which it includes soon dispose of wild theories.'[119] Another entry in the diary by Riddell seemed typical in this respect. On 6 March, at the lunch with Lloyd George, the latter strongly favoured peace with the Russian government anticipating its representatives 'to arrive in England at an early date to make arrangements regarding trade with Russia'.[120]

Summing up, one may conclude that the UK foreign policy stalled by the spring of 1920, for London had failed to assemble the 'Russian jigsaw' either by reconciling the Soviets with the Whites, or by providing armed, material and financial support to anti-Bolshevik forces, let alone an open intervention 'without agreement'.

Historians continue to debate the roots and reasons of the Entente's fiasco to overthrow the Bolshevik regime and introduce liberal democracy in Russia. While Soviet or European left-wing authors traditionally mentioned a decisive contribution of British workers and other social grassroots who appealed to ruling elites for the political recognition of the Bolshevik government, modern Western scholars mostly pointed out to the divergence of views among Entente politicians on the means and methods of Russia's appeasement.[121]

On 29 January 1920, a group of prominent Labour activists issued a manifesto welcoming the withdrawal of all British expeditionary forces from the Russian territory. They also warned the Government against preparing new armed intervention. On the other hand, the Scotland Yard reports to the Cabinet attested to trade unions overruling the conscription by the government for the cause of militarily interference in Russian affairs.[122] Smuts, an influential South African statesman and the Imperial Cabinet member, strongly recommended to London 'to leave Russia alone, lift the blockade and take the course of neutrality towards it'.[123]

Finally, even Churchill, the most stubborn opponent of the Bolsheviks among the ministers, confessed to Lloyd George in a letter dated to 24 March 1920: 'I should be prepared to make peace with Soviet Russia on the best terms available to appease the general situation, while safeguarding us from being poisoned by them', the phrase sounding ironically given his love for poison gas![124]

This author considers a unique combination of domestic and international conditions that made it possible for the Bolsheviks to survive in the civil war and intervention from abroad. This 'cocktail' comprised not only the peculiarities of Russian climate, the lack of clearly formulated objectives or poor support to the anti-Bolshevik armed resistance, as some authors believed.[125] The major 'ingredient' seemed to be Russia's general unpreparedness for the perception of industrial democracy on a Western pattern. Hence, all attempts by the British ruling elites to plant liberal order in the former half-medieval empire by force failed in contrast with the victorious norms of the Bolshevik dictatorship, disguised as people democracy.

Considering Russia's specific geostrategic position as a great power, none of the Entente leaders could neglect her state interests and ambitions, even seriously diminished because of the Bolshevik revolution. The fact that the allies and foremost Britain failed to convene an international forum to discuss the situation in Eastern Europe with Russia's participation also played a negative part for the maintenance of the Versailles international system.[126]

'What a black chapter in our history is all this Russian business', wrote Esher to Balfour following the latter's resignation as the foreign secretary.[127] An assessment of this kind strongly suggested that for the UK as well as for other Entente states and the

Figure 8 'Winston's Bag', Caricature, Star, 21 January 1920. Photo courtesy of Wikimedia Commons (public domain).

United States, the intervention in Soviet Russia became a 'stillborn crusade', as one historian entitled his academic monograph.[128]

The next chapter will demonstrate how the situation in Eastern Europe formidably affected the general course of relations between London and Moscow.

6

The Baltic problem, Soviet-Polish war and trade negotiations

> *Diplomacy and Bolshevism – does not a comparison between these two words include the most glaring contradiction?*
>
> Pavel Miliukov, 1927[1]

For several centuries, the Eastern Baltic has been a 'bone of contention' between European countries, including Russia and Britain. The collapse of empires and emergence of independent states on the Baltic coasts in the aftermath of the global war went hand in hand with the spread of the Bolshevik ideology, defying a sustainable regional sub-system of international relations within the frames of the Versailles world order.

Doubtlessly, political and economic contacts between Soviet Russia and the UK played an important role in the process. Yet each side perceived it according to its own political concept. For the Bolsheviks, whose chances to hold the Eastern Baltic seemed diminutive, at least in the immediate aftermath of the revolution, diplomatic recognition of the new sovereign states meant the opening of a 'window' to Western Europe through the local seaports – Revel, Riga and others. Besides, the Kremlin leaders regarded the Baltic countries, including Poland and Finland, as the most appropriate testbed to bring to life the project of a global anti-capitalist revolution. The British government, engaged in the demilitarization of national economy, in turn, considered the Baltic area not only as a valuable market but also as a bulwark to contain the penetration of subversive communist activity into Central and Western Europe. The burden of previous, unresolved political controversies along with overpowering ethnic and confessional diversity seriously debarred the Entente states from regional 'appeasement' which also arrested the yearns by the Foreign Office pundits to recommend certain diplomatic measures to British statesmen.[2]

The Brest treaty put the UK at a very disadvantageous position due to the occupation of a large part of the Baltic coastal area by German troops. Comparably to how London acted in other parts of the former tsarist empire, the Cabinet had often undertaken steps 'to touch', following the traditional method of 'trial and error' in the face of an acute shortage of experts on current developments. That is why Lloyd George, Balfour and Curzon cautiously probed regional political elites who were contacting London through 1918 in the search of guarantees for their independence from Russia.[3]

The vast bulk of evidence testifies to the various opinions on the solution of the Baltic problem. A minor part of Cabinet ministers, for instance, Churchill, Walter Long, the First Lord of Admiralty and senior military staffers advocated the independent status of Poland and Finland while neglecting that of Estonia, Latvia and Lithuania.[4] Others, Curzon as a paragon, shared the idea of political federalization of Russia's imperial outskirts along with the creation of the Baltic League under Britain's patronage.[5] The third group, such as Balfour and some high-ranking diplomats, supported the establishment of the sovereign states, which would be economically linked to the UK as a common market for the manufactured goods from Britain. Yet all of them were unanimous in the assumption that the Baltic states ought to act as a bulwark against westward advance of Bolshevism.[6]

As for the prime minister, he traditionally intended to find a compromise between the recognition of democratic regimes in response to Moscow's attempts to proclaim the Soviet republics and the refusal to form full diplomatic relations, dreading negative reaction by those anti-Bolshevik circles who projected the restoration of empire. Put it another way, British promises of support to the Baltic states left considerable room for interpretation and often might be regarded as a propaganda exercise.[7]

The final stage of the Great War and the beginning of the Entente's armed intervention in Russia nearly coincided with the consecutive declaration of independence by five regional states: Finland – on 6 December 1917, Estonia – on 24 February 1918, Poland – on 11 November, Lithuania – on 16 November 1918 and Latvia – two days later.[8] In a special memorandum for the Cabinet, dated back to 18 October the same year, Balfour observed the need for Russia to have a protracted recovery period. He further claimed that it could be achieved by the inclusion in the anticipated democratic Russian Federation of the so-called 'small nations' which had already declared or were about to predicate their sovereignty. As Balfour maintained, the only attainable British objective should be twofold: 'to supply arms and money [to anti-Bolshevist administrations], and to protect as far as we can the nascent nationalities with our fleet'.[9]

Apart from political and ideological motives, Balfour pointed out to the necessity of preventing Soviet-German reproachment as well as to new financial opportunities for British investors in the Baltic. He was confident that any kind of vacuum in the region – political or economic – would imply the inevitable arrival of Britain's competitors – France or the United States. It is worth noting that about 80 per cent of manufactured goods were imported to Soviet Russia through the Baltic seaports in 1920–24.[10]

The transformation of the Baltic Sea into the 'British lake' seemed a more lucrative outcome for the UK's ruling elites. The euphoria of war victory led the Cabinet ministers to adhere to Balfour's vision of the situation at the meeting on 14 November 1918, although some of them drew attention to high risks and colossal financial costs. As early as on 20 November, the Admiralty directed the Sixth Light cruiser squadron consisting of four battleships, nine destroyers and seven minesweepers under Rear Admiral Edwin Alexander-Sinclair to the Latvian and Estonian ports of Liepaja and Revel, respectively.[11] In the beginning of 1919, the First Light cruiser squadron commanded by another Rear Admiral, Walter Cowan, replaced it at the possible theatre of war. The British fended off all aggressive challenges by the Bolsheviks to local Estonian and Latvian harbours by the concentration of a hundred surface warships, submarines and hydroplanes of different models towards the end of February.[12]

Yet the pacification of the Baltic in accordance with the scheme proposed by Balfour was against the interests of three other geopolitical actors –the Soviets, the Russian Whites and the Germans. Lenin and Trotsky were the first who attempted to skew negotiations for Soviet Russia's benefit. Despite the Bolsheviks instigated civil war in Finland which ended in a complete fiasco to their sympathizers in the summer of 1918, the November anti-monarchist revolution in Germany opened new prospects for 'exporting' revolution to Europe. In the case of Latvia, the Soviet government appropriated 160 million gold roubles for its bolshevization and ordered the Red Army divisions to invade its territory in the direction of Riga and Jelgava on the eve of 1919. Simultaneously, on 25–27 December 1918, two destroyers of the Red Baltic Fleet bombarded Revel, albeit scored no success and were later captured by British battleships.[13]

Meanwhile a pro-German coup in Latvia and the formation of the White army under General Nikolai Yudenich in May 1919 led to lively discussions amid the Entente delegates to the Paris conference.[14] On 15 May, they resulted in the creation by the Entente Supreme Council of the Inter-Allied military commission on the Baltic problem with Major General Hugh Gough as its representative in the region. Instructed by both Curzon and Churchill to regard the 'small nationalistic states' of the region as the 'buffers' between Russia and Germany, although without official recognition of their sovereignty, he arrived in Helsinki ten days later.[15] The Bolsheviks' reaction to this mission was a decree adopted by the All-Russian central executive committee on 1 June 1919 proclaiming the 'integration of the Soviet republics of Russia, Ukraine, Latvia, Lithuania and Belarus to fight the world imperialism'.[16]

A total of 238 British battle and ancillary ships had been carrying out the naval blockade of Soviet Russia in the Baltic until the end of December 1919. The Royal Fleet lost a light cruiser, two destroyers, a submarine, two minesweepers, eight torpedo boats and three transports, while sixty-one men-of-war suffered various damages.[17] The War Office and the Admiralty intimately collaborated through the period of blockade, especially in the arrangement of unexpected assaults against the principal Soviet naval base of Kronstadt. Striking episodes of the undeclared war in the Eastern Baltic included attacks by hydroplanes and speedy torpedo boats under the command of Lieutenant Augustus Agar upon the Bolshevik warships anchored in the Kronstadt harbour on 14 May, 13 and 18 June 1919, when the British scuttled the heavy cruiser *Oleg*.[18] But the most tangible loss for the Baltic Fleet was the destruction of the battleship *Andrei Pervozvannyi* as well as severe damages caused to another men-of-war *Petropavlovsk* and the training vessel *Pamiat' Azova* during the famous raid on the night of 18 August. The British torpedo boats broke through Russian mine barriers at 40 knots' speed, losing nine marines who were taken captive and three vessels due to the artillery fire of the patrol destroyer *Gavriil*.[19] In addition to these skirmishes three Bolshevik cruisers were detonated by British mines in the Finnish Gulf on 31 October 1919.[20] As Lieutenant Colonel Stephen Tallents, the high commissioner to the Baltic region, recalled later, 'both the Estonian and Lettish governments owe their existence directly to the support of British sea power', since 'without that support, the territories controlled by them would long ago have been in either Bolshevik or German hands'.[21]

The chiefs of the Russian White movement were deeply embroiled in the settlement of the Baltic problem. Some of them succumbed to the temptation to use the German occupation forces stationed in the former Baltic provinces of Russia in order to wipe the Bolsheviks out of the region.[22] General Yudenich met Robert Clive, the counsellor of the UK diplomatic mission in Stockholm, accompanied by the military attaché in Sweden and his adjutant on 9 December 1918. Whereas approving temporary presence of the German military administration in the Baltic area as well as expressing intention to continue the struggle against the Bolsheviks as soon as possible, Yudenich proposed that the British should capture the most significant seaports, redeploying there 50,000 Entente soldiers and officers to arrange for a new Russian North-West army on the territory of Finland. About 15,000–20,000 former tsarist troops, including 2,000–4,000 officers, were still expecting on the spot for a call to fight the Soviets. Even more reserves of manpower could be enrolled in the numerous POWs' camps elsewhere in Germany and Austria. Yudenich estimated the monthly funding of the 'liberation military march' to Petrograd in cooperation with the Finns at 50 million roubles.[23]

Yet both Lloyd George and Balfour took these plans with restraint. Their stance could be explained by the ongoing debates with Britain's allies in Paris and Yudenich's refusal to recognize Estonia and Latvia as sovereign states.[24] Some former tsarist diplomats in London complained that 'England sympathises with us [the anti-Bolshevik forces] only in words and inspires the selfness of the Baltic provinces to the detriment of Russia'.[25]

Here it is appropriate to review the impact of Germany and those pro-German forces who constituted the so-called Russian Western volunteer army commanded by Prince Anatoly Lieven and later also by Colonel (then Major General) Pavel Bermondt-Avalov.[26] As the latter identified the wide-spread attitude towards Berlin, 'we [Russian nationalists] were disappointed by the ambivalent role of the Entente that dragged on the Russian crisis, while the Germans, with all burden of the signed peace treaty [in Versailles], being surrounded by foes, became ready in every way to help Russia's recovery'.[27] Known for his Germanophile position, Bermondt-Avalov commanded paramilitary units that attempted to capture Riga in mid-October. Defeated by the Latvian troops with the assistance of British and French naval squadrons, they were compelled to evacuate to East Prussia in the end of 1919.[28]

The collapse of the Russian North-Western government accompanied by a setback of the Yudenich troops' march to Petrograd in October 1919 led to the complete disarray of the White movement in the former Baltic provinces. Yet the desire of some top Red Army commanders to occupy Estonia and Latvia found no response in the Kremlin.[29]

The fiasco of the Entente's military campaign against Petrograd prompted the Cabinet to phase out military supplies to the regional forces ensuring an almost complete withdrawal of warships from the eastern waters of the Baltic Sea. On 26 February 1920, Curzon instructed Talents to confidentially apprise the local governments of

Whitehall's intention to recommence the Baltic transit of manufactured goods to and raw materials from Russia.[30]

While cherishing hopes to create a regional association of states, London took into consideration competitive projects, which regional statesmen suggested as early as in 1917–18.[31] The establishment of a defensive alliance between Estonia and Finland, proposed by the well-known Estonian politician Konstantin Pates, was widely discussed among the Baltic intellectuals and European experts on the sidelines of the Paris conference. In this light, the diplomatic recognition of the Baltic states by the League of Nations on 21 September 1921 became a decisive step forward.[32]

A series of consultations which were held in Helsinki and Bilduri (a town in the proximity of Riga) in January and August 1920, as well as the meetings in Revel and again in Helsinki and Warsaw in February and August 1921, then in March and June 1922, contributed to the institution of the Baltic League. It was proclaimed in the capital of Poland on 17 March 1922 with the involvement of Poland, Finland, Estonia and Latvia. As some British policymakers believed close geographical location, economic interdependence and cultural proximity facilitated the implementation of this partnership, not to mention the 'Soviet threat' to members of the alliance.[33] However, regional convocations under the aegis of the League of Nations on several occasions during 1920–5 never brought the Baltic states to become a counterbalance to the French idea of the Little Entente in Eastern Europe. Instead, these diplomatic manoeuvres arose suspicion of both leaders of the Russian White movement and the Kremlin mandarins, for they contradicted their projects either to reanimate an empire or to construct a federation of Soviet republics.[34]

The dissolution of the Yudenich's army along with the evacuation of White Russian troops from Arkhangelsk, Murmansk and Novorossiysk decreased already poor chances for London to mediate between the Reds and Whites.[35] An exchange of radiograms on this issue lasted for a few weeks until the beginning of bilateral trade negotiations in the summer of 1920.[36] Although Moscow initially agreed to confer with the representatives of Piotr Wrangel, the successor of Denikin as the Supreme commander of the survived anti-Bolshevik troops in the Crimea, the Red Army's counter-offensive on the Polish front, the capture of the Caspian seaport Enzeli by the marines of the Caspian Flotilla and the aggravation of situation around Batum in the Black Sea brought the diplomatic efforts to naught (see Chapter 7). However, another important episode – the Soviet-Polish war – deserves attention, having affected bilateral relations to a much greater extent.

Having toppled down the Provisional government, Lenin and his followers regarded Poland as an available westward canal for the expansion of Bolshevism. Some leading Polish statesmen, especially Joseph Pilsudski, who was proclaimed the supreme chief of state, believed, in turn, that the time had come for the restoration of Greater Poland within the borders of the eighteenth century. Willing to take advantage of Russia's political fecklessness and economic disorder, they yearned to make Poland a hegemon of Eastern Europe. Another plausible explanation for Warsaw's international politics at the time could be a general chaos in the region following the end of the world war. Indeed, born from the break-up of three empires, Poland became almost immediately involved in a sequence of local conflicts, not only with the traditional great powers but between themselves as well. Small wonder, Churchill sarcastically commented on the international situation in this part of Europe: 'When the war of giants is over, the wars of the pygmies will begin.'[37] Despite relatively extensive scholarship of the Soviet-Polish armed conflict, some aspects still need more profound study in the light of interaction between Moscow and London.[38]

Following the Bolshevik coup d'état, the Allies repeatedly made clear that Poland's independence from Russia, whether Red or White, was a settled matter. This approach broadly corresponded with the Cabinet's foreign policy since the end of 1917 when Lloyd George discussed the Polish issue with his colleagues on several occasions.[39] Symptomatically, one of the Versailles treaty's clauses stipulated that Poland's eastern borders were to be demarcated only by agreement with Russia. This proviso posed Warsaw in front of uneasy dilemma: what diplomatic partner would be more appropriate in the negotiations – the Bolsheviks or the Russian nationalists?

As most historians argue, a skirmish between the Red Army units and Polish mounted detachments on 4–6 January 1919 in the Vilna area set about an inevitable military confrontation, leading to a large-scale warfare a month later. While the Bolshevik troops were engaged mainly in fighting Denikin and Yudenich, Polish infantry and cavalry divisions steadily occupied the most part of Belarus and Lithuania. After the hostilities between Poland and the Ukrainian People's Republic erupted in the mid-1919, Pilsudski ordered his legions to temporarily cease the eastward offensive.

If the leaders of the anti-Bolshevik armed resistance rejected any idea of Poland's sovereignty, the Kremlin agreed to hold the Soviet-Polish diplomatic consultations in October 1919. But the euphoria of defeating the White armies made the Bolsheviks less compliant about the demarcation of the Polish eastern frontier. On the other hand, Warsaw abstained from attacking the Reds while they were fighting the Whites, which enabled the transfer of 43,000 infantry- and cavalrymen from the Polish front to blockade Wrangel's army in the Crimea by the beginning of 1920.[40]

The Entente Inter-Allied commission prepared a draft agreement on the demarcation of the eastern Polish border. Presented at the Paris conference special meeting on 22 April 1919, it envisaged to conduct the demarcation in accordance with the principle of ethnic homogeneity along the so-called 'Curzon line' running from Grodno through Bialystok, Brest-Litovsk, Rava-Russkaya and Przemysl. Approved by the Entente delegations on 8 December the same year, this solution of the problem found response neither in Moscow nor in Warsaw.[41]

Even though scarcely 5 per cent of the Poles inhabited the territory of 400,000 square kilometres with the total population of 20 million, Warsaw ignored both a new Bolshevik proposal of peace talks and British recommendations to start consultations with Moscow.[42] In January 1920, the meeting of Lloyd George and Stanislav Patek, Polish foreign minister, led to nothing. In fact, the British requests to Warsaw to abandon war preparations and resolve peacefully all disputable issues with the neighbouring states, above all Russia and Lithuania, fell on a deaf ear.[43] Moreover, the Polish government concluded a secret political alliance with Simon Petliura, the chief of the self-proclaimed Ukrainian People's Republic on 21 April 1920. Both sides took obligations to collaborate in a forthcoming military campaign against Soviet Russia. Shortly afterwards, the British Mediterranean squadron approached the southern coasts of the Crimean Peninsula to protect it from any potential amphibious operation by the Soviets.[44]

On 25 April 1920, Polish troops launched a general offensive against the Red Army, but the British government refrained from its immediate condemnation. Instead, Curzon wired to the British acting consul in Revel that 'the allies would not remain silent', should the Bolshevik armies invade the 'border states'.[45] Equally, the Cabinet declined the Kremlin's request to London to mediate in the conflict on the pretext of the Soviet non-recognition of the League of Nations, whereas King George V cabled greetings to Pilsudski, commemorating the second anniversary of the restored sovereignty.[46]

The paradox of the Soviet-British relations became obvious to the Cabinet members at the meeting on 21 May. No decision was made, though Lloyd George together with his colleagues hoped to clarify the matter during the trade negotiations with the Soviet delegation arriving in London.[47] In the conversation with Riddell, the prime minister argued that although 'communist was doomed to failure', 'it had to be tried and he [Lloyd George] did not object to the experiment so long as it was tried here'.[48] A similar discordance of views was evidenced in the Kremlin with regard to the war plans against Poland. If Chicherin meant to bolshevize it by territorial concessions, Trotsky was determined to crush Pilsudski by force.[49]

As the declassified political correspondence shows, British military strategists and diplomatic pundits were meticulously monitoring the developments at the Polish-Soviet theatre of war in the summer of 1920. Long claimed in the memorandum for the Cabinet that the Bolshevik submarines in the Baltic were about to carry out naval demonstrations to intimidate Poland, Finland and other 'small states' contiguous with Soviet Russia.[50] The Foreign Office analysts maintained, in turn, that notwithstanding obvious military and political preponderance of the Bolshevik regime in Russia, 'its economic feebleness seemed doubtless'. They argued furthermore that the mass revolts by disgruntled Russian peasants who joined numerous bands known as the 'Greens', sympathizing with neither the Reds nor the Whites, could erode the Soviet rule elsewhere in the country.[51]

As it was mentioned earlier in the chapter, the Cabinet was split in the perception of the Soviet-Polish war. While Lloyd George and Andrew Bonar Law, the then Lord Privy Seal and the Tory leader, pinned their hopes on the foreseeable diplomatic consultations with the Soviet delegation, Balfour, Lord President, and Austen Chamberlain, the minister without portfolio, advocated a cautious attitude. On the other side, Churchill together with Curzon and Montagu tended to militarily support Pilsudski.[52]

Owing to counter-offensive operations conducted by the Red Army in the mid-1920, the fundamental shift in the Soviet-Polish war triggered feverish diplomatic activities by the British government. As one British historian notes, 'trade was seen by Lloyd George and the Labour Party, as well as significant members of the Conservative Party as "stabilising Russia", encouraging what we might call "convergence" and "interdependence"'.[53] The gathering that Lloyd George and Curzon convened with the French premier Alexander Millerand accompanied by the Entente C-in-C Marshal Foch in Spa (Belgium) on 8–10 July 1920 drew the attention of leading European politicians, military experts and public. Vladislav Grabski, the Polish prime minister escorted by the chief of the General Staff, Stanislav Haller, was also invited to attend the conference.[54] Being short of funds and ill-equipped to launch a new large-scale military campaign to rescue their Polish associates, both British and French cabinets instead warned the Bolshevik government against crossing the 'Curzon line' to further bolshevize the provinces where the autochthon Polish population prevailed. The Spa declaration invited the delegates from Soviet Russia, Poland, Lithuania, Latvia and Finland to assemble in London as soon as possible for a peace conference under the League of Nations' aegis.[55]

This time it was Moscow that refused to follow the Spa recommendations. Encouraged by the successive operations on the Polish front, this disinclination could be seen in the Soviet diplomatic notes on 13 and 17 July. Moscow accused London of ongoing support to the White troops synchronizing it with the Polish invasion of Ukraine and Belarus.[56] Suffice it to say that Lenin demagogically commented on the British proposal to conclude immediate armistice on all fronts: 'Personally, I think it is a pure scam for Crimea's annexation ... They [the British] are going to snatch victory out of our hands by certain fraudulent promises.'[57] As the Soviet leader anticipated, the Red Army's invasion of Poland would 'blow up the Versailles system'.[58]

Joseph Stalin, then the political commissar of the South-Western front, shared this extremist view. Although some Bolshevik military commanders, for example Mikhail Tukhachevsky, suggested to halt the advance at the 'Curzon line', Stalin urged the offensive to be going on without recession to subsequently bolshevize Hungary, Czechoslovakia, Romania, Germany and even Italy. Following this decision, the Red troops were ordered to cross the Polish ethnic boundary on 23 July 1920.[59]

Concurrently, the Kremlin sent Julian Marchlevski, the chairman of the urgently established Polish Provisional revolutionary committee, to emulate peace negotiations with Pilsudski's emissaries. Moscow regarded this trip as an adequate response to Curzon's drastic note received by Chicherin on 20 July.[60] Analysing calls to immediately stop offensive on the Polish front added by the threats to break Soviet-British trade negotiations (see below in the chapter), Lenin instructed Chicherin:

> If Poland wishes peace, we are pro [here and further underlined by Lenin], we have said it clearly and now repeat, let them offer it. If you [the British] break the trade negotiations, we shall feel pity, but you expose yourself in the evasion of truth, for you started them during the war with Poland and promised armistice.[61]

Under strong diplomatic pressure, Moscow nevertheless declared its readiness to take part in the planned London conference. On 26 July, the Cabinet contemplated practical measures to be undertaken for its preparation. The British diplomacy craved for the role of impartial supreme arbiter between Russia and Poland.[62] As one Cabinet minister told Robert Sanders, the junior Lord of Treasury, 'with regard to Poland, we are gambling on the expectation that the Bolsheviks are so anxious to trade with us that they will give up military advantages to obtain our good will'.[63]

Before analysing the impact of the Soviet-Polish war upon bilateral relations, one should highlight their economic aspect, tightly bound with the concurrent political developments. As is well known, the Entente governments were motivated by commercial reasons to lift the blockade of Soviet Russia. These were demilitarization of national economics, reduction of unemployment as well as repayment of debts. A combination of industrial and currency crises in the aftermath of the Great War decreased living standards because of consumer prices' growth by 295 per cent in the UK, 510 per cent in France and 1,486 per cent in Germany in the end of 1920.[64]

The Bolshevik leaders, for their part, regarded the blockade's breakthrough to bring about diplomatic recognition which meant the regime's consolidation, taking also into account the UK share of Russia's foreign trade turnover averaging 40 per cent before the world war. That is why the Kremlin invited to Russia a TUC delegation headed by Benjamin Turner from the LP National executive committee. On 10 December 1919, the TUC annual meeting commissioned seven men and two women, including Ethel Snowden – the spouse of a prominent Labour activist, to make the trip. Bertrand Russel, the renowned philosopher, two members of the Independent Labour Party (ILP) and a couple of journalists from the left-wing periodicals also joined the delegation.[65]

Sailing off the British shores on 24 April 1920, the visitors passed via Estonia to Petrograd and henceforward to Moscow in mid-May. They were warmly welcomed in both Russian capitals with a succession of banquets, public ceremonial meetings and military parades. 'In short, everything was done to make us feel like the Prince of Wales did', Russell recalled later.[66] The British had an opportunity to speak to Trotsky, Kamenev, Chicherin and other top bureaucrats as well as to some Bolsheviks' opponents, for example, Prince Petr Kropotkin, the legendary Russian anarchist.[67] On 26 May, Russell was granted an hour tèt-a-tèt talk with Lenin who assured him that 'peace between Bolshevik Russia and capitalist countries would always remain insecure' and 'would be, therefore, of a brief duration'. 'I felt, concluded Russell, that he [Lenin] regarded the resumption of trade with capitalist countries as a mere palliative of doubtful value.'[68]

On 28 May, the guests set off on board a cruise steamer down the Volga to Nizhny Novgorod and further to Saratov. The Bolshevik authorities even permitted the members of the delegation to visit Smolensk in the immediate proximity to the Soviet-Polish front line. And two labour activists were allowed for a week sojourn in a village near Saratov. Although the trip's officially proclaimed purpose was the examination of Russian proletarians' working and living conditions, the British emissaries debated with certain Kremlin mandarins the integration of the ILP into the Communist International as well.[59]

After six weeks in Soviet Russia, the visitors drew the conclusion that armed intervention and economic blockade by the Entente would lead to the appeasement of Russia by no means. As they maintained in the final report, the previous measures by Western countries only contributed to its militarization and rapprochement with revanchist Germany.[70] Interestingly, one of this mission's practical results was the establishment of the so-called Red Profintern that embraced trade unions as national sections, the English one chaired by George Murphy, later a co-founder of the National Minority Movement.[71]

The high-ranking TUC activists travelled to Soviet Russia when both sides were engaged in intensive preparations for the first official diplomatic conference between London and Moscow. On 24 April, Krassin circulated a memorandum on trade relations with the UK. Having examined commercial offers from British companies, he recommended a purely professional, depoliticized approach to the upcoming negotiations.[72] But for Lenin and his associates, the political significance of the agreement with Britain substantially overwhelmed its economic value. To the Bolshevik leader, Krassin's point of view seemed 'extremely naive'.[73] Nonetheless, following the Soviet delegation's arrival in London on 26 May 1920, all practical work fell on his shoulders.[74]

Lloyd George, in turn, required the key ministers to draft a programme of Soviet-British consultations. Churchill became the first to respond arguing in the memorandum that 'UK subjects are the most hated foreigners in Russia, and the most persecuted'. The secretary for war manifested anxiety about the Comintern activities to undermine democratic regimes by means of revolutionary propaganda as well as by subversive anti-governmental actions all over Europe.[75]

But the prime minister paid much more attention to the note compiled by Edward Wise, who specified Russia's crucial role as a substantial market for manufactured goods exported not solely from the UK but also from the dominions.[76] Consequently, Robert Horne, the head of the Board of Trade, presented his vision of the situation with the Soviet foreign trade under the state control. He considered it along with transport's devastation and the disinclination to repay foreign debts to challenge the future of Soviet-British commercial relations most of all.[77]

On 27 May, Curzon focused on a possible Britain's interposition between the Bolsheviks and General Wrangel. The foreign secretary also cautioned the Cabinet against unwarranted expectations of the negotiations with Moscow, urging Lloyd George to demand from the Kremlin specific Soviet guarantees for the existence of 'small nations'.[78] In two other notes for the Cabinet, the First Sea Lord admiral David Beatty suggested to bind the Soviet government with an obligation to refrain from any aggressive action against Britain and coastal states in the Baltic. Basil Thomson from the Scotland Yard, for his part, argued that the relations with Moscow would only raise the Bolsheviks' prestige in the West, convincing the Russian people of the Bolsheviks' aptness to rule the country.[79] Nevertheless, as one historian correctly put it, a feeling took over in the entourage of Lloyd George that 'the hostile actions of the Russians, as with propaganda in the empire, could only be stopped by contact and "confidence building measures"'.[80]

The conference between Lloyd George and Krassin which continued from the end of May 1920 until mid-March 1921 has been properly studied by researchers.[81] It is necessary, therefore, to merely concentrate upon their principal or less known aspects. Above all, both negotiators had to jointly outline the main objectives of the conference. Maurice Hankey, the secretary of the Cabinet and Committee of Imperial Defence, described in his diary after the incipient meeting on 31 May 1920: 'I "grasped the hairy paw of the baboon" to use W. Churchill's picturesque phrase ... As Lloyd George remarked to me afterwards, he [Krassin] is the first Russian who we have ever heard state his case with real ability'.[82] An equally positive assessment of the Soviet emissary was given by Charles Scott, Lloyd George's associate, who remarked that 'the whole Cabinet was greatly impressed by Krassin – a far abler ambassador ... than any ever

Figure 9 'Russian Jazz', Caricature, *Star*, 31 May 1920. Photo courtesy of Wikimedia Commons (public domain).

sent to us under the old regime'.[83] And one British journalist even described Krassin as the 'best dressed Communist in the world.'[84]

The Soviet representative, in turn, was amazed with openness and trust demonstrated by most British ministers. Krassin considered Lloyd George to be 'a man who gives an impression of kindliness and shrewd intelligence'. Their mutual respect persisted during nearly all phases of their negotiations which in no small part allowed them to reach a final agreement.[85]

Already the first meeting demonstrated that the participants preferred not to confine themselves to debates on solely commercial issues. Apart from the Soviet-Polish war, the Bolshevik emissary raised the question of the British military support to Wrangel and Russian rights to Svalbard and the Aland Islands, whereas Lloyd George dwelt on the Comintern activities, including the Anglophobic propaganda in the UK, the promotion by Moscow of the nationalistic movements in Turkey and Persia. The implementation of Litvinov–O'Grady accord concerning repatriation of ex-POWs was on the agenda as well.[86]

Despite daily British periodicals posting rather ironic descriptions of negotiations, few contemporary observers denied its epochal significance.[87] The subsequent meetings on 7, 9, 16 and 26 June, along with private contacts being of priority to Lloyd George, intensified discussions which were proceeding nevertheless at a slow pace. As the prime minister supposed, Krassin 'was always looking over his shoulder as if he expected to be shot'.[88] However, the decision to institute the All-Russian Cooperative Society (ARCOS) in London on 9 June 1920 contributed to the development of commercial links. Registered as a private legal entity with limited responsibilities under the Soviet government's obligations, this enterprise became a universal trading company consisting of eight main and three ancillary departments with the incipient share capital of £15,000 reaching £100,000 by the turn of 1921.[89]

The Kremlin mandarins distrusted the British government, being vigilant about the 'intrigues of Lloyd George' while suspecting Krassin not to follow the 'revolutionary line' through the negotiations.[90] On the other hand, the classified telegrams between Chicherin, Litvinov and Krassin, intercepted by MI5 agents, demonstrated how the Bolshevik leaders were hesitating between their willingness to end the war against Britain and a bigger goal of carrying out the Communist revolution to Europe on the shoulders of the Red Army servicemen.[91] Krassin, in turn, strained every effort to dispel the Kremlin's suspicions of his putatively excessive compliance with the British side.[92] The hardest disputes between him and Lloyd George occurred on 16 and 29 June, resulting, nonetheless, in the clarification of their positions with Krassin being able to preliminarily concur with the prime minister on the convocation of a special seminar on Russian debts.[93]

Following this sitting, the members of the Soviet delegation were handed a memorandum with the necessary terms of a trade agreement which included the mutual suspension of any hostile actions and propaganda, the exchange of POWs and interned persons as well as a compensation for the confiscated British private property and manufactured goods.[94] Having requested the British side for a pause in negotiations, the Soviet delegation left London on board the HMS destroyer *Vimiera* on 2 July 1920. After their departure, Chicherin informed Curzon that the SNK principally endorsed the draft agreement.[95] Yet the head of the NKID revealed a 'hidden agenda' in a letter to Trotsky: 'Our game is to convince the English government that we shall pay our debts without concurrently binding ourselves to nothing.'[96]

At the same time, certain Cabinet ministers, for instance Churchill, continued to stubbornly oppose any possibility of dealing with Moscow. He kept on repeating that 'the Bolsheviks are fanatics', accusing the leader of the Cabinet of not knowing their true nature. 'Lloyd George thinks he can talk them over and that they will see the error of their ways and the impracticability of their schemes', Churchill maintained at a lunch with the King.[97] Despite all the critical arrows, the prime minister found it appropriate to resume diplomatic consultations early in August, emphasizing the aggravation of the situation in Eastern Europe due to the Red Army's general offensive on the Polish front and the approaching collapse of Wrangel's troops in the Crimea. Responding to allegedly peaceful intentions avowed by the Kremlin, the Cabinet decided to resume calls for London conference on the Polish problem. Meanwhile the Kremlin received intelligence about the German government's secret proposal to the War Office of a combined strike on the advancing Red Army divisions.[98] To raise the level of diplomatic representation, the Soviet leadership appointed Lev Kamenev, the chairman of the Moscow Soviet, to lead the delegation with Krassin as his deputy.[99]

Coming back to the British vision of the Soviet-Polish war, one should bear in mind the Cabinet's disinclination towards Warsaw's plans of excessive territorial expansion. This opposition revealed the British elite's anxiety about a permanent hotbed of tension emerging in Eastern Europe as well as eventual hegemony of France patronizing

Pilsudski's regime. Yet the threat of Poland's bolshevization and the prospect of a military alliance between Moscow and Berlin prevented the Cabinet from leaving Poland 'one to one' with the Soviets.[100]

Against the background of the Red Army contingents crossing the 'Curzon line' and of the Polish revolutionary committee proclaiming itself an alternative government in the town of Bialystok, the Kremlin sought to gain time expressing at the same time their willingness to immediately come to peace terms with Warsaw.[101] This position became clear in early August 1920 when Kamenev and Krassin's consultations with Lloyd George did not lead to a plausible solution of the problem, for the Soviet representatives skirted any concrete obligations to stop the Bolshevik troops' offensive.[102] However, Chicherin instructed Kamenev to keep on intimidating Lloyd George:

> You are authorised to stress in the talk to the British that if they open military hostilities against us, they won't be able to cause us serious harm in Europe, except for some 'pins' on the periphery. But if we take all the opportunities we have in the East, we can immediately and greatly damage England's world standing.[103]

The closer Soviet troops were approaching the Polish capital, the harder it was to untie the knot of contradictions in the triangle of relationship between Moscow, London and Warsaw. On 4 August, Lloyd George refused to proceed with trade negotiations, although Kamenev tried to privately convince him that the Red Army's invasion of Poland was a 'purely military operation' which did not put in doubt the independence and integrity of the Polish state within its ethnic borders.[104] Even Lloyd George's effort to cool down the interventionist zeal of Lenin and Trotsky by mentioning the eventual departure of the British naval squadron to patrol the Soviet territorial waters in the Baltic led to nothing.[105]

These diplomatic manoeuvres accompanied the ferocious and bloody battle for Warsaw that was going on in the mid of August. If Lloyd George insisted on halting the Bolshevik invasion of Poland, Kamenev focused on the demand to cease the Allied supply of weapons to Pilsudski.[106] At the same time, the Cabinet proved incapable to motivate Warsaw to accept the Soviet peace proposal resembling an ultimatum to the Poles. On 17 August, Kamenev startled Chicherin with information that a Soviet-British war seemed highly possible.[107] The following day Lloyd George put on the table his last trump-card when he suggested the cessation of support to anti-Bolshevik armed forces in exchange for easing the terms of the Soviet ultimatum to Warsaw.[108]

According to Jay Moffat, an American diplomat who witnessed the battle on the Vistula, 'it seemed as though nothing could save the city, and for three days [on 14–17 August] all Europe watched it with bated breath', since the fall of Warsaw to the Bolshevik hands might be regarded as 'the signal for uprisings in Germany, Austria and Northern Italy'. Rather pessimistically, Moffat remarked that 'the outlook for European civilization was in many ways as dark as when the Hun stood before Chalon, or the Saracens before Tours [in the fifth and eighth centuries, respectively]'.[109]

Luckily for the British government, the Red Army's defeat at Warsaw which was followed by the Soviet troops' eastward retreat far beyond the 'Curzon line' eliminated the problem of defending Europe from the Bolsheviks invasion and the prospect of

Britain's involuntary participation in a new conflict on a broader scale. As Horatio Rumbold, the British envoy to Warsaw, described his impression of the 'miracle on the Vistula' in a cable to Curzon on 24 August 1920: 'The battle of the Marne [in September 1914] was perhaps the nearest parallel in recent times but the almost miraculous change in the military situation in Poland had produced effects far greater than those of the battle of the Marne.' On likening the Bolshevik armies' destruction in 1920 to the defeat of the Turks under the walls of Vienna in 1683, Rumbold concluded that 'once again the flood of barbarism, which threatened to overwhelm Central Europe, had been rolled back'.[110]

In a survey of the British diplomacy during the Soviet-Polish war some historians pointed out the lack of the Cabinet's united vision of the situation in the east of Europe. By all odds, its most influential members simply underestimated the Red Army's combatant potential while simultaneously being unaware of the Polish government's strategic plans. As a British author correctly maintained, the Polish crisis became an ample embarrassment for Lloyd George which could destroy his trade policy with Russia.[111] The situation began to improve after following the dispatch to Warsaw of the British extraordinary military-diplomatic mission on 20 July. It consisted of Edgar D'Abernon, Division General Percy Radcliffe, director of the military operations at the War Office, and Maurice Hankey mentioned earlier in the chapter. The mission aimed to assist recruiting 200 British officers for drilling Polish military units in addition to redeploying the Entente four infantry and cavalry divisions to fight 'Bolshevik hordes'.[112]

It is hardly possible nevertheless to impute to the British government the intention to openly declare war on Soviet Russia in August 1920. At the same time, Britain's cautious perception of the Bolshevik diplomatic tricks during the Soviet-Polish military clashes might be also explained by a surge of domestic pacifist protests in the summer of 1920. Established in January of the previous year as a reaction to the Entente armed invasion of the former tsarist empire, the 'Hands off Russia' committees quickly assumed a key role in these protests, collaborating with local trade unions in rallying anti-war meetings and demonstrations, issuing political pamphlets and boycotting the delivery of war munitions to Polish troops.[113] On 23 June 1920, the Labour Party annual conference in Scarborough unanimously called for the Allied governments to restrain from any direct or implicit attacks against Soviet Russia.[114] In mid-August, a joint session of the Labour and trade-union activists alluded that 'war is being engineered between the Entente powers and Soviet Russia on the issue of Poland'. On declaring that 'such war would be against humanity', the meeting warned the Cabinet that 'the whole industrial power of the organised workers' would be applied to defeat it'.[115] On 11 August, the 'Hands off Russia' national committee's senior members assured Kamenev and Krassin of their disagreement with military preparations undertaken by the Cabinet.[116] The 'fuel to the fire' was added by a group of left extremists who formed the Communist Party of Great Britain just in the apogee of the considered armed conflict. Proclaiming their affiliation with the Comintern, they vociferously denounced Whitehall for the arrangement of a 'new crusade' against Bolshevik Russia.[117]

The conclusion of the long-awaited armistice between Moscow and Warsaw on 12 October 1920 led to the intensive diplomatic consultations which ended in signing the treaty of Riga on 18 March the following year. The way the British ruling circles tackled the Polish problem in the course of the Soviet-Polish armed confrontation suggested three alternatives: the one symbolized by Churchill who was eager to instigate a new round of military conflicts in Eastern Europe; the other related to certain LP front-runners along with some trade union leaders who showed their preparedness to go on a 'general strike' once Britain was involved in the war with Russia; and the third scenario provided for the settlement of the conflict at the international conference which was offered by Lloyd George to Moscow and Warsaw.

Besides the climax of the war, the second stage of diplomatic consultations between Lloyd George and the Bolshevik delegation was notable by the international scandal related to the smuggling of gold, platinum, diamonds and currency by the Soviet emissaries to back up social unrest in the UK.[118] It should be kept in mind that in addition to 500 tons of state gold reserves inherited by the Bolsheviks from the tsarist regime, Cheka agents regularly confiscated valuables from aristocratic Russian families, former high-ranking tsarist administrators and the Orthodox Church clergymen. Their total sum amounted to 18 million roubles, the main part of which was concentrated in the state reserve created by the SNK decree on 3 February 1920.[119] One of the Bolsheviks' secret directives prescribed to the Cheka to set up a network of clandestine informants and saboteurs with funds received from the sale of diamonds, gold jewelleries, furs and works of art, formerly belonging to the 'upper crust' of the empire. Being in full swing during 1919–20, this transfer included the valuables in double-bottom suitcases or shoe heels by Soviet diplomatic officials, their wives, private secretaries, couriers and the sailors of cargo merchant vessels to European countries and the British dominions.[120]

Furthermore, the MI5 agents reported on financial allocations to British Communists and left-wing Labours by the Comintern emissaries. Accordingly, these money tranches averaged 8,579,000 roubles in the period from September 1919 to June 1920. Suffice to say that the Comintern subsidized £55,000 for the establishment of the Communist Party in August 1920 only.[121] Additionally, the funds collected from the sale of diamonds through international 'black' syndicates enabled the Bolshevik leaders to sponsor the publication of the *Daily Herald*. George Lansbury, the founder and editor-in-chief, became the first Labour front-runner who visited Russia in the winter of 1920.[122] Later the same year, Lansbury and Francis Meynell, the deputy director of the newspaper, set up close contacts with Krassin and his associates at the friendly dinner on 9 June. As Litvinov claimed in a telegram to Chicherin, 'if we do not support the *Daily Herald* that again suffers a slump in circulation, it will have to apply to right-wing trade unions. Regarding the "Russian question", it works like our own organisation does.'[123]

The resumption of negotiations in August allowed to covertly deliver to London a new batch of diamonds, pearls and platinum bullions along with 620 Chinese state gold bonds of the 5 per cent series costing £20 each. After this information leaked to the British press, nearly all daily periodicals discussed the acquisition of Russian jewelleries for £8 million by London dealers. They also revealed a smuggling channel through a coal shop in Whitechapel whose owner, by a strange coincidence, joined the newly founded Communist party of Great Britain (CPGB).[124]

Kamenev's ciphered correspondence to Moscow, intercepted and decrypted by the MI5 pundits attested to £40,000 that were received from the sale of Russian valuables only to be further transferred to the *Daily Herald's* editorial board on the decision of the Kremlin.[125] Judging by Kamenev's estimation, he intended to get another £60,000 from the sale of platinum bullions, of which £10,000 were designated to the newspaper, whereas the rest cash should be allocated to other pro-Bolshevik political movements elsewhere in Europe.[126]

During the apogee of the battle for Warsaw, Churchill circulated a note to Lloyd George on the intervention of the Soviet emissaries in the UK domestic affairs, for example, on their contacts with the mentioned Committees of action. He was particularly enraged with the mailing of the *Daily Herald* copies to British soldiers in Germany as well as with the attempts to drive a wedge in the relations between the allies.[127] One could suggest that it was the war minister and his subordinates who regularly let the pieces of intelligence leak to *The Times* because it did not hesitate to publish on 19 August the intercepted and decrypted confidential mails between the Soviet delegates in London and the Kremlin.[128]

In response, the newspaper's editorial board rebated the allegations claiming that it had got from Moscow 'not a single bond, franc or rouble'.[129] The scandal surrounding the transfer of £75,000 to the *Daily Mail* periodical by the foreign government, especially of those procured from the illegal sale of the confiscated Russian valuables, shocked the UK public opinion. For example, the Social Democratic Federation of Great Britain withheld from any further contribution to the 'Hands off Russia' national movement until finding out the true source of funds at its disposal.[130]

On 30 August, new evidence of the smuggled valuables from Soviet Russia was presented to the Cabinet by the Scotland Yard who apprised the ministers of at least three portions of Russian diamonds having been sold through certain London black-market dealers totalling £2 million.[131] Concurrently, Curzon joined Churchill and the chorus of other tenacious opponents of the Soviet-British negotiations, offering to declare the members of the delegation *personae non grata*.[132]

Apart from funding the left-wing newspapers, the foreign secretary accused Kamenev and Krassin of inciting industrial workers to anti-constitutional activities on the direct instructions from the Kremlin, their insincerity during negotiations with Lloyd George as well as the instigation of uprisings against the British empire. On this occasion even Austen Chamberlain, who usually championed Lloyd George's moderate course towards Russia, adhered to the pleas by Churchill and Curzon to expel the Bolshevik delegates from Great Britain.

Consequently, the prime minister found himself in a difficult situation. On one hand, he was firmly convinced of the need to accomplish negotiations with signing a trade agreement. But on the other, the tough tone of conversation with Kamenev on 1 September along with the declaration of an ultimatum to the Bolshevik top emissaries a few days later attested to his worries about their illegal activities in Britain.[133]

The indignation of the Cabinet's head was easy to understand, for the Soviet delegates clandestinely supported the Irish liberation movement, aided British workers to rally demonstrations in big cities (for instance, Birmingham and Manchester), as well as disseminated the Bolshevik propaganda among naval crews encouraging demobilized soldiers and sailors not only to join the Communist Party, but also to set up secret cells of a subversive kind.¹³⁴ The hesitation ended in a 'judgement of Solomon' taken by the Cabinet under the influence of George V and public opinion. While choosing between the complete abrogation of diplomatic consultations and angry charges of inaction by many Conservative die-hards, Lloyd George announced the expulsion of Kamenev from the UK and the suspension of contacts with Krassin.¹³⁵

Although Kamenev attempted to fend off all accusations of his embroilment with diamond smuggling and funding anti-governmental groups in Britain, he had to inform Lloyd George of his departure to Moscow 'for consultations'.¹³⁶ On 10 September, they held a final conversation, and the following day Kamenev left the UK forever, albeit the NKID kept on arguing that the Cabinet and British public had fallen the 'victims of the dishonest machinations by MI5 and anti-Bolshevik emigrants'.¹³⁷

Nevertheless, all strenuous efforts undertaken by the adversaries of negotiations in the British governing circles repining at the resumption of negotiations as well insisting on the expulsion of Krassin from Britain following Kamenev's departure ended in a fiasco.¹³⁸ The prime minister took into consideration the armistice between Moscow and Warsaw and the defeat of Wrangel's troops in Crimea. On the other hand, Churchill's final attempt to use against the Bolsheviks the so-called Russian national volunteer army of 30,000 under the command of Colonel Stanislav Bulak-Balakhovich and Boris Savinkov also came to nothing when the Red Army divisions redeployed from Crimea after Wrangel's defeat pushed the last anti-Soviet military formations resembling criminal gangs rather than regular servicemen beyond the 'Curzon line'. Shortly afterwards the Polish government, unwilling to further aggravate relations with Soviet Russia, interned and disarmed them.¹³⁹

On receiving the radiogram about the Kremlin's desire to recommence trade negotiations on 25 September 1920, Lloyd George supposedly authorized the *The Times* to publish a draft trade agreement with Moscow which became a surprise for British public.¹⁴⁰ If Curzon kept on denouncing the Bolsheviks' foreign and domestic politics, Moscow let the Cabinet know about desirability 'to focus on economic issues while avoiding accentuating political contradictions'.¹⁴¹ Simultaneously, Krassin was working 'like a beaver' to draw British companies to the collaboration with Soviet Russia. In the article for the *Ekonomicheskaia Zhizn* (*Economic Life* – a Soviet weekly edition) he stated that the delegates in London had already contacted several famous engineering companies, for instance, *Marconi* and *Armstrong*, despite concerns about certain export staple-wares might be used for the Red Army's needs.¹⁴²

At the same time, the British governing elites were nervous at the prospect of Russia dragging the whole of Europe into the economic abyss.¹⁴³ *The Times*' editorial on 17 November 1920 reviewed three years of the Soviet rule concluding that Bolshevism could not be merely crushed by means of force but it would endure a long-time evolution, while the resumption of Anglo-Russian commercial relations might be a first step in this direction.¹⁴⁴ Another appeal by the Bolshevik government to London on 9 November to reanimate trade negotiations prompted the ministers to consider the issue afresh.¹⁴⁵ Arguing for the receipt of political assurances from Moscow, Curzon even warned Lloyd George of his imminent resignation, should the Cabinet give its consent to resume negotiations.¹⁴⁶ On 16 November, Churchill also vehemently deprecated contacts with the Bolsheviks, motivating his view like Curzon by the continuation of the Bolsheviks' subversive activities in Europe and Asia.[147] The following day, both foreign and war ministers threatened to Lloyd George with their resignation mentioning the decrypted Soviet diplomatic correspondence exposing the Kremlin's Anglophobic intrigues in the UK and elsewhere.[148] The dispute came to the point when certain authoritative Unionist leaders obtained their concord to return to the table of negotiations with Krassin.[149] Following two more intensive debates held by the Cabinet ministers, the amended draft agreement was at last handed over to the Soviet delegation on 30 November.[150]

The Polish and Irish crises as well as collisions in the Middle East that are spotlighted in Chapter 7 formed a backdrop to the terminal stages of negotiations. Regarding purely economic controversies, these were guarantees of the immunity of property that had passed under the jurisdiction of the Soviet Republic, the obligation by the Bolshevik government to compensate public and private debts to Great Britain, and the scheme to sell a part of the Russian gold reserve in the UK for the repayment of the British exports.[151]

A formidable 'stumbling block' was removed by Horne's initiative who, given the peculiarities of the Anglo-Saxon legal system, proposed to deprive private creditors of the opportunity to claim compensation for their lost property from Moscow with the help of a created judicial precedent. The decision was also found on the issue relating to the difference of 30–40 shillings for a Troy ounce (31.1 g) between market prices of gold and the costs of gold imported from Soviet Russia.[152] Emulating the commercial practice of Australian and South African mining companies, Krassin and Horne concurred in giving to Moscow a six months' export licence for gold transactions, although the ban on its free sale in the Entente states, as a part of the economic blockade of Soviet Russia, had not been lifted. The endorsed scheme included import of gold into the UK in coins averaging 200 million roubles which should be followed by smelting them in bullions under the supervision of the Bank of England and further re-exporting to the third countries at world prices for half a year.[153]

Despite George V refusing to grant an audience to Krassin as a *de facto* diplomatic representative of the Russian Soviet Socialist Federation,[154] both sides yearned to accelerate negotiations, which were dragging on mostly because of disagreement between Krassin and his Kremlin curators blaming the latter of 'unjustified and irrational concessions' to London.[155] On 13 December 1920, Krassin presented a Soviet draft agreement which envisaged to prolong a three-month notice period in case of its denunciation by one of the parties concerned to one year.[156] At the next meeting that was held eight days later, Krassin, Lloyd George, Bonar Law and Horne specified the clauses of the agreement.[157] Symptomatically, while speaking to the delegates of the Eighth All-Russian Congress of Soviets on 21 December, Lenin declared the Bolsheviks' main purpose to be the signing of a trade agreement with Britain in order to purchase the necessary technologic equipment as soon as possible. 'But we do not believe in any permanent commercial relations with imperialistic states … , for it will be just a temporary break in a series of wars which are inevitable', admonished the Soviet leader.[158]

Krassin, for his part, reported to Moscow that the negotiations 'have driven a wedge' between the members of the British government. Looking rather pessimistically at a new campaign of solidarity with Soviet Russia in the UK, he objected to the convocation of a special conference to recognize the Soviet regime *de jure* by the Entente states and depicted an illusory vision of Bolshevism prevailing among the Cabinet ministers: 'They suppose that as soon as our borders with Europe open and business relations prove our insecurities and the lack of organisation, Soviet Russia will naturally die.'[159]

Curiously, the Bolsheviks' officialdom accelerated the course of negotiations at the incipient stages, but Curzon accused Moscow of delaying the signing of agreement.[160] On receiving the Politburo's approval, Krassin returned to London on 4 March with the strong intention to reach the final decision of all disputable questions.[161] Being challenged by the intransigent position of Lloyd George and Horne, Krassin ventured to draw three important amendments in the preamble without the Kremlin's endorsement: to refrain from hostile activities towards Britain in Asia, repatriate all UK citizens and stop the Anglophobic propaganda all over the world. On 16 March 1921, Krassin and Horne signed the long-anticipated agreement comprising fourteen clauses in the presence of Lloyd George, albeit without the participation of Curzon, Churchill (who had recently become the secretary for colonies) and other prominent Cabinet members.[162]

Some historians believed that the agreement was more profitable to Moscow than to London. After all, the Bolsheviks, as they claimed, allegedly got everything they wanted in exchange for their vague pledges to abstain from supporting 'anti-capitalist' forces in the UK and the British colonies. In fact, their regime was recognized *de facto*, the bilateral commercial relations were reanimated, and the London bullion market was opened for Russian gold on terms even more beneficial to them than to the mining companies of British dominions. As one researcher remarked, perhaps oversimplifying the real picture, the Kremlin leadership aimed solely to break through the Entente's 'gold blockade', refusing at the same time to reaffirm Russian debt obligations.[163]

In the present author's view, however, the 1921 trade agreement was of a framework nature, recalling more a protocol of good intentions than a document of practical significance. The 1921–2 commercial statistics indicated the considerable increase of the bilateral trade turnover which also had positive impact on economic relations with other Western states, though the Russian recurred requests for the extension of British government credits to buy goods manufactured in the UK remained unreciprocated.[164] What seems even more important, the document put an end to the indefinite 'neither war, no peace' situation in Eastern Europe, which, in turn, catalysed a process of normalization between Moscow and other regional actors. The important point to note is that the conclusion of this diplomatic tractate took place two days before the Soviet-Polish peace treaty was signed in Riga. The termination of the London negotiations astonished both White emigrants and even certain Bolshevik leaders themselves. As Chicherin wired to Krassin: 'We did not expect you to have completed negotiations so suddenly.'[165]

Shortly afterwards the SNK adopted a decree on the measures to be undertaken focusing on the lift of all restrictions on Soviet overseas commercial shipping. Chicherin demagogically assured Krassin that 'we [the Kremlin] value our newly established relationship with Great Britain too much and are committed to peace and trade … '[166] On the British side, Lloyd George presented the contract to the House of Commons on

22 March. Given the condemnation of this action by France and the United States, he sought to obscure its political significance, calling the document 'purely commercial' that aimed at 'gradually educating Soviet leaders'. Following intense debates, the agreement received the approval of the Parliament's majority. Consequently, the Royal Navy suspended any hostilities against the Bolshevik men-of-war and submarines since 1 April 1921, and, a week later, both states resumed reciprocal mail traffic.[167]

At the end of the same month, the Foreign Office circulated to Krassin a register of the members of the first British official mission to Moscow headed by Robert Hodgson as the diplomatic agent. They arrived in the capital of Soviet Russia on 31 July 1921.[168] It should be mentioned that the opinions of contemporary observers as well as of historians about Hodgson's personality and qualities as a diplomatic representative were quite contradictory. If some authors called him a 'workhorse' who, albeit without much brilliance, faithfully performed his routine duties, other researchers emphasized a typical English poor readiness to contact the government whose ideology he did not understand at all.[169]

In any case, the settlement of the armed conflict with Poland and the conclusion of the trade agreement with the UK must be regarded as decisive steps towards the better Soviet-British relations, becoming a template for similar treaties with other great powers. However, as the next chapters will demonstrate, threatening tunes again sounded in the Soviet-British discourse after a short pause.

7

From bad to worse: Soviet-British relations in the Middle and Far East, 1919–22

The White Tsar was unpleasant enough for England as a neighbour in Asia Minor and Central Asia, but red Lenin promised her even less good.
                                                    Ivan Maisky, the Soviet diplomat, 1922[1]

The victory in the world war led to the UK acquisition of vast territories in Asia and Africa covering 1 million square miles with a population of 10 million. This amounted to 80 per cent of the lands and 50 per cent of the Entente's overall war 'booty'.[2] The British empire seemed to have achieved such geopolitical and economic power that no one could challenge it. Yet the euphoric impression was deceptive because of unprecedented war casualties, the transformation from a net creditor to a borrower with rather obscure prospects for refunding foreign debts and rapid increase in the share of imports from the dominions against the backdrop of the export's reduction.[3]

That is why the preservation of empire's overseas territories became of principal importance to British policymakers who were annoyed by the 'Bolshevik Leviathan' emerging on its borders. As an officer stationed in Transcaucasia wrote in a private letter on 13 February 1920, Soviet Russia would be more dangerous than imperial Russia because the Kremlin leaders were unscrupulous, taking no consideration of international treaties, bilateral agreements or diplomatic obligations.[4]

At the same time, there were pundits at Whitehall who pointed to Anglophobic deprecations among the peoples of the Near, Middle and Far East that were caused not only by a revolutionary upsurge in the aftermath of the world war but also by the disillusionment with the so-called mandate system, introduced by the Entente leaders at the Paris conference to prepare colonial territories for eventual sovereignty.[5]

The debates about the Bolsheviks' goals in the Orient have a lingering record. For example, Miliukov, mentioned repeatedly in the previous chapters, and many other political observers reduced them to merely 'setting the East ablaze'.[6] This position did not appear to be groundless, given Trotsky's intention to create 'the political headquarters of the Asian revolution' in Tashkent or Kabul. On 5 August 1919, he maintained that 'the road to India may be more passable and shorter now than the road to Soviet

Hungary'. Thus, from his point of view, it was necessary to commence preparations for 'a military strike on India to aid the Hindu revolution'.[7] On 20 September, Trotsky substantiated his opinion in the following way:

> England is actively working on the unification of Persia, Bukhara, Khiva and Afghanistan against Soviet Turkestan ... We can now undermine Britain's work to unite Asian states against us by establishing a strong military presence there, for which we already dispose of sufficient foundations.[8]

Not all Bolshevik leaders supported Trotsky's initiatives to conduct, so to say, forward policy in the East. For example, Stalin and Chicherin expressed a cautious attitude whereas Lenin preferred a westbound direction of foreign policy, at least until the bolshevization of the Baltic and Poland ended in nothing. Yet as the Versailles world order was undergoing stabilization, Lenin's attention shifted to Asian countries which could be proved by Mikhail Pavlovich, the editor-in-chief of the Comintern monthly journal *Vostok* (Orient):

> Not until the entire Black Sea is in Soviet hands, and a red Turkish banner or the banner of the Soviet Federations of the Black Sea states – Ukraine, the Caucasus, Turkish Anatolia – is raised over Constantinople, will these states begin to lead a peaceful life and be able to devote themselves to creative and constructive work.[9]

A significant cohort of historians described the Bolsheviks' goal in Asia as 'the Communist revolution'.[10] Other authors indicated the Kremlin's intention to play an ethnic or confessional card, using pan-Islamism, pan-Arabism or pan-Turkism to undermine British positions in Eastern countries.[11] A third part of scholars, in turn, emphasized the Bolsheviks' geopolitical interests to protect their southern borders.[12] There were also those researchers who attested to the equivalence of both vectors – westward and eastward – in the Kremlin's foreign policy during the Bolshevik dictatorship's early phase.[13]

To unravel intricacies, it is important to turn attention to Transcaucasia as the closest region to Russia's European part. According to Dunsterville, in response to British statements about their intention to merely restrain German influence in the area, the Bolsheviks indicted Whitehall of setting up the permanent control of oil in the Caspian area.[14] After the Mudros armistice with the Ottoman Empire had been signed, the British expeditionary troops captured Transcaucasia, re-entering Baku on 17 November 1918 together with the ministers of the Central Caspian government under the protection of the brigade commanded by Bicherakhov (see Chapter 4).[15] In the autumn of 1918, it served as a formation needed to shield Gorsk Republic in the Northern Caucasus with Makhachkala (former Petrovsk) as its capital. Yet looting and mass repressions against both the Russian Reds and Whites committed by this military unit led to the British military administration's decision to dissolve and withdraw it from the Caucasian region in the winter of 1918–19.[16]

Despite Bicherakhov's strenuous efforts to reorganize his brigade into the volunteer corps of 10,000 cavalrymen to fight Bolshevik troops in the region of the Terek- and

Kuban'-rivers, his request for 100 million roubles from the British military authorities seemed too audacious for the Treasury.[17] When forced to leave the Caucasian region shortly afterwards, Bicherakhov reached the UK by the autumn of 1919 where he later unsuccessfully solicited financial subsidies and military orders for the survived rank-and-file of his brigade.[18]

British task forces had been staying in Transcaucasia until August 1919. As Churchill noted in a memorandum for the Cabinet, 'the British division was the only guarantor of peace between the Georgians, Armenians, Azerbaijanis, other highlanders and Russians in the whole Caucasus between the Black and Caspian Seas'.[19] Meanwhile the British Eastern Committee actively debated various scenarios of further strategic moves to be taken in Transcaucasia. Concurrently, they envisaged three potential alternatives: the reunification of former imperial possessions with Russia, the establishment of a confederation between Moscow and these minor states or securing their true sovereign status.[20] Curzon supported the third scenario, not excluding the second alternative. On 9 December 1918, he told his colleagues: 'I do not want to protect them [the peoples of the Caucasus] against anybody, I want to give them a chance of standing on their own feet.'[21]

The future of these quasi-state entities depended largely on the general situation in the Middle East where Britain constantly competed with France for hegemony and access to rich deposits of raw materials. Even incomplete statistics showed that 13,284 tons of crude oil were transported by the British from Baku to Batum and Persia in 1918. A year later, this volume augmented to 375,309 tons, whereas in five months of 1920, before the Soviet regime was reinstated in Azerbaijan, it averaged 153,222 tons, although the British focused not only on the extraction of crude oil but on the control of refining industrial facilities in Baku as well.[22]

The developments in Transcaucasia remained in the focus of British public opinion through 1919 against the backdrop of the Entente powers conferring at the Paris conference while the armed intervention in Russia reached climax, exposing its ineffectiveness. It was Lloyd George who specified the need to withdraw expeditionary troops, including the British manpower, from the Caucasian region. This was pursued by the War Office in concord with the Admiralty in the period from August 1919 to July 1920.[23] Depicting the situation in Transcaucasia half a year later, *The Times* had to acknowledge that 'at present, we [the British] should be wary of the alliance between Russia and disgruntled elements of Islam.'[24]

The last round of discussions on the preservation of at least a symbolic expeditionary contingent in the region focused on Batum – a stronghold remaining under the Anglo-French joint protection since January 1919. Having deployed about 20,000 servicemen along the railway Batum – Baku as well as up to dozen men-of-war in the harbour, the British used it to transport lubricants to their troops.[25] On 25 April 1920, Curzon sent a note to Chicherin in the anticipation of the Kremlin's order to stop the Red Army's seizure of Batum.[26]

On 21 May, the Cabinet debated the UK Eastern policy. The discussion was prompted by the landing of the Red marines in the Persian port of Enzeli three days before, compelling the local garrison of several hundred Anglo-Indian infantry and cavalrymen to evacuate it (see further information below in this chapter).

The British troops' evacuation from Batum was ratified by the Cabinet ministers because of a plausible Bolsheviks' revolt and the Georgian government's noninterference. Whitehall defined the Allied policy in the Black Sea as 'unsecured from a military point of view and therefore far from safe', though the British forces were supported by a battalion of French colonial riflemen from Algeria.[27] While disapproving evacuation, Churchill complained to Curzon of being misunderstood about collaboration between the War and Foreign Offices.[28] It was nevertheless carried out in the summer of 1920. Two days before the operation was completed, the Georgian military units entered Batum, staying there until the collapse of the democratic regime in March 1921 when the Bolshevik troops occupied this bulwark of their influence.[29]

Here it is appropriate to draw the reader's attention to relations between Moscow and Angora which experienced their ups and downs during the period. On 20 September 1918, the Bolsheviks annulled the clauses of the Brest treaty concerning the interests of the Ottoman empire. This was done in response to the Turkish occupation of Baku.[30] Two years later, the Kremlin denounced the treaty of Sevres that was signed by the Entente powers and the sultan government on 10 August 1920. In the search for potential allies, Moscow developed contacts with various nationalist groups, although the British urged the sultan, as the sovereign of all Muslims, to issue *a fatwa* (decree) condemning Bolshevism as an ideological concept.[31] However, the Great National Assembly of Turkey dispatched a diplomatic mission to Soviet Russia to reaffirm the provisions of a bilateral pact agreed on 24 August 1920. Obviously, from Ankara's point of view, Bolshevism appeared a lesser threat than the traditional domination of European powers in the Near East.[32]

The establishment of sovereign Kurdistan became another burning issue of the day. Curzon urged its implementation in Eastern Anatolia, offering to bring this state entity under the protection of the British empire to prevent France, Italy and the United States from filling in the regional geopolitical vacuum.[33] At the international conference in the Italian resort of San-Remo, Lloyd George and Curzon favoured the transformation of South Kurdistan in a buffer state between Iraq and independent Arab countries. But the sharp objections from Tehran, which considered the Kurds to be a part of the ancient Persian ethnos, forced the Foreign Office to accept the option beneficial to the Shah. Because the region of Mosul was rich with oil deposits, Curzon as a shareholder of the *Turkish Oil Company* preferred to keep it under Britain's patronage, being even willing to sacrifice the whole idea of Kurdish sovereignty to the conservation of postwar *status-quo*.[34]

Enormous financial, military and diplomatic aid, which Moscow provided to Mustapha Kemal's republican government, especially in the armed conflict against Greece, has been extensively covered by historians.[35] It is worth adding only a curious detail, namely, a free passage of Muslims volunteers secretly heading from the British Raj to Anatolia through the territory of the Turkestan Soviet Republic to join Kemal's troops in the summer of 1920. At the same time, the Kremlin achieved a final agreement on the demarcation of boundaries between three Transcaucasian Soviet Republics and Turkey on 13 July 1921.[36]

As it has been noted above, the British military mission under Malleson was deployed in the northern Persian town of Mashhad since mid-1918. Following the withdrawal of the Ottoman troops from Transcaspia, one could expect the mission's role to increase, which was evidenced by Malleson's trip to Krasnovodsk. In fact, the War Office desired to turn this sea-port into a kind of 'Caspian Gibraltar'.[37] Even earlier, on 10–14 October, British forces rebuffed four attacks by the Turkestan Red Army at Dushak, captured Merv (Mara) and forced the Bolshevik troops' retreat to the railway station of Ravnina, where the hostilities had stopped until the spring of 1919.[38] In addition, Malleson reshuffled the Ashgabat government on 1 January 1919 by removing Funtikov and his 'ministers' from their posts. Moreover, they were put in prison on the charge of embezzlement of £10 million subsidies allocated to them by the Treasury. Instead, a military dictatorship of five persons was set up as the Directorate of public salvation.[39]

Another British military mainstay – the Caspian Naval Flotilla – included nine (according to other records – ten) armed steamships, two (or four) hydroplane carriers and twelve high-speed torpedo boats.[40] On 21 May, this naval squadron defeated the Reds in the Tuba-Karakhan Bay. The Bolsheviks lost seven warships and a torpedo boat while a British cruiser suffered a slight damage. Following the capture by the Denikin troops of Tsaritsyn on 30 June 1919, the combined British and White Russian naval squadron established the full command of the Caspian Sea and the lower Volga, albeit only for the second half of 1919.[41]

However, the empire's financial strain accompanied by the involvement in numerous local conflicts throughout the world urged the Cabinet to evacuate troops from Turkestan, like it had already happened in Transcaucasia.[42] As for Malleson's military mission, the repeated appeals to London by the viceroy Chelmsford and the subsequent memorandum by the India Office, attesting the uselessness of its further stay in the Middle East, played a crucial part in this decision on 9 February 1919. A month later, Malleson left Ashgabat following the removal from Transcaspia of the British colonial troops amounting 950 personnel. Krasnovodsk was the last bastion of the British regional influence whence the troops were evacuated on 3 August the same year.[43]

The withdrawal catalysed the general offensive by the Reds against the demoralized military units of the Ashgabat government whose position became hopeless after the departure of Malleson's mission.[44] After one of the talented military commanders, Mikhail Frunze, was appointed to command the Turkestan army, and a permanent railway communication was re-established between the Ural region and Turkestan in September 1919, nothing could prevent the collapse of the non-Soviet authorities in Transcaspia. On 6 February 1920, the Bolsheviks entered Krasnovodsk, eliminating the 'Caspian Gibraltar'.

It is time now to shortly describe the scramble for Persia. As early as on 30 December 1918, at a regular meeting of the Eastern Committee, Curzon suggested to build a national Persian army under the command of a British general and European military instructors. He also insisted on reforming the country's fiscal system by experts from the Bank of England.[45] As a well-known British diplomat later stressed, the head of the Foreign Office sincerely believed that 'by dint of a friendly alliance, by the exercise of prudent advice, by the encouragement of the flow of capital eastwards and by its application to purposes of ascertained stability, having for their object the reinvigoration of the country', Persia would be placed 'in a position which may render the hostile schemes of her neighbours, if not impossible, at least precarious'.[46]

Almost concurrently, Percy Cox, the envoy to Tehran, was commissioned to conduct negotiations resulting in the conclusion of a new Anglo-Persian agreement on 9 August 1919. In fact, Cox simply 'purchased' the consent of Ahmad Shah for monthly subsidies of 15,000 tomans (equivalent of £6,000). Additionally, the Persian prime minister along with two influential Kadzhar princes received a payment amounting to 400,000 tomans. The loan of £2 million was also promised by London to Tehran for twenty years.[47] In the memorandum for the Cabinet, Curzon insisted on the mutual benefits: Persia would get British military, technical, financial and consultative assistance, provided the Shah's government would guarantee the security of Britain's strategic position in the Middle East.[48]

The *Manchester Guardian* claimed on 16 August that if any other power had signed a similar treaty with Persia, one should have called it a 'hidden protectorate'.[49] For his part, Curzon regarded the Anglo-Persian rapprochement a 'complete triumph' that was achieved mainly by his own efforts.[50] But it was a Pyrrhic victory because the Bolshevik propaganda and the evacuation of British expeditionary troops from the Middle East caused the unprecedented rise of nationalist movements in Asia.[51]

On the other hand, Bolshevik emissaries proposed to the government of Persia in the autumn of 1920 to regulate Soviet-Persian relations by signing a treaty of friendship. On receiving intelligence about this request, Curzon drew Cabinet's attention to the eventual decrease of Britain's influence in Transcaucasia, Persia and in the rest of Asia. He further maintained that this process would not stop until India's mountain barriers were overwhelmed by revolutionaries from abroad.[52]

The diplomatic scramble between Moscow and London in the second half of 1920 as well as the military coup in February 1921 that brought the former colonel of the Persian Cossack brigade, Reza Khan Pahlavi, to the state power minimized chances for the ratification of the Anglo-Persian treaty. The delay infuriated Curzon complaining to Lloyd George that all his efforts had ended nevertheless in the diminution of Britain's regional prestige.[53] Yet two more events had a considerable impact on the Persian situation – the collapse of the Gillian republic in the north of the country and abovementioned Red Caspian marines' landing at the port of Enzeli.[54]

The leader of the Gillian separatist movement Kuchik Khan (see Chapter 4) declared the Soviet republic in Resht on 20 May 1920. Taking into consideration the disarray of the shah's administration while relying on the Bolsheviks' military aid, this adventurer promised to Moscow emissaries to embark on reforming his 'state' in accordance to their recommendation to make it a springboard for the subsequent Bolshevization of Persia.[55] Yet Moscow's reorientation towards the central authorities in Tehran led to the reduction of the military assistance to the Gillian republic, except for the Red Army's contingent staying there until 9 July 1921.[56] Despite the fact that Kuchik Khan allowed several Communists to enter his 'government', renaming his paramilitary bands into the Persian Red Army, the conclusion of the treaty between Moscow and Tehran in February the same year ended the Bolsheviks' short-term 'flirtation' with the chieftain. By the end of 1921, internal disputes sparked a civil war in Gillian, used by the Shah's troops to eliminate the separatist movement and their leader.[57]

Regarding the landing of Soviet marines at Enzeli, it should be noted that Trotsky himself prepared this operation in accordance with Lenin in April 1920. Besides purely military objectives, it aimed to intimidate the British commanders 'on the spot', stampeding their evacuation from Northern Persia. In fact, Moscow played a double game, explaining the assault against Enzeli by the persecution of the former White Russian's warships in the Caspian Sea. As Feodor Raskol'nikov, the commander of the Enzeli expedition, recalled later, he was instructed to merely enforce the British garrison to escape from Enzeli avoiding involvement in the open military clash.[58]

The unexpected Bolsheviks' landing on 18 May 1920 took the British by surprise, prompting a widespread response in the Cabinet and mass media.[59] The Cabinet minute stated that 'within the last few days, the Bolsheviks had disembarked a force of some 2,000 men some miles from Enzeli, which had cut the line of retreat of the British forces there'. As it followed from the received intelligence, the Anglo-Indian garrison of Enzeli 'had been allowed to march out to Rasht ... ', while three British officers and thirty men, who had been dispatched from Batum to take over the guns of the former anti-Bolshevik Caspian Flotilla, were arrested by Raskol'nikov *en route* to Enzeli and imprisoned in Baku.[60]

At the Cabinet meeting on 21 May, the chiefs of the Imperial General and Naval Staffs, Wilson and Beatty, pointed out to the danger of combined attacks by the Bolsheviks and Kemalists upon the British expeditionary troops in Persian Azerbaijan. The government sanctioned their transfer to Palestine, Iraq and the North-West Frontier Province of India. Concurrently, the Cabinet encouraged Tehran to condemn the Bolsheviks' seizure of Enzeli urging immediate evacuation. On 6 June, Trotsky ordered Raskol'nikov to withdraw from the Caspian port taking with them the captured battleships as military trophy.

The Second congress of the Comintern as well as the First congress of the peoples of the Orient that took place in Moscow and Baku, respectively, called on all nationalist leaders to 're-direct world revolution to the East'. On 9 September 1920, Karakhan submitted to the Politburo a memorandum considering two alternatives in the case of Persia – either to support pro-Communist groups in order to depose the Anglophile government or to wind down revolutionary activities in order to come to appropriate terms with Tehran. Karakhan himself strongly favoured the first variant which loosened the Bolsheviks' hands to politically intimidate Lloyd George and Curzon while 'responding with a strike to their attacks'.[61]

The Soviet-Persian treaty was signed on 26 February 1921, the day when Reza Shah denounced the 1919 agreement with the UK. The treaty's sixth article forbade the usage of Persian territory for an armed intervention against Soviet Russia. Significantly, in case of emergency, the Bolshevik government was allowed to deploy military contingents on the Persian territories adjacent to the Russian border. In reward, Moscow annulled Persian debts averaging 75 million gold roubles as well as consigned a strategic highway, a railroad and the Russian Bank of payments to Tehran.[62]

Most contemporary political observers disagreed with the Foreign Office politics in the Middle East. For example, while surveying world affairs after the Paris conference, Arnold Toynbee, a prominent historian and international expert, wrote that 'Great Britain not only failed to acquire Russia's inheritance in Persia, but lost her own sphere of influence in attempting to spread her net more widely'.⁶³ Another analyst stressed that 'all Curzon's efforts in the eastern sphere of imperial policy were geared to the achievement of an informal protectorate over Persia. It was on these grounds that he resisted the abandonment of the Caucasus and pleaded for the retention of the Batum – Baku line ... '⁶⁴ A third specialist argued that the strategy of agreements with regional rulers, which Curzon had successfully implemented in India during his time as viceroy, did not work because of the break-up of the Ottoman empire and the wave of nationalist movements in the Near and Middle East.⁶⁵

In the present author's view, the failure of the British policy in Persia may be explained by the deficit of 'hard and soft power' to bridge the political gap after the collapse of the Russian and Ottoman empires. Concomitantly, all attempts to instigate an anti-Bolshevik nationalist movement in the North Caucasus failed too, albeit certain isolated 'hotbeds', such as the one in the highlands of Chechnya, kept on smouldering through the 1920s. The recognition by Lenin's adepts of nations' right for self-determination, numerous resolutions by the Comintern, the foundation of the Russian Muslim Communist party in 1918–19, as well as the opening of the Communist university for the toilers of the East in Moscow on 10 February 1921, contributed to the shift of sympathies in Asia to the benefit of the Bolsheviks. This was also evidenced by a liberation movement in Iraq, Britain's mandate territory since 3 May 1920. According to intelligence sources, Moscow instigated the Kurds' uprising to prevent the Royal Air Forces from bombarding the Baku oil fields. Only an urgent transfer of 50,000 expeditionary corps to Iraq in the summer of 1920 enabled London to suppress the rebellion, though the situation in Mesopotamia continued to be far from stable.⁶⁶

In another state of strategic importance – Afghanistan – the situation remained tense and unclear as well. Like in adjacent Asian countries, the domestic struggle between various ethnic and confessional clans had a negative effect on Kabul's foreign policy. On the night of 21 February 1919, Emir Habibullah was assassinated not far from Jalalabad in the east of Afghanistan. This ruler used to receive annual subsidies of 1,800,000 rupees from the viceroy of India to maintain the Anglophile policy.⁶⁷ Amanullah Khan, his younger successor, who was proclaimed the Emir a week later, seemed unwilling to follow this path and broke all secret contacts with Britain. Searching for foreign support, he sent a message to Lenin on 7 April pleading for military backing and offering a new friendly agreement. Moreover, he allowed Indian extremists to openly enlist volunteers and drill them for being secretly transferred to the British Raj.⁶⁸

The third Anglo-Afghan war broke out on 3 May 1919 with Amanullah's troops attacking the Anglo-Indian garrison in the small town of Bag. The hostilities had lasted until 3 June. As some military experts believed, the British air raids on Kabul and Jalalabad on 17, 20 and 24 May forced the Emir to agree on peace negotiations.⁶⁹ But in order not 'to put all eggs in one basket', Amanullah dispatched a diplomatic mission to Moscow via Tashkent where the Afghan General consulate was established on 4 June.⁷⁰ By the beginning of October 1919, the Afghan delegates had reached the Soviet capital. They conferred with Trotsky, Chicherin and Karakhan and were received by Lenin on two occasions. Both sides did their best to gain strategic advantage by pushing each other against the British in the Middle East.⁷¹ Such an impression was highlighted by Trotsky's decision to consign three military airplanes to the Afghan government. Accordingly, Amanullah received the Soviet diplomatic agent Nikolai Bravin who assured the Emir that Moscow would provide Afghanistan with munitions and support it financially, should Kabul repeatedly attack Anglo-Indian troops.⁷²

However, the Afghan ruler did not feel like coming back to trenches because his army needed complete reorganization. All attempts by Yakov Suritz, a new Soviet representative in Kabul, to convince the Emir to challenge Britain fell on a deaf ear.⁷³ Nonetheless, Amanullah's reproachment with the Bolsheviks continued through the second half of 1919 – the first half of 1920. Under the pressure of his Kremlin friends, the Emir had to recognize the establishment of people's republics in the place of the Khanate of Khiva and the Emirate of Bukhara destructed by the Red Army. He even refrained from the prohibition of the pro-Bolshevik nationalist groups of Indian revolutionaries in the Afghan capital.⁷⁴

But despite the signing of the Soviet-Afghan treaty on 28 February 1921, shortly after a similar pact with Persia was concluded, Amanullah disbelieved the friendship with the Soviets. Although the Bolshevik military counsellors brought with them huge amounts of munitions for the Emir's troops and consigned to him the lavish annual financial subsidy of 1 million gold roubles, he finally preferred a policy of equidistance from Moscow and London, having also concluded an agreement with Henry Dobbs, the British commissioner to Afghanistan, on 22 November 1921.⁷⁵

In the evaluation of the treaties which both London and Moscow attempted to impose on Turkey, Persia and Afghanistan, one could heed their (British and Soviet) aspiration to avoid a new round of the Great Game while concurrently blocking other great powers' penetration in the Middle East. Although both Moscow and London often took spontaneous steps reacting to emergent situations without any persistent strategy, as further developments demonstrated, the existent treaties between the local states and Soviet Russia or the UK enabled Iran and Afghanistan to adhere to neutral status during the Second World War.

On the other hand, fanatic adepts of the 'immediate Communist revolution in the Orient' pressed the NKID to create a springboard in Turkey, Persia and especially Afghanistan for a decisive march to the Indian Ocean. It is important, therefore, to focus on the Bolsheviks' projects for Hindustan – equally the most fortified outpost of the British empire and simultaneously its Achilles' heel.

The activities of Indian nationalists in Tashkent where the Bolsheviks set up a training base for those willing to combat for 'the liberation of Hindustan from the British yoke' raised serious concerns in Chelmsford's administration. On 8 March 1919, the viceroy approved an act of legislation which gave the police extraordinary powers to eradicate anarchist and revolutionary propaganda. A month later, the colonial troops under Brigadier General Reginald Dyer dispersed the 8,000 crowd of people in the city park of Amritsar deprecating the prohibition of mass meetings. The conflict ended in the so-called Jallianwala Bagh massacre on 13 April, when the Anglo-Indian troops fired on unarmed demonstrators killing 379 people, including 40 children, and wounding 1,100 adults. This awful incident provoked the anti-colonial movement across India which opened new opportunities for the Comintern subversive actions.⁷⁶

It is known that the Indian centre for propaganda was instituted in Moscow in December 1918. Four months later, the two leaders of nationalist movement, Maharana Pratap and Mohammad Barkatullah, visited Soviet Russia. On 6 May, the latter gave an interview to the Bolshevik central press and the following day he met Lenin offering mediation between Moscow and Kabul.[77] In the summer, Barkatullah published a pamphlet that was translated into English. Along with countless denunciations of 'British imperialists', it contained a programme of their expulsion from Asia, postulating the conceptual proximity of Communism and Islam.[78] Curiously, one of eminent Muslim theologians, a professor at the university of Bombay, replied to Barkatullah in a pamphlet entitled *Islam and Bolshevism*, refuting the controversial concept of convergence between religion and ideology.[79] According to Miliukov, the Comintern circulated to the countries of the Middle East and South Asia more than 4 million copies of Anglophobic propagandist literature from late 1919 to the mid-1920s.[80]

The third Anglo-Afghan war gave Indian nationalists a good chance to relocate their base from Tashkent to Kabul where Barkatullah together with his associates attempted to set up the Provisional government of Indian peoples in the latter half of 1919. On 12 December, *The Times* informed readers that 400 trained fighters headed from Soviet Turkestan to Northern India via Kabul to instigate an uprising.[81] The British government's annual report stated that 'in the place of German military danger the new and more formidable menace of Bolshevism now threatened India'.[82]

Members of the Bolshevik Revolutionary military council presided by Trotsky were deeply engaged in drafting a scheme of 'marching to India' which needed a huge sum of 2 million gold roubles.[83] In fact, these projects were nothing but the reincarnation of analogous plans elaborated by the tsarist General Staff in the late nineteenth century.[84] Trotsky suggested to concentrate two or three mounted corps in the South Urals to remove them later towards India via Afghanistan and Kashgar.[85] After the British troops were withdrawn from Soviet Turkestan, the Kremlin intensified preparations for an invasion of the British Raj. The end of the Soviet-Polish war also made it possible to direct troops against India. Shortly afterwards the Comintern Central Asian bureau was established in Tashkent on the initiative of Zinoviev.[86]

Early in 1921, Roy as one of the most zealous Comintern activists, argued that the Anglo-Indian troops were unfit for a full-scale battle. He claimed that the 25,000 military contingents together with Afghan volunteers had real chances to invade North India to stampede an overall anti-British rebellion of the so-called free tribes. He even stipulated the exact quantity of weapons needed for the military operation in view: 5,000 rifles, fifty machine-guns, 500 pistols, 4,000 hand-grenades, six airplanes and eight portable radio-stations.[87]

By November 1920, a rear base for the march was established in Tashkent, where thirty-seven emigrants from India and Afghanistan had arrived to be drilled by the Comintern emissaries.[88] On 19 November 1920, the NKID's Eastern department requested the People's commissariat of nationalities for the publication of Persian, Kazakh, Tibetan and Hindi textbooks.[89] According to *The Times*, one of the Bolshevik top officials announced on 3 February 1921 about a wide-ranging network of propagandists engaged in subversive activities from Afghanistan to Ceylon. The same person claimed that the Comintern agents enticed 91,000 activists to local Communist cells.[90]

After the Tashkent centre was closed in May 1921, pursuant to the provisions of the Soviet-British agreement, most trainees removed to Samarkand on the territory of the officially independent Bokharian People's Republic, while another group, including Roy, headed to Moscow to enter the mentioned university for the toilers of the East. In March 1922, the last 200 students left Soviet Turkestan to join the troops under the order of Mustapha Kemal in the war against Greece.[91]

Actually, the Indian Communist movement achieved far less success than the campaign of unarmed protest initiated by Gandhi.[92] It may be explained by the profound disagreement that existed between various revolutionary groups as well as by the collision of nationalist leaders' ambitions who proved reluctant to unite all anti-British movements in the struggle for independence.[93] Moreover, the Kremlin officialdom appeared incapable of choosing a reliable figure who could enjoy its absolute confidence. A possible exception was Roy who proclaimed the establishment of the Communist party of India in Tashkent on 17 October 1920.

However, nearly all attempts by this young and ambitious activist to send specially equipped secret emissaries to India across the Pass of Khaybar, Karakorum Desert or the Persian Gulf ended in a fiasco. Assigned to expand a network of anti-government agents in the highly populated urban areas, such as Delhi or Calcutta, ten emissaries had been arrested by the British counter-intelligence almost immediately after their arrival in India. Detained in Peshawar in February 1922, one of them betrayed to police inspectors that Roy had provided him and other five members of his group with the sum of £1,400 and six rifles as well as with special messages to chieftains of frontier tribes, encouraging them to rebel against the British.[94] Four months later, the Indian police confiscated £6,600 out of the total £40,000, obtained by the Soviet trade delegation from the sale of diamonds and other jewellery in London and transferred to India through Afghanistan, to spur the mass revolutionary activity.[95]

Only two Roy's agents managed to escape the instant police persecution, succeeding in the creation of Communist cohorts in Calcutta, Benares and Chandpur. In addition to Indian workers not being prone to violence, the emissaries' personal agenda, unscrupulousness and greed had a decisive negative impact on the results of their mission. Typically, when a member of the CPGB came to India early in 1925, he could find only one ardently pro-Bolshevik person.[96] Finally, pressed by the British envoy, Amanullah ordered the members of the Provisional Indian government to depart from Kabul in October 1922.[97]

The situation in Chinese (Eastern) Turkestan, ranking among the main regions of the British struggle against Bolshevism in Asia, needs to be reviewed too.[98] The India Office records testified to the modest results of the Comintern activity in China by mid-1921, giving two reasons: the anarchists' influence on left-wing political groups linked to Chinese nationalists under Sun Yisian, and the weakness of the Bolsheviks' positions in Siberia. The only exception was Shanghai where the pro-Soviet newspaper *Shanghai Life* was published and the Comintern agents intensified activities into the Guomindang party cells.[99] Despite the British domination in China, which included the naval bases in Hong Kong and Weihaiwei, seven industrial concessions and nine settlements as well as twenty-five consulates and 115 trade missions in the main sea- and river-ports,[100] the Kremlin was eager to play on contradictions between the 'imperialist states'.[101] Not invited to participate in the Washington naval conference of 1921–2, Moscow wished to follow the course characterized by Adolph Ioffe, the Soviet plenipotentiary to Germany in 1918, later the special envoy to the Far East, in the following way: 'Regarding China as a tangle of world imperialist intrigues and, undoubtedly, the likely cause of a future war (if any), we should aspire for an even more destruction of the imperialist world, ... linking with none but tacking between all of them.'[102]

It was for this reason that the Bolsheviks agreed on a temporal existence of the buffer Far East Democratic Republic in 1920–2. They simply aimed to 'buy time' while their resources were too limited to embark on greater expansion in the Pacific region. Until the 1925–7 Chinese revolution, the Kremlin's principal goal remained to eliminate the remnants of the Russian White guards in the outskirts of the former empire and use Xinjiang routes for an intrusion into the British Raj. The consolidation of the Soviet rule and the overthrow of feudal monarchies in Turkestan raised a question of turning Xinjiang into a bridgehead for the Bolsheviks' march towards India.[103] On 17 May 1921, the Turkestan front commanders endorsed a deal with the local Chinese governor general to let the Red Army detachments enter the territory of the Chinese Republic to chase the retreated White troops. Nine days later, the so-called protocol of Ili was concluded in Kuldja to facilitate normal relations between Soviet Russia and Xinjiang. Curiously, some Politburo members suggested even to declare the establishment of the independent Kashgar and Dhungar republics, although this far-fetched idea was rejected by Lenin and Chicherin, both anxious about anti-Bolshevik guerilla movements in Turkestan backed by the British.

London, in turn, offered to channel the local population's discontent against the Bolshevik repressions into mutinies on several occasions.[104] It was general consul Percy Etherton who meticulously constructed a regional network of informants and saboteurs struggling against Comintern agents on the territory of Chinese Turkestan.[105]

The last Bokharian Emir, Said Alim Khan, appealed to Etherton for assistance in the struggle against the Bolsheviks' encroachments in the summer of 1920, pleading to safeguard his private belongings which averaged £35 million.[106] Besides lively contacts with nationalist chieftains, Etherton did his best to prevent Soviet diplomatic and trade missions from coming to Kashgar.[107] As he wrote in the diary, many local Chinese officials cooperated with him to thwart the subversive actions in Chinese Turkestan and India.[108] The British diplomat also undertook protective measures against opium traffic across the Russo-Chinese border which was allowed to exist by Soviet customs officers who demanded lavish bribes from smugglers. Yet, charged with illegal currency transactions, Etherton was finally recalled from Kashgar at the end of 1921.[109]

Thus, Soviet and British sides seemed to have swapped places by 1922: the former was defending themselves against Muslim rebels (or *basmachis*), and the latter was betting on their activities[110] In this respect, the story of Ismail Enver Pasha, the former prominent leader of the Turkish nationalist movement, who initially enjoyed the support of Moscow, might serve an example.[111] Very soon this man who proclaimed himself 'the C-in-C of all forces of Islam, the Son-in-Law of the Caliph, and the Deputy of the Prophet', became disillusioned with Bolshevism, launching a guerilla war against the Red Army troops which proceeded until the mid-1920s. Luckily for the Soviets, on 4 August 1922, he was killed in a skirmish near Kuliab.[112]

As this chapter repeatedly mentioned, the First congress of the peoples of the East, held in Baku early in September 1920, was important to the Bolshevik leadership for many reasons. As early as in November 1919, Lenin suggested to summon a congress under anti-imperialist slogans.[113] Many Communist front-runners from Western Europe were invited to the capital of Azerbaijan, including some CPGB top functionaries, who were given a chance to take the floor in Baku on two occasions.[114]

Zinoviev topped at all plenary sessions, addressing 1891 delegates of thirty-seven nations.[115] In one instance (on 1 September 1920), he delivered a lengthy speech on the Bolsheviks' preparedness to 'bolster up revolutionary struggle against the British government'. Calling upon the participants for a 'holy war' against British and French imperialists. Zinoviev's oration was accompanied by a storm of applause and enthusiastic roars.[116] Encouraged by Zinoviev and Radek, the delegates adopted several resolutions, the most important of which was the *Manifest of the peoples of the East*. It accused 'British imperialists' of the aspiration to 'keep colonial and dependent nations with brute force and bribery in disenfranchisement, ignorance and poverty'.[117] Apart from the manifest, the congress addressed a special message to the workers of Europe, America and Japan, and elected the Council for propaganda and action as an executive committee.[118]

The Foreign and India Offices closely followed the work of the Baku Congress through both mass media and intelligence channels.[119] In the diplomatic notes which Curzon sent to Chicherin on 2 and 9 October 1920, the Cabinet condemned those public speeches by the Bolshevik leaders at the congress that 'instigated a genuine hurricane of propaganda, intrigues and conspiracies against British interests and power in Asia'.[120]

One could hardly dismiss the Baku congress as being insignificant for further developments in Asia and the Soviet-British relations.[121] This author shares the view that 'the summons to Baku' aimed 'to organise a counterattack against the foreign invaders of Russia in order to expel them from the lands adjacent to the Soviet republics, including Turkey, Iran, Armenia, and Mesopotamia'.[122] Yet the described conflicts between Moscow and London in Asia cannot be defined as a new round of the Great Game since the latter process had taken place within a certain geographical scope and at the appropriate time, being driven not by ideological but geopolitical motivation.

In the meantime, the Bolshevik regime's consolidation in both domestic and foreign affairs prompted Whitehall to address the former irreconcilable opponent with invitations to attend international conferences which will be described in the next chapter.

8

Soviet Russia and Great Britain at the international conferences, 1922–3

> *Naivety, childish culture, childish cruelty, the complete lack of understanding, the inability to comprehend the necessity of working, slowness in reacting to new ideas – that is the 'log' which we have shown ourselves unable to move, notwithstanding all really heroic efforts which the party has made during these years.*
>
> Lenin in the letter to a correspondent in Switzerland, 1921[1]

One of this book's key points is that the Bolshevik government pursued a highly controversial foreign policy in the 1920s, combining the instigation of revolutionary crises abroad with attempts to consolidate the Soviet regime by political and economic means. Besides the armed intervention and blockade, the Russian population sustained mass famine and epidemics which undermined the Bolshevik rule in the situation of domestic unrest, separatist movement on the fringes of the former empire and possible military aggression from outside.[2]

The famine was caused by the long-lasting civil war, the devastation of prosperous provinces of Central Russia and Siberia due to peasant revolts, degraded agriculture and low standards of rural life along with the disruption of communications. An unprecedented drought added hardships for national economics through 1920–1. At the same time, the Kremlin leaders, imbedded with the fanatical determination 'to set capitalist states ablaze', contrived various projects to financially promote 'world revolution'. In December 1917, they allocated 2 million gold roubles for the propaganda campaign to be launched in the Scandinavian countries to prompt the Entente powers to stop war hostilities.[3]

In the autumn of 1920, when merely 40 per cent of the average annual grain crops were harvested, mass famine along with the epidemics of influenza, typhoid, cholera and even plague (in some regions of southern Siberia and Central Asia) affected about 18–19 million inhabitants of twenty-one provinces (fourteen in Russia and seven in Ukraine). The total rate of mortality from infectious diseases amounted to 2 million people in 1918–20, while 858,000 Russian citizens perished of hunger and exhaustion during 1921–2.[4]

The situation became even more aggravated after thousands of former POWs and interned persons set began their repatriation from the camps on the territory of

Germany, Austria, Czechoslovakia, France, Turkey and Egypt because of the general amnesty proclaimed by the Bolshevik government. On 17 June 1921, the critical situation made Chicherin to ask Curzon to raise the issue of 'the urgent material assistance to Russian refugees' before the Council of the League of Nations.[5]

On 10 July, Maxim Gorky, the world-known Russian belletrist and playwriter, published a proclamation *To All Honest Citizens*, calling for granting an immediate food aid to Soviet Russia, whereas Patriarch Tikhon dispatched special messages to the Archbishops of Canterbury and New York with the same plea.[6] Several nongovernmental organizations in the UK responded to these calls, such as the Imperial War relief fund, Save the children fund, the Friends' emergency and war victims committee, and the Workers' international famine relief committee.[7]

On 28 July 1921, Nikolai Klyshko, the secretary of the Russian trade mission, informed the NKID that the British Red Cross was expecting the Soviet authorities to allow for its activity in the areas influenced by starvation, most of all in the Volga region.[8] The following day he reported to Moscow about a conference of the International famine relief committee which established the body with similar functions.[9] Janis Berzin, the deputy diplomatic agent in London, for his part, notified Chicherin on 4 August about the initiative of the Save the children of Central Europe fund to send invitations to one thousand Soviet kids who could be accepted by English families for a period of a year.[10]

In mid-August 1921, the International Red Cross at last set up the Russian aid committee presided by the famous polar explorer Fridtjof Nansen, who initiated raising a £10 million fund.[11] Almost concurrently, on 20 August, the Soviet government signed an agreement with the American Relief Administration (ARA) to promote further collaboration in the humanitarian sphere.[12] Ten days later, a preparatory meeting of the Intergovernmental commission for famine rescue was held in Paris with delegates representing the Entente countries and the United States. The participants put forward two principal conditions of granting humanitarian aid to the Bolsheviks: their concord to fulfil financial obligations by all previous Russian governments and consent to the distribution of domestic food supplies under the appropriate supervision of international organizations.[13] Although Lloyd George termed a 'devilish matter' the plan to use hunger to impose debt recognition on Russia, he nevertheless added that Britain's business community still distrusted the Bolshevik government's ability to avoid corruption by local Soviet authorities.[14]

There were also voices within the Kremlin officialdom in favour of refusing foreign aid and of 'snatching bread by force of arms' from European countries, such as Poland, while simultaneously 'punishing it for the constant violations of the Riga peace treaty'.[15] Karl Radek who frequently acted as the Kremlin's mouthpiece also expressed disbelief in Western governments' genuine willingness to aid the starving Russian population. Condemning their reluctance, he compared the 'crumbs of charitable subsidies' to Soviet Russia to substantial financial backing of the Kolchak and Denikin armies.[16]

However, on 6 August 1921, the British Committee to help fight famine in Russia decided to set up branches for food and medicine supply in European and Asian countries.[17] The issue was also debated at the meeting of the Entente's Supreme economic council in the French capital on 10–12 August. Addressing the delegates, Curzon suggested to settle the problem by drawing from his experience as viceroy.[18] On 7 September, Josiah Wedgwood, who presided over the public Anti-Famine relief committee, requested James Masterton-Smith, the permanent under-secretary for the colonies, to recommend to all governors of British overseas possessions to donate to Russia's relief funds [19] After a tense discussion in Brussels, the Entente countries finally declared the establishment of the international commission for saving Russia from famine which began to operate on 10 September.[20]

British food delivery to the Russian population was carried out at two main levels: by governmental bodies and public organizations. In the first instance, the total amount of aid matched £400,000 (in comparison to £12 million from the United States and only £86,000 from France). In the second case, it could be estimated at a few tens thousand pounds.[21] In May 1922, British families accepted 250 Russian children (some historians give 500 instead). Several thousands of food parcels from Britain were shipped from the UK to Russia. The Soviet government also received an international humanitarian loan of £200,000 with 5 per cent annual interest rate for the purchase of industrial equipment to produce consumer goods. About 82,000 starving people were provided with hot meals on a regular basis by British trade-unions at the public canteens opened in Russia.[22]

Yet, when questioned of the Cabinet's overly cautious position in view of Russian famine, Austen Chamberlain gave the following counterarguments: the disastrous socio-economic situation in the UK, the ongoing financial subsidies to various European states, the high likelihood of the League of Nations requesting extra funds to fight typhoid, and finally the Soviet government's own resources being wasted on subversive actions abroad – all these aspects prevented the Cabinet from massive aid to Russian population. Obviously, Chamberlain's reservations predetermined the Cabinet's refusal to grant extra £350,000 to Russia for humanitarian purposes.[23]

Another project was submitted by Leslie Urquhart who chaired the Association of Russian bond holders and acted as the largest shareholder of the 'Russo-Asiatic Joint Mining Corporation' and the 'Lena Goldfields Company'. In the outburst of international sympathies with the suffering Russian citizens, he suggested to Moscow to build an international consortium with the capital of £25 million to finance the Central committee for the famine relief which the Bolsheviks established on 18 June 1921. However, Urquhart's personal contacts with Chicherin and Krassin late in August–early in September 1921 led to nothing.[24]

Meanwhile a short-term euphoria that emerged in the relations between Moscow and London after the conclusion of the trade agreement began to evaporate. As early as in April 1921, British conservative periodicals made public the Kremlin's 'instructions' to conduct revolutionary propaganda under the guise of commercial activities in the empire. Despite the rebuttal made by Krassin on 9 April as well as the public statement by Lloyd George who branded these 'instructions' as fake, mutual dissatisfaction with implementation of the agreement's provisions was growing day by day.[25] By 28 April, the Foreign Office employees notified the Cabinet about thirteen violations of the 1921 agreement by the Soviet side. For his part, Chicherin expressed the Soviet government's dissatisfaction with the British funding the 'White Russian scum' remaining in some neighbouring countries.[26] Moreover, on 2 July 1921, Krassin remitted a note of protest to the Foreign Office after the joint Soviet-Ukrainian trade delegation was arrested and deported from Constantinople by the British military administration, being charged with an attempted coup.[27]

Besides that, Curzon and his colleagues were gravely concerned about the Comintern propaganda in Asian countries. To counteract it, Henry Dobbs, the British diplomatic agent, arrived in Kabul in January 1921 to confer with the Afghan Prime Minister Mohammed Tarsier. As Raskol'nikov, the Soviet plenipotentiary to Afghanistan, informed Chicherin, the British did not skimp on the broad promises of assistance to the Emir, offering him 20,000 rifles, 4 million rupees annual subsidies, among other supplies.[28] The Soviet-Afghan treaty mentioned in the previous chapter annoyed Whitehall most of all. Under its terms, the Soviet consulates were established in the country's five principal administrative centres. The London top officials became fully aware that a diplomatic cover could be used by the Comintern activists for revolutionary activities.[29]

A note by Curzon to Chicherin on 7 September 1921 indicted the Kremlin of being responsible for subversive actions by the Comintern, including Anglophobic actions by Soviet representatives in various countries. For example, Theodor Rothstein, the plenipotentiary to Tehran, was accused of bribing Persian ministers as well as of urging local rulers to create 'a united front of the suppressed native peoples from the Ganges in the east to the Nile in the west'.[30]

After a fortnight pause, Litvinov repudiated these allegations claiming that the Comintern had nothing to do with the Soviet government, while 'all reports, speeches and declarations, registered in the British note, are deliberately fabricated'. Although he admitted some cases of 'inadvertent [?] violations by Soviet diplomats of Britain's interests'.[31]

Subsequent lively debates at several Cabinet sittings made Curzon repeat his denunciations in the subsequent note to the NKID. He referred to the intelligence about twenty Indian left-wing extremists staying in Moscow from May to September 1921.[32] Here it should be stressed that despite the considered diplomatic mission by Dobbs resulting in the conclusion of Anglo-Afghan treaty on 22 November the same year, the Kremlin did not abstain from regarding Amanullah as a potential ally. To dispel the Emir's concerns about pro-Communist political groups in Afghanistan, willing to overthrow monarchy on the pattern of Bokhara and Khiva, where the Bolsheviks managed to establish the so-called Peoples' republics, the Soviet plenipotentiary kept on reassuring Amanullah of the Bolsheviks' absolute support in the face of Britain's encroachments.[33]

Notwithstanding these diplomatic collisions, Berzin as Krassin's deputy, was instructed to notify Lloyd George about Moscow's readiness to fulfil Russian debt obligations in exchange for the Entente's official recognition of the Bolshevik regime and financial loans on special terms.[34] Just at that time, the prime minister was impressed by Lenin's lecture to the delegates of the Second All-Russian congress of political propagandists on 17 October, when the Bolshevik leader admitted the presence of market tendencies in the Soviet economy in the course of its transition to socialism.[35]

On 28 October, Chicherin issued another note which clearly indicated the Kremlin's willingness 'to recognise the obligations before foreign states and their subjects on the loans made by the tsarist government prior to 1914'. In response, Curzon expressed satisfaction with Moscow seemingly taking a U-turn on the debt repayment, although he asked his vis-a-vis to explain, whether this included all Russia's financial commitments.[36]

A monthly pause in the dialogue led to a new telegram by Krassin to Moscow on 26 November 1921. He mentioned that the British government was involved in the settlement of controversies in Ireland and the Near East, as well as in the preparation for the Washington naval conference which distracted the Cabinet from tackling the 'Russian problem'.[37] To restart diplomatic talks, Krassin gave an interview to a group of Labour activists, later published as a leaflet by the National committee 'Hands off Russia'. Among other statements, he argued that 'if normal political relations between Russia and the UK were to resume, the priority should be given to its economic revival', depending on British loans to Moscow.[38]

The Soviet leaders strived for permanent economic contacts with Britain since its share amounted to 33.4 per cent of Russian imports, and 44.2 per cent of exports by the end of 1921. Symptomatically, Russia's purchase of British manufactured production increased ten times from 6 to 61 million gold roubles during the same year.[39] Not surprisingly that Urquhart pitched to Krassin another project of an international financial syndicate as a collective sponsor of the Russian commercial revival. The British industrialist assured the people's commissar that the syndicate would deal with the Soviet government on the conditions adopted by the SNK on 23 November 1920, matching the principles of concession policy approved by the Soviet government on 29 March 1921.[40]

Almost concurrently, the *Daily Herald*, which was secretly subsidized by Moscow, proposed to convoke an all-European economic conference. Thus, the Kremlin cast a *ballon d'essai* on the recognition of Russia's commercial interests by the former allies. Lloyd George, Horne and Krassin resumed the exchange of opinions on a multisided consortium of financial companies that were eager to invest in Russian industry and agriculture on conditions of control over main national railways.[41] The Soviet emissary argued that the *de jure* recognition of the Soviet regime by London could be achieved without the establishment of such a consortium. 'It is absolutely obvious that the British themselves dispose of no concrete plans for Russia's economic revival, he wired to Chicherin on 17 December 1921, and some German "brains" work instead of them in this case'.[42] Ten days later, however, he advocated at least the partial acknowledgement of the Russian debt in exchange for Britain's financial assistance and diplomatic recognition.[43]

On 6 January 1922, the Entente Supreme council in Cannes endorsed the idea of conferring with Soviet Russia on Europe's economic revival. The forthcoming forum in Genoa was bound not only to reanimate international trade but also to unravel the tangle of mutual financial obligations and offer a scheme of war debts' repayment.[44] Four days later, the official letter of invitation was remitted to Moscow. Shortly afterwards Krassin and Edward Wise, the chief economic counselor to Lloyd George, deliberated on the terms of diplomatic consultations with some leading European financial experts.[45] At the same time, Soviet Russia's Supreme national economic council set up a special commission to prepare for the conference. Chaired by Chicherin, the delegation included Krassin and Litvinov together with abundant eminent experts working on the development of Russia's industry, financed by foreign loans and investments.[46]

Krassin's telegram to Chicherin apprised the Kremlin of his conversation with Lloyd George and Curzon on 13 February 1922. It was during this meeting that the

Figure 10 British delegation at the Cannes Conference, 1922. (left to right: George Curzon, Robert Horne, David Lloyd George). Photo courtesy of Wikimedia Commons (public domain).

Soviet representative finally abandoned the plan of Russian economic revival by means of financial credits which the projected international consortium was bound to grant to the Soviet government.[47]

The arguments against the international economic conference were heard from both the Western governments and the Soviets. If Lloyd George, Horne and Stanley Baldwin, the future prime minister, favoured cooperation with Russia, such staunch anti-Communists as Churchill and Curzon openly rejected any idea of the collaboration with Moscow.[48] Similarly, the antagonists of normalization influenced the Kremlin's position: Trotsky, Zinoviev and Stalin quibbled with pro-European Kamenev, Chicherin and Krassin, whereas Lenin traditionally held a middle view. Yet even the proponents of better relations with the Entente states seemed annoyed with even short delays in the organization of the conference, albeit caused by the necessity to synchronize positions of key Western actors – Britain, France, Italy and the United States.[49]

Many Kremlin pundits were nevertheless confident that the decrease of the British foreign trade by 40 per cent compared to 1913 would force London to seek for the improvement of commercial and then political relations with Russia, since the prolongation of a post-war economic reconversion could even lead to the disintegration of the British empire.[50] 'The idea of the Genoa conference, wrote a Soviet economic expert, is a project of British diplomacy, for the development of British foreign trade critically depends on Russia with its 140 million population being reintegrated in the world market'.[51]

In January–February 1922, the Foreign Office analysts drafted basic documents trying to meet expectations of both Western powers and Soviet Russia.[52] The opponents of conferring with the Soviets admonished the Cabinet ministers that 'their [Bolsheviks'] intention is to try and obtain *de jure* recognition first and credits afterwards, and to be able to dispose of these credits themselves'. As one of these antagonists argued in the memorandum for the government, Britain was obliged to make terms for three reasons – because it regarded the Russian side as its 'formidable adversary in the world of Islam', the British working class was able to lobby for cooperation with the Soviet republic and the 'British trade could only be saved by an agreement with Russia at any price'.[53]

Lloyd George, for his part, eager to use the conference to consolidate the Cabinet, made a statement in the Parliament on 3 March 1922 justifying the 'economic recognition' of Soviet Russia.[54] Four days later, the interdepartmental committee adopted the main clauses of the convention which was supposed to be concluded with Moscow in Genoa. One of the provisos which the British financial experts put forward was the establishment of an international commission on Russian foreign debts.[55] At the same time, the authoritative City bankers drafted a framework for financial conditions to be recognized by Moscow. While stipulating the legal insolvency of the Kremlin's refusal to repay its debt and the urgent need to abolish the state monopoly of foreign trade, they recommended to the Cabinet to agree on annual payments of 1.1–1.25 billion gold roubles to foreign creditors. Apart from that, the attention of the Cabinet members was drawn to the rights of property owners in Russia and their protection from confiscation.[56]

Queried by the King at a regular audience, Lloyd George did not reply clearly, if he would confer with Lenin or Trotsky at the conference. More importantly though, the prime minister regarded the upcoming multilateral negotiations as a major international event, which would not only bring the recognition of Soviet Russia but also benefit Europe by the conclusion of a universal non-aggression treaty. Describing his motivation, Lloyd George wrote to Horne on 22 March: 'It is an essential part of the Genoa programme that there should be a European pact of peace, which will involve an undertaking by Russia not to attack her neighbours, and by Poland and Romania not to attack Russia.'[57]

The most striking disagreement between key ministers became obvious during the Cabinet meetings on 27, 28 March and 2 April. Lloyd George, Austen Chamberlain and Hankey presented various scenarios of holding the conference. Addressing Lloyd George's claim that Lenin and his partisans 'were departing from the doctrine of Communism', Churchill remarked that the Bolsheviks were constantly violating the trade agreement, being conspirators by nature, trying to push Western powers with each other and expressing cynicism towards the UK, while 3 million Russian emigrants were appealing to Whitehall for humanitarian aid. Nevertheless, most of the Cabinet ministers approved the prime minister's programme to 'economically' recognize the Soviet regime. They decided to form a delegation presided by Lloyd George, which included Laming Worthington-Evans, the state secretary for war, Horne and Philip Lloyd-Graeme, who charged the Board of Trade department of overseas commerce.[58]

Since the history of the Genoa conference has been extensively studied by diplomatic historians over the last decades, the narration below focuses on merely Soviet-British diplomatic consultations.[59] In the speeches delivered by Lloyd George and Chicherin on 10 April 1922 – the opening day of the conference, both statesmen revealed contrasting difference in the approach to the forum's agenda. Responding to Chicherin's calls on the Entente members to drastically reduce military budgets and redistribute national gold reserves as long-term loans between all countries, Lloyd George mentioned wide-spreading rumours about plentiful revolutionary volunteers, preparing to subvert Europe to the same state of devastation as Russia had experienced after the world war. He further raised the issue of foreign debts as a necessary condition for bringing the Soviet republic to the fold of civilized interstate relations.[60]

However, during an informal conversation with Chicherin at Villa Alberti in the suburbs of Genoa, Lloyd George persuaded him to adhere to universal principles of collaboration between the states, acting simultaneously as both creditors and debtors. Interestingly, the prime minister referred to the historic precedents of Anglo-French relations, when neither London nor Paris usually refrained from mutual material claims for damages in the aftermath of bilateral war conflicts. To prove his arguments, the British leader equalled the Soviet request for 39 million gold roubles as compensation for the armed intervention with the Entente powers' demands to Germany. In fact, he offered a compromise: to discount all military loans to Russia, reducing the interest rates on the pre-war debt to foreign owners whose property was nationalized by Soviet authorities.

Sharing Lenin's opinion about the state monopoly of foreign trade, Chicherin nevertheless advocated partial recognition of tsarist debts. He also proposed to agree with the Entente countries on the scheme of their repayment after a five-year moratorium, later increased to thirty years on the instructions from the Kremlin. The people's commissar also harboured the idea of the nationalized foreign property should be converted into foreign economic concessions, given Moscow was lavishly subsidized by the City.[61]

But even this modified position seemed unacceptable to Lenin and most Soviet high-ranking mandarins because it would mean allocating up to 80 per cent of the budget expenses for annual debt repayments.[62] The Bolshevik leader moreover instructed Chicherin not to cede an iota more to Britain and the other Western delegations.[63] On 30 April, Lenin cabled to Genoa: 'A new round of conference in three months is the most profitable thing for us. Do not take financial obligations on the closing of the conference in any case, do not agree with even the half-recognition of debts and do not be scared by a [conference's] break-up at all.'[64]

The conclusion of a separate Soviet-German treaty in Rapallo on 16 April was a lightning-fast diplomatic move, albeit well prepared by Chicherin's visit to Berlin before coming to Genoa. It greatly impressed all delegates, especially the British, having an effect of a 'diplomatic bombshell' among them. The European press wrote about Chicherin's personal triumph, whereas the British periodicals dubbed him a hidden Germanophile.[65] The most important paragraph of the Rapallo agreement was a mutual debt and reparation's amnesty in the amount of 16 billion gold roubles. As Lloyd George and his colleagues supposed, this deal could set a dangerous precedent for other debtor states.[66] Meanwhile Lenin encouraged Chicherin in a telegram: 'The Russo-German treaty should serve as the only model of international agreement acceptable by the Soviet government.'[67]

On 18 April, the Entente top representatives conferred at the premises of Villa Raggi – the official residence of the Italian prime minister. The conversation focused on the Soviet-German reproachment which was regarded as a 'second Brest'. Lloyd George argued that 'the real danger was a combining of interests between Germany and Russia … ' 'Bolshevism, he continued, was a passing phase, and sooner or later – it might be two, it might be more years – there would be another government in Russia of a more stable kind … '[68] The following day, the Entente states declared their right to invalidate any provisions of the Rapallo treaty.[69]

To 'save face' and bring the forum to concrete decisions, Lloyd George was even ready to sign a pan-European pact of non-aggression, initiated by Moscow, albeit with its subsequent approval by the League of Nations General Assembly.[70] Two more memoranda presented by the Western delegations to Chicherin on 29 April and 3 May became the last attempts to break the deadlock. They reflected the opinion of Keynes who advocated a long-term moratorium on debt repayment, the issue of bonds to refund it and a £50 million urgent loan to Moscow. Put another way, the considered memoranda defined those 'red lines' that the Cabinet could not cross in any case.[71]

The first memorandum enumerated the terms of the financial agreement with Soviet Russia, providing for the reconstruction of national economy through a gold bond loan with an annual interest of 5 per cent. In fact, it emulated the aforementioned project of an international consortium with the initial capital of £15 million rejected by Moscow prior to the Genoa conference.[72] The second document proposed further reduction of Russia's foreign debt along with the simultaneous increase in the volume of credit borrowings for the Kremlin up to £25 million.[73] Significantly, Lloyd George announced at the press conference on 3 May 1922 that if Russia denied a final agreement under these circumstances, Britain would no longer let itself be snubbed.[74]

In response, the Soviet delegation justified the need for Moscow to obtain a loan totalling 8.8 billion gold roubles (equal to £880 million) with financial guarantees in the form of a special tax, the state platinum reserves and future industrial concessions to foreign companies.[75] Chicherin voiced this final condition at a conference's plenary session on 3 May. While finally acquiesced with the idea of an international consortium, he categorically ruled out the slightest possibility that the Kremlin would abandon the state monopoly of commerce and control over foreign currency transactions.[76]

It seems that the prime minister fully realized the Bolshevik leadership's incapability to reach an agreement with the Entente states during an informal meeting with Krassin on 5 May, when the latter petitioned Lloyd George of granting a £120 million government loan to Soviet Russia for three years. The stalemate of negotiations stripped the Cabinet leader of the last illusions. As he told Krassin, 'he had begun to despair of any settlement going through. If the Soviet government concluded that they could not meet the conditions of the memorandum [the first one dating to 3 May], there was no hope. England must fall back on her old policy of isolation.' At the end of the talk, Lloyd George expressed his bitter disappointment once again:

> All our efforts had been directed to bringing the other countries much further than they had ever gone before, and we had certainly produced a scheme which would enable the Russians to reconstruct their country, to secure peace, and at the same time to hold out the hope of a real settlement of European questions.[77]

Yet the Soviet diplomatic notes that were circulated to other delegations on 6 and 11 May accused the Entente of the unwillingness to admit the economic damage that the intervention brought to Russia, defining the Civil War, which prevented the Bolshevik government to repay debts, as the circumstances of irresistible force akin to the events of the Great French revolution.[78]

The conference's last plenary sitting took place on 17 May. It was marked by Chicherin's assurances of the importance of dialogue between 'the first socialist state and the capitalist world', as well as by Lloyd George's reciprocal lecture on the eventual continuation of debating the 'Russian question' at the next international forum in the light of the 'two systems' fundamental incompatibility'.[79]

The results of the pan-European economic congress found various assessments by contemporary observers. For example, one Bolshevik politician called it a 'profound reconnaissance mission in the rear of the enemy' and the 'victory of English liberalism over the French reaction'.[80] Some Russian emigrant leaders expressed their deep sorrow at the beginning of the actual dialogue between Europe and the Bolshevik regime.[81] Soviet official historians tried to convert the conference's fiasco into a 'triumph of the Leninist policy of peaceful coexistence', owing to Chicherin's diplomatic flexibility.[82] Keynes also avowed his point of view in a series of articles for leading Western journals.

On 10 June 1922, he published a summary in the *Manchester Guardian Commercial*. While not hiding his disappointment at the results, Keynes concluded:

> Never, I think, at any conferences the intellectual standard of the official policy sunk so low. The discussions – I am limiting myself in this commentary to the Russian question – seldom touched reality. The greater part of the time was occupied by excited and sometimes melodramatic controversy between the British and French delegations about alternative versions of a formula, of which it was certain beforehand that Russians would accept neither, and of which their acceptance would have led to no practical consequence.[83]

In fact, three opinions on relations between Russia and its former allies competed in the spring of 1922. The first meant fundamental impossibility of reconciliation due to the Kremlin's intention to crush the Versailles order and cancel all foreign debts.[84] In the second place, there existed a concept of a temporal, tactical settlement between the East and the West in the anticipation of a new military confrontation.[85] The third notion envisaged Soviet Russia's incorporation in the system of relations created by European and partly American politicians. It was Chicherin and Krassin, on one side, along with Lloyd George and Horne, on the other, who advocated bringing the latter project to life.

This study highlights the miniscule chances of scoring success at the Genoa conference – 'the largest since the crusades', as the *Manchester Guardian* coined it.[86] Given the goals of the Soviet and the UK political leadership as well as the prevailing moods of European, especially British public, its failure could have been predicted beforehand, although some statesmen, such as Churchill and Curzon, were annoyed at the prospect of Lloyd George and Chicherin reaching mutual accord.[87] It was not the inadequate preparation, inept conduct, disagreement among the Western delegations or the signature of a separate treaty in Rapallo, but this fundamental contradiction that caused the Cabinet's defeat at the first pan-European forum with the Bolsheviks' participation. In fact, the Genoa conference may be considered as the meeting which 'demonstrated that Britain could no longer exercise European, and still less global leadership in dealing with new phenomenon of international revolution'.[88]

Similar obstacles stood in the way of the delegates to the second round of the pan-European economic congress, which took place in The Hague two months later.[89] However, this time Litvinov headed the group of economists with Leonid Krassin and Nikolai Krestinsky as his deputies. Instead of the prime minister, Lloyd-Graeme chaired the British delegation facing an even tougher stance of the Soviet representatives. Denying foreign debts altogether, Moscow refused to restitute nationalized property to former owners, whereas requesting a loan of £330 million to restore industrial facilities and offering a limited number of industrial concessions to Western partners.[90]

The fruitless debates in three committees set up by the delegates compelled the French and Belgian representatives to indict the Kremlin of an inadmissible approach to the agenda. Despite certain controversies amid British financial experts, most part of them also became aware of the futility to reach an agreement with Moscow. Hence, they advised each Western government to separately negotiate with the Bolsheviks on the debts issue.⁹¹ In turn, the Soviet press-bureau pointed out that the conference scored no success because of 'the Entente powers' phantom hope to bully Moscow into any economic compromise'. Whereas *The Times* recommended the Cabinet to initially settle the problem of German reparations, the *Daily Telegraph* attributed the collapse of negotiations to Europe's fundamental disagreement with the Bolshevik regime.⁹² Yet the very fact of the Soviet participation in the multisided consultations enabled the Kremlin to obtain invaluable experience in conducting dialogue with Western political elites. Put another way, despite their obvious fiasco, both the Genoa and Hague conferences drew a line between confrontation and cooperation meaning Soviet Russia's *de-facto* returning to 'civilized diplomacy'.⁹³

Shortly afterwards Krassin and Urquhart resumed to privately contact on the financial compensation for the British tycoon's lost property. Since Urquhart was the largest Russian state bonds' holder, many political observers closely surveyed these negotiations in Moscow and Berlin from 20 August to 9 September 1922.⁹⁴ To the astonishment of sceptics, they succeeded in fixing a preliminary agreement of twenty-seven clauses. It obligated the Soviet government to contribute £3 million to the share capital of the 'Lena Goldfield Company' to 'facilitate the re-start of mining in Russia'. As the London *Evening Standard* commented on the bargain, Russia had made an important step on the way to return to normal commercial relations, trying to wipe off barriers to the country's reintegration in the world economic system.⁹⁵

However, the enthusiasm of British public again proved to be short-lived. Because of the two points, allegedly contradicting the Soviet laws, the SNK annulled the Krassin–Urquhart draft contract on 5 October 1922, even though the latter warned the Kremlin leaders that the coalition government would imminently fall not only because of the crisis in the Near East (see below in the chapter) but also following the Soviet rejection of the deal.⁹⁶ Similarly, negotiations about the organization of the 'Anglo-Russian Oil Company' in August 1922 ended in a fiasco. According to the report by a MI6 informant, Krassin shouted in a rage at Nikolai Bukharin and other Bolshevik party bosses at a regular Politburo meeting: 'If you think that I am incapable of signing contracts, then go to Berlin and London, and try to deal with Urquhart, Krupp and Stinnes about the "sacred rights" of the proletariat.'⁹⁷

A new round of Soviet-British diplomatic frictions related to the situation around Turkey. There a new government under Mustapha Kemal rescinded the treaty of Sevres in 1920 and counteracted the offensive of the Greek troops backed by Britain during 1921–2. These events led to the so-called Chanak crisis risking a new war and leading to the collapse of the Lloyd George's coalition.⁹⁸ It forced London to strain efforts for the conclusion of the Greco-Turkish peace treaty in Mudanya on 11 October 1922. A special conference on Turkey's territorial settlement was agreed to be held in the Swiss town of Lausanne.⁹⁹

The decryption of Soviet diplomatic correspondence by the GC&CS experts exposed the Soviet-Turkish rapprochement during the war against Greece. Some politicians considered Kemal a puppet of Moscow, whereas others pointed to the unnatural and provisional character of the Soviet-Turkish alliance. For instance, Curzon wrote to Austen Chamberlain on 26 May 1922 that 'Kemal was in the strong arms of the Bolsheviks', although further complications between Moscow and Angora did not attest to this unequivocal assessment. The foreign secretary referred to the expulsion of Cebesoi Ali Fuad, a diplomatic agent and Kemal's friend, from Soviet Russia, which might be interpreted as Moscow's disagreement with the prohibition by the Angora government of the Turkish Communist Party. Besides that, the Kremlin officialdom suspected Kemal of backing the pan-Islamist movement in the Caucasus and Central Asia.[100]

At the same time, the Bolsheviks annoyed London by their presumed accord with Angora, as it was demonstrated by Chicherin's message to Curzon on 12 September 1922.[101] In response, the British navy was ordered to destroy all Soviet surface and submarine ships navigating at the coast of Turkey. Moreover, Admiral Osmond Brock, the commander of the Mediterranean Fleet, did not rule out the interception of Soviet transports with weapons for the Kemalists on board. Additionally, the Admiralty requested a battle squadron in the Atlantic to defend commercial shipping in the Baltic Sea, should a war with Soviet Russia burst out.[102]

The escalation of tension in the autumn of 1922 required the NKID to appeal to several foreign ministers, including Curzon, despite the lack of diplomatic relations.[103] As some MI6 analysts predicted, Moscow strenuously pushed Angora to an open confrontation with London. One of the agency's reports stated that Karakhan assured the Turkish representative that the British were not going to voluntarily leave the Dardanelles. They could be, therefore, pressed to do so only by force, namely, by an assault on the neutral zone established around Constantinople under the treaty of Sevres, or by attacking the British positions in Iraq.[104] The MI6 agents managed to obtain a copy of the minute compiled by the staff of the Comintern Eastern department regarding allocating funds to the Communist party of Turkey.[105]

The crisis in the relations between this country, Soviet Russia and the Entente states had to be settled at an international conference in Lausanne. It was also significant for Soviet Russia and the United States, both the non-members of the League of Nations, that the conference would not be held in Geneva – the home place of this international organization.[106] The aggravation of situation around the Black Sea Straits against the background of the NKID's persistent efforts to attain the recognition of Russia's geopolitical interests prompted the Foreign Office to remit on 27 October 1922 an official invitation to Moscow, albeit confining the Soviet participation in debates to the problem of navigation through the Bosporus and the Dardanelles.

The presence at the opening ceremony of Raymond Poincaré, then the French prime minister, as well as Benito Mussolini, the new Italian leader, underlined the importance of the forum. Curzon, who headed the British delegation, was elected the acting chairman of plenary sittings. Delegates from nine countries took part in the congress (the Japanese and American diplomats acting as observers), while the joint Russo-Ukrainian-Georgian delegation led by Chicherin represented the Russian Soviet Socialist Federation. Three commissions worked from 20 November 1922 to 4 February 1923 and, after a short-term pause, from 23 April to 24 July the same year, focusing on Turkey's territorial settlement, the fate of the Mosul oil fields, and the mode of navigation in the Straits connecting the Black and Mediterranean Seas.[107]

According to many viewers, the Lausanne forum became the apogee of Curzon's diplomatic career. As his messages to Bonar Law demonstrated, the foreign secretary saw the task by yielding to the opinions of the Bolsheviks and Kemalists in procedural details, albeit firmly defending British positions on the main issues.[108] Despite persistent Turkish reluctance, Curzon managed to obtain Angora's concordance with the principal provisions of the international convention on maritime traffic, initiated by the British. Here a new barrier was caused by Chicherin who was given an opportunity to take the floor at the first sitting of the commission for the safety of the Straits' navigation on 4 December 1922. Spoken not only on behalf of Soviet Russia, but also Turkey as a presumed Moscow's ally, he maintained that the Black Sea Straits ought to be open to merchant transports and closed to battleships, except the Turkish men-of-war.[109]

After a response by the Romanian delegate insisting on the internalization of the Straits, Curzon addressed the audience. In the wire to the permanent under-secretary Eire Crow, the head of the Foreign Office described the situation in Lausanne:

> General impression produced by sitting was that Turkey had openly and unnecessarily placed herself in position of humiliating subjection to Russia and that latter had proposed a ridiculous plan designed only to convert the Black Sea into a fortified Russian lake, and to make Turkey her vassal.[110]

From Curzon's point of view, this would mean a return to the situation of Russia overseeing the Straits, like it occurred in the 1833 according to the treaty of Unkiar Skelessi. The hasty Turkish assurances that they did not consider their views identical to the Soviet intentions, as well as Angora's backstage notification about their readiness 'to break with Russia, renew a long-standing friendship with Britain and make peace with Greece', became the first diplomatic success scored by Curzon and the apparent defeat suffered by Chicherin in Lausanne.[111]

On 6 December, the chairman of the conference took the floor for his second programme speech on the problem of the Straits. This time Curzon presented a draft logically sound and agreed with the Allies of how to resolve this issue: always opening the Straits for any battleships and merchant vessels, except for those of the states at war with Turkey. The subsequent lecture by the French representative concurred with this vision.[112] As a result, Chicherin failed to amend the British draft. Yet Curzon would have breached his moral principles if he had not proposed to his Russian opponent a private conversation to discuss Chicherin's idea of a compromise regarding 'conditional closure of the Straits'.[113] Their meeting took place on 17 December at Beau Rivage Hotel where the British diplomatic mission resided.

It is quite clear that the conversation was interpreted differently by the British and Russian sides. According to the former, Curzon again drew Chicherin's attention to the constant violations of the commitments made by Moscow under the 1921 agreement, for example, those relating to the termination of Anglophobic propaganda. But the people's commissar traditionally rejected all allegations, adding that the Kremlin could not be responsible for the actions of 'every unofficial Soviet agent on the ground'. He moreover notified Curzon on Moscow's concerns about British intrigues in Transcaucasia, northern Persia and Afghanistan. In response, the foreign secretary again claimed that Britain 'harmed Russia nowhere', whereas Chicherin, even staying in Lausanne, published articles to impair bilateral relations.[114]

Chicherin, for his part, reported to Moscow that 'Curzon demonstrated only cold "woodiness," formalism and inability or reluctance to cover matters broadly politically, as Lloyd George had always done.' In defiance of seemingly positive intention to settle the problem of the Straits, the people's commissar had nothing to do but to agree with Curzon on the fact that Soviet Russia's isolation in Lausanne was 'incomparably more than during the period of Genoa and the Hague'. Two days later he wrote to Litvinov: 'The general impression I have of the conference is that there can be no serious agreement with England under Curzon at all.'[115]

As a result, the alternative draft presented by Chicherin on 18 December found no support, despite his assertion that Curzon contrived 'to make the defence of the Straits and Constantinople impossible and open Russia to attacks of large foreign fleets'.[116] Consequently, the foreign secretary wired to Crowe:

> I first rejected Russian scheme in toto as mere reproduction of Chicherin's original proposal for *mare clausum* in the Black Sea, remarking that it had not found a friend and was so inconsistent with Allied ideas that even consideration was useless. So, it perished without a sigh from anyone and with barely a groan from its authors.[117]

With the pledge to reduce the amount of war reparations from £15 to £12 million, Curzon managed to pull the Turkish delegation to the British side. The fact that Chicherin admitted diplomatic defeat in Lausanne, failing to play on the contradictions between Britain and other Entente states, particularly France, as he had originally planned, was evidenced by his telegram to Litvinov, dated 30 January 1923.[118] Although the head of the Soviet delegation refused to sign the final draft of the convention on the Straits, leaving Lausanne on 7 February, the Soviet delegation, this time chaired by the old Bolshevik of the Polish origins, Waclaw Worowski, had nothing to do but to return to Switzerland and take part in the second act of the conference which resulted in the conclusion of the convention on 24 July the same year.[119]

Diplomatic historians have divided into three cohorts on the evaluation of winners and losers in Lausanne. There were those who concentrated on the unconditional victory of the British diplomacy. Others assessed London's Near and Middle East policy much more cautiously, while the third group of scholars argued that Curzon's political course stalled in these regions. Some authors claimed that the Foreign Office destroyed the Russo-Turkish alliance and restored Britain's prestige in the Islamic world through the combination of diplomatic tact and detailed knowledge of the situation that Curzon displayed at the conference. They maintained that no other British foreign ministers until the Second World War could surpass him. In other words, his 'masterful' guidance of the Lausanne conference strengthened Britain's imperial positions, while Moscow suffered defeat, recognized by Chicherin himself.[120] Those analysts who viewed the state of affairs more pragmatically, for instance, Toynbee, regarded the congress as nothing but 'the salvation of the face of a nominally victorious Britain'.[121] Besides, many political observers, Churchill as an example, emphasized the negative reaction by the British dominions to Curzon's activities in Lausanne. While acknowledging the skillful conduct of the conference by his colleague, he nevertheless commented on the inconsistency and indecisive nature of the entire Asiatic policy pursued by Lloyd George and Curzon.[122] The Soviet supporters of the third concept diminished the importance of the Lausanne forum, emphasizing Soviet Russia's 'moral victory' (?) over Curzon's persistent pressure upon Turkey.[123]

From the present author's point of view, the Lausanne conference became a notable step in the process of restoring London's position in the Near and Middle East, although certainly not to the extent that the Cabinet had aspired for in the spring of 1923. Moscow's response to this diplomatic fiasco became the increasing assistance to nationalist movements under the banner of anti-colonial struggle. As the next chapter reveals, the so-called Curzon's 'ultimatum' reflected the British political elites' nervosity towards this subversive activity.

9

The 'Curzon ultimatum' of 1923

And here is the whole Curzon note,
There are signs of cold sweat on it.
Curzon suffers from hidden ailment,
His ultimatum is dictated by fright.

Demian Bednyi, the Soviet poet, 1923.[1]

For the fact that any reader can find more about George Curzon's life and political career in the available books and articles, a comprehensive assessment of his work as the foreign secretary is outside the scope of this study.[2] It is worth noting, however, that while holding this position during the first half of the 1920s, Curzon never changed his opinion about the Soviet regime calling it 'deplorable' at the Imperial conference of 1921. To his mind, Bolshevism presented an attractive ideology only to colonial nations, yet challenging Britain's 'great civilizing mission' there.[3]

As it has been noted in previous chapters, Curzon drew special attention to Afghanistan – a key regional area of the Anglo-Soviet geopolitical competition. Given Moscow's commitment to stop the overt anti-British activities, Soviet diplomatic agents opted for clandestine methods of agitation among local tribes, particularly in the proximity of the Indian north-western frontier.[4] The secret transfer of ten Indian revolutionaries through the Pamir mountains and the so-called Wakhan Mountain Corridor to Hindustan arranged by the Comintern agents in early August 1922 attested to Kremlin's endless attempts to weaken the British Raj.[5]

At the same time, recurrent punitive attacks conducted by the Anglo-Indian troops against tribal guerrillas to protect military checkpoints and police stations on the Afghan frontier worried the Bolshevik leaders. 'In the event of future world conflicts, Chicherin insisted in a letter to Stalin on 19 December 1923, it will be of the greatest importance to us, whether Afghanistan will represent an independent nation state, … or the British will completely occupy its territory, reaching the borders of Soviet Turkestan.'[6] Hence, the members of the Politburo commission on Afghanistan instructed Feodor Raskol'nikov, the plenipotentiary in Kabul, 'to immediately begin negotiations with the Afghan government on a secret agreement to counteract Britain's aggressive policy in the frontier area'.[7]

The 'machinations of imperialist powers' in the Far East during 1922 annoyed Moscow as well. Specifically, those Russian White guards who had escaped to Manchuria and Korea in the aftermath of the Civil War were eager to receive financial and military support sufficient to raid the Soviet territory and even recapture such big cities as Vladivostok, Khabarovsk or Blagoveshchensk.[8]

Meanwhile the Soviet authorities never stopped persecutions of social dissenters within Russia, despite the Kremlin repeatedly announcing about termination of political repressions. The British public opinion was particularly outraged by numerous cases of groundless arrests and tortures of the UK citizens by the Cheka (OGPU) agents on charges of counter-revolutionary activity and espionage.

The detention of Stan Harding, a British journalist working for the American periodical *World*, and of Charles Davison, an engineer at a Petrograd factory, were only two instances. Intended to better understand the 'Bolshevik social experiment', Harding arrived in Soviet Russia in the summer of 1920. Arrested on false accusations, she spent more than half a year in two ill-famous Moscow prisons – Lubyanka and Butyrka – suffering tiresome nightly interrogations and harassment.[9] It was only in February 1921, after her case had been spoken in the Parliament for eighteen times [*sic*!], when she was released owing to the Litvinov–O'Grady agreement. The British government's claim for financial compensation, sent to the NKID in September the same year, was ignored by Chicherin.[10]

Unlike his compatriot, Davison was much less fortunate because of his involvement in a fuel supply fraud. According to the Cheka version, some of the funds obtained from the sale of gasoline were channelled to MI6 agents in Russia. Arrested on the charge of contacting the Secret Intelligence Service, Davison was executed on the night of 17 January 1920 without a trial.[11]

In late 1922–early 1923, the persecution of Russian clergymen intensified as well. To the list of accusations against them was added espionage on the instructions from Poland and other European countries. These indictments were supported by the information about the Polish leader, Joseph Pilsudski's plan to invade Soviet Russia and Weimar Germany in the coming summer.[12] Equally tragic was the fate of Russian Orthodox and Greco-Catholic hierarchy, when they deprecated frequent requisitions by the Cheka of values in cathedrals and monasteries. At the demonstrative trial in Moscow late in March 1923, seventeen priests received long prison sentences. The campaign of persecution faced strong condemnation by the Archbishops of Canterbury and York.[13] Repeated arrests of Christian clergymen, including several high-ranking Catholic priests in Belorussia, added more 'fuel to the fire' of public indignation in the West. The execution of the prelate Konstantin Budkievicz and a ten-year prison sentence to archbishop Jan Cieplak, both widely known in Europe for their pacifist and charitable activities, as well as the house arrest of Patriarch Tikhon led to widespread indignation in the West, making Curzon to request Hodgson, the British representative in the USSR, to demand explanation from the Bolshevik rulers.[14]

Curzon's patience in the relations with Moscow finally ran out after the detention of two British trawlers in the Russian territorial waters near Murmansk on 28 March 1923. The case triggered a heated parliamentary debate, during which Ronald Macneill, the parliamentary under-secretary for foreign affairs, confronted the MPs' grievances about Britain's vulnerability to Bolshevik attacks.[15] The Kremlin, in turn, expressed displeasure with the Foreign Office's refusal to accept Litvinov's appointment as the head of the Soviet trade mission to London.[16] Additionally, the Bolshevik leadership was frustrated by the failed attempts to confer with Whitehall's top officials on recent political developments.[17]

London's condemnation of the repressions fell on a deaf ear in Moscow. Moreover, Grigory Weinstein, the acting head of the NKID sub-department for the Entente states, replied to it in a deliberately rude manner, going as far as to mention recent British atrocities against the Irish national movement.[18] As a result, Hodgson refused to accept his note, making Weinstein to repeat it three days later, this time reminding the British diplomat of the cruelties against Indian nationalists.[19]

On 9 April 1923, two senior diplomatic experts – John Gregory and Edward O'Malley – reviewed the current Russian policy in a memorandum for the Cabinet. They made a critical enquiry into the 1921 trade agreement, pointing out to its repeated violations by Moscow. Betting on the Bolshevik government's weakness because of mass domestic social unrest and isolated position in world politics, Gregory and O'Malley recommended to carefully weigh all pros and cons of the accord's prolongation. Shortly afterwards Curzon secured Hodgson's opinion on the matter as well.[20]

On 11 April, the Association of British creditors of Russia submitted a proposal, backed by the Russian section of the London chamber of trade and industry, to recall the diplomatic mission from Moscow.[21] By the middle of the month, the clouds that were gathering over the Soviet mission in London forced Berzin and Klyshko, the aforementioned Bolshevik diplomats, to petition some Labour leaders to oppose the anti-Soviet campaign launched by the conservative mass-media.[22] In response, Arthur Henderson together with Arthur Smith, the LP parliamentary faction's chief whip, appealed to Bonar Law to evaluate all consequences of a breach in the relations with Russia.[23]

Nevertheless, Macneill announced in the House of Commons that the Cabinet was going to remit a stern warning to Moscow.[24] By early May, the British ruling elite's concerns about Russia's inappropriate both internal and external policy reached such a high level that even Lloyd George in a letter to Curzon, the acting prime minister for a short period, urged him to show firmness in tackling the 'Russian question'.[25] Against the backdrop of the German Ruhr crisis in Europe and the problem of Ireland being far from resolved, the Soviet-British tensions were rapidly growing during April 1923.

Early the following month, Curzon convened a Cabinet meeting to adopt a draft note to the Soviet government. 'We were unanimous in our support for his hard message to Russia', Leo Amery, then the First Lord of the Admiralty, penned in the diary on 2 May.[26] Meanwhile some conservative MPs again urged the Soviet mission to be evacuated from the UK. These calls predetermined the ultimatum tone of the memorandum, personally edited by Curzon, who committed Robert Hodgson, the diplomatic agent in Moscow, to deliver it to the NKID.[27] Litvinov's belated attempt to find a plausible excuse for the British trawlers' arrest, referring to gaps in the international law could not prevent the impending diplomatic crisis, especially since the Soviet border guards captured one more fishing boat *Lord Astor* on 7 May.[28]

The memorandum that Hodgson handed Litvinov the following day became known as the 'Curzon ultimatum' because of Britain's unprecedented claims to the Kremlin to fulfil them within ten days.[29] The strong remonstration provided the disavowing of Weinstein's notes, paying monetary compensation to the families of British subjects persecuted in Soviet Russia, abandoning repressions against clergymen, reducing Russian territorial waters' area, terminating support to all anti-British nationalist movements in Persia, Afghanistan and India as well as the recalling of the Bolshevik plenipotentiaries from Tehran and Kabul.[30]

The possibility of a full-scale armed conflict was evidenced by Macdonald's urgent cable to Chicherin on 10 May. The Labour leader pledged the people's commissar not to undertake prompt actions threatening open military hostilities. On the other hand, the NKID informed the Soviet trade delegates in London of a real possibility to leave the British capital in case of diplomatic rupture.[31]

On 11 May, Krassin took the floor at the Politburo meeting to warn about the consequences of the Comintern's subversive activities in the Oriental countries. Responding to this statement, Trotsky nevertheless claimed: 'We must put pressure on Britain in its vulnerable points (India, Afghanistan, Persia and Egypt). It would be foolish of us not to take advantage of it. But we do not need to completely severe relations!' Sharing this adventurist point of view, Dzerzhinsky similarly insisted on the continuation of the Comintern seditious operations: 'We have to endure the work, for its reduction or termination will give native tribes an impression of the Soviet government's impotence and remove them far from Moscow.' As a result, a special commission was established to settle the crisis. Krassin was ordered to immediately set off for London to negotiate with Curzon, while Radek was directed to gauge the attitude of other European powers towards British demarche during his trip to Berlin.

It was Trotsky and Litvinov who drafted the response to Curzon's claims. Some historians believed that Ransome, the British left-wing journalist mentioned in the beginning of the book, who was staying in Moscow in May 1923, mediated between Litvinov and Hodgson. On one side, the response Soviet note denounced all responsibilities for the anti-British activities by the Comintern activists in the East. Yet on the other – apart from renouncing Weinstein's provocative assertions – the counterclaims were also put forward. Thus, Moscow urged appropriate financial reimbursement to the families of twenty-six Baku commissars. Moreover, the Bolsheviks' regular references to exaggerations regarding the scale of political repressions in the USSR were added by the arguments of Britain's disregard for Soviet interests in the Black Sea Straits, East Galicia, Memel (Klaipeda), Bessarabia, etc.[32]

At the same time, Chicherin and Litvinov did their best to merely 'buy time', making use of disputes between European states during the culmination of the Ruhr crisis which had led to the occupation of this German province by French and Belgian troops.[33] The murder of Worowski, who was appointed the Soviet representative at the Lausanne conference's second stage, also played into the Bolsheviks' hands. Committed on 10 May by a young Russian refugee to avenge the execution of the Tsar's family, this assassination enabled the Kremlin to link it to Curzon's diplomatic demarche. Two days later, the national daily *Izvestiya* published an editorial headlined

'A New Approach by the British Imperialism', blaming London for the deterioration of bilateral relations after receiving 'lopsided and tendentious pieces of information'.³⁴

In the meantime, reports by British journalists together with the telegrams by Hodgson from Moscow and Thomas Preston, the general consul, from Petrograd, described demonstrations that took place in many big cities, such as Moscow, Petrograd, Kharkov, Baku, Tashkent on 10 and 12 May. The participants chanted 'Hands off Russia!', 'Say No to war!', while carrying anti-British slogans, such as 'Down with English lords and their henchmen!', 'Do not joke with fire, Mr. Curzon!', 'Smash lords in the face!', 'We demand revenge for Worowski's murder!' and even 'No to fascism!' Referring to Zinoviev's harangue at the entrance of the Taurus Palace in Petrograd, Preston apprised the Foreign Office of the reasons for the 'ultimatum' in the view of the Bolsheviks' leadership. These were Whitehall's desire 'to distract the attention of the British people from the domestic economic crisis', 'the Russian White emigrants' pressure upon ruling elites' and 'the European bourgeoisie's disappointment of the new economic policy carried out by the Bolshevik government'.³⁵

In his speech at the Moscow Soviet emergency plenary session on 12 May, Chicherin concentrated almost entirely on Curzon's personality. 'This political proponent of extreme reaction in diplomacy remains, as he has been repeatedly called, a psychological viceroy of India.'³⁶ Yet in a private conversation with Ransome Chicherin admitted that the 'Curzon memorandum' raised Great Britain's prestige, especially in Asia due to the condemnation of Soviet actions. The head of the NKID called Curzon's note a 'punishment of a naughty child', meaning the Soviet state.³⁷

The Bolshevik proponents in the UK attempted to rally industrial workers at the meetings of solidarity with the Soviets. On 6 May, that is even before the official presentation of the Curzon note to Litvinov, a mass demonstration organized by the Communists and some left-wing LP members with the assistance of the Comintern activists took place in Birmingham. The protesters decried the Cabinet's aggressive political course, claiming that Britain could not afford the rupture of commercial relations with the Soviet republic which brought at least £12 million profit a year.³⁸ Shortly afterwards the TUC National united council unanimously endorsed continuation of economic collaboration at a meeting in the Trafalgar Square under the slogans 'Down with war!' and 'Anglo-Russian trade agreement must be maintained!'³⁹

On 25 May, another rally of several thousand took place in the British capital, during which some Labour activists called for a peaceful settlement of the conflict. Late in May–early in June, the Committees of action as well as the trade-union meetings in Nottingham, Liverpool, Newcastle, Dandy and other big cities petitioned the government for similar purpose.⁴⁰

Krassin, in his turn, gave an interview to the *Izvestiya* on the eve of his departure to London. He did not exclude the eventual reorientation of Soviet purchases to other European markets and the liquidation of ARCOS, in case Britain ventured to break up relations with Russia. The following day Krassin flew from Moscow to London, escorted by two leading Soviet economic experts.⁴¹ On 15 May, he conferred with some prominent UK politicians in London. Describing the unfavourable impression of these contacts in a letter to his spouse, Krassin remarked: 'Anxiety and excitement in England is tremendous; the majority certainly opposes the rupture, yet Curzon is strong enough to disrupt relations and will tear up [the trade agreement], should we not make concessions on all the important points.'[42]

At the Cabinet's sitting on the same day, the ministers criticized the Soviet government's reply. Curzon who chaired the meeting on behalf of diseased Bonar Law was supported by his colleagues in the dissatisfaction with the Kremlin's response. However, the ministers authorized him to hold a parley with Krassin and grant a few more days to Moscow to decide on the 'ultimatum'. Lloyd-Graeme, now the president of the Board of Trade, was assigned to explain to MPs that the UK benefited nothing from the Anglo-Soviet agreement of 1921.[43]

Two days later, Curzon met Krassin in the presence of Crowe, Macneill and Gregory. As if anticipating a tough discussion, the Soviet emissary immediately claimed that he had arrived not for closing the Russian mission in the event of rupture, but in order to understand the Cabinet's motivation for such a demarche.[44] As Gregory recalled later, 'Lord Curzon received Krassin like a gentleman, and watching them closely at the same table for two or three days in succession, I felt it was quite possible for them to do business together.'[45]

When the foreign secretary expressed his view on the anti-British propaganda launched by the Kremlin in Asia, Krassin tried to persuade Curzon that each case required a separate investigation. Nevertheless, the chef of the Foreign Office urged additional guarantees from the Soviet government. The most important was that Moscow should abstain from any action abroad which might be regarded as hostile to the UK's interests.[46] Krassin, in return, gained time for the continuation of discussion because the next meeting was appointed on 22 May, although it occurred a day later due to the government's crisis. It was caused by Bonar Law's resignation and Curzon's failed endeavour to replace him as a new prime minister.[47] Meanwhile the NKID received another British memorandum rejecting new Soviet guarantees.[48]

During his second meeting with Curzon, the Soviet emissary assured him of Moscow's willingness to release British trawlers, conclude a fishing convention and provide financial compensations of £3,000 to Harding and £10,000 to Davison's family. Weinstein's notes were officially disavowed while the Cabinet was offered to resolve all problems in the East at a special conference as soon as possible.[49] As a result, on 23 May, Krassin expressed cautious optimism for the first time during the trip in a message to his wife: 'I am still unable to tell you how the situation is going to develop, but it looks like there will be no breach.'[50] Concurrently, the Bolshevik diplomat circulated a summary of the talks with Curzon to Chicherin. As Krassin remarked he was confident in the relaxation of the Anglo-Soviet present because of the Soviet government's compliant stance and the shift of the Cabinet's head – Stanley Baldwin instead of Bonar Law, who was terminally ill, but in no case Curzon. Yet Krassin drew to the following conclusion: 'My overall impression, also shared by Berzin [his deputy in the UK], is that the break-up of the relations can only be avoided by our concessions on all the main points.'[51]

The Cabinet members presided by Baldwin vigorously debated the way out of the impasse. Contemporary analysts left no doubt about a possible rupture greatly annoying the Bolsheviks. The experts assumed the Kremlin was leaning towards a compromise, despite their open Anglophobia. Obviously, they were ready to make far-reaching concessions to Whitehall up to the consent to recall their plenipotentiaries in Tehran and Kabul.[52]

Reviewing Krassin's diplomacy from today's standpoint, one should take into consideration the fact that he fought simultaneously on the 'two fronts' – one against his British counterparts and the other against opponents inside the Soviet officialdom, such as Trotsky, Zinoviev, Kamenev, embarking on the unscrupulous inner-party race for leadership in the party and state. Besides that, Chicherin and Litvinov were engaged in their perpetual scramble for decisive influence upon the diplomatic staff.[53] However, both the people's commissar and his first deputy criticized Krassin for 'exceeding his commission' in dealing with Curzon. As Hodgson informed London, Krassin allegedly said before leaving for London: 'Whenever they [the Kremlin mandarins] get into a mess, they have to come to me to get them out.'[54]

On 28 May, Curzon and Krassin met for the third time to clarify all the remaining misunderstanding.[55] The following day, Gregory handed Krassin another memorandum, differing in tone from the previous two notes. The Cabinet agreed to cease indictments as well as to abandon antagonistic propaganda. However, it was reluctant to further postpone the final de-escalation of the diplomatic conflict.[56] Four days later, Krassin wrote to his wife: 'How long I shall stay here, it is not yet known; if the case is settled without a break with England, then, perhaps, I shall return to Moscow on 15 June.'[57]

Finally, the Soviet government remitted a memorandum to London which, according to Litvinov's revelation in a letter to Berzin, meant 'capitulation on all points'.[58] Drafted by Chicherin, it included a pledge to put an end to the anti-British propagandist campaign in Asian countries in return for the British denial of support to Russian emigrant groups in the UK. The note also restated the proposal to convene a bilateral conference to settle international problems of mutual concern.[59]

Five days later, the Politburo meeting presided by Trotsky endorsed the additional instructions to Krassin. They recommended not only to mobilize British left-wing factions to promote bilateral economic cooperation but also to address French diplomatic circles for mediation between Moscow and London. Concomitantly, Chicherin was ordered to immediately conclude the Soviet-Persian treaty and proceed with the development of the Soviet-Turkish collaboration as the countermeasures against Britain's expansion in the Middle East.[60] In the meantime, Hodgson informed Curzon of the rumours circulating in Moscow that the British government wanted to reduce pressure upon Moscow in order to deprive the most extreme Bolshevik leaders of a plausible excuse to oppose reconciliation with London. On the other hand, he warned the Foreign Office of the Kremlin's purpose to bully the Cabinet with a comprehensive Soviet-German trade agreement that would close the Russian market to the UK export.[61]

In reply to the Bolshevik memorandum, Curzon notified Krassin of the UK government's satisfaction with the acceptance of practically all British requests. To demonstrate it, the head of the Foreign Office allayed his position regarding financial compensation to British citizens (excluding Harding and Davison) for the loss of their property, insisting no more on the Soviet plenipotentiary's instant departure from Persia.[62] This gesture of 'good will' enabled Karakhan to communicate to Angora,

Tehran, Kabul and Peking that the conflict with Britain was over without 'great concessions' being made by Moscow to London.[63]

The settlement of the diplomatic conflict in a compromised manner was achieved owing to the British public fears of a new large-scale war between the West and Soviet Russia, which would inevitably cause huge casualties and financial loses. In the second place, the Bolshevik government met almost all the Cabinet's requests. Third, Curzon's personal fiasco to take the prime minister's office certainly reduced his interest in the crisis' prolongation, making it possible to shirk military confrontation with Moscow. Additionally, the disinclination of great powers to follow Britain in the conflict with Russia also defused tensions.[64]

At the same time, the Bolshevik propagandists interpreted their defeat as an unconditional victory. The Soviet press published 'letters by angry workers and peasants', unanimously condemning Whitehall, especially Curzon. Even matchboxes manufactured in the USSR during this period carried the image of an airplane with a fig sign of the propeller and the caption: 'Our reply to Curzon!'[65] As for the NKID's assessments, Chicherin and Karakhan instructed the plenipotentiaries in Turkey, Persia, Afghanistan and China on 4 September 1923: 'The crisis has revealed the power of those Cabinet ministers who value relations with the Soviet republic.' The peoples' commissar urged his colleagues to propagate 'peaceful coexistence', avoiding 'the petty clashes of Soviet agents with their British opponents, even if it was pursued in the core of revolutionary ideology'. It is worth mentioning his phrase about the need to fulfil the obligations before Britain in order Soviet Russia to be able to act as a bridge in the 'nonviolent mediation between the East and the West'.[66] However, all these revelations seemed merely an outlier contradicting the idea of 'world revolution'. Indeed, a few months later, after the Kremlin's anxiety had calmed down, Chicherin reiterated the previous assessments of the 'Curzon ultimatum' as 'the greatest attempt of adversaries to undermine our international position', which ended in their complete failure while 'demonstrating our [Soviet] strength'.[67]

It was this official perception of the conflict's outcome which configured grounds for the Soviet official consideration of the 1923 crisis.[68] According to British observers, it stunned the Soviet officialdom and most of all the NKID's top bureaucrats.[69] As, for example, one American journalist, personally acquainted with Chicherin and other Kremlin leaders, remarked in his book: 'The Bolsheviks, nevertheless, feared the political and economic consequences of a break to such an extent that they decided to do what was not consonant with right and national honour to satisfy claims which, in their opinion, had not the remotest justification.'[70] Some modern authors also emphasize that the 'Curzon ultimatum' compelled the Comintern to temporarily shut down its activities in Central Asia that was viewed as a bridgehead to India.[71]

Although it was Krassin who mostly contributed to the settlement of the international incident, he was given a cold reception after returning to Moscow. While talking to his closer relatives and friends, Krassin, in turn, pointed out that the Soviet mandarins' incompetence in the issues of domestic and foreign policy remained incredible.[72] At the same time, Weinstein, the 'hero' of the diplomatic scandal, was replaced in the NKID's staff by Santeri Nuorteva, a Swedish Communist, Karakhan was dispatched as a plenipotentiary to China, whereas Litvinov was suspended from office for two months for 'misconducting the Anglo-Soviet relations'.[73]

Summing up Britain's policy towards Soviet Russia from July 1921 to September 1923, the Foreign Office experts stressed the Kremlin's 'complete surrender' to Curzon's famous note. Indeed, they had every reason to maintain that 'the completeness of this surrender itself was unexpected, and perhaps of even greater importance than the surrender itself was the indication, which it gave of the extent to which the Soviet Government felt itself isolated amongst the nations and of the corresponding value which it placed on its relations with His Majesty Government'.[74] Even two years later when the Soviet-British relations deteriorated in a similar way, Gregory considered it necessary to refer to the precedent of the 'panic in the Bolsheviks camp' as well as to 'the concessions which they had made on all but two minor points'.[75] Curzon's letter to Robert Crew-Milnes, the ambassador to France, attested to his expectation of the Kremlin leaders to behave 'more carefully' in world politics, at least for some time, henceforth.[76] *The Times*, in turn, congratulated Curzon on the 'refreshing vigour' of his handling 'a tyranny more bloodthirsty than that of any tsar', while the Cabinet could 'record a highly successful issue to the dispute'.[77]

Regarding present views on the matter, it is worth drawing attention to several important details that have eluded historians' scope of research. First, it was the so-called Ten-Year Rule, adopted in August 1919. According to this regulation, any British government, regardless of party affiliation, was obliged to avoid a 'full-scale war' during the decade, which made it possible to avoid a military conflict with Soviet Russia in 1923.[78] Second, the German factor also contributed to the settlement of the conflict, since Whitehall was bound to concentrate on the situation in the frontier area between France, Belgium and the Weimar republic.[79] Finally, it is appropriate to correlate political developments in Europe with the situation in the Middle and Far East where both Russia and Britain confronted nationalist movements under the banner of Muslim radicalism.[80] Whereas the focus of the Comintern's anti-British activities was shifting towards China, Chicherin wrote to Stalin on 8 January 1924 about the projects of supporting the government of Sun Yisian by the establishment of a training centre, dispatching military instructors to the Far East and publishing pro-Communist newspapers there. For his part, Karakhan advertised the creation of a united anti-imperialist Soviet-Chinese front in the world politics.[81]

A notable development in the post-crisis period was the visit of eighty British top manufacturers and commercial managers to the USSR. Initiated by the newly appointed prime minister's cousin Francis Baldwin, himself an industrial tycoon, the trip was undertaken in August 1923, in order not only to alleviate the negative impression of the recent diplomatic scandal but to outstrip competitors in the scramble for the Russian market.[82] The visit was a success, as evidenced by Baldwin's interview to the leading newspapers, such as *The Times*, *Morning Post* and *Evening Standard*. He pointed out to a tremendous potentiality of mutual trade between the countries, able to 'work hand in hand in accordance with the interests of their nations'. The visitors returned home with a feeling of the USSR, proclaimed as early as on 30 December 1922, being ready to trade with Britain, although the turnover's volume appeared to be limited by Russia's solvency.[83]

Meanwhile the tension was about to escalate again in the end of summer because of the appointment of Christian Rakovski, the chairman of the Ukrainian SNK, to the post of the diplomatic agent in the UK.[84] The minutes of the Bolshevik Central committee's meetings attested to the serious disputes on domestic affairs between Stalin and Rakovski, who supported Trotsky in the inner-party struggle for Lenin's political legacy. It was no coincidence, therefore, that Stalin persistently secured Rakovski's promotion to the diplomatic position in Europe to keep him away from Moscow, as

Figure 11 Christian Rakovski, Soviet charge d'affaires, 1924. Photo courtesy of Wikimedia Commons (public domain).

Krassin confessed in a private letter to his spouse.[85] However, the two statesmen' views on international problems seemed practically identical, for Rakovski, as the former official leader of the Ukrainian republic, strongly criticized the British diplomacy in the diplomatic crisis around Curzon's note. Besides that, he even published an Anglophobe leaflet in mid-1923, branding Curzon as a 'die-hard colonial imperialist' and called for the destruction of the British empire by the Comintern.[86]

Nevertheless, on 25 June, Chicherin turned to the Foreign Office for the agreement on Rakovski's appointment.[87] Moreover, the NKID undertook urgent steps to convince London of the nominee's high-ranking status amongst the Soviet officialdom. Rakovski was promptly included in the NKID's collegium as one more Chicherin's deputy, while his anti-British pamphlet had been withdrawn from sale, being interpreted by the Kremlin as an excessive emotional reaction to the declaration of the 'infamous ultimatum'.[88]

On 11 August, Curzon demanded the Foreign Office and the MI6 to investigate whether Rakovski indeed vilified him at public rallies in Russia. Some Labour frontbenchers contributed to the settlement of the growing conflict. For instance, Henderson sent a message to Baldwin persuading him to permit Rakovski to come to the UK. Finally, Curzon appealed to the French authorities to clarify the situation with the Russian emigrant press demonizing Rakovski as a fanatical Anglophobe.[89] Having carefully examined the intelligence about him, while accepting Moscow's assurances of Rakovski's non-involvement in any anti-British action, did Curzon regard it possible to approve the Soviet emissary's arrival in the UK.[90]

But before Rakovski appeared on the banks of the Thames, the Bolshevik Central committee's plenary session took place on 23 September. Zinoviev spoke of the coming socialist revolution in Germany and avowed a provocative idea to create the United States of workers and peasants' republics with the USSR and the bolshevized Germany as their core. Regarding Britain, the chairman of the Comintern emphasized the menace of the Baltic Sea's occupation, despite the deficit of active land troops as well as the preponderance of pacifist sentiments among the UK middle-class.[91]

Rakovski's initial reports from London revealed the distasteful reception the Foreign Office and public had given to him. 'It is only after a few weeks, I am able to navigate more or less correctly in British domestic affairs,' he wired to Moscow on 6 October 1923. 'So far, I can hardly read English newspapers and ... conversations remain to me the main source of information.' Because of the lack of diplomatic experience, Rakovski naively intended to influence Whitehall's position on the Soviet Union's full recognition by official London through those representatives of dominions who had assembled in London for the regular Imperial conference.[92]

Meanwhile a notable event in the economic sphere of bilateral relations was the opening of the Soviet-British society for refunding grain export. It was set up in London on 15 October 1923, which signalled Russia's return to the world cereal markets after a decade-long pause. It is worth mentioning that the USSR provided the UK with significant volumes of raw materials during 1923–4: corn – by 2.3 per cent of the total British import, flax and hemp – 12.4 per cent, pressed cakes – 14.4 per cent, horse hair – 29.3 per cent, bristles – 34.3 per cent, oil products and timber – up to 50.1 and 52.6 per cent, respectively.[93] The importance of mutual economic collaboration was also demonstrated by the Anglo-Russian trade chamber's appeal to the British association of commercial chambers on 24 October to fully resume diplomatic relations as well as to increase the bilateral trade turnover to resolve the debt problem.[94]

Furthermore, the Society for Cultural Relations with the USSR was established in London in the second half of 1923. Some well-known writers, artists and academicians, such as Bernard Shaw, Herbert Wells, on the British side, Alexei Tolstoi, Valerii Briusov, Konstantin Yuon, Aleksander Fersman, Nikolai Marr, on the Soviet side, joined this organization from the very beginning. Four years later, it was converted into the Society of the Friends of the USSR.[95]

Despite these positive mutations, all Rakovski's attempts to get his credentials to be presented to Baldwin ended in a fiasco. That is why he sent them to the Foreign Office by a registered letter on 16 October – an unprecedented situation in diplomatic history.[96] Two weeks later, the Soviet diplomatic agent was finally able to confer with John Gregory, the head of the Foreign Office Northern department, who immediately raised the problem of the £180 million Russian debt to Britain and financial compensation to British citizens whose property was confiscated.[97] Yet Rakovski, for his part, reminded Gregory that the USSR needed foreign financial credits, without which Russo-British commercial relations could not be restarted.[98]

The most beneficial phenomenon for the Kremlin leadership was an evident consensus inside the LP on the full diplomatic recognition of the USSR, although various cohorts of politicians interpreted it in their own ways. For example, Henderson supported Russia's return to the comity of nations in order 'to resolve the problem of unemployment in Britain', 'to tame' the Bolsheviks and neutralize Communist influence in the UK. Macdonald pitched an idea to offer to the USSR the scheme of granting British loans, applied earlier to Austria. Some left-wing activists, such as Henry Brailsford, Arthur Ponsonby, George Trevelyan together with Sidney and Beatrice Webb, offered Rakovski their assistance as unbiased public intermediaries between London and Moscow.[99]

But the Tory staying in power prevented Whitehall from taking decisive steps towards diplomatic normalization. Only the formation of the first Labour government in January 1924 enabled both London and Moscow to bring the seven-year confrontation to an end.

10

The USSR's recognition by Britain and its repercussions

> *This agreement is the recognition by bourgeoisie of the gains which our revolution has scored because of our internal consolidation*
> Lev Kamenev in the public oration, 6 September 1924¹

The events of 1924 marked a turning point in the history of international affairs. The adoption of the reparation scheme by Charles Dawes' committee on 16 August, as well as the signing of the Geneva protocol on the prevention of military aggression by the League of Nations' General Assembly on 2 October, consolidated the Versailles world order. It was against this backdrop that Moscow and London made a breakthrough in their relations. Yet, as it had happened on many previous occasions, the euphoria was short-tempered, though both sides laid a seminal foundation for further collaboration.

Because the Tories were defeated at the general elections on 6 December 1923, three factions – Conservative, Liberal and Labour – divided their mandates in nearly equal proportion, which led to the so-called 'hung parliament'. Thus, Labour was given a chance to constitute the first socialist Cabinet, albeit of minority. As a result, they governed the UK for almost ten months – from 22 January to 8 November 1924 with Macdonald occupying a dual position – that of the prime and foreign minister. Like Lloyd George before him, he believed that London should encourage Moscow to develop political, economic and cultural ties with Western countries.²

Labour's rise to power almost coincided with a prolonged pause in the bilateral contacts. While the Soviet side anticipated a shift in the UK political course, the British had followed a line of 'aloofness' towards Russia until the scramble for Lenin's political legacy inside the Bolshevik officialdom came to an end, on the one hand, and the results of the new economic policy became evident, on the other.³ Nonetheless, the delegates of the TUC annual conference in September 1923 petitioned the government for a complete diplomatic recognition of the USSR by Britain. The resolution found response in various social cohorts which was evidenced by the statement of the Association of trade chambers on 15 January 1924.⁴ Rakovski also sought to open some promising vistas for eventual cooperation. While intensifying personal contacts with

Figure 12 James Ramsay Macdonald, prime minister, 1924. Photo courtesy of Wikimedia Commons (public domain).

public activists and journalists, he concentrated on the issues of disarmament as well as on the role of the League of Nations, not to mention the economic reconstruction of Europe.[5]

Requesting the Foreign Office for a review of the Soviet-British relations, Macdonald received a memorandum, composed by John Gregory. Among other important items, the head of the Northern department also mentioned the revision of treaties concluded by the UK with the Russian tsarist and Provisional governments, regulation of navigation and fishing in Soviet territorial waters, termination of Communist propaganda and financial compensation for British property confiscated by Bolshevik authorities.[6]

The pressure from left-wing MPs who believed in the necessity of reproachment prompted Macdonald to send a private message to Rakovski on 12 January. The coming prime minister assured the Soviet representative of his sympathy with the recognition of the USSR, adding that it dominated the minds of both the LP members and British public opinion.[7] Consequently, at the first audience with George V on 22 January 1924, Macdonald alluded to the earliest recognition of the USSR motivating it by the other Entente governments' willingness to undertake a similar step.[8] The King did not object to this opinion but noted the unacceptability of obtaining credentials from the emissary of the regime responsible for the murder of his cousin's family. In the sovereign's view, the level of diplomatic representation should not exceed charge d'affaires.[9]

It was Lenin's death on 21 January 1924 that accelerated the process.[10] Because no more substantial obstacles were standing in this way, Macdonald remitted a special note on the USSR's recognition to Moscow on 1 February, supplementing it with a notable formulation – 'on the former Russian Empire's territories, which accede to its [the Soviet government's] power'. This caveat provided London with a necessary room for political manoeuvres in the relations with the Baltic nations and other independent states that might emerge in case of Russia's overall break-up. At the same time, the status of both Soviet and British diplomatic agents was raised to the level of charge d'affaires.[11]

Additionally, Macdonald circulated a private letter to Chicherin, accentuating those spheres of economic and cultural relations which seemed to him particularly prospective.[12] The response by the peoples' commissar was full of elation: 'When I [Chicherin] learned the results of the elections, my first thought was: if we could only work together with the British Labour party for the sake of a comprehensive settlement! It is a unique opportunity … "The elephant" and "the whale" are striving together towards universal peace, what a sight!'[13]

On 11 February, Macdonald suggested to Rakovski to summon a conference aimed at the discussion of all current challenges which the UK and the USSR confronted.[14] Having considered the British draft, the Kremlin offered the so-called 'pacifist cooperation', while bearing in mind the precedent of the international seminar on naval armaments which was held in Geneva and Rome during the second half of the same month. In Moscow's view, the Soviet-British collaboration could lead to the universal disarmament as well as to granting financial loans to the states suffering from devastation caused by the world war, and to the revision of the maritime traffic through the Black Sea Straits.[15]

On 5 February, the Soviet daily *Izvestiya* published Rakovski's photo on the front page supplementing it with a triumphant commentary on the recognition of the Bolshevik regime by the 'most significant imperialist state'. The following day, it issued not only an interview with Krassin regarding the Soviet-British economic contacts, but also a letter by Hodgson to the editorial board about political consequences. The diplomat stressed that 'the complete and happy establishment of the Russo-British relations' meant the beginning of 'a new era'. 'I hope', wrote Hodgson, 'we will have the atmosphere that both Great Britain and the USSR so desperately want and need'.[16] However, in his secret reports, the Foreign Office political intelligence department informed London of different attitudes in the Soviet society to the recognition. If some Bolshevik top bureaucrats anticipated lavish financial credits, common public remained apathetic, while intellectuals, who had survived the Cheka repressions, were confused with Britain's 'betrayal' of their opposition to the Communist dictatorship.[17] Two weeks later, Rakovski gave an extensive interview to the *Izvestiya*. After dwelling upon the impact of the reparation crisis on the USSR's diplomatic recognition, he emphasized the unconditional nature of this political move.[18]

Pondering on the reasons for recognition, some researchers indicated the necessity to restore economic ties, maintain international order and settle political conflicts in the European central and eastern regions. The present author does not share the opinion that the recognition was just a gift from London.[19] Instead it was due to a combination of reasons, including people's craving for peace and public diplomacy.[20] At the same time, at least three different approaches were typical for British ruling elites: some politicians envisaged the further expansion of contacts without formulating surplus conditions, others advocated a limited collaboration, in case Moscow acceded to principal British demands, while a third group rejected any kind of cooperation.[21] Whitehall's deliberations on the coming conference with the Kremlin emissaries lasted several weeks. On 26 March, the Foreign Office presented a historical survey of the Anglo-Soviet relations, including the epic of the Entente's armed intervention against Russia.[22]

A week later, Gregory submitted the draft programme of diplomatic consultations to the Cabinet's attention.[23] In order to ensure domestic stability, the government set up a five-member committee on industrial conflicts, commissioning it to examine the ongoing surge of strikes. The committee's hidden agenda was the investigation of the Comintern's involvement in subsiding strikes through the clandestine channels supervised by the CPGB members.[24]

The Kremlin officials, in turn, established several working groups in the People's commissariats for foreign affairs and foreign trade. Their representatives were incorporated in the commission under Rakovski to draft the Soviet delegation's platform. A note by Rakovski on the tactics at the London conference was submitted to the Politburo and the SNK's consideration. On 1 April, Krassin presented his personal point of view as well.[25]

Chicherin suggested that the principles of 'peaceful coexistence', declared in Genoa two years ago, should form the basis for diplomatic bargaining with the British side. As Trotsky declared at the public meeting in Tiflis on 11 April 1924, the Labour Cabinet's staying in power created a favourable atmosphere to reconcile with the UK. Litvinov shared this view, calling for the development of relations with Britain and France, but not to the detriment of other great powers, especially, the United States.[26]

Because many authors have already narrated the history of the Soviet-British conference rather extensively, it appears unnecessary to describe its procedure in all details. Instead, this author prefers to focus on the episodes of critical importance for further developments.

To begin with the fact that the Bolshevik representatives outnumbered their British partners in the proportion of twenty to eighteen experts.[27] Rakovski led the Soviet delegation because of the Cabinet's disagreement with Litvinov's appointment, though the latter nevertheless arrived in London for a short period in June 1924 to help in the search of the way out of the conference's stalemate. Arthur Ponsonby, then the parliamentary under-secretary for foreign affairs, chaired the British delegates with Macdonald being the nominal head.[28] As Ponsonby considered, Britain spent more money and material resources on the intervention against Soviet Russia than any other Entente power had done. The UK ruling circles became, therefore, morally responsible for the former ally's reintegration to the family of European countries. In Ponsonby's view, isolated and humiliated Russia posed a serious threat to the international order, which required the normalization of relations with all leading geopolitical actors.[29]

As one of the Soviet experts described the situation in London, all the right-wing British newspapers unanimously declared that from now on His Royal Majesty's country and the British people were 'desecrated' because the 'most genuine sinners' – the Bolsheviks – were about to land 'on the banks of the Thames'.[30] Characteristically, the directors of City banks warned the Labour Cabinet against making an accord with the Bolsheviks too hastily. In their view, the government ought to start negotiations only on the terms of the Bolsheviks' acknowledgement of foreign debts. The bankers also called for the restitution of British citizens' property, supplying it with the proper guarantees against confiscation. They urged the restoration of independent courts and the abolition of the state trade monopoly as well as the real termination of anti-British propaganda.[31] Additionally, some key Cabinet members, such as Snowden, then the chancellor of the exchequer, objected to the allocation of loans to the USSR in exchange for the Soviet purchase of goods manufactured by British industrial companies.

The official heads of delegations – Macdonald and Rakovski opened the Anglo-Soviet conference on 14 April 1924. The delegates formed four groups which were to debate the UK debt claims to the USSR along with the Bolsheviks' plea for loans. The rest of the agenda included the regulation of trade, navigation and fishing, revision of previous treaties and measures to be taken for universal disarmament.[32]

Two weeks later, while speaking at the meeting of the Bolshevik party Leningrad committee, Kamenev amounted the UK financial requirements to the Soviet government to 10,639 billion gold roubles, including the pre-war loans of 2,450 billion, the war debts of 5,373 billion and the interest rate of 2,816 billion. At the same time, the Soviet counterclaims to Britain for the armed intervention averaged 2 billion gold roubles.[33] Besides, the Kremlin urged the UK to return the gold bullions that had been deposited by the tsarist government in the Bank of England in 1915. Simultaneously, Moscow implored London for a credit of £60 million to be granted in three annual tranches (soon after this sum was reduced to £30 million).[34]

Meanwhile dissonant views on the relations with Moscow contented among the Labour Party and the TUC activists, which was evidenced by the publication of the memorandum on 16 May 1924.[35] As Austen Chamberlain communicated to his sister while summing up the Labour government's diplomatic performance, 'Ramsay did well with the Dawes report [on German reparations] and Egypt, but he has left an awful mess about Russia and an equally bad and even more delicate situation in regard to the Geneva protocol'.[36]

In these circumstances, the position of the Liberal Party vacillating between the need for normalization with Moscow and the scare of the 'Bolsheviks' eventual aggression' seemed crucial for the success of negotiations.[37] While the resolution adopted by the annual congress of the National Liberal federation in May 1924 stated the significance of Russia's reconstruction for the consolidation of international order and appealed to the USSR 'to sincerely and energetically cooperate with the British people', the leading Liberals insisted on the Kremlin's recognition of foreign debts and the non-use of credit funds for the rearmament of the Red Army.[38]

Facing the criticism from the opposition, the Cabinet tried to shift the agenda from economic problems to international issues. Macdonald, Ponsonby and their colleagues argued in the left-wing newspapers that in order Russia could restore as a great power, Britain should bring Moscow to the League of Nations, erasing in every possible way the Russian people's historic memory of the British contribution to the Allied intervention.[39]

The Soviet delegates used the parleys for the settlement of geopolitical controversies as well. On 30 April, Rakovski raised the question of Bessarabia, occupied by the Romanian troops with the Entente's accord as early as in 1918, touching upon the reanimation of former Russian consulates in India and protesting the communists' persecution by the Scotland Yard.[40] Even though both sides intended to finish consultations in three months, most of the plenary sessions led to endlessly bickering and blaming the opposite side. 'The point was', recalled Gregory later, 'that it was only by utterly disregarding all received methods of diplomacy and business that we [the British] had any chance of establishing a genuine relationship with this abnormal state [the USSR]'.[41]

The scramble between Trotsky and the Kremlin 'triumvirate' of Stalin, Zinoviev and Kamenev also affected the diplomatic consultations because the extremists sharply criticized the 'Labour government's hypocrisy in dealing with Moscow'.[42] The Comintern instructions to the CPGB to 'politically grip the Workers' party by throat' in order to destabilize it from inside contradicted the NKID's official position. The Kremlin's disappointment with the negotiations proceeding at a slow pace as well as the declarations of the Comintern Fifth congress in the summer of 1924 shifted the earlier Kremlin's benevolent attitude to the socialist government. Trotsky and Zinoviev in their public lectures continued to regularly define the Labour policy as 'conformism in practice', stigmatizing the prime minister as 'a lackey of British rentiers and shareholders', or, what sounded even more dismissively – 'a butler of George V'.[43] Infuriated by these attacks, Macdonald wrote to Rakovski: 'I now note a recurrence of vituperation on the part of Mr. Zinoviev which passes all bounds of decent political controversy'.[44] Despite recommendations by Ponsonby regarding the government's guarantees for the loan that Moscow craved to receive in the Bank of England, Rakovski and Litvinov failed to find a way out of the impasse.[45]

A new round of talks with Leslie Urquhart that were conducted through the Main committee on economic concessions and joint-stock companies, established by the SNK decree on 4 April 1922, had additional impact on the Soviet-British negotiations.

Although Krassin criticized a new draft contract in the memorandum to the Politburo on 12 May 1924, the Kremlin leadership continued to discuss it, supposing the conclusion of accord with Urquhart would contribute to the successful termination of the Soviet-British negotiations. Interestingly, some Bolshevik officials even suggested to secretly purchase the shares in Urquhart's company to make him 'an ally' amid other European industrial tycoons.[46]

The negotiations paused for several weeks which allowed London and Moscow to draft treaties: the British project was presented to the public on 5 July and the Soviet – a week later. According to Gregory, the Cabinet advocated a kind of normalization, resembling the previous offer to Moscow by Lloyd George in 1922. As Ponsonby claimed on 18 July, both sides would miss a chance of rapprochement if they did not conclude a general treaty.[47] Having secured the consent of City bankers to accept the government's guarantees for the loan of £30 million, the ministers returned to debating the issue on 30 July.[48] Finally, a compromise was reached on two key conditions – the settlement of the Russian debt and the endorsement of the treaty by the dominions. While expounding Whitehall's position, Ponsonby stressed that the failure of the talks would destabilize the situation in Europe and lead to the rise of unemployment because of Russia consigning the contracts for manufactured goods and equipment to Britain's rivals. He recommended Macdonald to agree to a loan to the USSR if two-thirds of its volume were allocated to the purchase of goods manufactured in Britain. Ponsonby argued that the conference had to result in the conclusion of the diplomatic acts which would be collected in the official White Book and ratified by the Parliament in the autumn of 1924. Further consultations with the Russian bond's holders were to follow the signature of a special protocol about the non-existence of claims from British companies and individuals to the Soviet Union as the legal successor of the Russian empire.[49]

The Kremlin leaders, in turn, conceded a point regarding compensation for the damage caused by the Allied intervention that amounted to £180 million, as well as partly acquiesced with Russia's financial obligations to Britain which they were ready to discuss at a special meeting. All the considered compromises opened the door to the general treaty as well as to the agreement on navigation and trade.[50]

Yet the situation changed after Rakovski came back to London on 2 August 1924 with the instruction to recall the Soviet side's former promise to compensate British citizens, who had lost property in Soviet Russia. This time Moscow agreed to merely consider their petitions to the Bolshevik government without taking on any concrete obligations.[51] During the eighth plenary session on 4 August, which lasted nearly twenty hours, the Soviet draft did not consort with that amended by the British side.[52] The main stumbling block remained the problem of money compensation for nationalized property. Curiously, the Cabinet members split in their opinion almost evenly: if one half of ministers were insisting on the prolongation of negotiations, another demanded to stop them because of the impossibility to reach the solution appropriate to both sides.[53]

At that moment, the parliamentary backbenchers, mostly left-wingers, such as George Lansbury, Edmund Morel, Albert Purcell, intervened in the negotiations, urging the British delegation to continue discussion.[54] This demarche led to the conference's seminal plenary session on 7 August, which ended only by noon. At 3.30 pm Rakovski and Ponsonby fixed the treaties, one of which comprised eighteen and the other – twenty paragraphs. Four hours later, the under-secretary announced the closure of negotiations in the House of Commons. The 8th of August 1924 – the day when the final eleventh session was held – became the date of signing the treaties.[55]

Nearly all Soviet leading periodicals published the NKID's statement about this event, focusing on the Cabinet's assurances of granting a large loan to the USSR.[56] On 12 August, Rakovski avowed six political declarations on behalf of the Soviet government, regarding universal disarmament, the territorial controversies with neighbouring states and the regime of maritime traffic through the Black Sea Straits.[57] At the Moscow Soviet's plenary session on 20 August, Kamenev, Chicherin and Rakovski, who returned home for a short-term vacation, spoke about the diplomatic victory scored by the Kremlin in the negotiations with the British.[58] The proceedings of the Politburo's meeting on 21 August demonstrated the Kremlin leadership's desire to further diplomatic contacts with London. They planned to allocate 60 per cent of the loan to the purchase of British equipment as well as to grant an economic concession to the 'Becos' company, owned by the Baldwins and to organize the president of the Midland Bank's introductory tour across the USSR.[59]

The compromised nature of the Anglo-Soviet general treaty was seen in the Article 6 confirming the Kremlin's accord to expulse from the 1918 decree on nationalization of foreign property any reference to British subjects. Concomitantly, Moscow promised to recognize the claims by Russian bonds' holders in the amount of at least 50 per cent of their personal value. On the other hand, according to Article 12, the UK government committed itself to granting a loan to the USSR after the approval by the Parliament on conditions that would be discussed after the ratification procedure was over. Apart from economic items, the signatories pledged to refrain from any acts of hostility against each other on the territories of the British empire and the USSR.

However, no sooner than the ink had dried on the documents, they were mercilessly disparaged by Russian emigrant circles and British ruling elites, including the Liberals, whose pessimistic reaction became a cold shower to the Cabinet.[60] Symptomatically, conceptual divergences between the supporters of Lloyd George and Herbert Asquith within the Liberal Party did not prevent both statesmen from the condemnation of the treaties.[61] The Federation of industries issued a statement which maintained that they would not facilitate bilateral commercial ties while contradicting the principles of trade with other countries.[62] The Trade Chamber also argued that the agreements could not separate the issue of interstate claims from financial compensation to individuals.[63] Finally, many public associations as well as the governments of dominions expressed their deep concern about treaties' implementation.[64] Only the left-wing Labours, the National minority committees and the CPGB leadership congratulated Macdonald and Ponsonby on the results of the conference.[65]

In the meantime, the Cabinet suffered strong critics because of the so-called 'Campbell case'. John Campbell, a world war veteran, awarded for courage in the world war, joined the CPGB and was elected the member of its executive committee. Acting as the editor-in-chief of the *Workers Weekly*, he published on 25 July 1924 an open letter by Harry Pollitt, then the general secretary of the National minority movement, under the title 'Army and Industrial Conflicts'. Pollitt called on British soldiers and sailors 'not to turn arms against their proletarian brothers' and unite forces in a joint assault upon 'capitalists'.⁶⁶ As a result, on 5 August, the policemen examined the newspaper's editorial office, arresting Campbell for the alleged violation of the 1797 Incitement to Mutiny Act. He was jailed in defiance of the subsequent explanation that Pollitt merely urged British military not to be involved in the suppression of strikes by local authorities. A week later, however, the Attorney General, pressed by some Cabinet members, allowed Campbell to be released on bail of £200. This decision raised a public campaign of deprecations in mass media.⁶⁷

Because of the summer recess, the parliamentary debates had been delayed until 30 September. Shortly afterwards a series of public meetings and the newspaper publications demonstrated that British public was most outraged by the government's desire to hush up the scandal. After hearing Macdonald's slurred explanations on 8 October, the House of Commons established a commission to investigate the matter, which was regarded by the prime minister as a vote of no confidence to his Cabinet.

Even though Macdonald's decision to step down met a strong defiance by some Labour front-runners, he announced the dissolution of the Parliament which led to the snap election in two weeks. Yet this voluntary resignation by no means provided for a smooth return to power of the Tories. In fact, the British electorate needed a harsh shake to switch to the Conservatives. It was at this very moment that the ill-famous 'Zinoviev letter', also known as the 'Comintern' or 'Red letter', was published in the newspapers.⁶⁸ To understand the meaning of this puzzling matter which later received various interpretations, it is necessary, at least briefly, to expound the perception of the incident by ruling elites.⁶⁹

The Foreign Office permanent under-secretary Eire Crowe received a copy of the secret letter dispatched by Zinoviev to the CPGB activists. Otto Kuusinen, the secretary of the Comintern executive committee, and Ernst Reuter, one of its members, were responsible for the elaboration of the document together with Zinoviev. Apart from invectives against the LP for 'harmonious relations with bourgeoisie', the letter instructed British Communists to organize 'cells in all military units, particularly among those quartered in the large centers of the country, and also among factories working on munitions and at military store depots'.⁷⁰

Further evidence of the letter's authenticity was given to Ponsonby on 13 October. Deeply detesting Bolshevism, Crowe considered it significant to obtain a real evidence of the Kremlin's anti-British activities. For his part, Ponsonby decided to immediately inform Macdonald who was campaigning in industrial regions on the eve of the general election.⁷¹ Crowe recommended the prime minister to publish the copy of the letter in mass media and send a note of strong protest to the Soviet government.⁷²

Although Macdonald did not object to the publication, the Foreign Office top officials – Crow, Ponsonby and Gregory – focused on the note's wording as the original Comintern instructions. On 17 October, Whitehall was provided with the necessary confirmation of the letter's authenticity, and three days later, Gregory consigned a draft note to Crowe, who in turn mailed it to Macdonald, still on the electorate tour outside London.⁷³ Curiously, even before the notorious letter appeared in the newspapers, the MI5 sent the copies to the Home and War Offices as well as to the Admiralty with

Figure 13 Grigory Zinoviev, leader of the Comintern, 1924. Photo courtesy of Wikimedia Commons (public domain).

a request to distribute them to police stations, military units and navy crews. After the prime minister sent his response to the Foreign Office, Gregory dispatched it to Rakovski and, simultaneously, to the *Daily Mail*, which issued both documents on 25 October 1924.[74]

The publication became a shock to the Labours as well as to everyone who championed the treaties. It is small wonder that Macdonald expressed his utmost dissatisfaction with the dispatch of the note to Rakovski without his own authorization.⁷⁵ Yet while commenting on the 'Zinoviev case' at the polling rally in Cardiff, his explanations sounded so unconvincingly that some observers wished the stage would have 'swallowed Macdonald to conceal his disgrace'. According to Asquith, 'he could not remember to have read a more distracted, incoherent and unilluminating statement in the whole of his political experience'.⁷⁶

While seeking an appropriate way out of the scandal, Macdonald repeatedly claimed that it had taken him much time to examine the document's genuine origin, though it remained unclear why he preferred keeping in touch with Crowe and Ponsonby via mail instead of using telegraph or telephone. The situation led even to his proponents to openly resent the prime minister's perplexed behaviour.⁷⁷

Even before the receipt of urgent instructions from Moscow, Rakovski repudiated the British note on the night of 25 October, stating that the 'Comintern letter' had been fabricated by the foes of the Soviet-British rapprochement.⁷⁸ On 27 October, Rakovski dispatched the second, more urgent note to the British premier, not only rejecting Zinoviev's involvement in the matter but also blaming the Foreign Office staff for the falsification of the Zinoviev's appeal. Additionally, Rakovski offered the Cabinet to convey apologies to Moscow, conduct internal investigation and refer the whole case to impartial arbitration.⁷⁹

However, Macdonald refused to accept the second note as well. Meanwhile Albert Inkpin, the CPGB general secretary, categorically denied the receipt of any letter. As a result, the Cabinet constituted a commission to enquire into the problem, albeit its work had gone for naught. As Macdonald confessed to one of his subordinates, 'he felt like a man sewn in a sack and thrown into the sea'.⁸⁰

The Tories and the Liberals used the 'Red letter's' publication as a pretext to launch a vehement anti-Communist campaign. Practically all British newspapers, excluding the *Manchester Guardian* and *Daily Herald*, did not question its real origins, propagating the slogan: 'A voice for Labours is a voice for the Bolsheviks!' The *Punch* caricatures and newspaper articles disinformed the readership, reporting about the alleged construction of a monument to the biblical Judas Iscariot in the USSR, or about the plans to send the Bolshevik divisions to join anti-British guerillas in India and Egypt.⁸¹ Even Lloyd George, the earlier sympathizer of the 'Bolshevik experiment', declared at the Queen's Hall in London:

> The time has come for Liberalism to resume the leadership of progress – to lead away the masses from the chimer of Karl Marx and the nightmare of Lenin, and to carry on the great task, to which Gladstone and Bright dedicated their noble lives.⁸²

The Kremlin could not remain indifferent to the attacks against the Comintern in this regard. As early as on 25 October, the SNK members debated the matter, requiring an explanation from Zinoviev. He argued that the published document was a distorted version of the directives to the CPGB drafted by Arthur Macmanus, the first chairman of the CPGB, during his visit to Moscow in the autumn of 1924. According to Zinoviev, the secret instructions became known to MI6 agents thanks to the Comintern rank-and-file negligence or owing to a whistleblower in the CPGB central bodies.⁸³ As

Chicherin informed the Politburo, Zinoviev privately acknowledged the circulation of the Comintern memorandum to Britain, albeit with distorted content.[84]

On 30 October, the NKID's collegium assembled for a plenary session in the presence of the Politburo members, including Stalin and Zinoviev. The latter claimed for an immediate rupture with Britain, but most of the Kremlin leaders adhered to Chicherin's view of a high risk which this demarche would cause. Stalin's proposal to thoroughly enquire into the case was accepted by the majority. They appointed Karl Radek to chair a commission to investigate the incident. Concurrently, Rakovski was instructed to insist on an 'arbitration trial', whereas Dzerzhinsky was requested to collect intelligence attesting to the British espionage in the USSR.[85]

From 26 October on, the Soviet mass media published editorials defining 'Zinoviev letter' as a bogus faked by Russian emigrants in Britain with the help of some Whitehall top officials.[86] Meanwhile Zinoviev gave an interview to the *Izvestiya* accusing the emigrant circles, close to the Polish military intelligence, of its fabrication.[87]

It is well known that the snap elections brought a landslide victory to the Tories who scored 419 seats in the House of Commons. As Amery described the impact of the incident on electorate's preferences:

> The tide was flowing strongly in our favour when, on top of all the feeling about the Russian treaty and the 'Campbell case', came the notorious 'Zinoviev letter', exhorting British subjects to work for revolution and for the subversion of the armed forces ... It drove wavering Liberals in shoals to vote for the party that could best be trusted to oppose the Socialist menace.[88]

Most historians share this point of view, drawing attention to the Liberal Party's eventual transformation into a marginal political force when the voters from the middle class, scared by the Labours' reconciliation with the Bolsheviks, secured rescue under the 'Tories' wing'.

At the same time, Rakovski, still unaware of the polls' results, addressed Macdonald with one more protest which remained unanswered as well.[89] The 'cat-and-mouse' game came to an end only after Rakovski consigned the third note to the prime minister during their meeting on 2 November. Macdonald strenuously opposed the Kremlin's allegations that some employees inside Whitehall could have forged the notorious letter to discredit left-wing forces. Similarly, he was sceptical about certain Russian White emigrants being capable to fabricate the document. However, the Labour leader's opinion seemed no longer decisive, as Baldwin received the King's formal invitation to form his second Cabinet two days later. The outgoing Labours had only time to announce that it was impossible to prove the letter's authenticity. In response, Rakovski reaffirmed the proposal to conduct a joint Soviet-British impartial investigation of the case.[90]

The final phase of the 'Zinoviev incident' began on 12 November 1924, when Austen Chamberlain became the head of the second commission of experts to deal with the scandal. Its members reaffirmed the letter's authenticity that was declared by Chamberlain at the Cabinet sitting five days later.[91] As a result, Baldwin and his colleagues were challenged by three alternatives: to denounce the Soviet provocation which could lead to the rupture of relations, focus on the anti-Bolshevik campaign in the mass media or disassociate themselves from the matter by blaming the incompetent Labour ministers. On Chamberlain's recommendation Baldwin adopted the last scenario, albeit supporting the main principles of Anglo-Soviet relations announced by Macdonald in April 1924.[92] The Foreign Office was authorized to dispatch two more diplomatic notes to Moscow: one notifying the authenticity of the letter and the other denouncing the ratification of the Anglo-Soviet treaties.[93] As Chicherin declared at the Politburo meeting on 24 November, 'the English bomb had been dropped', the European press was instigating a new anti-Soviet campaign, and an armed conflict with Britain was again becoming a reality.[94]

An invitation of five top TUC officials to visit the USSR became the last attempt to save the Kremlin's face. Their trip took nearly four weeks – from 11 November to 15 December 1924, aiming to examine the correspondence at the Comintern headquarters. But any reference to the 'Red letter' was wiped out of all inventories and records of the Comintern secretariat on the eve of the delegation's arrival in Moscow, though the visitors were accorded a cordial welcome and given the opportunity to talk to Zinoviev.[95] Another immediate result of the visit became an agreement to constitute the Joint committee of Soviet and British trade unions on a permanent basis to develop a 'united anti-capitalist front'.[96] On the day of the delegation's departure, Mikhail Tomsky, the chairman of the All-Russian central council of trade unions, consigned to Purcell, who headed the delegation, an open letter running as follows:

> The investigation led you to the conclusion that the so-called 'letter' appeared to be a definite forgery. No one of progressed workers could doubt this even a minute before. Now, after you have rendered a trustworthy judgment, the issue is finally resolved both for British and Soviet workers, as well as for the proletarians all over the world.[97]

However, many observers, even in the ranks of the European social-democrats, condemned the British trade-union leaders trying to exonerate Zinoviev and other top Comintern officials from blame by the examination of select files.[98]

Six days after Austen Chamberlain made a speech at Westminster on 15 December 1924 announcing the Cabinet's imperative decision to put an end to all speculations about the 'Comintern letter', Rakovski attempted to reanimate the discussion. On behalf of the Kremlin, he suggested to ensure immunity of a secret informant amid the Comintern employees, identified under the letter 'M' in the MI6 intelligence reports, who might have escaped from Moscow with the original message by Zinoviev to the CPGB.[99]

But Baldwin and Chamberlain ignored the continuation of pointless debates, rejecting the Kremlin's proposal to carry on arbitration. The head of the Foreign Office once again notified Rakovski that the UK government strongly believed the 'Red letter' to be authentic.[100] In response, the SNK put embargo on the export contracts with British industrial companies. Although Rakovski was given one more chance to expound the Kremlin's position on the incident in the conversation with Chamberlain on 6 January 1925, the Soviet representative admitted the ineffectiveness of further attempts to develop cooperation in political and economic spheres.[101]

Regarding the ill-famous 'Zinoviev case', there still exist various interpretations of its origins suggested by politicians, journalists and historians. Some of them blamed the Foreign Office, others – the British, German or Polish intelligence and counter-intelligence officers, including the master-spies, such as Sydney Reilly. There are also authors who point to Russian White emigrants as the fabricators of the document.[102] It is beyond the chapter's scope to present all allegations in detail, though the bizarre version of Macdonald's contribution to the falsification or the version of the Americans attempting to disrupt the ratification of the Anglo-Soviet treaties does not stand up to criticism at all.[103] Nevertheless, the present author believes that the re-analysis of the 'Zinoviev case' remains essential for the understanding of the Anglo-Soviet relations in the 1920s, albeit some authors argued that the mystery of the Zinoviev letter would never be cleared up.[104]

Above all, it is necessary to compare the document, whether authentical or fabricated, with several analogous instructions that the Comintern leaders used to circulate to Communist parties. Typically, one of Macdonald's biographers ironically wrote of the 'Red letters fluttering around Whitehall for years to paper the walls of the Foreign Office'.[105] Moreover, the contents of this message completely corresponded to the Comintern principal resolutions adopted at the fifth congress in August 1924.[106] Besides that, there is good reason to believe that there existed at least three variants of the letter, each of them used by various political forces, anxious to prevent the Labour victory at the snap election.[107] The Tories and the right-wing Liberals, the officers of secret and security services, certain top Whitehall officials, especially those from the Foreign and India Offices – all of them seemed to be particularly displeased with the Cabinet's 'flirtation' with the Bolsheviks.

It is necessary to focus on the role of Macmanus who attended the Comintern congress and translated Zinoviev's speech into English. According to a certain MI5 agent, identified in the recently declassified records as CX/1174, Macmanus sent this translation to Inkpin, who after avowing it at the CPGB executive committee's extraordinary session destroyed the document.[108] Significantly, Zinoviev confessed to Chicherin that he had signed the translation without peering it. It is also highly likely that Macmanus, in turn, contacted an unidentified journalist of the *Daily Herald* after his visit to Moscow. One could suppose, therefore, that it was Macmanus who either voluntarily or unwittingly leaked the Comintern instructions to the British secret service and press.[109]

However, one could also believe that a 'mole' in the Comintern secretariat under the coded identification of FR/3/K copied both Russian and English variants of the letter. On 2 October, the informant circulated the Russian version to the MI6 Riga residentiary, where it was translated into English and dispatched to London.[110] Meanwhile another British agent identified as 'M' in the MI5 files rushed from Moscow to London via Berlin with another English translation of the letter.[111] The operation might have been planned by British intelligence structures and carried out in the cooperation with certain high-ranking Conservative officials, for example, by its chairman George Davidson, or by the Tory chief treasurer Lord Younger. Thus, apart from Macmanus' possible contribution to the letter's publication, two other alternative scenarios seemed to have been brought to life by some top functionaries and their assistants in MI5 and MI6. One of them was to send the document through a concatenation of proxies. Donald im Thurn, a retired counterintelligence officer, the owner of the 'Steamship and Trading Corporation', where Russian emigrants were engaged, seemed to have played a key role. It was im Thurn who consigned the English copy of the letter to Thomas Marlow, the *Daily Mail* editor-in-chief, in mid-October 1924.[112]

One more scenario envisioned sending several copies to the Foreign Office, MI5 and Scotland Yard on 9 October. But when Crowe, as Macdonald's deputy, requested the MI5 directorate for the testimony of the letter's authenticity, Major Desmond Morton, former Churchill's counsellor, quoted the secret report by the Riga residentiary. He also mentioned the letter's presentation at the CPGB executive committee's meeting early in October 1924.[113]

At the same time, the involvement of Russian White emigrants remains unclear. Given the route of the 'Red letter' to Britain, the Berlin group of former tsarist officers, experienced in forging various kinds of Soviet and Comintern documents, could have contributed to its fabrication. The fact was that Morton contacted their head, Vladimir Orlov, who, in turn, maintained links with another cohort of Russian expatriates staying in Riga headed by certain Lieutenant Ivan Pokrovsky.[114]

One could also point to Russian Major General Kornev (regretfully, his real name cannot be identified), who was granted British citizenship after 1917 in exchange for his service as the MI6 informant. Acting under the sobriquet Captain Black, Kornev suggested to Pokrovsky to concoct a document that could blow up the situation in the UK and trigger an internal political crisis. After the letter's compilation, Kornev (Black) and Pokrovsky allegedly received £500 with the MI6 obligation to pay to each of them a monthly subsidy of £15. Shortly after the 'Comintern letter' was published, they left Riga for Brazil, then removed to Argentina and finally settled down in Uruguay.[115]

Yet some writers conjectured the most probable version of the dual provocation, conceived not only by the UK politicians and intelligence officers but also by the opponents of Anglo-Soviet rapprochement inside the Bolshevik leadership. This explanation dates back to the hypothesis that was put forward by the journalists of the *Morning Post* and *Daily Chronicle* as early as on 4 November 1924. They suggested that Stalin and Dzerzhinsky, both ill-famed for their aversion to Britain, arranged the delivery of the 'Comintern letter' to the UK via Latvia, Poland and Germany, notifying the MI5 and MI6 double agents of its route to London.[116] Significantly, Zinoviev himself considered this explanation being true to life for several reasons. First, at least three Comintern officials, including Zinoviev's personal secretary, had been arrested and almost immediately executed on the charge of their involvement in the incident.[117] Second, some members of Orlov's group maintained close contacts with the OGPU agents.[118] Third, while craving for leadership, Stalin could use any possible means to discredit his inner-party rivals, such as Zinoviev.[119] Finally, one can also mention a bizarre attempt of two British citizens, who were OGPU agents-provocateurs, to blackmail Rakovski late in December 1924, which attested, though indirectly, to Stalin and Dzerzhinsky's intention to disrepute him in the internal struggle for power.[120] All in all, the 'Red letter' was never sent to the CPGB in the way that was presented to general public, though it contained the Comintern instructions, typical for all Communist parties subsidized by the Kremlin.

At the same time, the scandal with the 'Zinoviev letter' revealed once again the strong controversies in the higher echelons of the British and Soviet state power regarding bilateral relations in political, economic and cultural spheres. As sporadic ups and downs in their development demonstrated, the perpetual deficit of understanding and good-will on both sides always constituted the most formidable barriers on the way to collaboration.

Epilogue

This monograph covers the initial period of relations between Soviet Russia and the UK, focusing on their political side, but also taking into consideration economic and cultural issues. Nobody can deny that, as one modern Canadian historian maintains, 'Bolshevism had the greatest impact on Britain and British strategic foreign policy'. Likewise, it is true to conclude that 'Soviet Russia affected more issues of significance for Britain than did any other major power'.[1] In the first half of the 1920s, the bilateral relations underwent crucial transformation from an armed confrontation caused by mutual rejection of the Bolshevik dictatorship and the British parliamentary monarchy to humanitarian, then economic and finally political collaboration culminated in the USSR's diplomatic recognition by the Labour government in 1924.

During the years under consideration, Moscow and London took only the necessary first steps towards overcoming alienation that arose after the Bolsheviks took over in Russia, rescinding their military obligations to the Entente in 1917–18. The armed confrontation between our two countries could also be explained by their competing geopolitical interests not only in Europe, but in Asia too. Evidently, one should bear in mind the historical legacy of the Great Game that lasted several decades and came to an end only shortly before the world war. The formation of the Versailles system compelled both the Bolshevik leadership and the British ruling circles to strive for compromises on urgent problems of international affairs. If the Kremlin was paranoic about safeguarding the new regime, Whitehall was equally annoyed about the stabilization of the British Raj. Nonetheless, the UK was the first principal Entente power to both conclude a trade agreement with Bolshevik Russia and to grant full diplomatic recognition.

The turbulent development of the Soviet-British interaction, filled with unexpected conflicts and unreasonable clashes, seems extremely insightful. It presents an example of relations between the two great powers, although occupying the Eurasian continent but completely differing in the key aspects, such as geopolitical position, ethno-social composition of population, historical experience and cultural paradigm, but most importantly – the level of socio-economic development which had been proceeding for centuries on either continental or maritime patterns. When illustrating the main phases of the Soviet-British contacts in the aftermath of the Bolshevik revolution, one should mention the Entente armed intervention 'by agreement' in the spring – summer of 1918 that was followed by the full-scale 'crusade' in 1919 and the economic blockade through the Civil War.

Yet these collisions led to the conclusion of the trade agreement in March 1921, quite unexpectedly for most contemporary observers. Although Britain's attempts to settle the 'Russian question' at the international conferences in Paris, Genoa and the Hague through 1920–2 failed, they nevertheless brought the post-revolutionary Soviet republic back to the international community of nations. A series of further intensive diplomatic consultations and humanitarian contacts made it possible for both sides to procure stabilization, albeit tainted by the infamous incident with the 'Zinoviev letter' after the USSR's official recognition by the UK on 1 February 1924.

Judging by the proceedings of numerous meetings attended by statesmen, diplomats and public activists as well as by their personal diaries, letters and memoirs, the contribution of David Lloyd George and Leonid Krassin to the bilateral dialogue could be identified as decisive, so that the two statesmen became the genuine 'father-founders' of the new balance of power between Moscow and London. Maxim Litvinov and Christian Rakovski together with Ramsay Macdonald and James O'Grady also greatly contributed to the normalization of relations, developing both mutual political and social links. All of them harboured the idea of the inability to solve principal domestic and foreign problems without hammering out a constructive interaction, including the lifting of Russia's blockade, subsequent economic reconstruction of Europe, repatriation of former POWs, struggle with famine and pandemics and renewal of humanitarian as well as cultural collaboration. Here, the active role of various non-governmental organizations which were constituted by the prominent public figures, such as Maxim Gorky, Herbert Wells and many others, ought also to be considered.

On the other hand, the opponents of normalization, such as Lev Trotsky and Grigory Zinoviev in Soviet Russia, or Winston Churchill and George Curzon in Britain, strained every effort to either stop normalization or at least use it for their ambitious projects. Concurrently, there were those statesmen in both countries – Vladimir Lenin and Arthur Balfour, as examples, who traditionally occupied the 'middle' position, changing it for tactical, albeit not always appropriate reasons.

It should be also noted that the instabilities caused by the Great War and the Russian revolution had a significant impact on antagonizing the former friendly relations between London and Moscow which determined the vector of their evolution for decades. In this context, the Soviet-British collaboration on the territory of Asian countries, especially in the Middle East and Central Asia, was of particular significance. As this study strongly suggests, the intents by Trotsky to 'export' the communist revolution abroad or Lord Curzon's projects to counteract the 'Bolshevik menace' by the formation of buffer-states' belt on Russia's southern boundaries were doomed to failure because local nationalist leaders desired to disengage from the great powers' control. Not surprisingly that Robert Hodgson, the diplomatic agent in Moscow, reported to London of Chicherin's suggestion to reanimate the 1907 Anglo-Russian convention on the delimitation of the Soviet and British spheres of influence in Persia, Afghanistan and Chinese Turkestan after the end of the Russian civil war in 1922.[2]

Regretfully, Moscow and London slackened normalization by the end of 1924, instead of marking a real breakthrough in their relations. Nevertheless, the period of the Labour Cabinet in power went down in history as the time of missed opportunities and the general setback caused not only by the Comintern provocative appeals and subversive actions but also by the British political elites' reluctance to reconcile with the survival of Bolshevik Russia. On the one hand, the Kremlin's aspirations to improve relations with the 'capitalist world' remained unfulfilled because of the deep mistrust on the British side, which only intensified owing to the 'Zinoviev incident'. Certainly, nobody could expect Whitehall tolerating the numerous Comintern agents to wage propaganda all over the world as well as to instigate social unrest under Anglophobic slogans in many oriental countries. That is why all post-war British cabinets, regardless of party affiliation, claimed the dissolution of the Comintern to become a *sine qua non* condition for the normalization of Anglo-Soviet relations.³

Some Bolshevik publicists, for their part, strongly condemned the British counteracting the Soviet support to Indian and Chinese nationalists, attributing Whitehall's desire to encircle the USSR with unfriendly limitrophes.⁴ The apparent misunderstanding of British mentality, national character and political rituals remained perpetuated in the Soviet officialdom. This could be evidenced by Solomon Lozovsky, the secretary of the Communist international of trade unions who announced at the Anglo-Soviet conference held in Moscow in April 1925 that 'the reformist way has already been tried [by British workers], and no matter how their leaders treat Communism and revolutionary means of struggle … , life is stronger than any trade-union traditions or conservative notions'.⁵

As the diplomatic correspondence between London and Moscow reveals, both sides suspected each other in the activities that contradicted their interests which were voiced by Macdonald and Rakovski at the opening session of the conference in mid-April 1924. While the Kremlin presumed that Whitehall was forming a new anti-Soviet military alliance, the Cabinet charged the Bolshevik government with sponsoring the Communist groups in the countries from London to Peking.⁶ These statements once more attested to the pendulum nature of bilateral relations, swaying between reconciliation and alienation throughout the twentieth century.

The ongoing and even escalating confrontation between Moscow and London on the issues of European security in the mid-1920s was correctly summed up in Chamberlain's letter to his fellow-diplomat:

Casting an uneasy shadow westward, Soviet behaviour remained a highly uncertain 'factor' for British policy. The Foreign Office considered Soviet Russia a potentially dangerous power intent on exploiting German discontent to topple the international order.⁷

It is also significant to emphasize that since the early 1920s, Moscow's foreign policy was influenced not by two, as most diplomatic historians still consider, but by three conceptual alternatives: the internationalization of the Russian revolutionary movement; Soviet state's integration in the world order on the principles of maintaining *status-quo* in relations with leading powers; and the return to the maintenance of pan-Slavish geopolitical interests, similarly to how the tsarist government used to conduct its policy throughout the nineteenth century. Permanent rivalry between these imperatives played a key role in the understanding of how controversially Moscow perceived the West, and Britain in particular, while the third chauvinist tendency began to prevail in the Kremlin's foreign policy after Stalin had established full control over the Communist party and socialist state.

However, further developments required the reconsideration of historical experience of confrontation and collaboration by politicians, diplomats and public activists on both sides, while the ruling elites had to bear in mind the consequences of the armed conflicts in various regions of Transcaucasia, Central Asia and the Far East. In the later periods both Moscow and London became fully aware that they were bound to opt for pragmatic cooperation against the backdrop of contentious trends in world politics, in order to bring international problems to mutually beneficial settlement.

Notes

Introduction

1. Sidney Aster (comp., ed.), *British Foreign Policy, 1918–1945. A Guide to Research and Research Materials* (Tunbridge Wells – Wilmington, Del: Costello, Scholarly Resources Inc, 1984); Janet Harley, *Guide to Documents and Manuscripts in the United Kingdom Relating to Russia and the Soviet Union* (Mansell, 1987); Robert Johnson, *Soviet Foreign Policy, 1918–1945: A Guide to Research and Research Materials* (Tunbridge Wells – Wilmington, Del: Costello, Scholarly Resources Inc, 1991); A. V. Torkunov (ed.), *Izvestnye diplomaty Rossii. Ministry inostrannykh del. XX vek* (Moskovskie uchebniki, 2007); Jonathan Davis (comp.) *Historical Dictionary of the Russian Revolution* (Lanham, ML: Rowman and Littlefield Publishers, 2020); etc.
2. See, especially, S. V. Demidov, 'Vneshniaia politika i diplomatiia Velikobritanii mezhdu dvumia mirovymi voinami', in *Ocherki istorii Velikobritanii XVII – XX vv.*, ed. A. V. Nikitin, 158–207 (Prometei, 2002); N. K. Kapitonova and E. V. Romanova, *Istoriia vneshnei politiki Velikobritanii* (Mezhdunarodnye otnosheniia, 2016), 269–334.
3. For further information, refer to Richard Ullman, *Anglo-Soviet Relations, 1917–1921* (Princeton, NJ: PUP, 1961–72), 3 vols; Gabriel Gorodetsky, *The Precarious Truce. Anglo-Soviet Relations, 1924–1927* (Cambridge: CUP, 1977); Stephen White, *Britain and the Bolshevik Revolution. A Study in the Politics of Diplomacy, 1920–1924* (Macmillan, 1979); Curtis Keeble, *Britain and the Soviet Union* (Macmillan, 1990); etc.
4. For the rationale of the chosen temporal limits, see, especially, Sally Marks, *The Ebbing of European Ascendancy: An International History of the World, 1914–1945* (E. Arnold, 2002), 272–99; Zara Steiner, *The Lights That Failed. European International History. 1919–1933* (Oxford: OUP, 2005), 387–456.

Chapter 1

1. Winston Churchill, *The World Crisis. The Aftermath* (Thornton Butterworth, 1929), 71.
2. See Geoffrey Swain, *A Short History of the Russian Revolution* (I. B. Tauris, 2017).
3. Quoted in Ian Bullock, *Romancing the Revolution: The Myth of Soviet Democracy and the British Left* (Edmonton: AU Press, 2011), 41.
4. Willie Thompson, *The Good Old Cause. British Communism 1920–1991* (Pluto Press, 1992), 26. For more details, see Bullock, *Romancing the Revolution*, 45–55.
5. Memorandum by Curzon for the Cabinet, 12 May 1917, TNA, CAB 24/13, GT 703.
6. R. Warman, 'The Erosion of Foreign Office Influence in the Making of Foreign Policy, 1916–1918', *Historical Journal* 15, no. 1 (1972): 140.
7. Memorandum by Amery for the Cabinet, 20 May 1917, TNA, CAB 24/14, GT 831.

8   According to a certain contemporary observer, 'tall and distinguished in appearance, an excellent linguist, but not a Russian speaker, Buchanan combined courtesy and firmness in a measure which commanded respect both in Petrograd and in London'. Quoted in Keeble, *Britain and the Soviet Union*, 1.
9   Minutes of the Cabinet meeting, 17 September 1917, TNA, CAB 23/4/8. On the British attempt to mediate in the dispute between Kerensky and Kornilov, see A. F. Kerensky, *Rossiia na istoricheskom povorote. Memuary* (Zentrpoligraf, 1993), 384–5; Michael Kettle, *Russia and the Allies, 1917–1920* (A. Deutsch, 1981), 1: 36–69; Richard Abraham, *Alexander Kerensky: The First Love of the Revolution* (New York: Columbia University Press, 1987), 247–75; Geoffrey Swain, *The Origins of the Russian Civil War* (London–New York: Longman, 1996), 102–3; N. E. Bystrova, 'Ruskii vopros' v 1917 – nachale 1920 g.: Sovietskaia Rossiia i velikie derzhavy (Institut rossiiskoi istorii RAN, 2016), 17, 19–20.
10 Diary, 28 September 1917. Trevor Wilson (ed.), *The Political Diaries of C.P. Scott. 1911–1928* (Ithaca, NY: Cornell University Press, 1970), 304–5.
11 Frank Owen, *Tempestuous Journey. Lloyd George: His Life and Time* (Hutchinson, 1954), 447.
12 For Britain's motives, see Keith Neilson, 'Anglo-Russian Relations in the First World War', in *Russian International Relations in War and Revolution, 1914–22*, ed. David Schimmelpenninck van der Oye et al. (Bloomington, IN: Slavica Publishers, 2021), 1: 155–6.
13 *Daily Telegraph*, 30 November 1917.
14 For further information about the foreign policy of the Russian Provisional Government, see A. V. Ignatiev, '1917 god – politika Vremennogo pravitel'stva', in *Ocherki istorii MID Rossii*, ed. A. V. Torkunov (Mezhdunarodnye otnosheniia, 2002), 2, 30–2; B. I. Kolonitsky, 'Britanskie missii i A. F. Kerensky (March–October 1917 goda)', in *Rossiia v XIX – XX vv.*, ed. A. A. Fursenko (St Petersburg: D. Bulavin, 1998): 71–2.
15 Abraham, *Alexander Kerensky*, 241.
16 For further details, see William S. Maugham, *The Summing Up* (W. Heinemann, 1938), 202–5; Emanuel Voska, and Will Irwin, *Spy and Counter-Spy* (G. Harrap, 1941), 27–45; V. S. Vasiukov, *Predystoriia interventsii: fevral' 1917 – mart 1918* (Gospolitizdat, 1968), 181–92; Nigel West, *MI6: British Intelligence Service Operations* (Weidenfeld and Nicolson, 1983), 13–14; E. V. Sakhnovsky, 'Missiia Somerseta Maughama v Rossiyu v 1917 g.', *Novaia i noveishaia istoriia*, no. 5 (1987): 173–86; Michael Smith, *Six: The Real James Bond 1909–1939* (Biteback Publishing, 2011), 210; Giles Milton, *Russian Roulette. How British Spies Defeated Lenin* (Scepter, 2014), 53–64; Swain, *The Origins*, 10–11, 103–16.
17 Milton, *Russian Roulette*, 62–3.
18 George Buchanan, *My Mission to Russia and Other Memoirs* (Cassell, 1923), l: 2, 349.
19 Minutes of the Cabinet meeting, 7 November 1917, TNA, CAB 23/4/41.
20 *Morning Post*, 8 November 1917.
21 N. G. Dumova, and V. G. Trukhanovsky, *Churchill i Miliukov protiv Sovetskoi Rossii* (Nauka, 1989), 36; Walter Laquer, *The Fate of the Revolution. Interpretations of Soviet History from 1917 to the Present* (New York: C. Scribner's Sons, 1987), 157.
22 Bystrova, 'Russky vopros', 22.
23 Abraham, *Alexander Kerensky*, 321–2.
24 Lubov Krassin, *Leonid Krassin: His Life and Work* (Skeffington and Son, 1929), 77.
25 Robert Macdonell, *And Nothing Long* (A. Constable, 1938), 179.

26 Buchanan to the Foreign Office, 20 November 1917, *TNA*, FO 371/2999/398.
27 Page to the Foreign Office, 8 November 1917, *TNA*, ADM 116/1805; The Admiralty memorandum, 22 November 1917, ibid., CAB 24/33 GT 2715. On the possibility of the Russian battleships' transition to the Germans by the Bolshevik leaders as well as on the Admiralty's probable response, see David Jones (comp., ed.), 'Documents on British Relations with Russia 1917–1918. F.N.A. Cromie's Letters', *Canadian – American Slavic Studies* 7 (1973): 350–75, 498–510; Roy Bainton, *Honoured by Strangers. The Life of Captain Cromie 1882–1918* (Shrewsbury: Airlife Publishing, 2002), 190.
28 Memorandum by General William Robertson, the head of the General Staff, for the Cabinet, 19 November 1917, *TNA*, CAB 27/8. See also Neilson, 'Anglo-Russian Relations': 1, 158.
29 Philip Reynolds, *British Foreign Policy in the Inter-Wars Years* (Longmans, Green and Co., 1954), 60.
30 Kerensky, *Rossiia na istoricheskom povorote*, 412.
31 On the Entente diplomats' concerns about Russia, see Meriel Buchanan, *Petrograd: The City of Trouble 1914–1918* (W. Collins, 1918), 197–8; Morton Price, *My Reminiscences of the Russian Revolution* (G. Allen and Unwin, 1921), 153–4; T. Rose (ed.), *Morton Price. Dispatches from the Revolution: Russia 1916–18* (Pluto Press, 1997); Louis de Robien, *Journal d'un diplomate en Russia (1914–1918)* (Paris: Michel, 1967), 143–7.
32 *The Times*, 9 November 1917.
33 Robert Page Arnot, *The Impact of the Russian Revolution in Britain* (Lawrence and Wishart, 1967), 97–100.
34 See Nicola Lenin, alias Vladimir Ilich Ulianov, 23 August 1915–15 December 1917, *TNA*, KV 2/585; Nicola Lenin, alias Vladimir Ilich Ulianov, 27 May 1920–3 January 1921, ibid., KV 2/587.
35 Zinoviev Life, 15 November 1917–6 May 1959, ibid., KV 2/501; Lev Davidovich Bronstein, alias Leon Trotsky, 13 May 1915–16 February 1918, ibid., KV 2/502; Leonid Krassin, 21 May 1918–13 December 1920, ibid., KV 2/571.
36 The Bolsheviki Party, 22 July 1917–18 April 1918, ibid., KV 2/498.
37 Quoted in Ullman, *Anglo-Soviet Relations*, 1: 3.
38 George Hill, *Go Spy the Land. Being the Adventure of IK8 of the British Secret Service* (Biteback Publishing, 2014), 179; Milton, *Russian Roulette*, 69.
39 For the reassessment of this reorganization, see Michael Hughes, 'From the February Revolution to the Treaty of Brest-Litovsk', *Russian International Relations in War and Revolution*: 2, 32–5.
40 L. D. Trotsky, *Moia Zhizn'. Opyt avtobiografii* (Berlin: Granit, 1930), 2: 63–4; William Oudendyk, *Ways and By-Ways in Diplomacy* (P. Davies, 1939), 244.
41 Trostky's diplomatic note to the Entente Ambassadors, 21 November 1917, in *DVP SSSR*, ed. A. A. Gromyko (Gospolitizdat, 1957), 1: 16–17.
42 *Daily Mail*, 23 November 1917.
43 On the projects of the South-Eastern Union of Russia, see Ia. A. Ioffe, *Organizatsiia interventsii i blokady Sovetskoi respubliki, 1918–1920. Ocherk* (Moscow – Leningrad: Voenizdat, 1930), 103; Kettle, *Russia and the Allies*, 1: 128–47; Swain, *The Origins*, 111.
44 Buchanan to the Foreign Office, 23 November 1917, *TNA*, FO 371/3018. See also Michael Occleshaw, *Dances in Deep Shadows. The Clandestine War in Russia, 1917–20* (New York: Carrol and Graf Publishers, 2006), 308.
45 Michael Hughes, *Inside the Enigma. British Officials in Russia, 1900–1939* (London – Rio Grande: The Hambledon Press, 1997), 123.

46 For this diplomatic note, refer to Yu. V. Kliuchnikov and A. V. Sabanin (comps), *Mezhdunarodnia politika noveishego vremeni v dogovorakh, notakh i deklaratsiiakh* (Litizdat NKID, 1926), pt 2, 92.
47 See Etienne Antonelli, *Bolshevik Russia* (New York: A. Knopf, 1920), 194–5.
48 *The Times, Manchester Guardian*, 24 November 1917. See also M. Yu. Levidov, *K istorii soyuznoi interventsii* (Leningrad: Priboi, 1925), 1: 14; Page Arnot, *The Impact of the Russian Revolution*, 109.
49 Buchanan, *My Mission to Russia*, 2: 367–8.
50 The Foreign Office memorandum for the Cabinet, March 1919, TNA, OUBL, MS. Milner, B. J-2. See also Ullman, *Anglo-Soviet Relations*, 1: 46; Lloyd Gardner, *Safe for Democracy. The Anglo-American Response to Revolution, 1913–1923* (New York – Oxford: OUP, 1987), 153.
51 Ullman, *Anglo-Soviet Relations*, 1: 28–9.
52 Minutes of the Cabinet meeting, 6 December 1917, TNA, CAB 23/4/67.
53 Buchanan, *My Mission to Russia*, 2: 372–6; Levidov, *K istorii soyuznoi interventsii*, 1: 22; Keeble, *Britain and the Soviet Union*, 5–6.
54 Memoranda and telegrams relating to the civil war in Russia, 1919, TNA, PRO 30/30/15.
55 Diary, 10 January 1918, in *The Diary of Beatrice Webb*, ed. Norman and Jeanne Mackenzie (Cambridge, MA: HUP, 1984), 3: 292.
56 Quoted in Martin Gilbert (ed.), *Winston S. Churchill. A Companion* (Boston: Houghton Mifflin, 1975), 4, pt1: 219.
57 Diary, 4 January 1918, TNA, CU CAC, AMEL 7/14.
58 *New York Times*, 28 November 1917.
59 Quoted in Stephen White, *The Origins of Detente. The Genoa Conference and Soviet-Western Relations* (Cambridge: CUP, 1985), 18.
60 Balfour's memorandum to the Cabinet, 9 December 1917, TNA, CAB 23/4. W.C. 295; ibid., CAB 23/295; ibid., CAB 24/35/GT 2932. On Balfour's Russian policy, refer to David Lloyd George, *War Memoirs* (New York: AMS, 1982), 5: 2565; George Kennan, *Soviet-American Relations, 1917–1920* (New York: Athenaeum, 1967), 1: 169; Swain, *The Origins*, 121–2.
61 Francis Bertie, *Za kulisami Antanty. Dnevnik britanskogo posla v Parizhe*, transl., ed. K. V. Miniar-Beloruchev (Izdatel'stvo Gosudarstvennoi publichnoi istoricheskoi biblioteki, 2014), 303–4.
62 See Cedrick Lowe and Michael Dockrill, *The Mirage of Power* (London – Boston: Routledge and Kegan Paul, 1972), 2: 304; Keeble, *Anglo-Russian Relations*, 14; Bystrova, 'Russkii vopros', 238–55.
63 See, for example, B. E. Shtein, *'Russkii vopros' na Parizhskoi mirnoi konferentsii* (Moscow: Gospolitizdat, 1949), 29; F. D. Volkov, *Tainy Whitehall i Dawning*-street (Mysl', 1980), 28–31. More arguments for this concept may be found in Bystrova, 'Russkii vopros', 38–9.
64 Convention between France and England, 23 December 1917, in *DBFP, 1919–1939*, ed. E. L. Woodman, R. Butleret et al. (HMSO, 1949), First ser.: 3, 369–70. For the detailed analysis of this document, see Louis Fischer, *The Soviets in World Affairs. A History of the Relations between the Soviet Union and the Rest of the World. 1917–1929* (Princeton, NJ: HUP, 1951), 1: 836; Ullman, *Anglo-Soviet Relations*, 1: 46, 54–5; Kennan, *Soviet-American Relations*, 1: 168; David French, *The Strategy of the Lloyd George Coalition, 1916–1918* (Oxford: Clarendon Press, 1995), 240; Kettle, *Russia and the Allies*, 1: 148–75; Richard Debo, *Revolution and Survival. The Foreign Policy of Soviet Russia 1917–1918* (Liverpool: Liverpool University Press, 1979), 41–2.

65 Milner to Lloyd George, 23 December 1917, *TNA*, PA, LG F/38/2/27.
66 Debo, *Revolution and Survival*, 241–2; Keeble, *Britain and the Soviet Union*, 20–1. Characteristically, Lockhart described Millner as his 'patron and idol', see Robert Bruce Lockhart, *Agoniia Rossiiskoi imperii, vospominaniia ofitsera britanskoi razvedki*, trans. V. N. Karpov (Algoritm, 2016), 170–5, 207, 216; N. N. Berberova, *Zheleznaia zhentschina* (Izdatel'stvo Sabashnikovykh, 2001), 217–55.
67 Meriel Buchanan, *Petrograd*, 253–62.
68 See, for example, John Wheeler-Bennett, *Brest-Litovsk. A Forgotten-Peace, March 1918* (London: Macmillan, 1939), 286–304; John Long, 'Searching for Sidney Reilly: The Lockhart Plot in Revolutionary Russia, 1918', *Europe – Asia Studies* 47, no. 7 (1995): 1227; Hughes, *Inside the Enigma*, 129–32; Occleshaw, *Dances in Deep Shadows*, 77–95, 180–2.
69 Memoranda on the political situation in Russia and notes on Lord Milner's defence of the Allies' policy in Russia, December 1917–February 1918, *TNA*, OUBL, MS Milner, dep. 372. See also Lockhart, *Agoniia Rossiiskoi imperii*, 207–8; Berberova, *Zheleznaia zhentschina*, 223.
70 Quoted in Roland Chambers, *The Last Englishman: The Double Life of Arthur Ransome* (Faber and Faber, 2009), 223.
71 Lindley to the Foreign Office, 13 January 1918, *TNA*, FO 800/205/235–36.
72 A. M. Fomin, 'Voenno-politicheskie tseli Velikobritanii na zavershaiutschem etape Pervoi mirovoi voiny', *Novaia i noveishaia istoriys*, no. 3 (2012): 75–7.
73 Quoted in A. W. Ward and G. P. Gooch (eds), *The Cambridge History of British Foreign Policy, 1783–1919* (Cambridge: CUP, 1923), 3: 522.
74 Frederick Northedge and Audrey Wells, *Britain and Soviet Communism: The Impact of a Revolution* (London – Basingstoke: Macmillan, 1982), 3; A. B. Davidson, 'Obraz Velikobritanii v Rossii XIX – XX stoletii', *Novaia i noveishaia istoriia*, no. 5 (2005): 56.
75 V. I. Lenin, 'K istorii voprosa o neschastnom mire', in *Polnoe sobranie sochinenii*, ed. V. I. Lenin (Gospolitizdat, 1971), 35: 247.
76 G. N. Mikhailovsky, *Zapiski. Iz istorii rossiiskogo vneshnepoliticheskogo vedomstva, 1914–1920* (Mezhdunarodnye otnosheniia, 1993), 2: 56.
77 Minute of the Russia Committee, 17 January 1918, *TNA*, FO 95/802. For further information about this structure and later established Caucasian Committee, see Ullman, *Anglo-Soviet Relations*, 1: 84; Terence O'Brien, *Milner. Viscount Milner of St James's and Cape Town 1854–1925* (Constable, 1979), 292.
78 Diary, 1 January 1918, in Middlemas, Keith (ed.), *Thomas Jones. Whitehall Diary* (London – Oxford: OUP, 1969), 1: 41–2.
79 Robert Bruce Lockhart, *Memoirs of a British Agent, Being an Account of the Author's Early Life in Many Lands and of His Official Mission to Moscow in 1918* (London – New York: Putnam, 1932), 231.
80 Buchanan to the Foreign Office, 4 January 1918, *TNA*, T 1/12126. On Litvinov's appointment and activities in the UK, see Peter Scheffer, 'Maxim Litvinov: An Intimate Study', *Current History* 34, no. 4 (1931): 671; S. Yu.Vygodsky, *U istokov sovetskoi diplomatii* (Gospolitizdat, 1965), 45; Richard Debo, 'Litvinov and Kamenev – Ambassadors Extraordinary: The Problem of Soviet Representation Abroad', *Slavic Review* 34, no. 3 (1975): 466; Z. S. Sheinis, *Maxim Maximovich Litvinov: revoliutsioner, diplomat, chelovek* (Gospolitizdat, 1989), 104–14; A. V. Torkunov (ed.), *Izvestnye diplomaty Rossii. Ministry inostrannykh del XX veka* (Mezhdunarodnye otnosheniya, 2007), 181.
81 *TNA*, FO 371/3298/1957. See also Debo, 'Litvinov and Kamenev', 466.

82 G. Z. Besedovsky, *Na putiakh k Termidoru (iz vospominanii byvshego sovetskogo diplomata)* (Paris: Mishen', 1930), 1: 218–21; Scheffer, 'Maxim Litvinov', 677; Fischer, *The Soviets in World Affairs*, 1: 124; G. A. Solomon, *Sredi krasnykh vozhdei* (Sovremennik, 1995), 475–6. For Litvinov's political views, see also Jonathan Haslam, 'Litvinov, Stalin and the Road Not Taken', in *Reexamining the Soviet Experience. Essays in Honor of Alexander Dallin*, ed. David Holloway and Norman Naimark (Boulder, CO – Oxford: Westview Press, 1996), 56.
83 Diary, 10 February 1918, in *The Diary of Beatrice Webb*, 3, 293.
84 Kliuchnikov and Sabanin, *Mezhdunarodnaia politika*, pt 2, 114, 119.
85 Litvinov to Balfour, 5 January 1918, *AVPRF*, f. 05, op. 1, pap. 155, d. 2, ll. 1, 4; Hardinge to Litvinov, 10 January 1918, ibid., f. 69, op. 3, d. 2, l. 2.
86 K. D. Nabokov, *Ispytanie diplomata* (Stockholm: Severnye ogni, 1923): 190–2, 196, 199; Ullman, *Anglo-Soviet Relations*, 1: 60; I. M. Maisky, *Puteshestvie v proshloe* (Izdatel'stvo AN SSSR, 1960), 72.
87 *Daily Herald*, 12 January 1918.
88 Litvinov to Balfour, 13 February 1918, *DVP SSSR*, 1, 103–4. On the initial weeks of Litvinov's diplomatic activity, see also I. M. Maisky, 'Anglo-sovetskoe torgovoe soglashenie 1921 g.', *Voprosy istorii*, no. 5 (1957): 63, footnotes 8, 72, 75.
89 Ullman, *Anglo-Soviet Relations*, 1: 79.
90 Page Arnot, *The Impact of Russian Revolution in Britain*, 122–4; Bullock, *Romancing the Revolution*, 88–9.
91 TNA, FO 371/3299/33471; ibid., OUBL, MS Milner, Box B. See also Debo, 'Litvinov and Kamenev', 467–9.
92 Levidov, *K istorii soyuznoi interventsii*, 1: 44–5. On the Bolsheviks' alleged cooperation with the Germans, see Edgar Sisson, *One Hundred Red Days. A Personal Chronicle of the Bolshevik Revolution* (New Haven: YUP, 1931).
93 Bertie, *Za kulisami Antanty*, 314.
94 Debo, 'Litvinov and Kamenev', 472.
95 Wheeler-Bennett, *Brest-Litovsk*, 284–6.
96 Ibid., 286.
97 Diary, 27 February 1918, *The Diary of Beatrice Webb*, 3: 298–9.
98 Lloyd George, *War Memoirs*, 5: 98–9.
99 Lockhart to the Foreign Office, 6 February 1918, in A. A. Ivanov, 'Russkaia revolutsiia i konflikt v britanskom razvedyvatel'nom soobstchestve v 1917–1918 gg.', *Voprosy istorii*, no. 10 (2012): 153–4.
100 Curzon to Balfour, 10 February 1918, in Norman Davies, *White Eagle, Red Star. The Polish – Soviet War, 1919–1920* (London: Macdonald, 1972), 90. On Lloyd George's positive attitude towards the Soviet Government, see also John Campbell, *Lloyd George: The Goat in the Wilderness, 1922–1931* (J. Cape, 1977), 103.
101 Diary, 8 February 1918, *Thomas Jones. Whitehall Diary*, 1: 49–52.
102 Memorandum by the Foreign Office, 9 February 1918, TNA, FO 800/205. See also Trotsky, *Moia zhizn'*, 2: 103; Alfred Dennis, *The Foreign Policy of Soviet Russia* (New York: J. M. Dent and Sons, 1924), 165–76; Fischer, *The Soviets in World Affairs*, 1: 78–81; R. Girault, and R. Frank, *Turbulente Europe et nouveaux mondes. Histoire des relations internationals contemporaines* (Paris, etc.: Masson, 1988), 2: 54: Debo, *Revolution and Survival*, 125.
103 The Foreign Office report, 8 February 1918, TNA, FO 175/6.
104 In the final count, they set off by train to Vladivostok on 9 March 1918, see Allan Monkhouse, *Moscow, 1911–1933* (V. Gollancz, 1933), 70–3.

105 Kettle, *Russia and the Allies*, 1: 220–49.
106 Lockhart, *Agoniia Rossiiskoi imperii*, 260.
107 Berberova, *Zheleznaia zhentschina*, 218, 220.
108 See, for example, Long, 'Searching for Sidney Reilly', 1227.
109 Oclleshaw, *Dances in Deep Shadows*, 36.
110 Ian Buikis, 'Proschet Lockharta', in *Osoboe zadanie*, ed. I. E. Polikarpenko (Moskovskii rabochii, 1968), 84.
111 Lockhart, *Memoirs of a British Agent*, 209–10.
112 Balfour to Lockhart, 21 February 1918, *TNA*, FO 371/3199/32015.
113 Lockhart, *Istoriia iznutri*, 209–10; Ullman, *Anglo-Soviet Relations*, 1: 49, 72–3.
114 Robert Warth, *The Allies and the Russian Revolution. From the Fall of the Monarchy to the Peace of Brest-Litovsk* (Durham, NC: Duke University Press, 1954), 235.
115 Minutes of the Bolshevik Central Committee meetings, 22 and 23 February 1918, in *Protokoly TsK RSDRP(b). August 1917–February 1918*, ed. M. A. Saveliev (Moscow – Leningrad: Gospolitizdat, 1929), 243–52. See also Lockhart, *Agoniia Rossiiskoi imperii*, 263; Debo, *Revolution and Survival*, 140.
116 Lockhart, *Memoirs of the British Agent*, 213.
117 Antonelli, *Bolshevik Russia*, 201; Berberova, *Zheleznaia zhentschina*, 226. On the Entente diplomatic missions' evacuation to Vologda, see A. V. Bykov and L. S. Panov, *Diplomaticheskaia stolitsa Rossii* (Vologda: Ardvisura, 1998), 11–14.
118 Quoted in Lloyd George, *War Memoirs*, 5: 220, 252. On this meeting, see also Wheeler-Bennett, *Brest-Litovsk*, 284; Warth, *The Allies and the Russian Revolution*, 227; Swain, *The Origins*, 135.
119 Minutes of the Cabinet meeting, 4 March 1918, *TNA*, CAB 23/5. See also, Occleshaw, *Dances in Deep Shadows*, 91.
120 Diary, 4 April 1918, *TNA*, CU CAC, AMEL 7/14.
121 Blanche Dugdale, *Arthur James Balfour* (Hutchinson, 1936), 2: 258.
122 William and Zelda Coates, *Armed Intervention in Russia 1918–1922* (V. Gollancz, 1935), 63–9.
123 Minutes of the Russia Committee meeting, 7 March 1918, *TNA*, FO 95/802.
124 Swain, *The Origins*, 119.
125 William and Zelda Coates, *Armed Intervention*, 70–1; Bystrova, 'Russkii vopros', 68–71.
126 Warth, *The Allies and the Russian Revolution*, 240–1; Northedge and Wells, *Britain and the Soviet Communism*, 28.
127 Kliuchnikov and Sabanin, *Mezhdunarodnaia politika*, pt 2, 135–7.
128 Review of Soviet–British relations, end of 1917 – beginning of 1918, January 1918, *AVPRF*, f. 69, op. 3, pap. 2, d. 7, ll. 31–7.
129 On the negotiations in Brest-Litovsk, see Wheeler-Bennett, *Brest-Litovsk: The Forgotten Peace*, 268–304; Warth, *The Allies and the Russian Revolution*, 196–241; A. O. Chubarian, *Brestskii mir* (Gospolitizdat, 1963); Yu. G. Fel'shtinsky, *Krushenie mirovoi revoliutsii: Brestskii mir, October 1917 – November 1918* (Terra, 1992). For recent reassessment of the Brest problem, see L. V. Lannik, *Posle Rossiiskoi imperii: germanskaiya okkupatsiya 1918 g.* (St Petersburg: Eurasia, 2020), 33–70; Hughes, 'From the February Revolution', 3–35, especially, 25–31; John Steinberg. 'The Treaty of Brest-Litovsk: The Wilsonian Moment before Wilson', *Russian International Relations in War and Revolution*, 2 (2021): 135–63.
130 P. N. Miluikov, *Rossiia na perelome* (Paris: Imprimerie d'Art Voltaire, 1927), 1: 266; French, *The Strategy of the Lloyd George Coalition*, 173.
131 Swain, *The Origins*, 132.

132 French, *The Strategy of the Lloyd George Coalition*, 173–4.
133 Quoted in Northedge, and Wells, *Britain and the Soviet Communism*, 27. There were historians who related the conclusion of the Brest treaty to the 'real establishment of the young Soviet state', see Adam Ulam, *Expansion and Coexistence. The History of Soviet Foreign Policy, 1917–67* (New York – Washington: F. Praeger, 1968), 75.
134 Oudendyk, *Ways and By-Ways in Diplomacy*, 259.
135 Lockhart, *Memoirs of the British Agent*, 203.
136 Ibid., 230, 248. See also William and Zelda Coates, *Armed Intervention*, 79.

Chapter 2

1 Quoted in Antonelli, *Bolshevik Russia*, 203.
2 V. N. Brovkin, *The Bolsheviks in Russian Society. The Revolution and the Civil War* (New Haven – London: YUP, 1997), 1.
3 See, for example, E. Yakunin and S. Polunin, *Angliiskaia interventsiia v 1918–1920 gg* (Moscow – Leningrad: Gosudarstvennoe izdatel'stvo, 1928); I. I. Minz, *Angliiskaia interventsiia i severnaia kontrrevoliutsiia* (Moscow – Leningrad: Gosudarstvennoe sotsial'no-ekonomicheskoe izdatel'stvo, 1931); B. E. Stein, *Vneshniaia politika SSSR 1917–1923 gg* (Gospolitizdat, 1945); etc. Regretfully, some modern Russian historians still adhere to the traditional Soviet concept of the armed intervention in Soviet Russia, see, for example, O. V. Vasilenkova, 'Anglo-sovetskie otnosheniia v 1918–1921 gg.' (Avtoref. diss. kandidata istoricheskikh nauk, Vladimirskii gosudarstvennyi pedagogicheskii universitet, Vladimir, 2007); S. A. Mironiuk, 'Interventsiia v Rossiiu v politicheskikh diskussiiakh praviatschikh krugov Velikobritanii (1917–1919 gg.)' (Avtoref. diss. kandidata istoricheskikh nauk, Rossiskii universitet druzhby narodov, 2021).
4 Fomin, 'Voenno-politicheskie tseli Velikobritanii na zavershayutschem etape Pervoi mirovoi voiny', 86–7; E. Yu. Sergeev, 'Sovetsko-britanskie otnosheniia na rubezhe 1917–1918 gg', *Vestnik Moskovskogo universiteta* 1, ser. 25, no. 1 (2018): 42–71; Idem., 'Britaniia i nachalo interventsii v Rossii v pervoi polovine 1918 g', *Rossiskaia istoriia*, no. 1 (2019): 43–59.
5 See, for example, Kennan, *Soviet-American Relations*, 2: 245–76; Idem., *Russia and the West under Lenin and Stalin* (Boston – Toronto: Little, Brown and Co., 1961), 64–79; Ullman, *Anglo-Soviet Relations 1917–1921*, 1: 191–229; George Brinkley, *The Volunteer Army and Allied Intervention in South Russia, 1917–1921* (Notre Dame, Ind.: University of Notre Dame Press, 1966); etc.
6 Winston Chamberlin, *The Russian Revolution, 1917–1921* (Macmillan, 1935), 2: 150–72; Frederick Schuman, *Russia since 1917. Four Decades of Soviet Politics* (New York: A. Knopf, 1957), 105; Denna Fleming, *The Cold War and Its Origins, 1917–1960* (G. Allen and Unwin, 1961), 1: 31; Ullman, Anglo-Soviet Relations, 1: 185; Kettle, *Russia and the Allies*, 2: 25–48; Michael Carley, *Silent Conflict: A Hidden History of Early Soviet-Western Relations* (Langham, MD.: Rowman and Littlefield Publishers, 2014), 1–28; etc.
7 Michael Reynolds, *Shattering Empires: The Clash and Collapse of the Ottoman and Russian Empires, 1908–1918* (Cambridge: CUP, 2011), 61.
8 Gardner, *Safe for Democracy*, 149–50.
9 Richard Pipes, *Russia under the Bolshevik Regime, 1918–1924* (Harvill Press, 1997), 63; Howard Fuller, 'Great Britain and Russia's Civil War: The Necessity for a Definite and Coherent Policy', *The Journal of Slavic Military Studies* 32, no. 4 (2019): 553–9.

10 Ilia Somin, *Stillborn Crusade. The Tragic Failure of Western Intervention in the Russian Civil War, 1918-1920* (New Brunswick, NJ - London: Transaction Publishers, 1996), 20.
11 Jonathan Smele, *The 'Russian' Civil Wars, 1916-1926: Ten Years that Shook the World* (Hurst, 2015), 1-16.
12 A. J. Plotke, *Imperial Spies Invade Russia: The British Intelligence Interventions, 1918* (Westport, Conn: Greenwood Press, 1993), 83-105, 107-24.
13 Alston, Charlotte, 'International Intervention in Russia's Civil War: Policies, Experiences, and Justifications', *Russian International Relations in War and Revolution*, 2: 276.
14 O'Brien, *Milner*, 319.
15 For the chronology of the Allied intervention in Russia, refer to John Silverlight, *The Victor's Dilemma: Allied Intervention in the Russian Civil War* (Barrie and Jenkins, 1970); Robert Jackson, *At War with the Bolsheviks. The Allied Intervention into Russia 1917-20* (London: T. Stacey, 1972); Kettle, *Russia and the Allies*, 2; Smele, *The 'Russian' Civil Wars*, 49-103.
16 Ibid., 25-48; A. F. Rotshtein, *Kogda Angliia vtorglas' v Sovetskuyu Rissiyu* (Progress Publishers, 1982), 93-116; Christopher Dobson and John Miller, *The Day We Almost Bombed Moscow. The Allied War in Russia 1918-1920* (Hodder and Stoughton, 1986), 39-51; Dumova and Trukhanovsky, *Churchill i Miliukov*, 49.
17 Price, *My Reminiscences*, 277.
18 V. I. Goldin (comp., ed.), *Bely Sever, 1918-1920: memuary i dokumenty* (Arkhangelsk: Izdatel'stvo 'Pravda Severa', 1993), 1: 8.
19 G. V. Chicherin, *Vneshniaia politika Sovetskoi Rossii za dva goda* (Gosizdat, 1920), 16; Michael Graham, *The League of Nations and the Recognition of States* (Berkeley: UCP, 1941), 3: no. 2, pt I, 122. For the recent evaluation of these projects, see Steven Balbirnie, 'British Imperialism in the Arctic: The British Occupation of Arkhangelsk and Murmansk, 1918-1919'. PhD diss., University College Dublin, 2016.
20 Goldin, *Bely Sever*, 1: 6.
21 Ullman, *Anglo-Soviet Relations*, 1: 112, 114.
22 *The Times*, 10 January 1918 (clippings in GARF, f. 6302, op. 1, d. 3, ll. 1-198).
23 Quoted in Goldin, *Bely Sever*, 1: 7. It should be mentioned that the stockpiles of munitions in Arkhangelsk and Murmansk amounted to 160,000 and 450,000 tons, respectively, to a value of 2 and 6 billion roubles (compared to 800,000 tons to a value of 10 billion roubles in Vladivostok), see Somin, *Stillborn Crusade*, 34.
24 M. S. Kedrov, *Za Sovetskii Sever. Lichnye vospominaniia i materialy o pervykh etapakh grazhdanskoi voiny 1918 g* (Leningrad: Priboi, 1927), 7-8.
25 Ullman, *Anglo-Soviet Relations*, 1: 113.
26 Karl Mannerheim, *Memoirs* (Vagrius, 2003), 84-135; John Long, 'Civil War and Intervention in North Russia, 1918-1920' (PhD diss., Columbia University, New York, 1972); V. I. Goldin et al. (eds), *Russkii Sever v istoricheskom prostranstve rossiiskoi grazhdanskoi voiny* (Arkhangelsk: Solty, 2005), 69.
27 Ibid., 68.
28 Correspondence between the Murmansk Soviet and the SNK, 1-2 March 1918, in *DVP SSSR*, 1: 221. See also, Ullman, *Anglo-Russian Relations*, 1: 117.
29 William and Zelda Coates, *History of Anglo-Soviet Relations* (Lawrence and Wishart, The Pilot Press, 1943), 1: 82; Dennis, *The Foreign Policies of Soviet Russia*, 59.
30 Report on the Anglo-French armed intervention in Murmansk, 15 January 1918-28 January 1919, *RGVA*, f. 1, op. 1, d. 141, ll. 1-96. On the beginning of the armed

intervention in the north of Russia, see Levidov, *K istorii souznoi interventsii*, 1: 99–100; Goldin et al., *Russkii Sever*, 67.
31 Minutes of the Russia Committee's meetings, 4, 10 April 1918, TNA, FO 95/802. See also Goldin et al., *Russkii Sever*, 233.
32 Ibid., 69; Nick Baron, *The King of Karelia. Colonel P.J. Woods and the British Intervention in North Russia, 1918–1919. A History and Memoir* (F. Boutle Publishers, 2007), 263.
33 Chicherin, *Vneshniaia politika Sovetskoi Rossii*, 12.
34 On further details of the Allied landing operations in Karelia, see Levidov, *K istorii soyuznoi interventsii*, 1: 142; Fleming, *The Cold War and Its Origins*, 26; Baron, *The King of Karelia*, 143.
35 Jackson, *At War with the Bolsheviks*, 32–42; Goldin et al., *Russkii Sever*, 72; S. Idem., *Belyi Sever*, 2: 16; Baron, *The King of Karelia*, 112–15; Dobson and Miller, *The Day We Almost Bombed Moscow*, 61.
36 Churchill's speech in the Parliament, 29 July 1919, in Great Britain. War Office. *Army. The Evacuation of North Russia, 1919*, Cmd. 818 (HMSO, 1920), 3–4.
37 For further arguments, see Kennan, *Russia and the West*, 80–90.
38 A. I. Cherepanov, *Zapiski voennogo sovetnika v Kitae* (Nauka, 1964), 5–6.
39 See, for example, Kettle, *Russia and the Allies*, 2: 13.
40 V. A. Antonov-Ovseenko, *Zapiski o Grazhdanskoi voine 1917–1918* (Kuchkovo pole, 2016), bk. 1, 285; Karl Helferich, 'Moia moskovskaia missia', *Grani*, no. 155 (1990): 266; S. Page, *The Formation of the Baltic States. A Study of the Effects of Great Power Politics upon the Emergence of Lithuania, Latvia, and Estonia* (Cambridge, MA: HUP, 1959), 84–5.
41 On the collaboration between the Allied intelligence agencies during the First World War, see E. Yu. Sergeev, 'Russian Military Intelligence in the Coalition War, 1914–1918', *Russian International Relations in War and Revolution*, 1: 299–316.
42 Composition and activities of the British intelligence mission in Petrograd, 29 January 1917, TNA, CUL, HP, pt II, Russia, files 1/1–11.
43 Hill, *Go Spy the Land*, 182.
44 Joseph Noulens, *Mon Ambassade en Russie Sovietique: 1917–1919* (Paris: Plon, 1933), 2: 28, 53–6.
45 Quoted in Martin Gilbert, *Churchill. A Life* (Minerva, 1991), 389.
46 Ibid., 389–90.
47 Lockhart, *Agoniia Rossiiskoi imperii*, 263.
48 Levidov, *K istorii soyuznoi interventsii*, 1: 106; Kennan, *Russia and the West*, 95.
49 On pro-Bolshevik guerrillas on the occupied territories, see Price, *My Reminiscences*, 277–8; I. Ia. Korostovetz, *Seed and Harvest* (Faber and Faber, 1931), 337; Hill, *Go Spy the Land*, 190–5; Richard Deacon, *A History of the Russian Secret Service* (Grafton, 1987), 160–1; Swain, *The Origins of the Russian Civil War*, 132–3; A. A. Sikorsky, 'Smolenskii raion oborony. Organisattsiia partisanskogo dvizheniia v prifrontovoi polose Zapadnoi oblasti v marte – noiabre 1918 g', *Voenno-Istoricheskii zhurnal*, no. 3 (2004): 22–4; Macdonald and Dronfield, *A Very Dangerous Woman*, 88.
50 Minute of the Cabinet meeting, 12 April 1918, TNA, OUBL, MS Milner, dep. 364 B/221.
51 Lockhart to the Foreign Office, 13 April 1918, TNA, FO 371/3285/68677.
52 Balfour to Lockhart, 13 April 1918, in Keeble, *Britain and the Soviet Union*, 31.
53 Lockhart to the Foreign Office, 17 April 1918, TNA, FO 371/3285/69968.
54 Debo, *Revolution and Survival*, 254; Goldin et al., *Russkii Sever*, 234.

55 Milner to Bertie, 9 May 1918, *TNA*, OUBL, MS Milner, dep. 141.
56 Cecil to Balfour, 13 May 1918, *TNA*, FO 800/205.
57 Reclamations of the British companies to the Russian government, 1916–August 1918, ibid., MUN 4/6976/141, 143, 146, 148, 151, 152, 198. On the early contacts between the Bolsheviks and the British in the economic field, see Anthony Heywood, 'Russian and Soviet Foreign Trade, 1914–28: Rethinking the Initial Impact of the Bolshevik Revolution', *Russian International Relations in War and Revolution*, 2: 407–8.
58 Inter-Departmental Russian trade committee, 1918–1920, ibid., MUN 4/7000, 1917–18; T 1/12616.
59 Report by Urquhart, 9 May 1918, ibid.
60 Note of the Board of Trade, 3 May 1918, *TNA*, FO 800/205.
61 Price, *My Reminiscences*, 275–6.
62 *Izvestiya*, 17 May 1918.
63 Report on British Mission to Northern Russia, June 1918–31 March 1919, Lindley to Curzon, 25 April 1919, *TNA*, T 1/12349.
64 Chicherin to Lindley, 14 June 1918, in *DVP SSSR*, 1: 396.
65 Ioffe, *Organisatsiya interventsii*, 28.
66 See Nabokov, *Ispytanie diplomata*, 299–301; Chicherin to Lockhart, 12 June 1918, in *DVP SSSR*, 1: 360–2.
67 For further information about the trade negotiations in Moscow, refer to Lockhart, *Agoniia Rossiiskoi imperii*, 322–3; Ullman, *Anglo-Soviet Relations*, 1: 232–4; O. F. Soloviev, 'Iz istorii bor'by Sovetskogo pravitel'stva za mirnoe sosustchestvovanie s Angliei', *Voprosy istorii*, no. 12 (1965): 62–3; V. A. Shishkin, *Stanovlenie vneshnei politiki poslerevoliutsionnoi Rossii (1917–1930-e gody) i kapitalisticheskii mir: ot revoliutsionnogo 'zapadnichestva' k 'natsinal-bol'shevismu'* (St Petersburg: D. Bulavin, 2002), 78–9; Macdonald and Dronfield, *A Most Dangerous Woman*, 109.
68 Smele, *The 'Russian' Civil Wars*, 67–77.
69 Price, *My Reminiscences*, 275–6.
70 Diary, 6 May 1918, in Kenneth Young (ed.), *The Diaries of Sir Robert Bruce Lockhart* (Macmillan, 1973), 1: 36.
71 Price, *My Reminiscences*, 275–6.
72 Lloyd George, *War Memoirs*, 6: 91.
73 I. I. Minz (ed.), *Iaponskaia intervenysiia, 1918–1922 gg. v dokumentakh* (Zentrarchiv, 1934), 208. See also William and Zelda Coates, *A History of Anglo-Soviet Relations*, 1: 109–10; G. K. Gins, *Sibir', soyuzniki i Kolchak. Povorotni moment russkoi istorii. 1918–1920 (Vpechatleniia i mysli clean Omskogo pravitel'stva)* (Iris-Press, 2013), 51–64.
74 See A. V. Ignatiev, *Russko-angliiskie otnosheniia nakanune Oktiabr'skoi revoliutsii (February–October 1917 g.)* (Nauka, 1966), 329.
75 Wilson, *The Political Diaries of C.P. Scott*, 337.
76 Minute of the Cabinet meeting, 5 March 1918, *TNA*, CAB 23/5. See also, Occleshaw, *Dances in Deep Shadows*, 91.
77 Quoted in Richard Connaughton, *The War of the Rising Sun and Tumbling Bear. A Military History of the Russo-Japanese War, 1904–1905* (London – New York: Routledge, 1988), 274.
78 Wheeler-Bennett, *Brest-Litovsk*, 295.
79 Minz, *Iaponskaia interventsiia*, 201, 205. On how the Japanese intervention affected Soviet-British relations, see Dumova and Trukhanovsky, *Churchill i Miliukov*, 48–9.

80 Kennan, *Soviet-American Relations*, 1: 81–2; Keeble, *Britain and the Soviet Union*, 29–30.
81 Diary, 9 March 1918, in Bertie, *Za kulisami Antanty*, 253; Diary, 21 March 1918, in Wilson, *The Political Diaries of C.P. Scott*, 338.
82 For more details, see Chicherin, Vneshniaia politika Sovetskoi Rossii, 10; M. Pavlovich, *Sovetskaia Rossiia i kapitalisticheskaia Angliia (ot epokhi tsarisma do pravitel'stva Chemberlena – Bolduina 1925 g.*) (Gosudarstvennoe izdatel'stvo, 1925), 25; Levidov, K istorii soyuznoi interventsii v Rossiyu, 1: 53; Monkhouse, Moscow, 85–6; Jan Meijer (ed.), *The Trotsky Papers. 1917–1922* (Mouton, 1964), 1: 36–7; P. M. Nikiforov, Zapiski prem'era DVR. Pobeda leninskoi politiki v bor'be s interventsiei na DVR (1917–1922) (Gospolitizdat, 1974), 44–5; Ullman, Anglo-Soviet Relations, 1: 82–109, 144–6; Bradley, Allied Intervention in Russia, 24–47; Warth, The Allies and the Russian Revolution, 58; Debo, Revolution and Survival, 241; Kettle, Russia and the Allies, 2: 35.
83 Minz, *Iaponskaia interventsiia*, 203–4; William and Zelda Coates, *History of Anglo-Soviet Relations*, 1: 102–3; Dumova and Trukhanovsky, *Churchill i Miliukov*, 50; Debo, *Revolution and Survival*, 249–50.
84 Minz, *Iaponskaia interventsiia*, 204.
85 Ibid., 203, William and Zelda Coates, *History of Anglo-Soviet Relations*, 1: 100; Smele, *The 'Russian' Civil Wars*, 67–77.
86 Swain, *The Origins of the Russian Civil War*, 111. For the saga of the Czechoslovak Legion in Russia, see Chamberlin, *The Russian Revolution*, 1: 427; Ullman, *Anglo-Soviet relations*, 1: 168–71; Bradley, *Allied Intervention in Russia*, 65–105; Jackson, *At War with the Bolsheviks*, 43–9; Kettle, *Russia and the Allies*, 2: 49–154; Swain, *The Origins of the Russian Civil War*, 141, 156–60.
87 Goldin et al., *Russkii Sever*, 70–1.
88 Dennis, *The Foreign Policy of Soviet Russia*, 61; Bystrova, *'Russky vopros'*, 104; Macdonald and Dronfield, *A Very Dangerous Woman*, 77.
89 'Protokoly zasedanii ZK RKP(b), March 1918–March 1919', *Izvestiya ZK KPSS*, no. 4 (1989), 141.
90 Lenin, *Polnoe sobranie sochinenii*, 3: 323.
91 Karl von Bothmer, *S grafom Mirbakhom v Moskve* (Knigovek, 2010), 59–60.
92 Ibid., 49.
93 Ibid., 67, 75. See also Kettle, *Russia and the Allies*, 2: 137.
94 Swain, 'An Interesting and Plausible Proposal': Bruce Lockhart, Sidney Reilly and the Latvian Riflemen, Russia 1918', *Intelligence and National Security* 14, no. 3 (1999): 86.
95 Lockhart, *Istoriia iznutri*, 253. On Cromie's contribution to the annihilation of the British submarines, stationed in Helsingforse, see Dobson and Miller, *The Day We Almost Bombed Moscow*, 104; L. H. Ashmore, *Forgotten Flotilla: British Submarines in Russia 1914–1919* (Portsmouth: Manuscript Press in association with Press Navy Submarine Museum, 2001); D. Yu. Kozlov, *Britanskie podvodnye lodki na Baltiiskom more 1914–1918* (St Petersburg: Izdatel'stvo LeKo, 2006), 150; Macdonald and Dronfield, *A Very Dangerous Woman*, 70–1.
96 Lockhart, *Agoniia imperii*, 294; Kettle, *Russia and the Allies*, 2: 117–18; Swain, 'An Interesting and Plausible Proposal', 85; Macdonald and Dronfield, *A Very Dangerous Woman*, 83.
97 Cecil to Lloyd George, 30 May 1918, TNA, PA, LG F/6/5/27.
98 On the Anglo-French willingness to abet the Czechoslovaks in a mutiny against the Bolsheviks, see Price, *The Truth about the Allied Intervention in Russia* (Tipografiia

Tovaritschestva Riabushinskogo, 1918), 13; William and Zelda Coates, *History of Anglo-Soviet Relations*, 1: 110–11; Dumova and Trukhanovsky, *Churchill i Miliukov*, 57.
99   *Daily Telegraph*, 27 May 1918.
100 For the assessments of the mutiny, see William and Zelda Coates, *Armed Intervention in Russia*, 104, 107–8; Warth, *The Allies and the Russian Revolution*, 59–60; Debo, *Revolution and Survival*, 271–2.
101 Chicherin to Lockhart, 28 May 1918, in *DVP SSSR*, 1: 327. See also William and Zelda Coates, *Armed Intervention in Russia*, 109; Warth, *The Allies and the Russian Revolution*, 59–60; Debo, *Revolution and Survival*, 275, 277–8.
102 Swain, *The Origins of the Russian Civil War*, 57; Goldin et al., *Russkii Sever*, 72.
103 Chicherin to Lockhart, 2 April 1918, in *DVP SSSR*, 1: 222.
104 See Debo, *Revolution and Survival*, 255–8.
105 Chicherin to Yuriev, 12 May 1918; Chicherin to Yuriev, 22 May 1918, in *DVP SSSR*, 1: 286, 313.
106 Memorandum by the ASWC, 31 May 1918, *TNA*, FO 800/205/289–295.
107 See Debo, *Revolution and Survival*, 269–70; Dobson and Miller, *The Day We Almost Bombed Moscow*, 52.
108 Chicherin to Lockhart, 6 June 1918, *AVPRF*, f. 69, op. 3, pap. 2, d. 3, l. 17; Lockhart to Chicherin, 7 June 1918, ibid., d. 4, ll. 15–16. See also Lockhart, *Agoniia Rossiiskoi imperii*, 303; Kedrov, *Za Sovetskii Sever*, 8–9, 15–17, 70–4.
109 Chicherin to Lockhart, 12, 14 June 1918, *AVPRF*, f. 69, op. 3, pap. 2, d. 3, ll. 27–27ob., 28–28ob.
110 Report on the attack of five British destroyers against Revel, 12 May 1918, *RGAVMF*, f. R-342, op. 1, d. 168, ll. 1–14.
111 Ioffe to Chicherin, 20 May 1918, in *DVP SSSR*, 1: 311–13. See also Ullman, *Anglo-Soviet Relations*, 1: 190.
112 On the prospects of Soviet – German economic cooperation in mid-1918, see Keeble, *Britain and the Soviet Union*, 35; Debo, *Revolution and Survival*, 282.
113 Levidov, *K istorii soyuznoi interventsii v Rossiyu*, 1: 113–14; Goldin et al., *Russkii Sever*, 75.
114 Ye. N. Bystrova, 'Iz istorii diplomaticheskikh otnoshenii Sovetskoi Rossii 1917–1918 gg', *Rossiiskaia istoriia*, no. 5 (2012): 135.
115 Churchill's memorandum for the Cabinet, 22 June 1918, quoted in Gilbert, *Winston S. Churchill*, 4: pt 1, 333.
116 Kerensky, *Rossiia na istoricheskom povorote*, 469; Berberova, *Zheleznaia zhentschina*, 254; Warth, *The Allies and the Russian Revolution*, 275–6; Macdonald and Dronfield, *A Very Dangerous Woman*, 113. For a detached narration of the former Russian prime-minister's staying in the British capital, see Jonathan Smele, 'Mania grandiose and "The Turning Point in World History": Kerensky in London in 1918', *Revolutionary Russia* 20, no. 1 (2007): 1–34. For further details of these meetings, see Note on the conversation between Lloyd George and Kerensky, 24 June 1918, *TNA*, PA, LG F/201/3/8; Note on the conversation between Kerr and Kerensky, 25 June 1918, ibid., LG F/201/3/9.
117 Lockhart to Chicherin, 25 June 1918, *AVPRF*, f. 69, op. 3, pap. 2, d. 4, l. 22; Chicherin to Lockhart, 27 June 1918, ibid., f. 069, op. 2, pap. 1, d. 1, ll. 43–43ob.; Chicherin to Lockhart, 29 June 1918, in *DVP SSSR*, 1: 377–8.
118 Lenin's telegraphic conversation with Yuriev, 26 June 1918, in *DVP SSSR*, 1: 376.
119 Keeble, *Britain and the Soviet Union*, 36–8; Fleming, *The Cold War and Its Origins*, 21; Goldin et al., *Russkii Sever*, 75–6; Bystrova, 'Iz istorii diplomaticheskikh otnoshenii', 135.

120 Agreement between the Murmansk Regional Soviet and the military representatives of Britain, France and the United States, 7 July 1918, *AVPRF*, f. 069, op. 2, pap. 1, d. 1 ll. 44–6. On the controversies between the Murmansk Soviet and the Kremlin, see Chicherin to Lockhart, 12 July 1918, in *DVP SSSR*, 1: 389. For a fuller description, see also Maisky, *Vneshniaia politika RSFSR*, 49–51; Goldin et al., *Russkii Sever*, 75, 169–70.
121 Lindley to the Foreign Office, 9 July 1918, *TNA*, FO 175/1.
122 William and Zelda Coates, *Armed Intervention in Russia*, 86; Debo, *Revolution and Survival*, 289–90.
123 French, *The Strategy of the Lloyd George Coalition*, 240.
124 For further information about the Allied diplomats staying in Vologda, see Lindley to Curzon, 25 April 1919, *TNA*, T 1/12349; Bykov and Panov, *Diplomaticheskaia stolitsa Rossii*, 155–62. See also Debo, *Revolution and Survival*, 291–2; Hugh Brogan, *The Life of Arthur Ransome* (Pimlico, 1992), 149–205, especially, 203–4; Chambers, *The Last Englishman*, 182–190, 222–3, 230; Smith, *Six*, 257–72; Milton, *Russian Roulette*, 85.
125 See Maisky, *Vneshniaia politika*, 58.
126 *The Times*, 13 August 1918. See also Berberova, *Zhelesnaia zhentschina*, 263; Macdonald and Dronfield, *A Very Dangerous Woman*, 112.
127 *Izvestiya*, 1 August 1918. See also Kliuchnikov and Sabanin, *Mezhdunarodnaia politika*, II: 159–60; Dennis, *The Foreign Policy of Soviet Russia*, 64; Debo, *Revolution and Survival*, 297.
128 See Hellferich, 'Moia moskovskaia missiia', 2; Ullman, *Anglo-Soviet Relations*, 1: 285; Debo, *Revolution and Survival*, 296.
129 Kedrov, *Za Sovetskii Sever*, 90; Idem., *Pod igom britanskikh gromil* (Moscow – Leningrad: Gosudarstvennoe izdatel'stvo, 1927), 28–9.
130 For Kedrov's own explanation of his narrow escape from Arkhangelsk, see Kedrov, *Za Sovetskii Sever*, 65–6.
131 Goldin, *Belyi Sever*, 2: 204–5; Levidov, *K istorii soyuznoi interventsii v Rossiyu*, 1: 115.
132 Charles Maynard, *The Murmansk Venture* (Hodder and Stoughton, 1928), 310–11. See also Goldin et al., *Russkii Sever*, 77; William and Zelda Coates, *Armed Intervention in Russia*, 91–2.
133 John Ward, *With the 'Die-Hards' in Siberia* (Cassell, 1920), 3–5; Nikiforov, *Zapiski premiera DVR*, 60.
134 Minz, *Iaponskaia interventsiia*, 9–10. See also William and Zelda Coates, *Armed Intervention in Russia*, 124–5; Gilbert, *Winston S. Churchill*, 4: pt 1, 386, 764; Dobson and Miller, *The Day We Almost Bombed Moscow*, 233; A. I. Deriabin, *Grazhdanskaia voina v Rossii 1917–1922. Voiska interventov* (AST, 1999), 12–24.
135 Maisky, *Vneshniaia politika*, 51; Keeble, *Britain and the Soviet Union*, 40.
136 British Government's declaration to the peoples of Russia, 9 August 1918, *TNA*, FO 371/3287.
137 Findlay to Balfour, 19 August 1918, Great Britain. Foreign Office. *A Collection of Reports on Bolshevism in Russia*, Russia no. 1 (1919), Cmd. 8 (HMSO, 1919), 1.
138 Cromie to the Admiralty, 5 August 1918. Quoted in Michael Kettle, *Sidney Reilly: The True Story* (Corgi Books, 1983), 33–4.
139 The SNK declaration, 8 August 1918, in *DVP SSSR*, 1: 421.
140 Chicherin to Lockhart, 9 August 1918, *TNA*, FO 370/2320.
141 Lockhart to Chicherin, 5 August 1918, ibid., FO 370/2320. See also Keeble, *Britain and the Soviet Union*, 42.
142 Kedrov, *Za Sovetskii Sever*, 129–32, 191–2; Swain, 'An Interesting and Plausible Proposal', 94.

143 Lockhart, *Istoriia iznutri*, 284.
144 Quoted in Ullman, *Anglo-Soviet Relations*, 1: 286.
145 Ian Moffat, *The Allied Intervention in Russia, 1918–1920: The Diplomacy of Chaos* (Houndsmills, Basingstoke, Hampshire: Palgrave Macmillan, 2015), 36–46.
146 Ibid., 349–50.

Chapter 3

1   M. Ya. Latsis, *Dva goda bor'vy na vnutrennem fronte* (Gosudarstvennoe izdatel'stvo, 1920), 23.
2   On Reilly's life, refer to Norman Thwaites, *Velvet and Vinegar* (Grayson and Grayson, 1932), 181–5; Lockhart, *Agoniia Rossiiskoi imperii*, 339–41; Berberova, *Zheleznaia zhentschina*, 256–8; Robin Bruce Lockhart, *Ace of Spies* (Hodder and Stoughton, 1967); Edward van der Rhoehr, *Master Spy. A True Story of Allied Espionage in Bolshevik Russia* (New York: C Scribner's Sons, 1981), 23–35; Long, 'Searching for Sidney Reilly', 1225–41; Alexander Orlov, *The March of Time. Reminiscences* (St Ermin's Press, 2004), 124–35; Jeffrey, *MI6*, 178–84; George Brook-Shepherd, *Iron Maze. The Western Secret Services and the Bolsheviks* (London: Macmillan, 1998), 13–27; Alan Judd, *The Quest for C. Sir Mansfield Cumming and the Founding of the British Secret Service* (HarperCollins Publishers, 1999), 441; Andrew Cook, *Ace of Spies: The True Story of Sidney Reilly* (Stroud: Tempus, 2004); Robert Service, *Spies and Commissars. Bolshevik Russia and the West* (Basingstoke – Oxford: Macmillan, 2011), 146–54; Milton, *Russian Roulette*, 93–119, 148–67, 174–9.
3   Orlov, *The March of Time*, 127; Judd, *The Quest for C.*, 415.
4   Robin Bruce Lockhart, *Ace of Spies*, 63; Judd, *The Quest for C.*, 437–8; Smith, *Six*, 213.
5   Milton, *Russian Roulette*, 100.
6   Long, 'Searching for Sidney Reilly', 1227; Brook-Shepherd, *Iron Maze*, 27; Macdonald and Dronfield, *A Very Dangerous Woman*, 80; Milton, *Russian Roulette*, 110.
7   Long, 'Searching for Sidney Reilly', 1236.
8   Quoted in Richard Debo, 'Lockhart Plot or Dzerzhinskii Plot?', *Journal of Modern History* 43, no. 3 (1971): 427.
9   Berberova, *Zheleznaia zhentschina*, 246–7.
10 On Dzerzhinky's elaboration of similar conspiracy schemes, see Debo, 'Lockhart Plot or Dzerzhinskii Plot?', 423, 432; Long, 'Searching for Sidney Reilly', 1230; Berberova, *Zheleznaia zhentschina*, 255; Macdonald and Dronfield, *A Most Dangerous Woman*, 84, 89, 118; Chambers, *The Last Englishman*, 225.
11 The NKID notice of the 'Lockhart coup', September 1918, RGASPI, f. 495, op. 100, d. 1073, l. 9; *Pravda*, *Izvestiia*, 3 September 1918.
12 Long, 'Searching for Sidney Reilly', 1226.
13 M. I. Latsis, *Dva goda bor'by na vnutrennem fronte* (Gosudarstvennoe izdatel'stvo, 1920), 21–3.
14 Yakov Peters, 'Vospominaniia o rabote v VCheka v pervi god revolutsii', *Proletarskaia revolutsiia* 33, no. 10 (1924): 20–5, 31–2.
15 P. D. Mal'kov, *Zapiski komendanta Moskovskogo Kremlia* (Molodaia gvardiia, 1959), 238–61, especially, 255.
16 See, for example, N. D. Kondratiev, *Tovaritsch Peterson* (Riga: Latviiskoe gosudarstvennoe izdatel'stvo, 1959), 255–85; F. S. Pokrovsky (comp.), 'K istorii

zagovora R. Lockharta (1918 g.)', *Istoricheskii arkhiv*, no. 4 (1962): 234–7; I. Buikis, 'Proschet Lockharta', in *Osoboe zadanie*, ed. I. E. Polikarpenko (Moskovskii rabochii, 1968), 78–88.

17 A. A. Zdanovich, "Latyshskoe delo". Nyuansy Raskrytiia 'zagovora poslov', *Voenno-istoricheskii zhurnal*, no. 3 (2004): 25–32; V. K. Vinogradov et al. (eds), *Arkhiv VCheka* (Kuchkovo pole, 2007), 489–592; I. S. Rat'kovsky, *Krasnyi terror i deiatel'nost' VCheka v 1918 g* (St Petersburg: Sankt-Peterburgskii gosudarstvenni universitet, 2006), 148–222.

18 See, for example, Michael Sayers and Albert Kahn, *Great Conspiracy: The Secret War against Soviet Russia* (New York: Boni and Gaer, 1946), 23–35, 38–54; Kennan, *Soviet-American Relations*, 1: 62–3.

19 Robin Bruce Lockhart, *Ace of Spies*, 65–8; Debo, 'Lockhart Plot or Dzerzhinskii Plot?', 413–39; Idem. *Revolution and Survival*, 294–378; Rhoer, *Master Spy*, 36–56; Kettle, *Sidney Reilly*, 28–51; William Corson and Robert Crowley, *The New KGB: Engine of Soviet Power* (New York: Morrow, 1985), 31–80; Dobson, Miller, *The Day We Almost Bombed Moscow*, 156–84.

20 Long, 'Searching for Sidney Reilly', 1225–41; Idem., 'Plot and Counter-Plot in Revolutionary Russia: Chronicling the Bruce Lockhart Conspiracy', *Intelligence and National Security* 10, no. 1 (1995): 122–43; Hughes, *Inside the Enigma*, 129–32; Brook-Shepherd, *Iron Maze*, 56–78, 80–118; Judd, *The Quest for C.*, 431–48; Swain, 'An Interesting and Plausible Proposal', 81–102; Bainton, *Honoured by Strangers*, 238–43; Cook, *Ace of Spies*, 155–93; Occleshaw, *Dances in Deep Shadows*, 210–34; Smith, *Six*, 222–56; Milton, *Russian Roulette*, 74–90, 120–35, 148–67, 174–93; Macdonald and Dronfield, *A Very Dangerous Woman*, 17–31.

21 Service, *Spies and Commissars*, 155–65.

22 Vladimir Orloff, *The Secret Dossier: My Memory of Russia's Political Underworld* (G. Harrap, 1932), 301. See also, Smith, *Six*, 215, 219.

23 Cook, *Ace of Spies*, 161.

24 For further information, see George Leggett, *The Cheka: Lenin's Political Police: The All-Russian Extraordinary Commission for Combatting Counter-revolution and Sabotage (December 1917 to February 1922)* (Oxford: Clarendon Press, 1981), 286, Smith, Six, 187–205.

25 Judd, *The Quest for C*, 288–90, 311–12, 415.

26 See Peter Beesly, *Room 40. British Naval Intelligence 1914–18* (Oxford: OUP, 1984), 182.

27 Rat'kovsky, *Krasnyi terror*, 13–14.

28 Brook-Shepherd, *Iron Maze*, 111; Boynton, *Honoured by Strangers*, 207–18, 220–34.

29 Red Navy registration office's report to the Naval General Staff, 8 August 1918, RGVA, f. 3, op. 2, d. 2, ll. 7–7ob.; Northern and Petrograd district registration office report to the Red Army Main Staff, 3 September 1918, ibid., ll. 39–39ob.

30 Swain, 'An Interesting and Plausible Proposal', 86.

31 For further assessments of Latvian riflemen's mentality, see Zdanovich, 'Latyshskoe delo', 25–6; Swain, 'An Interesting and Plausible Proposal', 81–102; A. V. Shubin, 'Latyshskie strelki mezhdu rodinoi i revolutsiei', in *Rossiia i Latviia v potoke istorii: vtoraia povina XIX – pervaia polovina XX v*, ed. E. L. Nazarova (Institut vseobtschei istorii, 2015), 167.

32 Macdonald, Dronfield, *A Very Dangerous Woman*, 122.

33 Hill's report to Smith-Cumming, 26 November 1918, TNA, FO 371/3350/203967.

34 Helfferich, 'Moia moskovskaia missiia', 282.

35 Swain, 'An Interesting and Plausible Proposal', 90–1, 97; Macdonald, Dronfield, *A Very Dangerous Woman*, 83.
36 See Chicherin's conversation with Peters, October 1918, AVPRF, f. 69, op. 3, pap. 3, d. 10, ll. 12–14.
37 Zdanovich, 'Latyshskoe delo', 27. Interestingly, some authors argued that Reilly closely contacted the leaders of the left Socialist revolutionaries, see Robin Bruce Lockhart, *Ace of Spies*, 68.
38 See Lockhart, *Agoniia Rossiiskoi imperii*, 327.
39 For further details, see Bobadila Reilly (ed.), *The Adventures of Sidney Reilly, Britain's Master Spy* (E. Mathew and Marrot, 1931), 25; Pokrovsky, 'K istorii zagovora Lockharta', 235; Debo, 'Lockhart Plot or Dzerzhinskii Plot?', 430; Long, 'Searching for Sidney Reilly', 1232–3; Swain, 'An Interesting and Plausible Proposal', 82; Zdanovich, 'Latyshskoe delo', 29–32; Lockhart, *Agoniia Rossiiskoi imperii*, 331–2.
40 On the role of Maria Zakrevskaia in the plot and her affection to Lockhart, see Peters, 'Vospominaniia', 28–9; Berberova, *Zheleznaia zhentschina*, 225, 228, 305; Lockhart, *Agoniia Rossiiskoi imperii*, 305; Macdonald and Dronfield, *A Very Dangerous Woman*, 40, 122–3, 358.
41 Brook-Shepherd, *Iron Maze*, 104.
42 John Gregory, the head of the Foreign Office Northern Department, to Lockhart, 30 July 1918, TNA, FO 371/3287/129986.
43 Debo, 'Lockhart Plot or Dzerzhinskii Plot?', 429–30; Service, *Spies and Commissars*, 122; Dobson and Miller, *The Day We Almost Bombed Moscow*, 161.
44 Report by Lockhart to the Foreign Office, 5 November 1918, TNA, FO 371/3348/190442.
45 Lord Clive, the Home Secretary, to the Foreign Office, 7 September 1918, TNA, FO 371/3336/158837. On Lockhart's direct involvement in the preparations for the coup, see Hughes, *Inside the Enigma*, 139; Occleshaw, *Dances in Deep Shadows*, 230; Macdonald and Dronfield, *A Very Dangerous Woman*, 127–8.
46 Berberova, *Zheleznaia zhentschina*, 262–3; Swain, 'An Interesting and Plausible Proposal', 92.
47 See, for example, Hill, *Go Spy the Land*, VIII. On the British and American espionage networks in Soviet Russia, see David Foglesong, 'Xenophon Kalamatiano: An American Spy in Revolutionary Russia', *Intelligence and National Security* 11, no. 1 (1991): 159.
48 For the plot's details, refer to N. D. Kondratiev, *Tovaritsch Peterson*, 279; Berberova, *Zheleznaia zhentschina*, 262–3; Robin Bruce Lockhart, *Ace of Spies*, 72–3; Kettle, *Sidney Reilly*, 36–7; Dobson and Miller, *The Day We Almost Bombed Moscow*, 159; Brook-Shepherd, *Iron Maze*, 107.
49 Pokrovsky, 'K istorii zagovora Lockharta', 236; Long, 'Searching for Sidney Reilly', 1232; Occleshaw, *Dances in Deep Shadows*, 230.
50 Ferguson, *Operation Kronstadt*, 2.
51 Hill's report to Smith-Cumming, 26 November 1918, TNA, FO 371/3350/203967. On the plotters' intention to overthrow the Bolshevik Government, see also Peters, 'Vospominaniia o rabote v VCheka', 23; Mal'kov, *Vospominaniia*, 255, Robin Bruce Lockhart, *Ace of Spies*, 73; Long, 'Plot and Counter-Plot in Revolutionary Russia', 143; Dobson and Miller, *The Day We Almost Bombed Moscow*, 160.
52 Hill's report to Smith-Cumming, 26 November 1918, TNA, FO 371/3350/203967.
53 Hill, *Go Spy the Land*, 219–33. For further details of the 'Red terror' in Soviet Russia during 1918, see Rat'kovsky, *Krasnyi terror*, 117–18.

54 Yu. G. Fel'shtinsky (ed.), *L. D. Trotsky. Dnevniki i pis'ma* (Izdatel'stvo gumanitarnoi literatury, 1994), 117–18; Bothmer, *S grafom Mirbakhom*, 188, 304–5.
55 Richard Pipes, 'Unpublished Lenin', in *The Bolsheviks and Russian Society. The Revolution and the Civil Wars*, ed. V. N. Brovkin (New Haven – London: YUP, 1997), 206.
56 There is another evidence of forty British citizens detained in Petrograd, see Berberova, *Zheleznaia zhentschina*, 278. On the mass confiscation of private households and belongings, see Latsis, *Dva goda bor'by*, 24; Peters, 'Vospominaniia o rabote v VCkeka', 32.
57 On Lockhart's detentions in the Lubianka prison, see Lockhart, *Agoniia Rossiiskoi imperii*, 337; Mal'kov, *Vospominamiia*, 245–7; Berberova, *Zheleznaia zhentschina*, 271; Macdonald, Dronfield, *A Very Dangerous Woman*, 135–8, 142, 146–7. For the evaluation of the damage to the Soviet-British relations caused by Lockhart and Litvinov's reciprocal deportations, see Paget to Balfour, 3 September 1918, in Great Britain. Foreign Office. *A Collection of Reports on Bolshevism in Russia. Russia*, no. 1 (1919). Cmd. 8 (HMSO, 1919), 3; Telegram by Oudendyk, the Dutch Minister in Petrograd, 9 September 1918, *TNA*, FO 371/3336/154776.
58 *Morning Post*, 6 September 1918. See also Debo, 'Lockhart Plot or Dzerzhinskii Plot?', 415; Dobson and Miller, *The Day We Almost Bombed Moscow*, 166–7; Macdonald and Dronfield, *A Very Dangerous Woman*, 133.
59 Dobson, Miller, *The Day We Almost Bombed Moscow*, 165.
60 Gilbert, *Winston Churchill*, 4: 224–5.
61 Chamberlain to his sister Hilda, 24 September 1918, in Robert Self (ed.), *The Austen Chamberlain Diary Letters. The Correspondence of Sir Austen Chamberlain with His Sisters Hilda and Ida, 1916–1937* (Cambridge: CUP, 1995), 94.
62 The NKID statements on the internment of foreign citizens, 7 and 12 September 1918, in Kliuchnikov, Sabanin, *Mezhdunarodnaia politika noveishego vremeni*, 2: 170–1, 171–4.
63 Corson and Crowley, *The New KGB*, 52.
64 Zinoviev's speech at the meeting of the Petrograd Soviet, 1 November 1918, *RGASPI*, f. 324, op. 1, d. 13, ll. 1–4. For the official Soviet interpretation of Cromie's death, see Chicherin, *Vneshniaia politika Sovetskoi Rossii*, 18.
65 Peters, 'Vospominaniia o rabote v VCheka', 80.
66 British acting consul in Petrograd to the Foreign Office, 1 September 1918, *TNA*, FO 371/3337/168181/1–2.
67 Hall's report to Smith-Cumming, October 1918, *TNA*, ADM 223/637. For further details of the Cheka raid upon the British embassy, see Bainton, *Honoured by Strangers*, 250–7; Occleshaw, *Dancers in Deep Shadows*, 229; Ferguson, *Operation Kronstadt*, 1–6; Milton, *Russian Roulette*, 175–8; Macdonald and Dronfield, *A Very Dangerous Woman*, 132–5.
68 Wardrope, the general consul in Moscow, to the Foreign Office, 7 September 1918, *TNA*, FO 371/3337/168181. For further information, refer to Bainton, *Honoured by Strangers*, 258–64, 298; Dobson and Miller, *The Day We Almost Bombed Moscow*, 163–4.
69 Unauthorized telegram to the Foreign Office, *TNA*, FO 371/3337/168481, 1 September 1918. On the damage to the embassy building caused by the Cheka raid, see Anthony Cross, 'A Corner of a Foreign Field: The British Embassy in St Petersburg 1863–1918', *Slavonic and East European Review* 88, nos. 1–2 (2010): 352–3.
70 Quoted in Legget, *The Cheka*, 111; Rat'kovsky, *Krasnyi terror*, 121.

71 Lockhart's statement on being in custody, September 1918, AVPRF, f. 69, op. 3, pap. 3, d. 10, l. 22.
72 Rat'kovsky, *Krasnyi terror*, 159–60.
73 Legget, *The Cheka*, 114; Milton, *Russian Roulette*, 230.
74 Alston, High Commissioner in Siberia, to the Foreign Office, 1 February 1919, *TNA*, FO 608/195, f. 213. For further documentary evidence of the Bolshevik atrocities against foreign citizens, see the US consular reports and the dispatches of the American Red Cross delegation in Russia to the president administration, ibid., ff. 215–17, 221, 268.
75 Corson and Crowley, *The New KGB*, 53–63; Foglesong, 'Xenophon Kalamatiano', 165–6, 178; Brook-Shepherd, *Iron Maze*, 230–45.
76 Quoted in A. A. Ivanov, 'Organisatsiia sovetskoi kontrrazvedki na Severe Rossii (1918–1920 gg.)', *Novyi istoricheskii vestnik* 21, no. 3 (2009): 67.
77 The chief of the Naval General Staff to Trotsky and Peters, October 1918, *RGVA*, f. 1, op. 1, d. 141, ll. Л. 70–6.
78 On Lockhart's interrogation by Chekists and their attempts to recruit him, see Vinogradov, *Archiv VCheka*, 516–17.
79 Telegrams on the exchange of Lockhart for Litvinov, September–October 1918, *TNA*, FO 370/2320. Lockhart's report to the Foreign Office, October 1918, ibid., FO 371/3337/166847.
80 Diary, 29 September 1918, in Young, *The Diaries of Sir Robert Bruce Lockhart*, 1: 44–5.
81 Poiasnenie k prigovoru Verkhovnogo revolutsionnogo tribunala pri VTsIK RSFSR, 3 December 1918, *AVPRF*, f. 69, op. 3, pap. 3, d. 10, ll. 20–1.
82 Quoted in A. S. Gasparian, *Operatsiia 'Trest'. Sovetskaia razvedka protiv russkoi emigratsii. 1921–1937* (Veche, 2008), 191.
83 Vinogradov, *Archiv VCheka*, 592.
84 Macdonald and Dronfield, *A Very Dangerous Woman*, 241, 252.
85 On Marchand's letter, see Hill, *Go Spy the Land*, 236; Berberova, *Zheleznaia zhentschina*, 283; Robin Bruce Lockhart, *Ace of Spies*, 79; Kettle, *Sidney Reilly*, 39; Vinogradov, *Archiv VCheka*, 535–41; Brook-Shepherd, *Iron Maze*, 106, 108; Milton, *Russian Roulette*, 162, 187–8.
86 Lockhart's report to the Foreign Office, 5 November 1918, *TNA*, FO 371/3348/190442.
87 Hill's report to Smith-Cumming, 26 November 1918, *TNA*, FO 371/3350.
88 See, for example, Kettle, *Sidney Reilly*, 11; Dobson, Miller, *The Day We Almost Bombed Moscow*, 177.
89 Berberova, *Zheleznaia zhentschina*, 260; Debo, 'Lockhart Plot or Dzerzhinskii Plot?', 427–8.
90 The Soviet Government to President Wilson, 24 October 1918, in *DVP SSSR*, 1: 549, 556.
91 Buchanan to Cecil, 28 October 1918, *TNA*, FO 800/205/406–410.

Chapter 4

1 Quoted in *Dvadtsat' shest'. 1918–1928. Sbornik poem i stikhov pamiati 26-ti Bakinskikh komissarov* (Baku: TsK MOPR ASSR, 1928), 12.
2 On the comprehensive academic interpretation of the Great Game, see Evgeny Sergeev, *The Great Game 1856–1907: Russo-British Relations in Central and East*

Asia (Washington, DC: Woodrow Wilson Center Press – Baltimore, MD: The Johns Hopkins University Press, 2013). For the survey of the recent scholarship on the subject, including alternative points of view, see Daniel Waugh, 'Britain Confronts Bolsheviks in Central Asia: Great Game Myths and Local Realities', *Russian International Relations in War and Revolution*, 2: 341–58.

3   A. M. Fomin, 'Derzhavy Antanty i Blizhnii Vostok v 1918– 1923 gg', *Novaia i noveishaia istoriia*, no. 4 (2010): 80; V. V. Mikhailov, 'Rossiskie i britanskie vooruzhennye soedineniia v srazheniiakh protiv turok pri oborone Baku v 1918 g', *Klio* 32, no. 1 (2006): 196.

4   Basil Dmitrishyn and Frederick Cox (comps), *The Soviet Union and the Middle East. A Documentary Record of Afghanistan, Iran and Turkey, 1917–1985* (Princeton, NJ: Kingston Press, 1987), 244–5.

5   See V. A. Gurko-Kriazhin, 'Angliiskaia interventsiia v Zakaspii i Zakavkaz'e, (na osnovanii sledstvennykh materialov Verkhovnogo suda SSSR)', *Istorik-Marxist*, no. 2 (1926): 116–18.

6   On Curzon's activity as the foreign secretary in 1919–24, see David Gilmor, *Curzon* (J. Murray, 1994), 501–67; Gaynor Johnson, 'Preparing for Office: Lord Curzon as Acting Foreign Secretary, January – October 1919', in *The Foreign Office and British Diplomacy in the Twentieth Century*, ed. Gaynor Johnson (London – New York: Routledge, 2005), 53–73; E. Yu. Sergeev, *George Nathaniel Curzon – poslednii rytsar' Britanskoi imperii* (Tovaritschestvo izdatelei KMK, 2015), 206–70; etc.

7   On the Eastern Committee's establishment and functions, refer to John Fisher, 'Interdepartmental Committee on Eastern Unrest and British Responses to Bolshevik and Other Intrigues against the Empire during the 1920s', *Journal of Asian History* 34, no. 1 (2000): 1–34; A. A. Ulunian, *Turkestanskii platsdarm. 1917–1922: Britranskoe razvedyvatel'noe soobtschestvo i britanskoe pravitel'stvo* (LELAND, 2019), 22–4.

8   Houshang Sabahi, *British Policy in Persia 1918–1925* (F. Cass, 1990), 8; John Fisher, *Curzon and the British Imperialism in the Middle East, 1916–19* (London – Portland, Or.: F. Cass, 1999), 42–62.

9   S. V. Lavrov, 'Politika Anglii na Kavkaze i v Srednei Asii v 1917–1921 gg', *Voprosy istorii*, no. 5 (1979): 81–2.

10 Minutes of the War Cabinet Eastern Committee, March 1918–Janurary 1919, TNA, CAB 27/24. For these activities, see Ullman, *Anglo-Soviet Relations*, 2: 67–8; Goldstein, *Winning for Peace*, 156–7; Fisher, *Curzon and the British Imperialism*, 27.

11 Quoted in Ullman, *Anglo-Soviet Relations*, 2: 69.

12 George Curzon, *The Place of India in the Empire* (J. Murray, 1909), 12–13. For the apprehension of the Bolshevik threat by Curzon, see M. Pavlovich, *'Russkii vopros' v angliiskoi vneshnei politike (1922–1924)* (Vsesoyuznaia nauchnaia assotsiatsiia vostokovedov, 1924), 3–9.

13 P. M. Gusterin, 'Politika Sovetskogo gosudarstva na musul'manskom Vostoke v 1917–1921 gg', *Voprosy istorii*, no. 1 (2010): 92–110.

14 On Karakhan's diplomatic activity, see Besedovskii, *Na putiakh k Termidoru (iz vospominanii byvhego sovetskogo diplomata)*, 1: 222–4.

15 Isaiah Friedman, *British Miscalculations. The Rise of Muslim Nationalism, 1918–1925* (New Brunswick – London: Transaction Publishers, 2012), 87–103.

16 Dmitrishyn, Cox, *The Soviet Union and the Middle East*, 1.

17 S. S. Shaumian, *Bakinskaia kommuna* (Baku: Gosudarstvennaia tipographiia 'Krasni Vostok', 1927); A. B. Kadishev, *Interventsiia i grazhdanskaia voina v Zakavkazie*

(Voenizdat, 1960), 83–112; Ronald Suny, *The Baku Commune, 1917–1918. Class and Nationality in the Russian Revolution* (Princeton, NJ: PUP, 1972), 214–33; Dobson and Miller, *The Day We Almost Bombed Moscow*, 83–90; A. V. Shubin, 'Bakinskaia kommuna i vozniknovenie Azerbaijanskoi respubliki: perekrestie faktorov', in *Evropeiskie sravnitel'no-istoricheskie issledovaniia*, ed. A. A. Ulunian and E. Yu. Sergeev (Institut vseobstchei istorii RAN, 2014), 4: 22–5.
18   Mikhailov, 'Rossiiskie i britanskie vooruzhennye sordineniia', 197.
19   Alf Brun, *Troublous Times: Experience in Bolshevik Russia and Turkestan* (Constable, 1931), 49; Richard Koestenberger, *Mit der Roten Armee durch die Russisch-Zentralasien* (Graz: Verlag von U. Mosers Buchhandlung, 1925), 1; George Lenczowski, *Russia and the West in Iran, 1918–1948. A Study in Big-Power Rivalry* (Ithaca, NY: Cornell University Press, 1949), 31–3.
20   For further information on the Bolsheviks' military activity in Persia, refer to V. L. Genis, *Krasnaia Persiia: Bol'sheviki v Giliane 1920–1921. Dokumental'naia khronika* (Tsentr strategicheskikh i politicheskikh issledovanii, 2000); Ulunian, *Turkestanskii platsdarm*, 450–84.
21   Latham Blacker, 'Wars and Travels, 1918–1920', *Journal of the Central Asian Society* 9, pt. 1 (1922): 8; Percy Etherton, *In the Heart of Asia* (Constable, 1925), 151–2; Frederick Bailey, *Mission to Tashkent* (J. Cape, 1946), 44.
22   L. P. Morris, 'British Secret Missions in Turkestan, 1918–19', *Journal of Contemporary History* 12, no. 2 (1977): 365.
23   Alfred Rawlinson, *Adventures in the Near East, 1918–1922* (J. Cape, 1934), 57.
24   Morris, 'British Secret Missions in Turkestan', 364; L. I. Miroshnikov, *Angliiskaia expansiia v Irane (1914–1920)* (Vostochnaia literatura, 1961), 72.
25   Occleshaw, *Dances in Deep Shadows*, 39. On Dunsterforce's military-political activity in the Middle East, see, especially, Lenczowski, *Russia and the West in Iran*, 16–22; Plotke, *Imperial Spies Invade Russia*, 125–58; Timothy Winegard, 'Dunsterforce: A Case Study of Coalition Warfare in the Middle East, 1918–1919', *Canadian Army Journal* 8, no. 3 (2005): 93–109; Idem., *The First Oil War* (Toronto – Buffalo: University of Toronto Press, 2016); Alan Stewart, *Persian Expedition: The Australians in Dunsterforce, 1918* (Loftus, NSW: Australian Military History Publications, 2006); Edward Lemon, 'Dunsterforce or Dunsterfarce? Re-Evaluation of the British Mission to Baku, 1918', *First World War Studies* 6, no. 2 (2015): 133–49; Preston Lim, 'Upon the Altar of British Prestige: A Re-Evaluation of Dunsterforce's Exploits and Legacy', *Caucasus Survey* 5, no. 2 (2017): 103–20.
26   M. H. Donohoe, *With the Persian Expedition* (E. Arnold, 1919), 4, 203; Lionel Dunsterville, *The Adventures of Dunsterforce* (E. Arnold, 1920), 9–10.
27   Kennan, *Soviet-American Relations*, 1: 187.
28   See, for example, Suny, *The Baku Commune*, 274.
29   Ibid., 277.
30   Dunsterville, *The Adventures of Dunsterforce*, 16; William and Zelda Coates, *Soviets in Central Asia* (Wishart and Lawrence, 1951), 75; E. L. Shteinberg, *Istoriia britanskoi agressii na Srednem Vostoke* (Voenizdat, 1951), 179; Chattar Samra, *India and Anglo-Soviet Relations (1917–1947)* (Bombay, etc.: Asia Publishing House, 1959), 25; Kadishev, *Interventsia i grazhdanskaia voina*, 80–2; Charles Ellis, *The Transcaspian Episode, 1918–1919* (Hutchinson, 1963), 20–1; Winegard, 'Dunsterforce', 103.
31   Miroshnikov, *Angliiskaia expansiia v Irane*, 71; A. K. Babokhodzhaev, *Proval angliiskoi politiki v Srednei Asii i na Srednem Vostoke (1918–1924)* (Vostochnaia literatura, 1962), 61; Winegard, 'Dunsterforce', 103.

32 On the Russo-British military interaction in Persia, see A. G. Emelianov, *Persidskii front (1915–1918)* (Berlin: Gamayun, 1923), 51, 55; Miroshnikov, *Angliiskaia expansiia v Irane*, 11–46; V. V. Mikhailov, 'Vostochnyi vopros i positsii Velikobritanii i Rossii v Pervoi mirovoi voine,' (Avtoref diss. kandidata istoricheskikh nauk, Sankt-Peterburgskii gosudarstvenni universitet, St Petersburg, 2010), 30–1.

33 Dunsterville, *The Adventures of Dunsterforce*, 72–3; Emelianov, *Persidskii front*, 197–9, Miroshnikov, *Angliiskaia expansiia v Irane*, 53–4.

34 Donohoe, *With the Persian Expedition*, 70–2.

35 Dunsterville, *The Adventures of Dunsterforce*, 122–3; Gurko-Kriazhin, 'Angliiskaia interventsiia', 122; A. A. Ivanov (comp.), 'Gorskaia kontrrevolutsiia i interventy', *Krasnyi arkhiv* 68, no. 1 (1935): 139–40; A. Yu. Besugolny, *General Bicherakhov i ego Kavkazskaia armiia: neizvestnye stranitsy istorii Grazhdanskoi voiny i interventsii na Kavkase: 1917–1919* (Zentrpoligraf, 2011), 46–7.

36 Certificate of Major General Bicherakhov's merits to the Allies, early 1919, TNA, PA, STH, DS, STH/DS/2/2/4. On Bicherakhov's joint operations with the British troops, see Donohoe, *With the Persian Expedition*, 196–7; 203–7; Lionel Dunsterville, 'Military Mission to North-West Persia, 1918', *Journal of the Central Asian Society* 8, pt. 2 (1921): 79–98; Rawlinson, *Adventures in the Near East*, 3–106; Winegard, 'Dunsterforce', 10.

37 S. S. Shaumian, *Bakinskaia kommuna*, 114; Mikhailov, 'Rossiiskie i britanskie vooruzhennye soedineniia', 196–7, 199.

38 Sean Macmeekin, *The Ottoman Endgame. War, Revolution and the Making of the Modern Middle East, 1908–1923* (G. Allen and Unwin, 2015), 315–40; Taline Ter Minassian, 'From the Transcaspian to the Caucasus; Reginald Teague-Jones's Secret War (1918–21)', *Russian International Relations in War and Revolution* 2 (2021): 366–9.

39 S. S. Shaumian, *Bakinskaia kommuna*, 42; Kadishev, *Interventsiia i grazhdanskaia voina*, 117–18; Shubin, 'Bakinskaia kommuna', 34, 36.

40 Robert Johnson, *Spying for Empire. The Great Game in Central and South Asia, 1757–1947* (Greenhill Books, 2006), 230.

41 Rawlinson, *Adventures in the Near East*, 59.

42 S. S. Shaumian, *Bakinskaia kommuna*, 117; Besugolny, *General Bicherakhov*, 73–4, 81–2.

43 Rawlinson, *Adventures in the Near East*, 64–7; Gurko-Kriazhin, 'Amgliiskaia interventsiia', 123; Firouz Kazemzadeh, *The Struggle for Transcaucasia (1917–1921)* (Anglo-Caspian Press, 2008), 133–5; Goekay, *A Clash of Empires*, 30–1.

44 Macdonell, *And Nothing Long*, 210–12; Suny, *The Baku Commune*, 279–80.

45 L. S. Shaumian, *Rasstrel 26 bakinskikh komissarov angliiskimi interventami* (Pravda, 1949), 11–12.

46 Rawlinson, *Adventures in the Near East*, 65; Macdonell, *And Nothing Long*, 232; Johnson, *Spying for Empire*, 231; Goekay, *A Clash of Empires*, 30.

47 A. I. Mikoian, *Dorogoi bor'by* (Gospolitizdat, 1971), 146, 169.

48 I. Ratgauser, *Arest i gibel' komissarov Bakinskoi kommuny* (Baku: Otdel TsK i BK Azerbaidzhanskoi KP(b), 1928), 10, 15; Mikoian, *Dorogoi bor'by*, 176–7.

49 Rawlinson, *Adventures in the Near East*, 67.

50 Macdonell, *And Nothing Long*, p. 267.

51 L. M. Lifshits, *Geroicheskii podvig bakinskikh bolshevikov* (Baku: Azerneshr, 1964), 238; Miroshnikov, *Angliiskaia expansiia v Irane*, 117.

52 See, for example, R. Begak, *Sud and anglichanami, sdavshimi Baku turkam v 1918 g* (Baku: Azgiz, 1927), 65.

53 Dunsterville, *The Adventures of Dunsterforce*, 239–62; Suny, *The Baku Commune*, 259–92.
54 S. S. Shaumian, *Bakinskaia kommuna*, 58–60.
55 Ratgauser, *Arest i gibel'*, 22–3; Kadishev, *Interventsiia i grazhdanskaia voina*, 138–43.
56 Ratgauser, *Arest i gibel'*, 29; Bukshpan, *Poslednie dni*, 161–5.
57 Donohoe, *With the Persian Expedition*, 217–18; Macdonell, *And Nothing Long*, 61–6; Miroshnikov, *Angliiskaia interventsiia v Irane*, 118, 122; Johnson, *Spying for Empire*, 232; Shubin, 'Bakinskaia kommuna', 39–40.
58 Note by Lieutenant-General Cox on Malleson's mission, 20 December 1918, BLAAS. L/MIL/7/16919, ff. 158–60. See also Wilfrid Malleson, Twenty-Six Commissars, *Fortnightly Review*, 11, no. 133 (1933). http://turkmeny.h1.ru/memuar/m1.html (accessed 11 May 2017).
59 Report on military mission at Mashed, 1918–1931, BLAAS. L/MIL/7/16900, ff. 1–299; Malleson, 'The British Military Mission to Turkestan, 1918–20', *Journal of the Central Asian Society* 9, pt. II (1922): 96; Ellis, *The Transcaspian Episode*, 22–3.
60 See, Waugh, 'Britain Confronts Bolsheviks in Central Asia', 2: 349.
61 Note by Lieutenant-General Cox, 20 December 1918, BLAAS. L/MIL/7/16919, f. 160. On the Kremlin's negative reaction to Malleson's mission, see, Gurko-Kriazhin, 'Angliiskaia interventsiia', 137; Timoshkov, *Bor'ba s angliiskoi interventsiei v Turkestane*, 27; A. N. Kheifets, *Sovetskaia Rossiia i sopredel'nye strany Vostoka. 1921–1927* (Nauka, 1968), 201.
62 N. N. Lishin, *Na Kaspiiskom more. God beloi bor'by* (Prague: Izdadel'stvo Morskogo zhurnala, 1933), 35–6; Ellis, *The Transcaspian Episode*, 27.
63 Quoted in S. Tashliev (ed.), *Turkmenistan v period inistrannoi voennoi interventsii i grazhdanskoi voiny. 1918–1920* (Ashgabat: Turkmengosizdat, 1957), 65.
64 Ellis, The Transcaspian Episode, 31; Tashliev, Turkmenistan v period, 93–7; T. E. Yeleulov, and K. S. Inoiatov (eds), *Inostrannaia voennaia interventsiia i grazhdanskaia voina v Srednei Asii i Kazakhstane. Dokumenty i materialy* (Alma-Ata: Izdatel'stvo AN Kazachskoi SSR, 1963), 1: 333–6.
65 Skeleton Map of Russia and Northern Asia. Situation in Russia and Siberia from information received to 21 April 1919, TNA, FO 418/53. On the operations of the British expeditionary forces in Central Asia in the autumn of 1918, see, especially, Etherton, *In the Heart of Asia*, 153, 155; Blacker, *On Secret Patrol in High Asia*, 26–8, 134, 137–68; A. E. Knollys, 'Military Operations in Transcaspia', *Journal of the Central Asian Society* 13, pt. II (1926): 95–115; Bailey, *Mission to Tashkent*, 51–2; William and Zelda Coates, *Soviets in Central Asia*, 75; Hopkirk, *The Spy Who Disappeared*, 102–12; Johnson, *Spying for Empire*, 233.
66 Quoted in Hopkirk, *The Spy Who Disappeared*, 11. On Teague-Jones' life and activity, see, especially, Taline Ter Minassian, *Reginald Teague-Jones. Au service secret de l'Empire britannique* (Paris: Grasset, 2012); Idem., 'From the Caspian to the Caucasus: Reginald Teague-Jones's Secret war', 2: 359–75.
67 Hopkirk, *The Spy Who Disappeared*, 35, 62–8, 71–6. See also Johnson, *Spying for Empire*, 231–2.
68 Peter Hopkirk, *On Secret Service East of Constantinople. The Plot to Bring Down the British Empire* (J. Murray, 1994), 361–5; Johnson, Spying for Empire, 233; Ter Minassian, Reginald Teague-Jones, 123.
69 Malleson to the Indian Army General Headquarters, 18 September 1918, BLAAS. L/MIL/17/559. See also Tashliev, *Turkmenistan v period*, 127; M. I. Lifshits, *Kto vinovat v ubiistve 26-ti?* (Tiflis: Aktcionernoe obtschestvo 'Zakkniga', 1926). 12.
70 Macdonell, *And Nothing More*, 258–9; S. S. Shaumian, *Bakinskaia kommuna*, 64.

71 *BLAAS*. L/PS/10/741. See also Malleson, Twenty-Six Commissars', http://turkmeny.h1.ru/memuar/m1.html (accessed 11 May 2017).
72 Begak, *Sud nad anglichanami*, 44; Bukshpan, *Poslednie dni*, 75, 81; Tashliev, *Turkmenistan v period*, 127; Shaumian, *Rasstrel 26 bakinskikh komissarov*, 19.
73 Teague Jones – to the Under-Secretary of the India Office, 7 June 1922, *TNA*, FO 371/8204, ff. 174–9; Great Britain. Foreign Office, *Correspondence between His Majesty's Government and the Soviet Government Respecting the Murder of Mr. C.F. Davison in January 1920*, Russia no. 1 (1923), Cmd. 1846. London: HMSO, 7–11. See also Hopkirk, *The Spy Who Disappeared*, 120–2.
74 Bukshpan, *Poslednie dni*, 84.
75 Jarvis – to Pike, September 1918, *BLAAS*. Mss Eur. Major Jarvis Papers, D/942/6A.
76 Teague-Jones to the Permanent Under-Secretary for Foreign Affairs, 11 February 1923, *TNA*, FO 371/8205/78–84. The alternation of date was explained by the Foreign Office's desire to support their position in the acute controversy with the NKID.
77 *BLAAS*. Mss Eur. R. Sinclair (Teague-Jones) Papers, C 313/12, ff. 11–14.
78 Minassian, 'Some Fresh News about the 26 Commissars: Reginald Teague-Jones and the Transcaspian Episode', 71–2.
79 Mikoian, *Dorogoi bor'by*, 227; Ter Minassian, 'Some Fresh News about the 26 Commissars', 73–4.
80 Peters, acting diplomatic agent in Russia, to Litvinov, 20 December 1922; Litvinov to Peters, 12 January 1923, Great Britain. Foreign Office, *Correspondence between His Majesty's Government and the Soviet Government Respecting the Murder of Mr. C.F. Davison*, 11–12; Peters – to Curzon, 16 January 1923, *TNA*, FO 371/9357/161; Chicherin to the Foreign Office, 24 January, 13 February, 23 March 1919, *AVPRF*, f. 0528, op. 1, pap. 1, d. 2, l. 110; ibid., f. 69, op. 4, pap. 4, d. 2, ll. 1, 4, 6.
81 V. Chaikin, *Kazn' 26 bakinskikh komissarov* (Moscow: Izdatel'stvo I. Grzhebina, 1922).
82 Malleson, 'The Twenty-Six Commissars', – http://turkmeny.h1.ru/memuar/m1.html (accessed 11 May 2017). See also History of Dunsterforce, April 1922, *BLAAS*. Mss Eur C 313/12. F. 422. On the attempts by the Kremlin to offer the exchange of political prisoners, see Kadishev, *Interventsiia i grazhdanskaia voina v Zakavkazie*, 143.
83 Quoted in Malleson, 'The Twenty-Six Commissars', – http://turkmeny.h1.ru/memuar/m1.html (accessed 11 May 2017).
84 Malleson to the Chief of the General Staff in India, 23 September 1918, *BLAAS*. L/PS/10/741.
85 Ibid., Chief of the General Staff in India to Malleson, 24 September 1918.
86 Ibid., Grant, The Foreign Secretary of the Government of India, to Malleson, 24 September 1918.
87 The Foreign Office of the Government of India to Malleson, 30 September 1918, *BLAAS*. L/MIL/17/559. See also Brian Pierce, 'The 26 Commissars: On the Fate of the 26 Commissars', in *Papers of the Sixth and Seventh International Conferences of the Study Group on the Russian Revolution* (Leeds: Leeds University Press, 1981), 104.
88 Chicherin to Balfour, 21 April 1919, *AVPRF*, f. 69, op. 4, pap. 4, d. 2, ll. 10–11; ibid., f. 0528, op. 1, pap. 1, d. 2, ll. 136–7.
89 *Izvestiya*, 23 April 1919, Joseph Stalin, 'K rasstrelu 26 bakinskikh tovaritschei agentami angliiskogo imperializma', 1.
90 G. Z. Sorokin, *Pervi s'ezd narodov Vostoka* (Vostochnaia literatura, 1961), 43; K. G. Vezirov (ed.), *Pamiati 26 bakinskikh kommissarov. Dokumenty i materialy* (Baku: Azerbaidjanskoe gosudarstvennoe izdatel'stvo, 1968), 41–2; Hopkirk, *The Spy Who Disappeared*, 215.

91 Official reply by the India Office to the NKID, 15 June 1922, *TNA*, FO 371/8204, f. 190.
92 Hodgson to Curzon, 4 August 1922, ibid., FO 371/8205, f. 34.
93 Peters to Curzon, 17 July 1923, ibid., FO 371/9357, f. 175. See also Clifford Kinvig, *Churchill's Crusade: The British Invasion of Russia, 1918–1920* (Continuum, 2006), 328–9.
94 Ter Minassian, *Reginald Teague-Jones*, 106; Idem., 'Some Fresh News about the 26 Commissars', 65–6.
95 Frederick Bailey, 'In Russian Turkestan under the Bolsheviks', *Journal of the Central Asian Society* 8, pt 1 (1921): 49–69. On Bailey's travels in Asia since 1904, see Frederick Bailey, *No Passport to Tibet* (R. Hart-Davis, 1957); Karl Meyer, and Sharon Brysac, *Tournament of Shadows. The Great Game and the Race for Empire in Asia* (Abacus, 2001), 338–9, 430–2; Sergeev, *The Great Game*, 217–38; Waugh, 'Britain Confronts the Bolsheviks in Central Asia', 350–1, etc.
96 Quoted in Hopkirk, *Setting the East Ablaze*, 9.
97 Etherton, *In the Heart of Asia*, 7, 123, 225–7; Bailey, *Mission to Tashkent*, 43–6.
98 Report on the Kashgar mission, 1918–20, *BLAAS*. Mss Eur. Bailey's Papers. F 157/275, ff. 1–17. For the typical Soviet publications, see Timoshkov, *Bor'ba s angliiskoi interventsiei*, 61–2; Shteinberg, *Istoriia britanskoi agressii*, 180; N. Ia. Mil'stein, *Iz istorii Turkestanskoi Cheka* (Tashkent: Nauka, 1965), 21–2; L. N. Khariukov, *Anglo-russkoe sopernichestvo v Zemtal'noi Asii i ismailism* (Izdatel'stvo MGU, 1995), 118–19. For the recent Western studies of Bailey's mission to Tashkent, see Bush, *From Mudros to Lausanne*, 41; Johnson, *Spying for Empire*, 239–43.
99 Report on the Kashgar mission, 1918–20, ff. 19–27, *BLAAS*. L/PS/10/722, pt I.
100 Diary, 18 August 1918, in Brun, *Troublous Times*, 138; Blacker, *On Secret Patrol in High Asia*, 23–4; Bailey, *Mission to Tashkent*, 31, 54–5.
101 Bailey, *Mission Tashkent*, 142; Hopkirk, *Setting the East Ablaze*, 36; Milton, *Russian Roulette*, 216–17.
102 Report on the Kashgar mission, 1918–20, f. 19, *BLAAS*. L/PS/10/722, pt I.
103 Bailey, *Mission to Tashkent*, 146–7; Hopkirk, *Setting the East Ablaze*, 54–5; Johnson, *Spying for Empire*, 240.
104 Yeleulov, Inoiatov, *Inostrannaia voennaia interventsiia*, 1: 91.
105 Report on the Kashgar mission. 1918–20, f. 20, *BLAAS*. L/PS/10/722, pt. 1; Bailey, *Mission to Tashkent*, 81.
106 Morris, 'British Secret Missions in Turkestan', 373–4.
107 On Barkatullah's subversive activities in Asian countries, see V. V. Damie, 'Mandiama Prativadi Bkhaiankara Tirumala Aiariia: ot bolshevisma k anarkhismu', *Novoe literaturnoe obozrenie*, no. 52 (2017): 143–4.
108 For further information about Soviet intrigues in Persia and Afghanistan, see B. Z. Shumiatskii, *Na postu sovetskoi diplomatii* (Leningrad: Priboi, 1927), 5; Miroshnikov, *Angliiskaia expansiia v Irane*, 56; Volodarskii, *Sovety i ikh yuzhnye sosedi*, 45–6; Johnson, *Spying for Empire*, 241.
109 Report on the Kashgar mission. 1918–1920, *BLAAS*. L/PS/10/722, pt. I, ff. 23–5; Notes on foreign relations of the Turkestan Republic with Afghanistan, Bokhara, Khiva, Persia and China, ibid., ff. 25–7; Note on the Government of the Turkestan Republic, ibid., ff. 70–87; Communications from Lieutenant-Colonel Bailey, May–November 1919, ibid., f. 123-5. See also Bailey, *Mission to Tashkent*, 260; Brun, *Troublous Times*, 164–70; Hopkirk, *Setting the East Ablaze*, 91–5; Johnson, *Spying for Empire*, 242.
110 Richard Popplewel, *Intelligence and Imperial Defence. Defence of the Indian Empire, 1904–1924* (F. Cass, 1995), 307.

111 Quoted in Cecil Kaye, *Communism in India* (Delhi: Government of India Press, 1926), 1.
112 Hopkirk, *Setting the East Ablaze*, 175.
113 K. M. Troianovsky, *Vostok i revolutsiia. Popytka postroeniia novoi politicheskoi programmy dlia tuzemnykh stran Vostoka – India, Persia i Kitai* (Izdatel'stvo VTsik RSFSR, 1918), 20.
114 Idem., Plan organisatsii i programma deiatel'nosti revolutsionnoi ekspeditsii v Indiyu, April 1918, *AVPRF*, f. 90, op. 1a, pap. 1, d. 1, ll. 1–3.
115 On the Bolsheviks' projects regarding India, refer to Harish Kapur, *Soviet Russia and Asia, 1917–1927. A Study of Soviet Policy towards Turkey, Iran and Afghanistan* (London – Geneva: M. Joseph for the Geneva Graduate Institute of International Studies, 1966), 230–41; Zafar Imam, *Colonialism in East-West Relations A Study of Soviet Policy towards India and Anglo–Soviet Relations, 1917–1947* (Delhi: Patriot Publishers, 1987), 102–6. It should be noted that Persia was regarded by the Bolsheviks as another 'Suez Canal of Revolution', see Lenczowskii, *Russia and the West in Iran*, 10. On the Bolsheviks' policy in Afghanistan, see S. B. Panin, *Sovetskaia Rossiia i Afghanistan 1919–1929* (Moscow – Irkutsk: Izdatel'stvo Irkutskogo gosudarstvennogo pedagogicheskogo universiteta, 1998).
116 Manabendra Roy, *Memoirs* (Bombay: Allied Publishers, 1964), 286–94; Popplewel, *Intelligence and Imperial Defence*, 166, 216–35.
117 Imam, *Colonialism in East-West Relations*, 57.
118 *Morning Post*, 30 July 1918.
119 Lenczowski, *Russia and the West in Iran*, 39; Popplewel, *Intelligence and Imperial Defence*, 166, 307–8. On the activities of the Indian revolutionaries in Russian Turkestan, see M. A. Perciz, *Revolutionery Indii v Strane Sovetov. U istokov indiiskogo kommunisticheskogo dvizheniia* (Nauka, 1973); G. L. Dmitriev, *Indian Revolutionaries in Central Asia* (Calcutta: Greenwich Millennium Press, 2002), 40–67; Ulunian, *Turkestanskii platsdarm*, 600–38.
120 Quoted in Samra, *India and Anglo-Soviet Relations*, 25.
121 See D. I. Abrikosov, *Sud'ba russkogo diplomata* (Russkii Put', 2008), 317.

Chapter 5

1 www.commons.vikimedia.org (accessed 18 November 2021).
2 Price, *My Reminiscences*, 332.
3 Quoted in Jeffrey, *MI6*, 272.
4 Victor Madeira, *Britannia and the Bear. The Anglo–Russian Intelligence Wars 1917–1929* (Woodbridge, Suffolk: The Boydell Press, 2014), 18.
5 Chamberlin, *The Russian Revolution*, 1: 151. See also A. M. Fomin, 'Voenno-politicheskie tseli Velikobritanii', 88–9.
6 Minutes of the War Cabinet's meeting, 14 November 1918, *TNA*, CAB 23/8. See also Keeble, *Britain and the Soviet Union*, 49.
7 PD, Fifth ser., CX: 1547.
8 Gilbert, *Winston S. Churchill*, 4: pt 1, 226–7.
9 Great Britain. War Office, *Army. The Evacuation of North Russia, 1919*, Cmd. 818 (HMSO, 1920). Some historians wrote about 16,000 or even 20,000 British military servicemen in Russia, see Gilbert, *Churchill. A Life*, 405, 411; Keeble, *Britain and the*

Soviet Union, 47. According to contemporary observers, there were 22,000 British military volunteers in the south of Russia, 15,000 – in the north of the country, and 7,000 in Siberia by the end of 1918, see Bennett, *Freeing the Baltic*, 25. The Soviet researchers estimated the number of the British military in Russia at 14,000, see Trukhanovsky, *Winston Churchill*, 177. The leading British military historian considered this number to be correct, see Briand Bond, *British Military Policy between the Two World Wars* (Oxford: Clarendon Press, 1980), 14.

10 Memorandum by Crowe for the Cabinet, 7 November 1918, *TNA*, CAB 29/1; Reply by the War Office, 5 December 1918, ibid., CAB 27/38. See also Ullman, *Anglo-Soviet Relations*, 2: 86; Miroshnikov, *Angliiskaia expansiia v Irane*, 126; Figes, *A People's Tragedy*, 574; D. A. Mal'tsev, 'Entente i boevye deistviia na yuge Rossii v 1918–1920 gg.', in *Voennaia interventsiia i grazhdanskaia voina v Rossii (1918–1920 gg.)*, ed. G. I. Bordiugov (AIRO-XXI, 2009), 103–4.

11 Memorandum by Churchill for the Cabinet, 19 November 1918, in Gilbert, *Winston S. Churchill*, 4: pt. I, 418. See also Mannerheim, *Memoirs*, 143; Kinvig, *Churchill's Crusade*, 103–95.

12 Memorandum by Curzon for the Cabinet, 13 November 1918, *TNA*, CAB 24/70.

13 Pipes, *Russia under the Bolshevik Regime*, 68.

14 Ironside to the War Office, 8 March 1919, *TNA*, WO/33/966; Ullman, *Anglo-Soviet Relations*, 2: 201–3; Trukhanovsky, *Winston Churchill*, 178; Gilbert, *Winston S. Churchill*, 4: pt I, 261; Chambers, *The Last Englishman*, 2.

15 Klugman, *History of the CPGB*, 1: 79; Pipes, *Russia under the Bolshevik Regime*, 69.

16 Quoted in Gilbert, *Winston S. Churchill*, 4: pt I, 230. See also minutes of the War Cabinet meeting, 31 December 1918, *TNA*, CAB/23/42/48.

17 *Daily Express*, 3 January 1919.

18 Gilbert, *Winston S. Churchill*, 4: pt I, 230–31, 240–1.

19 Quoted in Jeffrey, *The Military Defence of the British Empire*, 200.

20 Churchill to Lloyd George, 17 January 1919, *TNA*, PA. LG/F/24/4/4. See also Henry Wilson's diary, 13 February 1919, in Gilbert, *Winston S. Churchill*, 4: pt I, 241.

21 Ibid., 240, 271–2, 303; Robert Dutton, *Austin Chamberlain: Gentleman in Politics* (Bolton: R. Anderson, 1985), 159.

22 Montagu to Lloyd George, 14 February 1919, *TNA*, PA. LG/F/40/2/35. Quoted in Gilbert, *Winston S. Churchill*, IV: pt I, 251. During one of his parliamentary orations, Lloyd George called the military intervention in Russia 'the greatest act of stupidity that any government could possibly commit', see Anthony Lentin, *Lloyd George and the Lost Peace. From Versailles to Hitler, 1919–1940* (Palgrave, 2001), 9.

23 Owen, *Tempestuous Journey*, 509–10.

24 Borden to Lloyd George, 13 February 1919, *OUBL*, MS. Milner, dep. 143; Hughes to Lloyd George, 5 March 1919, *TNA*, PA. LG F/28/3/6; Botha to Lloyd George, 1 April 1919, ibid., PA LG F/5/5/5. See also Jeffrey, *The Military Defence of the British Empire*, 51.

25 Quoted in Lenin, *Lenin o vneshnei politike Sovetskogo gosudarstva*, 185. See also Andrew Thorpe, *The British Communist Party and Moscow, 1920–43* (Manchester – New York: Manchester University Press, 2000), 29.

26 Kerensky, *Rossiia na istoricheskom povorote*, 493.

27 Memorandum by the War Office General Staff, 12 January 1919, *TNA*, FO 608/196, f. 4.

28 Chicherin, *Vneshniaia politika Sovetskoi Rossii*, 26; Dennis, *The Foreign Policies of Soviet Russia*, 73; Fleming, *The Cold War and Its Origins*, 30–1; Page Arnot, *The Impact of the Russian Revolution in Britain*, 161.

29 Lloyd George, *Memoirs of the Peace Conference* (New York: H. Fertig, 1972), 1: 213–14.
30 Chicherin, *Vneshniaia politika Sovetskoi Rossii*, 26; Ioffe, *Organisatsiia interventsii*, 79.
31 Lloyd George, Memoirs of the Peace Conference, 1: 118, 133. See also Stein, '*Russkii vopros' na Parizhskoi mirnoi konferetsii*, 52.
32 Dennis, *The Foreign Policies of Soviet Russia*, 76–80.
33 Charles Hardinge, *Old Diplomacy* (J. Murray, 1947), 234–5.
34 U.S. Department of State, *Papers Relating to the Foreign Relations of the United States (FRUS). The Paris Peace Conference. 1919* (Washington, DC: Department of State, 1942), III: 676; Lloyd George, Memoirs of the Peace Conference, 1: 238–9. On the organization of the Prinkipo conference, see, especially, Hardinge, Old Diplomacy, 235; Henry Steed, *Through Thirty Years. 1892-1922. A Personal Narrative* (London – New York: W. Heinemann – Doubleday, Page and Co., 1924); William and Zelda Coates, *Armed Intervention in Russia*, 146–60; Owen, *Tempestuous Journey*, 510; Kennan, *Russia and the West under Lenin and Stalin*, 126–35; Ullman, *Anglo-Soviet Relations*, 2: 99–135; Mowat, *The Cambridge Modern History*, 12: 212; Gardner, *Safe for Democracy*, 237; Macmillan, *Peacemakers*, 84–8; etc.
35 A. Borman, *A. V. Tyrkova-Williams po eio pis'mam i vospominaniiam syna* (Louven – Washington: A. Rosseels Printing, 1964), 169; A. I. Denikin, *Ocherki russkoi smuty* (Berlin: Slovo, 1925), 4: 340–5; Leonid Strakhovsky, *The Story of Allied Intervention and Russian Counter-Revolution in North Russia 1918–1920* (London – Oxford – Princeton, NJ: H. Milford – PUP, 1944), 139–52.
36 Memorandum of the Russians residents in London, February 1919, *TNA*, CUL. Lord Templewood (Samuel Hoare) Papers, pt II, file 3, 1919.
37 Macmillan, *Peacemakers*, 74–5.
38 Memorandum by the Foreign Office political intelligence department, 15 February 1919, *TNA*, CAB 24/75/48.
39 Radiogram by the Soviet government to the Entente leaders, 4 February 1919, *AVPRF*, f. 69, op. 4, pap. 4, d. 1, ll. 4-5 Stein, '*Russkii vopros*', 97; S. V. Listikov, 'Velikie derzhavy i "russkii vopros": resheniia Versal'skoi mirnoi konferentsii 1919–1920 godov i ikh posledstviia', *Rossiiskaia istoriia*, no. 5 (2011): 17.
40 Zinoviev's speech at the Petrograd Soviet meeting, 27 January 1919, *TNA*, FO 418/53, pt. I, ff. 1–5.
41 Gilbert, *Churchill. A Life*, 407–8.
42 Ibid., 408–9.
43 Owen, *Tempestuous Journey*, 507–8.
44 Ibid., 507; Gilbert, *Winston S. Churchill*, 4: pt I, 243–56.
45 Ioffe, *Organisatsiia interventsii*, 67; Stein, '*Russkii vopros*', 134–5; Stanley Roskill, *Hankey, Man of Secrets* (W. Collins, 1972), 2: 69; Keeble, *Britain and the Soviet Union*, 60.
46 Owen, *Tempestuous Journey*, 511–13; Gilbert, *Churchill. A Life*, 409–10.
47 Churchill to Lloyd George, 17 February 1919 (draft), *CU*, CAC. CHAR 16/21.
48 Quoted in Owen, *Tempestuous Journey*, 514.
49 Bullitt's proposals to Soviet Government, 9 March 1919, *DBFP*, First ser., III: 426–9. See also Pipes, *Russia under the Bolshevik Regime*, 66–7; S. V. Listikov, 'Missiia Williama Bullita v Sovetskuyu Rossiyu, 1919 g.', in *Amerikanskii ezhegodnik*, ed. V. V. Sogrin (Ves' Mir, 2013), 216.
50 For further details of Bullitt's mission to Russia, see Draft of the agreement between the Entente and the Government of Russian Federation, 12 March 1919, in ed.

Kliuchnikov, Sabanin, *Mezhdunarodnaia politika noveishego vremeni*, II: 235-7; William Bullitt, *The Bullitt Mission to Russia* (New York: B. Hübsch, 1919); Steed, *Through Thirty Years*, 2: 301-7; Fischer, *The Soviets in World Affairs*, 1: 171-3; Stein, 'Russkii vopros', 94-139; Ullman, *Anglo-Soviet Relations*, 2: 136-52; Debo, *Survival and Consolidation*, 34-54; Kettle, *Russia and the Allies*, 3: 54-99, 192-216; Brook-Shepherd, *Iron Maze*, 175.
51 Ibid., 176, 357.
52 *The Times*, 29 March 1919.
53 Bullitt, *The Bullitt Mission to Russia*, 66-7, 73; Debo, *Survival and Consolidation*, 50; Listikov, 'Missiia Williama Bullita', 226.
54 Macmillan, *Peacemakers*, 78.
55 William and Zelda Coates, *A History of Anglo-Soviet Relations*, 1: 141.
56 Quoted in Roskill, *Hankey*, 2: 77.
57 Lloyd George's speech in the House of Commons, 16 April 1919, *DBFP*, First ser., III: 308-11.
58 Memorandum by the Foreign Office political intelligence department, 22 April 1919, *TNA*, FO 608/181/6.
59 Correspondence on relations with Admiral Kolchak, January-June 1919, ibid., FO 608/188/7, ff. 157, 176-8, 179-519.
60 Appeal of the great powers to Admiral Kolchak, 27 May 1919, *GARF*, f. 5827, op. 1, d. 171, ll. 1-2; *DBFP*, First ser., III: 312-19; The Kolchak government's response to the Allied states' diplomatic note, 4 June 1919, *GARF*, f. 5827, op. 1, d. 171, ll. 2-2ob.; The official recognition by the Entente states of the Kolchak government, 12 June 1919, ibid., ll. 2ob.-3.
61 Knox to the War Office, 14 May 1919, *TNA*, FO 608/205.
62 *The Times*, 15 February, 27 May 1919. See also William and Zelda Coates, *Armed Intervention in Russia*, 201-2; Pipes, *Russia under the Bolshevik Regime*, 45.
63 Fleming, *The Cold War and Its Origins*, 20; Dumova, Trukhanovsky, *Churchill i Miliukov*, 80-95; Dobson, Miller, *The Day We Almost Bombed Moscow*, 232-46.
64 Quoted in G. K. Gins, *Siberia, soyuzniki i Kolchak. Povorotnyi moment russkoi istorii. 1918-1920 gg.* (AIRIS-Press, 2013), 475-6. On the 'Kolchak's spring of 1919', also see Smele, *The 'Russian' Civil Wars*, 110-19.
65 Curzon to Balfour, 1 July 1919, *DBFP*, First ser., III: 409-10; Denikin, *Ocherki russkoi smuty*, 5: 167-73. On the problem of the Entente's diplomatic recognition of Kolchak, see Gardner, *Safe for Democracy*, 252-8; Kinvig, *Churchill's Crusade*, 291-314. The Cabinet decided to transfer British military support from the Kolchak troops to the army under Denikin on 27 July 1919, see Memorandum by Harvey for the Cabinet, 29 July 1919, *DBFP*, First ser., III: 460-4. For further important details of this support, see also Pipes, *Russia under the Bolshevik Regime*, 96-7; Smele, *The 'Russian' Civil Wars*, 119-26.
66 Sablin to the Department of Foreign Affairs at the AFSR, 4 October 1919, *GARF*, f. 5805, op. 1, d. 315, ll. 47; Sablin to the AFSR Department for Foreign Affairs, 10 October 1919, in M. Kim (comp.), 'Iz archiva organizatorov grazhdanskoi voiny i interventsii v Rossii', *Istoricheskii archive*, no. 6 (1961): 92. For further information about Denikin's Moscow offensive, see Smele, *The 'Russian' Civil Wars*, 119-26.
67 *The Times*, 14 October 1919; *Daily Telegraph*, 16 October 1919. See also Kinvig, *Churchill's Crusade*, 207-35.
68 General Wilson's diary, 16 October 1919, in Gilbert, *Winston S. Churchill*, 4: pt II, 348; Sablin to Sazonov, 24 October 1919, *AVPRF*, f. 069, op. 3, pap. 3, d. 2, l. 15.

69 Memorandum by Halford Mackinder, 21 January 1920, *DBFP*, First ser., III: 768–87; Aleksandr Sevriuk, Minister Extraordinary of the Ukrainian Republic, to the Council of Ten, 9 April 1919, *TNA*, FO 608/207, ff. 85–90.
70 Memorandum by Halford Mackinder, 21 January 1920, *TNA*, FO 418/54, ff. 17–29; Notes of points, supplementary to Mackinder's memorandum of 21 January 1920, made by Mackinder in reply to questions put to him at the Cabinet meeting, 29 January 1920, ibid., FO 800/251, ff. 60–6.
71 Conclusions of a Cabinet meeting, 29 January 1920; *TNA*, CAB 23/20/7. See also Anthony Adamthwaite (comp.), *The Lost Peace: International Relations in Europe, 1918-1939* (E. Arnold, 1980), 38.
72 Figes, *A People's Tragedy*, 573; Gilbert, *Winston S. Churchill*, 4: pt II, 303–19.
73 Hudson, *Intervention in Russia*, 145; Kettle, *Russia and the Allies*, 3: 414–59; Jeffrey, *The Military Defence of the British Empire*, 256–65.
74 Jackson, *At War with the Bolsheviks*, 177; Dobson and Miller, *The Day We Almost Bombed Moscow*, 15–23; Dumova and Trukhanovsky, *Churchill i Miliukov protiv Sovetskoi Rossii*, 164.
75 For further information about the Civil War and British intervention in the north of Russia, see Smele, *The 'Russian' Civil Wars*, 132–4; Balbirnie, 'British Imperialism in the Arctic'.
76 Lindley to Miller, 23 March 1919, in I. Minz (comp.), 'Anglichane na Severe (1918–1919)', *Krasnyi arkhiv* 19, no. 6 (1926): 46–7.
77 Keeble, *Britain and the Soviet Union*, 60.
78 Churchill to Wilson, 12 May 1919, *TNA*, WO 32/5184; Churchill to Wilson, 22 May 1919, ibid., WO 32/5185.
79 Correspondence between War Office and Air Ministry on the use of chemical bombs, 6–8 August 1918, ibid., WO 32/5184; The War Office to Poole, 27 March 1919; Poole to the War Office, 2 April 1919; The War Office to Poole, 11 April 1919, *TNA*, WO 32/5749.
80 Proceedings of the Cabinet meeting, 12 May 1919, ibid., WO 32/5185; Reports on the use of chemical shells in Russia, 20 June 1919, *ibid.*, WO 32/5184; Hollman to Churchill, 18 November 1919, *CUL*. CAC. CHAR/16/13.
81 Denikin, *Ocherki russkoi smuty*, 5: 171.
82 Memorandum by Pares to the Foreign Office, 2 March 1919, *TNA*, FO 608/196.
83 Memorandum by Simpson to the Foreign Office, 18 July 1919, *TNA*, FO 418/53.
84 Lenin's speech at the conference of Moscow Province executive committees, 16 October 1920, in Lenin, *Polnoe sobranie sochinenii*, 41: 350.
85 See Gilbert, *Winston S. Churchill*, 4: pt II, 726–31, 736–9; 747–8; 752–6; 757–64; 766–74; Minutes of the Cabinet meeting. 4 July 1919, *TNA*, CAB 23/15. W.C. 588A.
86 Keeble, *Britain and the Soviet Union*, 57–8.
87 Diary, 14 August 1919, in Wilson, *The Political Diaries of C.P. Scott*, 276.
88 Quoted in Churchill, *The World Crisis*, 237.
89 Review by Curzon of the situation in Russia and the prospects of British policy, 12 September 1919, *TNA*, PA. LG F/202/1/9.
90 On the British officers' overall fatigue of war, see Admiral Zelenoi to the Russian Federation Revolutionary Soviet, 24 August 1919, *RGA VMF*, f. R-342, op. 1, d. 614, l. 6; Summaries of British press, 23 October–5 November 1919, *GARF*, f. 5936, op. 1, d. 290, ll. 1–100. On the evacuation of British expeditionary forces from the north of Russia, see General Rawlinson's journal, 31 July– 11 October 1919, *CU*, CAC, RWLN/1/13.
91 Gilbert, *Churchill. A Life*, 415–16.

92 British casualties during the intervention in the north of Russia totalled 106 officers and 877 rank-and-file, see Great Britain. War Office, Army. *The Evacuation of North Russia, 1919*, 13.
93 William and Zelda Coates, *Armed Intervention in Russia*, 227; Ullman, *Anglo-Soviet Relations*, 2: 24–5; Gilbert, *Churchill. A Life*, 415; Jeffrey, *The Military Defence of the British Empire*, 204; Dobson and Miller, *The Day We Almost Bombed Moscow*, 267–76; Kinvig, *Churchill's Crusade*, 237–69.
94 Leonid Krassin to Lubov' Krassin, 25 October 1919, in L. B. Krassin, 'Pis'ma k zhene i detyam', *Voprosy istorii*, no. 3 (2002): 90–1.
95 Proposed telegram to Wilson on the blockade of Russia, 25 July 1919, *DBFP*, First ser., I: 202–3.
96 Exchange of radiograms between Chicherin, Litvinov, the Foreign Office and O'Grady, 8 June–19 September 1919, *DVP SSSR*, 2: 190, 202–3, 226–7, 236–7, 249.
97 Quoted in Ullman, *Anglo-Soviet Relations*, 2: 311.
98 Judd, *The Quest for C.*, 437.
99 Proceedings of the meeting of the heads of delegations on the evacuation of the Baltic provinces, 11 November 1919, *BDFP*, II: 268–9; Temperley, *A History of the Peace Conference of Paris*, VI: pt II, 312–35.
100 Keeble, *Britain and the Soviet Union*, 61.
101 S. V. Lavrov, 'Bor'ba v politicheskikh krugakh Velikobritanii vokrug anglo-sovetskikh peregovorov 1920–1921 gg.', *Voprosy istorii*, no. 6 (1977): 64.
102 Denikin, *Ocherki russkoi smuty*, 5: 172.
103 Nabokov to Chaikovsky, 18 November 1919, *GARF*, f. 5805, op. 1, d. 147, ll. 9–16.
104 Meetings in London of the Allied prime ministers and ministers for foreign affairs, 11–13 December 1919, *DBFP*, First ser., II: 736, 744–8, 764–5, 776–8.
105 Correspondence on the repatriation of Russian ex-POWs, February–December 1919, *TNA*, FO 608/201, ff. 250–563; Sub-Committee for the repatriation of Russian ex-POWs, July 1919, ibid., FO 608/259, ff. 533–624; Diplomatic correspondence on Russian POWs and refugees in Germany, 29 November, 29, 31 December 1919, *DBFP*, First ser., II: 426–8, 431–4, 625, 651–2.
106 Correspondence on the repatriation of Russian ex-POWs, 1919, *TNA*, FO 608/203, ff. 1–319, especially ff. 250–2; Radiograms between Curzon, Chicherin and Litvinov, July–October 1919, *AVPRF*, f. 04, op. 4, pap. 17, d. 243, ll. 27–9, 47.
107 Curzon to Chicherin, 10 October 1919, *AVPRF*, f. 04, op. 4, pap. 17, d. 243, ll. 49–50; The NKID statement on the negotiations with O'Grady, 19 December 1919, *DVP SSSR*, 2: 311–12; Correspondence on Litvinov's negotiations with O'Grady, 1–31 December 1919, *GARF*, f. 5936, op. 1, d. 292, ll. 1–174. On the British intentions in the talks with Litvinov, see especially, Richard Debo, 'Lloyd George and the Copenhagen Conference of 1919–1920: The Initiation of Anglo-Soviet Negotiations', *Historical Journal* 24, no. 2 (1981): 429–41.
108 Curzon to O'Grady, 13 November 1919, *DBFP*, First ser., III: 643–4; Curzon to Watson, 26 November 1919, ibid., 663–4; Curzon to O'Grady and Watson, 6 December 1919, ibid., 687–8; Litvinov to O'Grady, 22 December 1919, ibid., III: 738–40; Statements by the NKID on the negotiations on the exchange of POWs and civil persons, 25 January, 6 February 1920, *DVP SSSR*, 2: 329–30, 359–62.
109 O'Grady to Curzon, 18 January 1920, *DBFP*, First ser., III: 762–3; Conclusions of a meeting on the exchange of POWs, 5 February 1920, *TNA*, CAB/23/20/9; Curzon to Watson, 7 February 1920, *DBFP*, First ser., III: 812–14; Great Britain. Foreign Office, *Agreement between His Britannic Majesty's Government and the Soviet Government of*

Russia for Exchange of Prisoners, Russia, no. 1 (1920), Cmd. 587 (HMSO, 1920). For further correspondence between Litvinov and O'Grady on the repatriation of Russian ex-POWs in 1920, see AVPRF, f. 168, op. 1, pap. 3, d. 34, ll. 1–203.
110 Quoted in Middlemas, *Thomas Jones. Whitehall Diary*, 105.
111 Report by Litvinov, 6 February 1920, *AVPRF*, f. 4, op. 4, pap. 19, d. 264, ll. 11–16.
112 Timothy O'Connor, *The Engineer of Revolution: L.B. Krasin and the Bolsheviks, 1870–1926* (Boulder, CO: Westview Press, 1992), 210, 230.
113 Meeting of the heads of delegations of the five great powers, 13 January 1920, *DBFP*, First ser., II: 874.
114 Note on the conversation between Wise and the top managers of the Central union of Russian consumer societies, 13 January 1920, *GARF*, f. 5906, op. 1, d. 104, l. 197.
115 Decision of the Entente Supreme Council, 16 January 1920, *TNA*, FO 418/54, f. 193; Allied agreement to enter trading relations with the cooperative movement in Russia, 16 January 1920, *DBFP*, First ser., II: 894–6. See also Keeble, *Britain and the Soviet Union*, 64.
116 Diary, 22 January 1920, in Riddell, *Intimate Diary*, 15.
117 Note by Hankey, 23 January 1920, *TNA*, CAB 24/96/94; MUN 4/3751. It is important to note that the Bolsheviks were even prepared to transfer the Baltic Fleet (twenty-six battleships and eight submarines) under the control of the British naval officers in exchange for the diplomatic recognition by Britain, see Memorandum by Long for the Cabinet, 23 January 1920, *TNA*, CAB 24/96/99; Reply from the Soviet Government, 26 January 1920, *TNA*, CAB 24/97/5.
118 Minute of the Cabinet meeting, 24 February 1920, *DBFP*, First ser., II: 899.
119 *The Times*, 11 February 1920. See also, Dennis, *The Foreign Policies of Soviet Russia*, 383.
120 Diary, 6 March 1920, in Riddell, *Intimate Diary*, 175.
121 See, for example, Moffat, *The Allied Intervention in Russia*, 229–50.
122 White, *Britain and the Bolshevik Revolution*, 31.
123 Quoted in Goode, *Bolshevism at Work*, 135.
124 Quoted in Gilbert, *Churchill. A Life*, 421.
125 See, for example, Jackson, *At War with the Bolsheviks*, 236.
126 Marks, *The Ebbing of European Ascendancy*, 84.
127 Esher to Balfour, 19 November 1919, Esher, *Journals and Letters of Reginald Viscount Esher*, 4: 325.
128 Somin, *Stillborn Crusade*, 179–84.

Chapter 6

1 Miliukov, *Rossiya na perelome*, 1: 258.
2 On the Baltic issue in the context of the Soviet-British relations, refer to Page, *The Formation of the Baltic States. A Study of the Effects of Great Power Politics upon the Emergence of Lithuania, Latvia, and Estonia*; Geoffrey Bennett, *Cowan's War. The Story of British Naval Operations in the Baltic, 1918-1920* (W. Collins, 1964); Idem, *Freeing the Baltic* (Edinburgh: Birlinn, 2002); Hugh Rodgers, *Search for Security. A Study in Baltic Diplomacy, 1920-1934* (Hamden, CT: Archon Bools, 1975); Stanley Vardys, and Romuald Misiunas (eds), *The Baltic States in Peace and War, 1917-45* (University Park – London: Pennsylvania State University Press, 1978); Olaf Hovi,

The Baltic Area in British Foreign Policy, 1918-21 (Helsinki: SHS, 1980); Merija-Liisa Hinkkanen-Lievonen, *British Trade and Enterprise in the Baltic States, 1919-1925* (Helsinki: SHS, 1984), 49-86; John Hidden, and Alexander Loit (eds), *Contact or Isolation? The Baltic in International Relations between the Two World Wars* (Stockholm: Stockholm University Centre for Baltic Studies, 1988); Debo, Survival and Consolidation, 85-105, 119-42; P. Vares and O. Osipova *Pokhitschenie Evropy, ili Baltiikii vopros v mezhdunarodnykh otnosheniiakh XX veka* (Tallinn: Izdatel'stvo Estonskaia entsklopediia, 1992); Christine White, 'The Gateway to Russia. The Baltic States as a Conduit for British and American Trade with Soviet Russia, 1918-1924', in *Emancipation and Interdependence. The Baltic States as New Entities in the International Economy. 1918-1940*, ed. Anders Johansson (Upsala: Stockholm university centre for Baltic studies, 1994), 41-62; David Kirby, *The Baltic World, 1772-1993: Europe's Northern Periphery in an Age of Change* (London – New York: Longman, 1995); Evgeny Sergeev, 'Great Britain and the Baltic States, 1918-22', in *From Versailles to Munich. Twenty Years of Forgotten Wars*, ed. David Artico and Brunello Mantelli (Wroclaw: UTET SpA, 2010), 17-36; etc.

3 Sforza, *Diplomatic Europe since the Treaty of Versailles*, 71; Hinkkanen-Lievonen, *British Trade and Enterprise*, 11; Anderson, 'British Policy toward the Baltic States', 276; Vares, Osipova, *Pokhitschenie Evropy*, 15, 25-8.
4 Anderson, 'British Policy toward the Baltic States', 282.
5 Curzon to Balfour, 28 March 1919, *TNA*, FO 418/53.
6 Hankey to Lloyd George, 19 March 1919, *TNA*, LG F/23/4/39.
7 Graham, *The League of Nations and the Recognition of States*, 3: no. 4, 410-13, 430-1; Anderson, 'British Policy toward the Baltic States', 263; Hovi, *The Baltic Area in British Policy*, 39.
8 Ullman, *Anglo-Soviet Relations*, 2: 51-8; Vares, Osipova, *Pokhitschenie Evropy*, 15. On the creation of pro-Soviet republics in the Eastern Baltic, see Page, *The Formation of the Baltic States*, 62-8, 69-85, 91-7; Debo, *Survival and Consolidation*, 85-105; Vares and Osipova, *Pokhitschenie Evropy*, 19-20.
9 Memorandum by Balfour, 18 October 1918, *TNA*, CAB 24/70; *FRUS*, Russia, 1918, II: 841-2. See also Ullman, *Anglo-Soviet Relations*, 2: 54; Bennett, *Cowan's War*, 31; Hovi, *The Baltic Area in British Policy*, 48-9; Sergeev, 'Great Britain and the Baltic States', 22-3.
10 See Christine White, 'The Gateway to Russia', 47.
11 Kirby, *The Baltic World*, 277.
12 Anderson, *British Policy toward the Baltic States*, 280; Kirby, *The Baltic World*, 280; Bennett, *Cowan's War*, 28; Hovi, *The Baltic Area in British Policy*, 48.
13 Anderson, 'British Policy toward the Baltic States', 279; F. Raskol'nikov, *Rasskazy michmana Il'ina* (Goslitizdat, 1936), 56-96; Idem., *Na boevykh postakh* (Voenizdat, 1964), 287-95; Bennett, *Freeing the Baltic*, 39-40.
14 Page, *The Formation of the Baltic States*, 151-3; Sharp, *The Versailles Settlement*, 152-5; Vares Osipova, *Pokhitschenie Evropy*, 22-3, 29.
15 Ruediger von der Goltz, *Meine Sendung in Finnland und im Balticum* (Leipzig: K.F. Köhler Verlag, 1920), 198-9; Hugh Gough, *Soldiering On* (A. Barker, 1964), 190-202; Ullman, *Anglo-Soviet Relations*, 2: 287-93. On the activities of the Inter-Allied Baltic Commission, see also the Final report of the Inter-Allied Baltic Commission, 8 December 1919, *TNA*, FO 608/200.
16 Shubin, 'Latyshskie strelki mezhdu Rodinoi i revolutsiei', 178.

17 Anderson, 'British Policy toward the Baltic States', 287; Ullman, *Anglo-Soviet Relations*, 2: 287–93; Gilbert, *Winston S. Churchill*, 4: 308; V. A. Shishkin, *Stanovlenie vneshnei politiki*, 69; Bennett, *Freeing the Baltic*, 6, 54–69, 237–8.
18 Kettle, *Russia and the Allies*, 3: 347, 460–87; Dobson and Miller, *The Day We Almost Bombed Moscow*, 247–66.
19 Admiral Zelenoi to the Commander of Naval Forces, 18 August 1919, RGA VMF, f. R-342, op. 1, d. 291, l. 4.
20 Ioffe, Organisatsiia interventsii, 108–9; Augustus Agar, *Baltic Episode: A Classic of Secret Service in Russian Waters* (Hodder and Stoughton, 1963), 80–97, 98–125, 152–79, 233; Jackson, *At War with the Bolsheviks*, 211–27; Bennett, *Freeing the Baltic*, 148–56.
21 Quoted in Bennett, *Cowan's War*, 205.
22 Quoted in A. V. Smolin, *Beloe dvizhenie na severo-zapade Rossii (1918–1920 gg.)* (St Petersburg: D. Bulavin, 1999), 316.
23 Gough, *Soldiering On*, 190–1; Smolin, *Beloe dvizhenie na severo-zapade Rossii*, 61, 81–2, 90.
24 Meetings of the heads of delegations of the five great powers, 5, 10, 19 November 1919, *DBFP*, First ser., II: 268–9, 272, 354–5. See also memorandum by the Foreign Office, 16 December 1919, TNA, CAB 24/95/32.
25 Quoted in Smolin, *Beloe dvizhenie na severo-zapade Rossii*, 301.
26 For further information, see Goltz, *Meine Sendung im Finland*, 221–9; P. V. Avalov (Bermondt), *V bor'be s bol'shevizmom* (Glückstadt – Hamburg: Izdatel'stvo I. I. Augustina, 1925); Stephen Tallents, *Man and Boy* (Faber and Faber, 1943); Herbert Watson, *An Account of a Mission to the Baltic States in the Year 1919, with a Record of Subsequent Events* (Waverley Press, 1958).
27 Avalov, *V bor'be s bol'shevizmom*, 150.
28 Goltz, *Meine Sendung im Finland*, 282–3; Anderson, 'British Policy toward the Baltic States', 284–5, 287; Kirby, *The Baltic World*, 282; Bennett, *Freeing the Baltic*, 172–93.
29 Christine White, 'The Gateway to Russia', 45. See also Smele, *The 'Russian' Civil Wars*, 126–32.
30 Curzon to Tallents, 26 February 1920, *DBFP*, First ser., XI: 230.
31 Sforza, *Diplomatic Europe since the Treaty of Versailles*, 69.
32 See Hinkkanen-Lievonen, *British Trade and Enterprise in the Baltic States*, 101; Vares, Osipova, *Pokhitschenie Evropy*, 49–51, 51–71.
33 Sforza, *Diplomatic Europe since the Treaty of Versailles*, 73; Dennis, *The Foreign Policies of Soviet Russia*, 130; Simpson, *Great Britain and the Baltic States*, 620.
34 Xenia Joukoff Eudin and Harold Fisher (comps, ed.), *Soviet Russia and the West. 1920–1927. A Documentary Survey* (Stanford, CA: Stanford University Press, 1957), 48–51; Vares, Osipova, *Pokhitschenie Evropy*, 52.
35 Notes by Curzon to Chicherin, 21 February, 11, 14 April 1920, *DVP SSSR*, 2: 385, 454–5; Curzon to Admiral de Robeck, British high commissioner for South Russia, 31 March 1920, *DBFP*, First ser., XII: 691–2.
36 Exchange of radiograms between Curzon and Chicherin, 18, 28 April, 4, 5, 8, 9, 17 May 1920, *DVP SSSR*, 2: 471, 490–1, 502–4, 510–11; AVPRF, f. 4, op. 4, pap. 17, d. 246, l. 4; TNA, WO 32/5715.
37 Quoted in Artico and Mantelli, *From Versailles to Munich*, 9.
38 See Bradley, *Allied Intervention in Russia*, 184–210; Hugh Elcock, 'Britain and the Russo-Polish Frontier, 1919–1921', *Historical Journal* 12, no. 1 (1960): 137–54; Norman Davies, *White Eagle, Red Star. The Polish-Soviet War 1919–1920*

(Macdonald, 1972); Jackson, *At War with the Bolsheviks*, 228–33; Ullman, *Anglo-Soviet Relations*, 3: 135–83; Debo, *Survival and Consolidation*, 213–47; Yu. V. Ivanov, *Ocherki istorii rossisko- (sovetsko) pol'skikh otnoshenii v dokumentakh. 1914–1945* (Mezhdunarodnye otnosheniya, 2014); etc.

39   Alexander Gurschin, Ustanovlenie vostochnykh granits nezavisimogo pol'skogo gosudarstva v 1918–1923 gg., *Vestnik RGGU*, no. 7 (2012): 51.
40   Quoted in Zubachevsky, *Politika Rossii*, 73.
41   Joukoff Eudin, Fisher, *Soviet Russia and the West*, 16; Davies, *White Eagle, Red Star*, 167–8; Ivanov, *Ocherki istorii*, 56.
42   Snowden, *An Autobiography*, 2: 559; Lowe, Dockrill, *The Mirage of Power*, 2: 329; Debo, *Survival and Consolidation*, 191–212; Ivanov, *Ocherki istorii*, 56.
43   Appendix to conclusions of the Cabinet meeting, 29 January 1920, *TNA*, CAB 23/20/7, ff. 7–8; Curzon to Rumbold, British Minister in Poland, 27 January 1920, ibid., PA, LG F/201/1/6.
44   Admiralty to the C-in-C in the Mediterranean, 25 April 1920, *TNA*, PA, DAV /108. See also, Mannerheim, *Memoirs*, 188; Brinkley, *The Volunteer Army*, 241–74; Ivanov, *Ocherki istorii*, 70.
45   Curzon to Porter, British Acting Consul in Revel, 7 May 1920, *DBFP*, First Ser., XI: 308.
46   *The Times*, 3 May 1920.
47   Conclusions of the Cabinet meeting, 21 May 1920, *TNA*, CAB 23/21/13.
48   Diary, 30 May 1920, in Riddell, *Lord Riddell's Intimate Diary*, 198.
49   Rumbold, British Minister in Warsaw, to Lloyd George, 26 April 1920, *TNA*, CAB 1/20/25.
50   Memorandum by Long, for the Cabinet, 1 May 1920, *TNA*, CAB 24/105/9.
51   Memorandum by the Foreign Office political intelligence department, 12 May 1920, ibid., CAB/24/106/27.
52   Preliminary conversations in London between British Ministers and a Soviet Russian Trade Delegation, 31 May–7 June 1920, *DBFP*, First ser., VIII: 280.
53   Andrew Williams, *Trading with the Bolsheviks. The Politics of East-West Trade, 1920–39* (Manchester – New York: Manchester University Press, 1992), 88.
54   D'Abernon, *An Ambassador of Peace*, 1: 69. See also Davies, *White Eagle, Red Star*, 69; Lowe, Dockrill, *The Mirage of Power*, 2: 330.
55   Curzon to Chicherin, 10 July 1920, *TNA*, FO 371/4058/207846; Curzon to Chicherin, 10–11 July 1920, *DVP SSSR*, 3: 54.
56   Hardinge to Litvinov, 2 July 1920; Chicherin to Curzon, 11, 13, 17 July 1920, *DVP SSSR*, 3: 42–3, 43–4, 47–53, 54–5; Hardinge to Litvinov, *AVPRF*, f. 168, op. 1, pap. 1, d. 3, l. 42, 1 July 1920.
57   Lenin to Stalin, 13 July 1920, in Lenin, *Lenin o vneshnei politike*, 314.
58   Speech at the Congress of leather workers, 2 October 1920, Lenin, *Polnoe sobranie sochinenii*, 41: 324–5.
59   Georgy Adibekov et al. (eds), *PB TsK RKP(b) – VKP(b) i Komintern 1919–1943. Dokumenty* (ROSSPEN, 2004), 54–5.
60   Curzon to Chicherin, 20 July 1920; Chicherin to Curzon, 23 July 1920; Curzon to Chicherin, 26 July 1920; Curzon to Chicherin, 29 July 1920, Kamenev to Curzon, 3 August 1920, *DVP SSSR*, 3: 63–4, 80; Chicherin to the British Government, 24 July 1920, *TNA*, PA, LG F/201/1/9. See also William Medlicott, *British Foreign Policy since Versailles, 1919–1963* (Methuen, 1968), 9–10.
61   Lenin to Chicherin, 22 July 1920, in Lenin, *Lenin o vneshnei politike*, 331.

62 Curzon to Chicherin, 30 July 1920, *AVPRF*, f. 4, op. 4, f. 17, d. 247, l. 57.
63 Diary, 1 August 1920, in Ramsden, *Real Old Tory Politics*. 141.
64 Shishkin, *Sovetskoe gosudarstvo i strany* Zapada, 245-6.
65 Ethel Snowden, *Through the Bolshevik Russia* (Cassell, 1920), 1-2; P. V. Gurovich, 'Pervaia delegatsiia tred-unionov i leiboristskoi partii v Sovetskoi Rossii', *Novaia i noveishaia istoriia*, no. 4 (1973): 71.
66 Bertrand Russell, *The Practice and Theory of Bolshevism* (G. Allen and Unwin, 1920), 1: 24-5.
67 ibid., 27. See also Charles Buxton, *In a Russian Village* (Labour Publishing, 1922).
68 Russell, *The Practice and Theory*, 1: 26, 32, 39-40.
69 Memorandum by Robert Horne, 9 February 1920, *TNA*, CAB 24/97/95.
70 *British Labour Delegation to Russia 1920. Report* (Office of the Trade Union Congress and Labour Party, 1920), 5-27. For further information, see Stephen Graubard, *British Labour and the Russian Revolution, 1917-1924* (Cambridge, MA: HUP, 1956), 214-19; Gurovich, 'Pervaia delegatsiia tred-unionov', 71-7; Morton Cowden, *Russian Bolshevism and British Labour 1917-1921* (Boulder, CO: East European Monographs, 1984); White, 'British Labour and Russian Revolution', 231-48.
71 A. Lozovsky, *Anglo-Sovetskaia konferentsiia professional'nykh soyuzov* (Gosudarstvennoe izdatel'stvo, 1925), 5-8. On the establishment of the National minority movement in Britain, see Northedge, Wells, *Britain and Soviet Communism*, 197; Thorpe, *The British Communist Party and Moscow*, 27, 35-8.
72 Memorandum by Krassin, 24 April 1920, *AVPRF*, f. 4, op. 4, pap. 19, d. 267, ll. 1-16.
73 Lenin to Chicherin and the members of the TsK RKP(b) Politburo, late in April 1920, ibid., l. 24.
74 Lubov Krassin, *Leonid Krassin*, 124.
75 Memorandum by Churchill and the War Office for the Cabinet, 11 May 1920, *TNA*, CAB 24/105/54; Memorandum by Churchill for the Cabinet, 26 May 1920, in Gilbert, *Winston S. Churchill*, 4: 1130-1.
76 Memorandum by Wise for the Cabinet, 18 April 1920, *TNA*, PA. LG F/202/3/3; Memorandum by Wise for the Cabinet, 21 May 1920, ibid., LG F/202/3/5. See also Andrew Williams, 'The Genoa Conference of 1922: Lloyd George and the Politics of Recognition', in *Genoa, Rapallo, and European Reconstruction in 1922*, ed. Carole Fink, Axel Frohn and Juergen Heideking (Washington, DC – Cambridge: German Historical Institute – CUP, 1991), 31-4.
77 Horne to Kerr, 26 May 1920, *TNA*, PA. LG F/27/6/35; Memorandum by the Board of Trade for the Cabinet, 26 May 1920, ibid., T/160/3.
78 Memorandum by Curzon for the Cabinet, 27 May 1920, *DBFP*, First ser., XII: 723-6.
79 Special report by the Home Office to the Cabinet, no. 18, June 1920, *TNA*, CAB 24/108/89.
80 Williams, *Trading with the Bolsheviks*, 63.
81 See, for example, Maisky, 'Anglo-Sovetskoe torgovoe soglashenie 1921 goda', 60-77; Dennis, *The Foreign Policies of Soviet Russia*, 377-407; Lubov Krassin, *Leonid Krassin*, 124-48; William and Zelda Coates, *A History of Anglo-Soviet Relations*, 1: 26-54; Glenny, 'The Anglo-Soviet Trade Agreement', 62-83; Roskill, *Hankey*, 2: 170-3; Ullman, *Anglo-Soviet Relations*, 3: 184-209; 397-453; Debo *Survival and Consolidation*, 248-71; Christine White, *British and American Commercial Relations with Soviet Russia, 1918-1924* (Chapell Hill – London: The University of North Carolina Press, 1992); Macmeekin, *History's Greatest Heist*, 168-98; Service, *Spies and Commissars*, 318-28.

82 Quoted in Roskill, *Hankey*, 2: 170–1. On Hankey's long-term career as the chief government counsellor, see also Richard Naylor, *A Man and an Intrusion. Sir Maurice Hankey, the Cabinet Secretariat and the Custody of Cabinet Secrecy* (Cambridge: CUP, 1984).
83 Diary, 31 May 1920, in Wilson, *The Political Diaries of C.P. Scott*, 387.
84 Quoted in Stafford, *Churchill and Secret Service*, 109.
85 Lubov Krassin, *Leonid Krassin*, 125; O'Connor, *The Engineer of Revolution*, 219–20; Shishkin, *Stancvlenie vneshnei politiki poslerevoliutsionnoi Rossii*, 98.
86 Provisional answers to questions raised by the head of the British Government at a conference held on 31 May 1920, 5 June 1920, *DBFP*, First ser., VIII: 281–90; *TNA*, CAB 24/107/21.
87 See, *The Manchester Guardian*, 1 June 1920.
88 Diary, 13 June 1920, in Riddell, *Lord Riddell's Intimate Diary*, 204. On the first stage of the negotiations, see *DBFP*, First ser., VIII: 292–306; Glenny, 'The Anglo-Soviet Trade Agreement', 68; O'Connor, *The Engineer of Revolution*, 217.
89 *All-Russian Cooperative Society Ltd. Memorandum and Articles of Association* (S. l., 1920); British companies' proposals to purchase machines and equipment, 11 February – 25 October 1920, *AVPRF*, f. 168, op. 1, pap. 3, d. 36, ll. 1-135. On the history of ARCOS, see also Shishkin, *Stanovlenie vneshnei politiki poslerevoliutsionnoi Rossii*, 99–100; Smith, *Soviet Foreign Trade*, 58–9; O'Connor, *The Engineer of Revolution*, 223; Macmeekin, *History's Greatest Heist*, 172.
90 Chicherin to Krassin, 6 June 1920, *AVPRF*, f. 4, op. 4, pap. 18, d. 251, l. 7–8.
91 Krassin to Chicherin, 26 November 1920, in Madeira, *Britannia and the Bear*, 89–106.
92 Chicherin to Krassin, 24, 27 June 1920, *AVPRF*, f. 4, op. 4, pap. 18, d. 251, ll. 23, 27.
93 Lloyd George and Krassin meeting, 16 June 1920, *TNA*, PA. LG F/202/3/19, ff. 327–64; *DBFP*, First ser., VIII: 380–8; Memorandum by Krassin to the British Government, 29 June 1920, *DVP SSSR*, 2: 593–8.
94 Memorandum by the British Government to the Soviet Government, 30 June–1 July 1920, *AVPRF*, f. 4, op. 4, pap. 17, d. 246, ll. 10–13; *DVP SSSR*, 3: 17–19; Krassin to Chicherin, 1 July 1920 (decrypt), *TNA*, HW 12/11.
95 On Krassin's impression of the return voyage to Soviet Russia on board the British warship, see Krassin to Lubov Krassina, 2 July 1920, in Lubov Krassin, *Leonid Krassin*, 126–7; Chicherin to Curzon, 7 July 1920, *DVP SSSR*, 3: 16–17. See also Glenny, 'The Anglo-Soviet Trade Agreement', 70.
96 Chicherin to Trotsky, 2 July 1920, *AVPRF*, f. 4, op. 4, pap. 17, d. 247, l. 54.
97 Diary, 23 July 1920, in Riddell, *Lord Riddell's Intimate Diary*, 224.
98 Curzon to Chicherin, 20 July 1920, Curzon to Chicherin, 29 July 1920, Kamenev to Curzon, 3 August 1920, *DVP SSSR*, 3: 63–4, 80; Chicherin to the British Government, 24 July 1920, *TNA*, PA. LG F/201/1/9.
99 Negotiations with the Soviet Government, 26 July 1920, *TNA*, CAB/23/37/47; Minute of the Cabinet meeting, 26 July 1920, in Middlemas, *Thomas Jones. Whitehall Diary*, 1: 118–19.
100 Elcock, 'Britain and the Russo-Polish Frontier', 138–9; Robert Boyce, *The Great Interwar Crisis*, 139–40.
101 Curzon to Chicherin, 3 August 1920, *DVP SSSR*, 3: 86.
102 Krassin to Chicherin, 1 August 1920, *AVPRF*, f. 4, op. 4, pap. 18, d. 253, ll. 1-2.
103 Chicherin to Kamenev, 3 August 1920, ibid., d. 251, ll. 47–8.
104 Kamenev to Chicherin, 4 August 1920, ibid., ll. 26–7; Note by Kamenev to Lloyd George, 5 August 1920, *DBFP*, First ser., VIII: 670–80.

105 Proceedings of the Anglo-Soviet meeting, 6 August 1920, *AVPRF*, f. 4, op., f. 17, d. 248, ll. 81–106; ibid., d. 249, ll. 1–26; *DBFP*, First ser., VIII: 695–708.
106 Memorandum by Lloyd George to the Soviet Government, 6 August 1920, in Gilbert, *Winston S. Churchill*, 4: 412–35; Chicherin to Curzon, 8 August 1920; Kamenev to Lloyd George, 9 August 1920; Lloyd George to Kamenev, 11 August 1920; Note by the Soviet Government to the British Government, 15 August 1920. Quoted in Shishkin, *Sovetskoe gosudarstvo i strany Zapada*, 98–9, 100–1, 123, 131–5,
107 Kamenev to Chicherin, 17 August 1920, *AVPRF*, f. 4, op. 4, pap. 17, d. 248, ll. 137–8.
108 Note by Lloyd George to Kamenev, 18 August 1920, *DVP SSSR*, 3: 135–6.
109 Norman Hooker (ed.), *The Moffat Papers. Selections from the Diplomatic Journals of Jay Pierpont Moffat 1919-194* (Cambridge, MA: HUP, 1956), 30.
110 Rumbold to Curzon, 24 August 1920, *DBFP*, First ser., XI: 522–4.
111 Davies, *White Eagle, Red Star*, 93–4, 167.
112 Curzon to Rumbold, 21 July 1920, *TNA*, FO 688/6/1.
113 Bulletins of the National Committee 'Hands off Russia', February–August 1920, *RGASPI*, f. 495, op. 100, d. 20, ll. 1-9. See also Page Arnot, *The Impact of the Russian Revolution*, 149, 170–3; L. J. Macfarlane, 'Hands off Russia': British Labour and the Russo-Polish War, 1920', *Past and Present*, no. 38 (1968): 126–52.
114 William and Zelda Coates, *A History of Anglo-Soviet Relations*, 1: 31.
115 Philip Snowden, *An Autobiography*, 560.
116 The appeal by the 'Committee of action' to the Russian delegation, 11 August 1920, *RGASPI*, f. 495, op. 100, d. 20, ll. 13–14.
117 Thorpe, *The British Communist Party and Moscow*, 30-2.
118 On the 'diamond scandal', see Miliukov, *Rossiia na perelome*, 1: 287–8; Andrew, Gordievsky, *KGB: The Inside Story*, 90–1; O'Connor, *The Engineer of Revolution*, 229–30; Solomon, *Sredi krasnykh vozhdei*, 336–9; Kevin Quinlan, *The Secret War between the Wars. MI5 in the 1920s and 1930s* (Woodbridge, Suffolk: The Boydell Press, 2014), 17, 26–7; E. A. Susloparova, 'Skandal s "bol'shevistskim zolotom" v istorii britanskoi gazety Daily Herald', in *Britaniia i Rossiia: sovremennye issledovaniia sotsiokul'turnykh aspektov vzaimodeistviia*, ed. M. P. Aisenstadt and T. L. Labutina (Institut vseobtschei istorii RAN, 2015), 147–53.
119 Macmeekin, *History's Greatest Heist*, 54–91.
120 Roy, *Memoirs*, 198–203; Costello, *Mask of Treachery*, 40.
121 Thorpe, *The British Communist Party and Moscow*, 44. On the early British Communist party, also see Bullock, *Romancing the Revolution*, 307–32.
122 Special report by the Home Office to the Cabinet, 22 March 1920, *TNA*, CAB 24/101/28; Chicherin to Lenin, March 1920, *RGASPI*, f. 159, op. 2, d. 27, l. 26. See also Arnot, *The Impact of the Russian Revolution*, 151–2.
123 Litvinov to Chicherin, 11 July 1920 (decrypt), *TNA*, PA. DAV/117. On the subsides to the *Daily Herald* by Moscow, see Kenneth Morgan, *Bolshevism and the British Left* (Lawrence and Wishart, 2006), 1: 88–113.
124 Yu. Dioneo (Shklovsky), *Angliia posle voiny* (Prague: Plamia, 1924), 29.
125 Snowden, *An Autobiography*, 538–9.
126 Kamenev to Lezhava, Chairman of the All-Russian Cooperative Society, 20 August 1920 (decrypt), *TNA*, PA. DAV/117.
127 Note by Churchill for the prime minister, 18 August 1920, *TNA*, PA. LG F/203/1/10. See also Gilbert, *Winston S. Churchill*, 4: 1175–6; Stafford, *Churchill and Secret Service*, 112, 115.

128 *The Times*, 19 August 1920. For the intercepted decrypted correspondence of the Soviet delegation in London, see Decrypts, July–August 1920, *TNA*, HW 12/11, HW 12/14; Classified correspondence between the NKID and the trade delegation in London, 1921, *AVPRF*, f. 4, op. 4, pap. 20, d. 273, ll. 1–350. See also Christopher Andrew, 'The British Secret Service and Anglo-Soviet Relations in the 1920s', *Historical Journal* 20, no. 3 (1977): 686.
129 *Daily Herald*, 20 August 1920.
130 Dioneo, *Angliia posle voiny*, 29.
131 Thomson to Davidson, 30 August 1920, *TNA*, PA. DAV/117. See also Christine White, '"Riches Have Wings": The Use of Russian Gold in Soviet Foreign Trade, 1918–1922', in *Contact or Isolation? Soviet-Western Relations in the Interwar Period*, ed. John Hidden and Alexander Loit (Uppsala: Stockholm University Centre for Baltic Studies, 1989), 122.
132 For further Churchill's critical commentaries on the trade negotiations with Krassin, see Memoranda by Churchill for the Cabinet, 24 August, 21 September 1920, *TNA*, CAB 24/111.
133 Lloyd George to Bonar Law, 4 September 1920, *TNA*, PA. DAV/117.
134 Memorandum by Lloyd George, late August 1920, *TNA*, CAB 63/29/75–80. See also Childs, *Episodes and Reflections*, 198.
135 On the King's role in Kamenev's extradition, see Ullman, *Anglo-Soviet Relations*, 3: 303.
136 Kamenev to Lloyd George, 9 September 1920, *TNA*, PA. DAV/118.
137 Conversation between Lloyd George and Kamenev, 10 September 1920, *DBFP*, First ser., VIII: 783–91; Note by the Soviet government to the British government, 9 January 1921, *DVP SSSR*, 3: 458–61.
138 Memorandum by Curzon for the Cabinet, 16 September 1920, *TNA*, PA. LG F/203/1/14, ff. 307–15; Memorandum by Churchill for the Cabinet, 21 September 1920, ibid., PA. DAV/118; Memorandum by Curzon for the Cabinet, 27 September 1920, ibid., T 160/3.
139 Memorandum by Churchill, 16 November 1920, in Gilbert, *Winston S. Churchill*, 4: 1237–41; Note by the Soviet Government to the British Government, 28 October 1920, *DVP SSSR*, 3: 300–1.
140 Chicherin to Curzon, 25 September 1920, *DVP SSSR*, 3: 208–10; *The Times*, 5 October 1920.
141 Note by Curzon to the Soviet government, 26 September 1920, *DVP SSSR*, 3: 287; Note by the Soviet government to the British government, 6 October 1920, ibid., 237–42; Note by Curzon to the Soviet Government, 9 October 1920, ibid., 317–20; Note by the Soviet government to the British government, 13 October 1920, Note by the Soviet government to the British government, 19 October 1920, ibid., 258–9. See also correspondence between Krassin and Chicherin, 30 September–11 January 1921, *AVPRF*, f. 4, op. 4, pap. 18, d. 254, ll. 1–178; Note by Curzon to the Soviet Government, 1 October 1920, *TNA*, FO 371/5435/4512; Chicherin to Krassin, 5 October 1920, *DVP SSSR*, 3: 233–4; Curzon to Chicherin, 9 October 1920, *TNA*, FO 371/5431/118.
142 Memorandum by Horne, 27 September 1920, *TNA*, CAB 24/111/93; Memorandum by the General Staff, October 1920, ibid., CAB/24/112/36; Memorandum by Horne, 3 November 1920, ibid., CAB 24/114/56.
143 Diary, 14 November 1920, Riddell, *Lord Riddell's Intimate Diary*, 248–9.
144 *The Times*, 17 November 1920.

145 Note by the Soviet Government to the British Government, 9 November 1920, *DBFP*, First ser., XII: 795–6.
146 Memorandum by Curzon for the Cabinet, 14 November 1920, *TNA*, CAB 24/114; FO 371/5433. On the contradictions between Lloyd George and Churchill in the first half of the 1920s, see Richard Toye, *Lloyd George and Churchill. Rivals for Greatness* (Basingstoke – Oxford: Macmillan, 2007), 195–271.
147 Memorandum by Churchill for the Cabinet, 16 November 1920, *TNA*, CUL. CAC. CHAR C/16/53.
148 Diary, 17 November 1920, in Roskill, *Hankey*, 2: 172.
149 Diary, 18 November 1920, ibid., 172–3. See also Glenny, 'The Anglo-Soviet Trade Agreement', 71–3; Gilbert, *Winston S. Churchill*, 4: 1241.
150 Diary, 19, 25 November 1920, in Roskill, *Hankey*, 2: 173; Proceedings of the Cabinet meeting, 25 November 1920, *TNA*, CAB 23/38/13; Draft agreement between His Majesty's government and the Russian Soviet government, 30 November 1920, ibid., CAB 24/114/87. See also Glenny, 'The Anglo-Soviet Trade Agreement', 74–5.
151 Krassin to Wise, 30 November 1920, *DVP SSSR*, 3: 351–3; Chicherin to Politburo, 2 December 1920, *RGASPI*, f. 159, op. 2, d. 27, ll. 77–80. Chicherin to Politburo, 3 December 1920, *AVPRF*, f. 168, op. 1, pap. 1, d. 3, l. 81–2.
152 Krassin to Chicherin, 29 May 1920, *AVPRF*, f. 4, op. 4, pap. 18, d. 252, l. 21.
153 Lubov Krassin, *Leonid Krassin*, 131–2; Christine White, 'Riches Have Wings', 124–30.
154 Klyshko to Chicherin, 9 December 1920, AVPRF, f. 04, op. 4, pap. 20, d. 282, l. 42.
155 Chicherin to Krestinsky, 12 December 1920, *AVPRF*, f. 168, op. 1, pap. 1, d. 3, ll. 39–40; Chicherin to Krestinsky, 16, 19 December 1920, *GARF*, f. 9462, op. 1, d. 61, ll. 7–8, 12–13.
156 Draft agreement by the Soviet Government, 14 December 1920, *TNA*, FO 418/54, ff. 265–72; Draft agreement by the Soviet Government, 5 January 1921, *TNA*, FO 418/54, ff. 5–8; Krassin to Lloyd George, 20 December 1920, *DVP SSSR*, 3: 399–404.
157 Krassin and Klyshko's meeting with Lloyd George, Bonar Law and Horne, 21 December 1920, *DBFP*, First ser., VIII: 879–92.
158 Lenin's speech at the Eights All-Russian congress of Soviets, 21 December 1920, *DVP SSSR*, 3: 411–13.
159 Krassin to Chicherin, 29 December 1920, AVPRF, f. 4, op. 4, pap. 19, d. 261, ll. 9–17.
160 Curzon to Chicherin, 7 January 1921, ibid., f. 69, op. 6, pap. 13, d. 10, l. 9.
161 Krassin to Chicherin, 1 February 1921, ibid., f. 4, op. 4, pap. 19, d. 268, l. 1; Chicherin to Curzon, 4 February 1921, *TNA*, FO 418/55.
162 Krassin to Chicherin, 16 March 1921, *AVPRF*, f. 4, op. 4, pap. 19, d. 268, ll. 5–8. See also Great Britain. Foreign Office. *Trade Agreement between His Britannic Majesty's Government and the Government of the Russian Socialist Federal Soviet Republic*, Cmd. 1207 (HMSO, 1921).
163 Glenny, 'The Anglo-Soviet Trade Agreement', 82. See also Macmeekin, *History's Greatest Heist*, 180–2.
164 Service, *Spies and Commissars*, 319.
165 Chicherin to Krassin, 20 March 1921, *DVP SSSR*, 4: 11–12.
166 The decree by the SNK, 11 April 1921, *RGAE*, f. 413, op. 17, d. 106, l. 107; Chicherin to Krassin, 18 April 1921, *DVP SSSR*, 4: 72–3.
167 PD, The Fifth ser., CXXXIX: 2506, 2511–12; The agreement between the government of the Russian Federation and the General Directorate of British Mail was signed on 16 August 1921, *DVP SSSR*, 4: 618–19.

168 Curzon to Hodgson, 22 June 1921, *TNA*, FO 418/55, ff. 144–5.
169 Stephanie Salzman, *Great Britain, Germany and the Soviet Union. Rapallo and After, 1922–1934* (Woodbridge, Suffolk – New York: The Boydell Press, 2003), 23–5.

Chapter 7

1. Maisky, *Vneshniaia politika*, 67.
2. A. G. Sudeikin, *Kolonial'naia politika leiboristskoi partii Anglii mezhdu dvumia mirovymi voinami* (Nauka, 1976), 19.
3. Ibid., 21.
4. T. Rawlinson to H. Rawlinson, 13 February 1920, quoted in Jeffrey, *The Military Defence of the British Empire*, 199.
5. For further reading, see Debo, *Survival and Consolidation*, 168–90; Gusterin, 'Politika Sovetskogo gosudarstva', 97; A. M. Fomin, 'Formirovanie mandatnoi sistemy na Blizhnem Vostoke. 1920-1924', *Novaia i noveishaia istoriia*, no. 1 (2014): 17–36.
6. Miliukov, *Rossiia na perelome*, 1: 258–400; Dennis, *The Foreign Policies of Soviet Russia*, 201–33; Fischer, *The Soviets in World Affairs*, 1: 415–34.
7. Note by Trotsky, 5 August 1919, *RGASPI*, f. 325, op. 1, d. 47, ll. 1–2ob. See also Meijer, *The Trotsky Papers*, 1: 622–4; G. M. Adibekov et al. (eds, comps), *Politbiuro TsK RKP(b) – VKP(b) i Komintern 1919–1943. Documents* (ROSSPEN, 2004), 30.
8. Note by Trotsky, 20 September 1919, Meijer, *The Trotsky Papers*, 1: 672; Adibekov, *Politbiuro TsK RKP(b) – VKP(b) i Komintern*, 30–1.
9. Quoted in Friedman, *British Miscalculations*, 95.
10. Kapur, *Soviet Russia and Asia*, 13, 245.
11. Park, *Bolshevism in Turkestan*, 204–48; Jacobson, *When the Soviet Union Entered World Politics*, 115; Friedman, *British Miscalculations*, 49–71, 87–103.
12. See, for example, Kadishev, *Interventsiia i grazhdanskaia voina*, 164–77; Vygodsky, *U istokov sovetskoi diplomatii*, 261–320; Lavrov, 'Politika Anglii na Kavkaze i v Srednei Asii', 92; Gusterin, 'Politika Sovetskogo gosudarstva na musul'manskom Vostoke', 99.
13. Jacobson, *When Soviet Union Entered World Politics*, 107; Carley, *Silent Conflict*, 65–6.
14. Dunsterville, *The Adventures of Dunsterforce*, 190–1.
15. Bush, *Mudros to Lausanne*, 47, 111.
16. Ivanov, 'Gorskaia kontrrevolutsiia', 136–40.
17. Memorandum by Lieutenant-Colonel C. Clutterbuck, 9 October 1918, *TNA*, FO 371/3334; Correspondence between Major General Thompson and Major General Bicherachov, 23 December 1918–2 January 1919, ibid., PA. STH/DS 2/2/4, ff. 1–5.
18. Bicherachov to Curzon, 1920, ibid., ff. 6–8.
19. Quoted in Arhkipova, 'Britanskii sled na Yuzhnom Kavkaze (1918–1919 gg.)', *Novaia i noveishaia istoriia*, no. 3 (2016): 217–18.
20. Denikin, *Ocherki russkoi smuty*, 4: 142.
21. Quoted in Ullman, *Anglo-Soviet Relations*, 2: 72.
22. A. Raevsky, *Angliiskaia interventsiia i musavatistskoe pravitel'stvo: iz istorii interventsii i kontrrevolutsii v Zakavkazie* (Baku: Gosudarstvennaia Tipografiia 'Krasnyi Vostok', 1927), 20.
23. Curzon to Balfour, 12 August 1919, *DBFP*, First ser., III: 482–4.
24. Quoted in Raevsky, *Angliiskaia interventsiia*, 16.

25 *Severnaia Zhisn'*, 28 February 1919. See also Bush, *Mudros to Lausanne*, 263–4.
26 Curzon to Chicherin, 25 April 1920, *DVP* SSSR, 2: 491–2.
27 Conclusions of the Cabinet meeting, 21 May 1920, *TNA*, CAB 23/21/13.
28 Churchill to Curzon, 21 May 1920, *TNA*, BL. Curzon Papers, F 112/236/3/3.
29 Bush, *Mudros to Lausanne*, 153–61; Friedman, *British Miscalculations*, 96–7.
30 Chicherin, *Vneshniaia politika Sovetskoi Rossii*, 21.
31 Roskill, *Hankey*, 2: 188–98.
32 Kemal', *Put' novoi Turtsii*, 3: 27, 93; Kapur, *A Study of Soviet Politics towards Turkey, Iran and Afghanistan*, 46–7.
33 Curzon to de Robeck, 26 March 1920, quoted in M. S. Lasarev, *Imperialism i kurdskii vopros*, 172.
34 Ibid., 177–80, 257–326, especially, 309.
35 See, for example, Maisky, *Vneshniaia politika*, 161–7; Fischer, *The Soviets in World Affairs*, 1: 382–403; Kapur, *A Study of Soviet Politics towards Turkey, Iran and Afghanistan*, 87–142; Bush, *Mudros to Lausanne*, 62–105; Dockrill, Goold, *Peace without Promise*, 131–79; 181–252; Goekay, *A Clash of Empires*, 63–91; Macmeekin, *The Ottoman Endgame*, 439–81; etc.
36 Imam, *Colonialism in East – West Relations*, 144–5; Bush, *Mudros to Lausanne*, 268.
37 Report by Teague-Jones to Malleson, 22 October 1918, in Eleulov, Inoiatov, *Inostrannaia voennaia interventsiia*, 343–4.
38 Malleson, 'The British Military Mission to Turkestan', 99–100; G. I. Karpov (ed.), *Sbornik statei i vospominanii uchastnikov grazhdanskoi voiny v Turkmenii (nachalo Zakaspiiskogo fronta)* (Ashgabat: Turmengiz, 1937), 1, no. 3, 58–66.
39 Note on the improvement of the financial situation in Transcaspia, 8 June 1919, *GARF*, f. 9431, op. 1, d. 14, ll. 14–14ob.
40 Miroshnikov, *Angliiskaia ekspansiia v Irane*, 129.
41 D. Norris, 'Caspian Naval Expedition', *Journal of the Central Asian Society* 10, pt 1 (1923): 3–15; Gurko-Kriazhin, 'Angliiskaia interventsiia', 130–1; Lishin, *Na Kaspiiskom more*, 166–8; J. Guard, 'The Royal Navy in the Caspian Sea 1918–1920', – http://www.gwpda.org/naval/caspian.htm (accessed 22 August 2017).
42 Correspondence on the Situation in Transcaspia, 1918–1919, *BLAAS*. L/MIL/7/16920.
43 Memorandum by the India Office, 6 February 1919, ibid., L/P&S/10/108; Malleson, 'The British Military Mission to Turkestan', 100–2; Ellis, *The Transcaspian Episode*, 164.
44 Malleson to Chelmsford, 9 August 1919, *BLAAS*. L/MIL/7/16922.
45 Memorandum by Curzon, 31 December 1918, *DBFP*, First ser., III: 468.
46 Nicolson, *Curzon*, 122–3.
47 Bush, *Mudros to Lausanne*, 131–43; L. G. Bondarevskaia, 'Anglo-iranskoe soglashenie 1919 g.', in *Problemy britanskoi istorii*, ed. V. G. Trukhanovsky (Nauka, 1987), 83–4.
48 Memorandum by Curzon, August 1919, BL F 112/253. See also Nicolson, *Curzon*, 136–7.
49 *Manchester Guardian*, 16 August 1919.
50 Lord Curzon to Grace Curzon, 17 August 1919, BL. F 112/793.
51 Quoted in Gilmour, *Curzon*, 517.
52 Minutes of the Cabinet meeting, 17 November 1920, *TNA*, CAB 23/23.
53 Minute by Curzon, 26 October 1922, *TNA*, FO 371/7810.
54 On the activities of the Red Caspian Flotilla during the Russian civil war, refer to A. K. Semyanichev, *Volzhsko-Kaspiiskaia flotiliia v bor'be za Kaspii. 1918–1920 gg.* (Voenmorizdat, 1952).

55 See V. L. Genis, *Krasnaia Persia: Bol'sheviki v Giliane. 1920–1921. Dokumental'naia khronika* (Tsentr strategicheskikh i politicheskikh issledovanii, 2000); M. A. Persiz, and M. S. Meier (comps), *Persidkii front mirovoi revolutsii. Dokumenty o sovetskom vtorzhenii v Gilian (1919–1921). Sbornik dokumentov* (Kvadriga, 2009).
56 Diplomatic note by the Soviet government to the government of Persia, 9 June 1921, AVPRF, f. 94, op. 5, pap. 3, d. 12, ll. 21–2.
57 Joukoff Eudin and North, *Soviet Russia and the East*, 96; Volodarsky, *Sovety i ikh yuzhnye sosedi*, 95; M. A. Persiz, *Zastenchivaia interventsiia* (Muravei-Gaid, 1999).
58 Raskol'nikov, *Na boevykh postakh*, 326.
59 *The Times*, 27 May 1920.
60 Conclusions of the Cabinet meeting, 21 May 1920, TNA, CAB 23/21/13.
61 Karakhan to Politburo, 9 September 1920, in Kvashonkin, *Bolshevistskoe rukovodstvo*, 159.
62 The Soviet-Persian Treaty, 26 February 1921, AVPRF, f. 94, op. 5, pap. 3, d. 5, l. 3.
63 Arnold Toynbee, *The World after the Peace Conference* (H. Milford – OUP, 1926), 42.
64 Darwin, *Britain, Egypt and the Middle East*, 167.
65 Monroe, *Britain's Moment in the Middle East*, 58–9; Bush, *Mudros to Lausanne*, 269–90.
66 Sudeikin, 'Politika Anglii na Blizhnem Vostoke', 217–20; Jeffrey, *The Military Defence of the British Empire*, 74, 277–93.
67 Panin, *Sovetskaia Rossiia i Afghanistan*, 7–8, 13.
68 Samra, *India and Anglo-Soviet Relations*, 41.
69 For the full report of this military action, refer to the cable by General Charles Monroe to the secretary of the government of India, 1 November 1919, in A. L. P. Burdett (ed.), *Afghanistan Strategic Intelligence. British Records 1919–1970* (Chippenham: Archive Editions, 2002), 1: 33–57; Blacker, *On Secret Patrol in High Asia*, 185–95; George Molesworth, *Afghanistan, 1919. An Account of Operations in the Third Afghan War* (London–Bombay: Asia Publishing House, 1962), 31–179.
70 Panin, *Sovetskaia Rossiia i Afghanistan*, 15–16; Gusterin, 'Politika Sovetskogo gosudarstva', 98.
71 Bolshevik Propaganda in Central Asia, 1919, BLAAS. L/PS/11/159.
72 Panin, *Sovetskaia Rossiia i Afghanistan*, 21–3.
73 V. L. Genis, *Vice-Consul Vvedenskii. Sluzhba v Persii i Bukharskom khanstve (1906–1920 gg.)* (Izdatel'stvo sotsial'no-politicheskaia mysl', 2003), 176–7.
74 On Bolshevik relations with Afghanistan, see Miscellaneous intelligence summaries, reports and minutes, August–November 1919, in ed. A. L. P. Burdett, *Afghanistan Strategic Intelligence. British Records 1919–1970* (Chippenham: Archive Editions, 2002), 1: 61–86; Suritz to Chicherin, January 1920, AVPRF, f. 090, op. 3, pap. 1, d. 5, ll. 1–55. See also Bush, *Mudros to Lausanne*, 290–301; Volodarsky, *Sovety i ikh yuzhnye sosedi*, 169.
75 Miscellaneous intelligence records (diary, telegrams), January–August 1921, Burdett, *Afghanistan Strategic Intelligence*, 1: 147–88; Karakhan to Politburo members, 26 January 1921, in Kvashonkin, *Bolshevistskoe rukovodstvo*, 176; Stalin to Trotsky, 2 November 1921, ibid., 214.
76 Popplevell, *Intelligence and Imperial Defence*, 301. See also Chelmsford to Montague, 28 May 1919, BLAAS. L/PS/10/836; Note by India Office experts, 31 October 1919, ibid., L/MIL/17/14/91/1. On the plans of Indian nationalists, see Barkatullah to Suritz, 1 June 1919, AVPRF, f. 090, op. 3, pap. 1, d. 3, ll. 24–8; Barkatullah to Chicherin, 3 June 1919, ibid., d. 4, ll. 1–3.

77 Kapur, *Soviet Russia and Asia*, 231.
78 Etherton, *In the Heart of Asia*, 159-60.
79 Note by India Office experts, 29 October 1919, *BLAAS*. L/PS/10/741.
80 Miliukov, *Rossiia na perelome*, 1: 294. See also Bureau of information. Measures against Bolshevist propaganda in India, June 1919-May 1921, *BLAAS*. L/PJ/6/1635.
81 *Times*, 12 December 1919.
82 Quoted in Imam, *Colonialism in East-West Relations*, 68.
83 Smith, *Six*, 5.
84 For further information, see Sergeev, *The Great Game*, 199-217.
85 Latyshev, *Rassekrechennyi Lenin*, 195-6.
86 Roy, *Memoirs*, 391; Imam, *Colonialism in East-West Relations*, 111-12, 138; Panin, *Sovetskaia Rossiia i Afghanistan*, 83-4.
87 Note by Roy to Politburo, early 1921, *RGASPI*, f. 5, op. 3, d. 577, ll. 19-24. See also Roy, *Memoirs*, 419-26.
88 Review by Leaper, the official of the Foreign Office, 16 March 1920, *TNA*, FO 371/6019; Proceedings of the meeting of the Indian revolutionary association, 2 December 1920, *RGASPI*, f. 17, op. 170, d. 120, ll. 1-2ob. See also Damie, 'Mandiama Prativadi Bkhaiankara Tirumala Achariia', 202.
89 Yanson, the head of the NKID Eastern department to the Peoples' commissariat of nationalities, 19 November 1920, *AVPRF*, f. 94, op. 1, pap. 3, d. 11, l. 29.
90 *Times*, 3 February 1921.
91 Roy, *Memoirs*, 429-38; Jacobson, *When Soviet Union Entered World Politics*, 116; Dmitriev, *Indian Revolutionaries in Central Asia*, 125.
92 Clippings from foreign newspapers, January-December 1921, *AVPRF*, f. 90, op. 4a, pap. 1, d. 1, ll. 1-34. See also, Popplevell, *Intelligence and Imperial Defence*, 297-320.
93 Suritz to Karakhan, June 1920, *AVPRF*, f. 090, op. 3, pap. 1, d. 3, ll. 14; Kaye, *Communism in India*, 5-6.
94 David Petrie, *Communism in India, 1924-27* (Calcutta: Government of India Press, 1927), 12; Popplevell, *Intelligence and Imperial Defence*, 311.
95 Petrie, *Communism in India*, 16.
96 Popplevell, *Intelligence and Imperial Defence*, 312-13.
97 Roy, *Memoirs*, 486-93; Popplevell, *Intelligence and Imperial Defence*, 308.
98 Ibid., 311.
99 *Shanghai Life*, May-June 1921, *BLAAS*. L/PJ/12/45, ff. 1-75, esp. ff. 2-5, 10-11, 41-4.
100 M. I. Sladkovsky, *Kitai i Angliia* (Nauka, 1980), 151-3, 157-9.
101 Kapur, *Soviet Russia and Asia*, 54-72.
102 Report by Ioffe to Politburo, 1921, in Kvashonkin, *Bolshevistskoe rukovodstvo*, 261.
103 Reports by Etherton, 1, 20 August 1920; 10, 20 October 1921, *BLAAS*. L/PS/10/836; Kashgar monthly diaries by Etherton, 1919-1920, ibid., L/PS/10/825; Kashgar monthly diaries by Etherton, 1921-2, ibid., L/PS/10/976.
104 Mil'stein, *Iz istorii Turkestanskoi Cheka*, 36.
105 Hopkirk, *Setting the East Ablaze*, 95-6.
106 William and Zelda Coates, *Soviets in Central Asia*, 79.
107 Etherton, *In the Heart of Asia*, 63-4, 229-32.
108 Etherton's diary, August 1920, *TNA*, FO/371/5318. See also Nyman, *Great Britain and Chinese*, 64.
109 Etherton, *In the Heart of Asia*, 138; Correspondence between Etherton and Bailey, 1920, *BLAAS*. Bailey Papers, F157/232.

110 On the British support to *Basmachis*, see Lenczowski, *Russia and the West in Iran*, 38; Babokhodzhaev, *Proval angliiskoi politiki*, 78–92; Panin, *Sovietskaia Rossiia i Afghanistan*, 93–110; D. V. Shevchenko, 'Basmacheskoe dvizhenie. Politicheskie process i vooruzhennaia bor'ba v Srednei Asii. 1917–1931 gg.', Avtoref. diss. kandidata istoricheskikh nauk (Irkutsk: Irkutskii gosudarstvenni pedagogicheskii universitet, 2006), 18–19.
111 Pervyi s'ezd narodov Vostoka v Baku, 1–8 September 1920. Stenographicheskie otchety (Petrograd: Izdatel'stvo Cominern, 1920), 108–12; John Riddell (ed.), *To See the Dawn: Baku, 1920 – First Congress of the Peoples of the East* (New York–London, etc.: Pathfinder, 1993), 23.
112 Etherton, *In the Heart of Asia*, 236–7; Lenczowski, *Russia and the West in Iran*, 37–8; William and Zelda Coates, *Soviets in Central Asia*, 79–80; Hopkirk, *Setting the East Ablaze*, 152–66.
113 G. Z. Sorokin. *Pervyi s'ezd narodov Vostoka* (Vostochnaia literatura, 1961), 14.
114 William Gallaher, *The Rolling of the Thunder* (Lawrence and Wishart, 1948), 15.
115 *Pervyi s'ezd narodov Vostoka v Baku*, 8. The American historian wrote about 55 per cent of Communists, 20 per cent of sympathizers and 25 per cent of non-party delegates of the Baku Congress, see Riddell, *To See the Dawn*, 23.
116 Ibid., 42–8; Dmitrishyn and Cox, *The Soviet Union and the Middle East*, 7–15.
117 Spector, *The Soviet Union and the Muslim World*, 288–98. See also Sorokin, *Pervyi s'ezd narodov Vostoka*, 62–7; Hopkirk, *Setting the East Ablaze*, 108–19.
118 *Pervyi s'ezd narodov Vostoka v Baku*, 211–12.
119 Weekly summary of intelligence report, no. 5, 8 September 1920, TNA, FO 371/5177; Political report on the Baku Congress, 30 October 1920, ibid., FO 371/5178/E.
120 Curzon to Chicherin, 2 October 1920, AVPRF, f. 4, op. 4, pap. 18, d. 258, ll. 13–14; Curzon to Chicherin, 9 October 1920, *DVP SSSR*, 4: 318.
121 Figes, *A People's Tragedy*, 703–4.
122 Spector, *The Soviet Union and the Muslim World*, 46; Jacobson, 'When Soviet Union Entered World Politics', 51–80.

Chapter 8

1 Lenin to his correspondent in Switzerland, 10 June 1921, TNA. PA. LG F/203/2/12, ff. 420–5. The Cabinet members were notified of this letter on 2 August 1921, ibid., CAB 24/126/94.
2 William and Zelda Coates, *A History of Anglo-Soviet Relations*, 1: 55–60; Klugman, *History of the CPGB*, 1: 130–236; Williams, 'The Genoa Conference of 1922: Lloyd George and the Politics of Recognition', 35; Anne Orde, *British Policy and European Reconstruction after the First World War* (Cambridge, MA: HUP, 2002), 162–3.
3 Trofimova, *Pervye shagi sovetskoi diplomatii*, 43.
4 Leaflet 'Help for Russia', 27 March 1922, RGASPI, f. 5, op. 3, d. 699; Alfred Mond, minister of health, to Lloyd George, 4 April 1922, TNA, PA. LG F/37/2/11. See also S. G. Wheatcroft, 'Population Loses, 1914–22', in *The Economic Transformation of the Soviet Union, 1913–1945*, ed. R. W. Davies et al. (Cambridge: CUP, 1994), 63.
5 Correspondence on the traffic of Russian POWs from France to the Black Sea ports, and the Europeans to the south of France, March–August 1921, *RGA VMF*, f. R-1, op. 3, d. 468, ll. 1–92.

6   The annual report by the NKID to the Ninth All-Russian congress of Soviets (December 1920–December 1921), *DVP SSSR*, 4: 673–4.
7   William and Zelda Coates, *A History of Anglo-Soviet Relations*, 1: 57; Graubard, *British Labor and the Russian Revolution*, 224–8.
8   Klyshko to Chicherin, 28 July 1921, *AVPRF*, f. 4, op. 4, pap. 20, d. 291, l. 64.
9   Klyshko to Chicherin, 29 July 1921, ibid., ll. 10–11.
10 Berzin to Chicherin, 4 August 1921, *RGASPI*, f. 495, op. 100, d. 25, l. 80.
11 Correspondence on Nansen's committee, August–September 1921, *DBFP*, First ser., XX: 718–40; Hodgson to Curzon, 14 August 1922, ibid., 909–12. See also Klugman, *History of the CPGB*, 1: 132–3.
12 William and Zelda Coates, *A History of Anglo-Soviet Relations*, 1: 59.
13 Report by Lloyd-Graeme, 3 September 1921, *TNA*, FO 418/56. Ff. 70–1.
14 Lloyd George's speech in the House of Commons, 16 August 1921, in Gilbert, *Winston Churchill*, 4: 775.
15 Klyshko to Chicherin, 29 July 1921, *AVPRF*, f. 4, op. 4, pap. 20, d. 291, l. 11.
16 *Pravda*, 17 August 1921.
17 Meeting of the Committee on the Russian Famine, 6 August 1921, *DBFP*, First ser., XX: 705–9.
18 Harding to Crow, 10 August 1921, ibid., 714.
19 Colonel Josiah Wedgwood, Chairman of the Russian famine relief committee, to the Russian branch of Imperial War relief fund and the permanent under-secretary of the Colonial Office, 7 September 1921, *TNA*, CO 323/88/32.
20 *Daily Telegraph*, 10 October 1921.
21 Leaflet 'Help for Russia', 27 March 1922, *RGASI*, f. 5, op. 3, d. 699, l. 25.
22 Agreement of the British government to permit the acceptance of 250 children from Russia by British families, May 1922, *TNA*, FO 371/8205, ff. 115–27.
23 The annual report by the NKID, *DVP SSSR*, 4: 671–682.
24 Martin Thomas, 'The Urquhart Concession and Anglo-Soviet Relations, 1921–1922', *Jahrbuecher fuer Geschichte Osteuropas* 20, no. 4 (1972): 551–70; Keeble, *Britain and the Soviet Union*, 89.
25 Shishkin, *Sovietskoe gosudarstvo i strany Zapada*, 256.
26 Quoted in B. E. Stein, *Vneshniia politika SSSR, 1917–1923* (Gospolitizdat, 1945), 141. See also Williams, *Trading with the Bolsheviks*, 60.
27 Note by Krassin to Curzon, 5 July 1921, *DVP SSSR*, 4: 211–4.
28 Raskol'nikov to Chicherin, 25 August 1921, *AVPRF*, f. 152, op. 3, pap. 1, d. 10, l. 52.
29 Memorandum by Montagu for the Cabinet, August 1921, *TNA*, CAB 24/127/48.
30 Curzon to Chicherin, 7 September 1921, *TNA*, FO 418/56, ff. 79–85; *DBFP*, First ser., XX: 741–7.
31 Litvinov to Curzon, 27 September 1921, *DVP SSSR*, 4: 374–80.
32 Memorandum by Curzon for the Cabinet, 27 October 1921, *TNA*, CAB 24/129/43; Curzon to Chicherin, 2 November 1921, ibid., FO 418/56, ff. 163–5; Curzon to Hodgson, 2 November 1921, ibid., FO 371/8204, ff. 7–10; Minutes of the Cabinet meeting, 3 November 1921, ibid., CAB 23/27/12.
33 Suritz to Chicherin, 26 December 1921, *DVP SSSR*, 4: 350–5.
34 Chicherin to Berzin, 4 September 1921, ibid., 306.
35 Lenin's speech at the Second All-Russian congress of political propagandists, 17 October 1921, in Lenin, *Polnoe sobranie sochineniii*, 44: 155–75.
36 Chicherin to Curzon, 28 October 1921, Curzon to Krassin, 1 November 1921, Great Britain. Foreign Office, *Correspondence with M. Krassin respecting Russia's Foreign*

Indebtedness, Russia (1921), no. 3. Cmd. 1546 (HMSO, 1921), 3-5, 5-6; Chicherin to Krassin, 27 October 1921, *DVP SSSR*, 4: 492-3. See also A. S. Sokolov and Yu. P. Golitsyn, 'Problema dorevoliutsionnogo dolga v sovetsko-britanskikh otnosheniyakh v 1920-e gg', *Istoriya* 7, no. 2 (2016), http://history.jes.su (accessed 6 October 2017).

37 Krassin to Chicherin, 26 November 1921, AVPRF, f. 0418, op. 1, pap. 1, d. 20, ll. 1-4.
38 Krassin's reply to the questions of Labour leaders, 29 November 1921, *DVP SSSR*, 4: 547-57.
39 The annual report by the NKID, 1922. Ibid., 764-5.
40 Lubov Krassin, *Leonid Krassin*, 185-6.
41 William and Zelda Coates, *A History of Anglo-Soviet Relations*, 1: 64-5; Orde, *British Policy and European Reconstruction*, 177.
42 Krassin to Chicherin, 17 December 1921, *DVP SSSR*, 4: 580-2.
43 Krassin to Chicherin, 28 December 1921, ibid., 605-6.
44 G. B. Sandomirsky (ed.), *Genuezskaia konferentsiia 1922 g. Materialy i dokumenty* (NKID, 1922), 3-4; Lorain - to Curzon, 7 January 1922, *TNA*, FO 418/57, ff. 110-12. See also B. E. Stein, *Genuezskaia konferetsiia* (Gosudarstvennoe izdatel'stvo, 1922), 3.
45 Wise to Krassin, 17 January 1922, *AVPRF*, f. 0418, op. 1, pap. 1, d. 20, ll. 6-8; Krassin to Chicherin, 17 January 1922, *DVP SSSR*, 5: 33; Chicherin to Krassin, 21 January 1922, *AVPRF*, f. 0418, op. 1, pap. 1, d. 20, ll. 15-16; Gregory to Krassin, 22 January 1922, *DVP SSSR*, 5: 60.
46 Documents on the preparations of the Soviet delegation for the Genoa conference, January-April 1922, *RGAE*, f. 2305, op. 1, d. 1194, ll. 5, 6-7, 28-31, 47-48ob. See also Stein, *Genuezskaia konferetsiia*, 16-20; N. N. Lubimov and A. N. Erlikh, *Genuezskaia konferetsiia. Vospominaniia uchastnikov* (Izdatel'stvo Instituta mezhdunarodnykh otnoshenii, 1963), 20.
47 Krassin to Chicherin, 13 February 1922, *DVP SSSR*, 5: 102-3.
48 Chamberlain to Lloyd George, 21 March 1922; UB CRLSC. AC 23/6/18; Chamberlain to Lloyd George, 24 March 1922, ibid.; Curzon to Chamberlain, 13 May 1922, ibid., AC 23/6/34.
49 Trotsky's speech at the meeting of Politburo, 9 February 1922, in Meijer, *The Trotsky Papers*, 2: 674-6; Chicherin to Curzon, 15 February 1922, *DVP SSSR*, 5: 113-15; Summary of the conversation between David Soskice and James Ramsey Macdonald, 19 March 1922, *TNA*, PA. STH/DS 2/2/9.
50 E. A. Preobrazhensky, *Itogi Genuezskoi konferentsii i khoziastvennye perspektivy Evropy* (Gosudarstvennoe izdatel'stvo, 1922), 5.
51 Ibid., 6.
52 Gregory to Curzon, 26 January 1922, in Orde, *British Policy and European Reconstruction*, 186.
53 Memorandum by Gregory to the Cabinet, 12 February 1922, *DBFP*, First ser., XX: 849-53.
54 Diary, 23 March 1922, in Riddell, Intimate Diary of the Peace Conference, 368. See also Stephen White, *Origins of Détente: The Genoa Conference and Soviet-Western Relations, 1921-1922* (Cambridge: CUP, 1985), 94-6.
55 Articles of agreement to form the basis of a treaty with Russia, 7 March 1922, *DBFP*, First ser., XIX 199-206.
56 Decisions taken at the meeting of experts in London on the 'Russian question', 20-28 March 1922, AVPRF, f. 0418, op. 2, pap. 8, d. 25, ll. 1-10; Memorandum by Preobrazhensky, early April 1922, AVPRF, f. 418, op. 2, pap. 8, d. 27, ll. 21-4. See also Preobrazhensky, *Itogi Genuezskoi konferentsii*, 23.

57 Quoted in William Beaverbrook, *The Decline and Fall of Lloyd George* (Collins, 1963), 293.
58 Minutes of the Cabinet meetings, 27, 28 September 1922, *TNA*, CAB 23/29; Drafts of the British programme for the conference in Genoa by A. Chamberlain, Hankey and Lloyd George, 27 March 1922, ibid., UB CRLSC. AC 23/6/12, 13, 14; Curzon to Lloyd George, 12 April 1922, *TNA*, PA. LG F/150/2/196.
59 On the Anglo-Soviet relations in the context of the Genoa conference, see especially A. A. Ioffe, *Genuezskaia konferentsiia* (Krasnaya nov', 1922); Steed, *Through Thirty Years*, 2: 380–4; Gregory, *On the Edge of Diplomacy*, 194–215; Fischer, *The Soviets in World Politics*, 2: 318–54; Owen, *Tempestuous Journey*, 615–20; Roskill, *Hankey*, 2: 266–76; Williams, *Trading with the Bolsheviks*, 64–71; Orde, *British Policy and European Reconstruction*, 183–207; Salzman, *Great Britain, Germany and the Soviet Union*, 7–32; etc.
60 Chicherin's speech, 10 April 1922, *AVPRF*, f. 418, op. 2, pap. 9, d. 37, ll. 6–12.
61 Declaration by the Soviet delegation, 17 April 1922, ibid., d. 38, ll. 1–4.
62 Memorandum by the Soviet delegation, 20 April 1922, ibid., d. 39, ll. 1–10; Chicherin to Lloyd George, 20 April 1922, ibid., d. 41, l. 4; Chicherin to Lloyd George, 22 April 1922, ibid., d. 43, l. 1; *DBFP*, First ser., XIX: 518–22.
63 Lenin to Stalin (for Chicherin), 21 April 1922, *DVP SSSR*, 5: 261; Draft of the telegram by Lenin to Chicherin, 2 May 1922, in Lenin, *Polnoe sobranie sochinenii*, 45: 172.
64 Lenin to Chicherin, 30 April 1922, in *ibid.*, 171.
65 Minutes of the British delegation, 16 April 1922, *TNA*, PA. LG F/150/1.
66 Stein, *Genuezskaia konferentsiia*, 17.
67 Lenin to Chicherin, 9 May 1922, in Lenin, *Polnoe sobranie sochinenii*, 45: 185.
68 Meeting of the Entente delegations at Villa Raggi, 18 April 1922, *TNA*, PA. LG F/145/1, ff. 87–9; *DBFP*, First ser., XIX: 446–58, especially, 447.
69 Collective note by the Entente representatives to the Russian delegation, 19 April 1922, *TNA*, PA. LG F/145/2, ff. 142–4.
70 Draft of the European pact of non-aggression, 26 April 1922, *AVPRF*, f. 418, op. 2, pap. 9, d. 44, l. 3.
71 *Manchester Guardian*, 19 April 1922. For more details, see Lubimov, Erlikh, *Genuezskaia konferentsiia*, 145; Stephen White, *The Origins of Détente*, 208–9.
72 Meeting of the Entente delegations at the hotel *Miramare*, 29 April 1922, *TNA*, PA. LG F/150/4/3, ff. 365–8; Drafts of the British and French memoranda to the Russian delegation, 27–28 April 1922, *DBFP*, First ser., XIX: 612–18, 618–24; The Entente powers' memorandum to the Russian delegation, 29 April 1922, *AVPRF*, f. 418, op. 2, pap. 9, d. 46, ll. 25–31.
73 The Entente powers' memorandum to the Russian delegation, 3 May 1922, *TNA*, PA. LG F/145/4, ff. 380–95. See also Sandomirsky, *Genuezskaia konferentsiia*, 216–24; A. A. Ioffe, *Genuezskaia konferentsiia*, 51; Fink, *The Genoa Conference*, 209–13.
74 Vygodsky, *U istokov sovetskoi diplomatii*, 235.
75 Memorandum by Rakovski to the president of the Genoa Conference Financial Commission, 3 May 1922, *TNA*, PA. LG F/145/4, ff. 415–24.
76 Chicherin's speech, 3 May 1922, *AVPRF*, f. 418, op. 2, pap. 9, d. 48, ll. 1–3.
77 Minute of the informal meeting of Lloyd George and Krassin, 5 May 1922, *DBFP*, First ser., XIX: 751–5.
78 Memoranda by the Soviet delegation, 6, 11 May 1922, *AVPRF*, f. 418, op. 2, pap. 9, d. 49, ll. 1–7; ibid., d. 50, ll. 5–8; Litvinov to the NKID, 8 May 1922, *DVP SSSR*, 5: 360.

79 Proceedings of the Genoa conference, 17 May 1922, *TNA*, PA. LG F/145/1, ff. 582–7; *DBFP*, First ser., XIX: 953–69. See also Owen, *Tempestuous Journey*, 620–1; Stephen White, *The Origins of Détente*, 192–4; Fink, *The Genoa Conference*, 169–91.
80 A. A. Ioffe, *Genuezskaia konferentsiia*, 61, 126.
81 See Maklakov to Bakhmeteff, 24 May 1922, in M. M. Kononova, *Russkie diplomaticheskie predstaviteli*, 67.
82 K. B. Vinogardov, *David Lloyd George* (Nauka, 1970), 348.
83 Keynes, 'Reconstruction in Europe', *The Manchester Guardian Commercial*, 10 June 1922, no. 3: 132–3.
84 Fink, *The Genoa Conference*, 129.
85 Evgeny Chossudovsky, 'Genoa Revisited: Russia and Coexistence', *Foreign Affairs* L no. 3 (1972): 560.
86 Stephen White, *The Origins of Détente*, VII.
87 Nicolson, *Curzon*, 245.
88 See Williams, *Trading with the Bolsheviks*, 89.
89 Chicherin's speech, 17 May 1922, AVPRF, f. 418, op. 2, pap. 9, d. 51, ll. 1–4. On the Hague conference of 1922, see B. E. Stein, *Gaagskaia konferentsiia* (Gosudarstvennoe izdatel'stvo, 1922); Maisky, *Vneshniaia politika*, 124–9; Fischer, *The Soviets in World Affairs*, 2: 355–72; etc.
90 Report by the Russian delegation to the SNK about the Hague Conference, 27 July 1922, in ed. G. N. Lashkevich, *Gaagskaia konferentsiia 1922 g. Polnyi stenographicheskii otchet (materialy i dokumenty)* (NKID, 1922), 7–14. See also Williams, *Trading with the Bolsheviks*, 70.
91 Maxse to O'Malley, 10 July 1922, *DBFP*, First ser., XIX: 1097.
92 *Izvestiia*, 18 July 1922.
93 I. A. Khormach, 'Bor'ba i sotrudnichestvo sovetskogo gosudarstva s Ligoi Natsii v 1919–1934 godakh', *Rossiiskaia istoriia*, no. 5 (2011): 31; Kocho-Williams, *Russian and Soviet Diplomacy*, 82–4, 87–9.
94 O'Connor, *The Engineer of Revolution*, 242–3.
95 Quoted in Khromov, *Leonid Krassin*, 35.
96 On the negotiations between Krassin and Urquhart in 1922, refer to Lubov Krassin, *Leonid Krassin*, 186, 188–9, 192–4; William and Zelda Coates, *A History of Anglo-Soviet Relations*, 1: 98; Shishkin, *Sovetskoe gosudarstvo i strany Zapada*, 335; Williams, *Trading with the Bolsheviks*, 71–2; Khromov, *Leonid Krassin*, 40–2.
97 Ibid., 72.
98 On the Chanak crisis, see Bennett, *British Foreign Policy during the Curzon Period*, 76–94; Rose, *Conservatism and Foreign Policy during the Lloyd George Coalition*, 245–6; Ferris, '"Far Too Dangerous a Gamble?" British Intelligence and Policy during the Chanak Crisis, September–October 1922', in *Power and Stability*, Goldstein, Mackercher, 139–84; Darwin, *The Empire Project*, 359–64.
99 On the conference in Lausanne, see Dennis, *The Foreign Policies of Soviet Russia*, 232–3; Lawrence Ronaldshay, *The Life of Lord Curzon. Being the Authorised Biography of George Nathaniel Marquise Curzon of Kedleston, K. G* (London – New York: E. Benn, 1928), 3: 322–43; Harold Nicolson, *Some People* (Boston – New York: Mifflin, 1926), 187–213: Idem., *Curzon*, 281–350; Fischer, *The Soviets in World Politics*, 2: 403–14; Aralov, *Vospominaniia*, 158–202; Trukhanovsky, *Vneshniaia politika Anglii*, 105–8; Vygodsky, *U istokov sovetskoi diplomatii*, 308–15; Bush, *Mudros to Lausanne*, 359–89; Dockrill and Goold, *Peace without Promise*, 236–47; Goekay, *A Clash of Empires*, 145–56; Erik Goldstein, 'The British Official Mind and

the Lausanne Conference', in *Power and Stability*, Goldstein, Mackercher, 185–206; Macmeekin, *The Ottoman Endgame*, 483–95; etc.
100 Alexander Yegorov, the commander of the Red Caucasian army, to Chicherin, 27 November 1922, *RGASPI*, f. 159, op. 2, d. 56, ll. 86–9.
101 Karakhan to Curzon, 12 September 1922, *DVP SSSR*, 5: 574–7.
102 Admiralty to Admiral Brock, 19 September 1922, *TNA*, WO 106/1503; Admiral Brock to Admiralty, 8 October 1922, ibid., FO 371/7900. For further information, see Ferris, 'Far Too Dangerous a Gamble?', 163.
103 A circular note by the Soviet government to foreign states, 24 September 1922, *DVP SSSR*, 5: 593–5.
104 Ferris, 'Far Too Dangerous a Gamble?', 173.
105 Correspondence with the Foreign Office, December 1922–December 1923, *BLAAS*. L/PJ/12/119.
106 Goldstein, *The British Official Mind*, 193.
107 Ibid., 201.
108 Curzon to Bonar Law, 28 November 1922, *TNA*, PA. Bonar Low Papers, F 111/12/35, ff. 1–11.
109 Chicherin's speech, 4 December 1922, *AVPRF*, f. 421, op. 1, pap. 2, d. 22, ll. 14–16.
110 Curzon to Crow, 5, 6 December 1922, *DBFP*, First ser., XVIII: 369–70, 374–5.
111 Nicolson, *Curzon*, 306–12.
112 Curzon's speech, 6 December 1922, *AVPRF*, f. 421, op. 1, pap. 2, d. 22, ll. 36–46; Chicherin to Stalin, 22 June 1923, ibid., f. 04, op. 4, pap. 23, d. 331, ll. 24–25.
113 Soviet delegation's proposal, 7 December 1922, *AVPRF*, f. 0421, op. 1, pap. 2, d. 24, l. 3.
114 Curzon to Crow, 17 December 1922, *TNA*, FO 418/58; FO 839/26; *DBFP*, First ser., XVIII: 397.
115 Chicherin to Litvinov, 9 December 1922, *AVPRF*, f. 0421, op. 1, pap. 1, d. 6, ll. 332–5; Chicherin to Litvinov, 17 December 1922, *DVP SSSR*, 6: 82–90.
116 Soviet delegation's draft convention on the Straits, 18 December 1922, in Dmitrishyn, Cox, *The Soviet Union and the Middle East*, 194–9; Chicherin's speech, 19 December 1922, ibid., 501–7.
117 Curzon to Crow, 19 December 1922, *DBFP*, First ser., XVIII: 398.
118 Chicherin to Litvinov, 15 January 1923, *AVPRF*, f. 0421, op. 1, pap. 1, d. 6, ll. 85–6; Chicherin to Litvinov, 30 January 1923, *DVP SSSR*, 6: 169–70.
119 Curzon to Crow, 5 February 1923, *DBFP*, First ser., XVIII: 504–7.
120 Dennis, *The Foreign Policies of Soviet Russia*, 227–8; Nicolson, *Curzon*, 292–3; Sharp, *The Versailles Settlement*, 173–4; Conte, *Christian Rakovski*, 253.
121 Quoted in Goekay, *A Clash of Empires*, 164.
122 Churchill, *The World Crisis*, 388, 391–2, 413, 438; Idem., *Great Contemporaries*, 273–88.
123 S. V. Zarnitskii and A. N. Sergeev, *Chicherin* (Molodaia gvardiia, 1968), 218.

Chapter 9

1 *Pravda*, 15 May 1923.
2 See, especially, Ronaldshay, The Life of Lord Curzon; Gilmor, Curzon, Idem., *Curzon: Imperial Statesman, 1859–1925* (Farrar, Straub and Giroux, 2003); Sergeev, George Nathaniel Curzon – poslednii rytsar' Britanskoi imperii.

3   Memorandum by Curzon for the Cabinet, 14 November 1920, BL., F 112/236. See also Ronaldshay, *The Life of Lord Curzon*, 3: 355; Stephen White, *Britain and the Bolshevik Revolution*, 151–8.
4   Raskolnikov to Safarov, the head of the Comintern Eastern department, 11 May 1923, in *Sovetskaia Rossiia v bor'be za 'afganskii koridor' (1919–1925)'*, comp. Yu. N. Tikhonov (Kvadriga, 2017), 373.
5   Goldenberg, the senior official in the staff of the Comintern Turkestan bureau, to Bolotnikov, political commissar of the Red Army, 4 August 1922, ibid., 393–5.
6   Chicherin to Stalin, 19 December 1923, *RGASPI*, f. 159, op. 2, d. 49, l. 26.
7   Minute of the meeting of the RCP(b) Commission on Afghanistan, 28 February 1923, in Tikhonov, *Sovetskaia Rossiia v bor'be*, 409.
8   Minute of the SNK meeting, 1 December 1922 (decrypt); Far Eastern and Northern Summary, no. 1136, 12 April 1923, *TNA*, WO 106/5556.
9   Stan Harding, 'The Case of Mrs. Stan Harding', *Nineteenth Century and After* 92, no. 1 (1922): 1–16.
10 Idem., 'The Moscow Trial', ibid., 280. On Harding's case see also, Lubov Krassin, *Leonid Krassin*, 145; Stephen White, *Britain and the Bolshevik Revolution*, 152–3.
11 On Davison's case see Curzon to Leslie, general consul in Revel, 2 October 1920; Chicherin to Curzon, 3 November 1920, 26 December 1920; Curzon to Hodgson, 3 January 1922, in Great Britain. Foreign Office, *Correspondence between His Majesty Government and the Soviet Government respecting the Murder of Mr. C. F. Davison in January 1920*, Russia, no. 1 (1923), Cmd. 1846 (HMSO, 1923), 3–6.
12 Preston to Curzon, 13 December 1922, *TNA*, FO 418/59, ff. 1–2; Peters to Curzon, 16 January 1923, ibid., ff. 25–6; Radek to Litvinov, 3 March 1923, *RGASPI*, f. 17, op. 170, d. 196, l. 15.
13 Hodgson to Curzon, 21 August 1922, *TNA*, FO 418/58.
14 Hodgson to Curzon, 20 March 1923, ibid., FO 418/59. As Hodgson informed the Foreign Office, Vatican suggested to Moscow to purchase the property of all Catholic parishes in the Soviet Republic to raise funds for assistance to the starving population, see Hodgson to Weinstein, 30 March 1923, *TNA*, FO 418/59.
15 PD, Fifth ser., CLXII: cols. 877–80.
16 Gregory to Curzon, 15 March 1923, *DBFP*, First ser., XXV: 52–3.
17 Conte, *Christian Rakovski*, 266–7.
18 Weinstein to Hodgson, 31 March 1923, *TNA*, FO 418/59; *DVP SSSR*, 6: 117.
19 Hodgson to Weinstein, 1 April 1923, *Anglo-sovetskie otnosheniia*, 31–2; Weinstein to Hodgson, 4 April 1923, FO 418/59. On Hodgson's impression of Weinstein, see *DBFP*, First ser., XXV: 58. See also Great Britain. Foreign Office. *Correspondence between His Majesty Government and the Soviet Government Respecting the Relations between the Two Governments*, Russia, 1923, no. 2. Cmd. 1869 (HMSO, 1923), 3–13. For the whole correspondence between Hodgson and Weinstein, see BL. F 112/236, nos. 1–5.
20 Curzon to Hodgson, 10 April 1923, *TNA*, FO 418/59, f. 113; *DBFP*, First ser., XXV: 60–1.
21 Shishkin, *Stanovlenie vneshnei politiki*, 167.
22 Berzin and Klyshko to Henderson, 17 April 1923, *AVPRF*, f. 05, op. 3a, pap. 1a, d. 4, ll. 5–6; Berzin to Litvinov, 23 April 1923, ibid., ll. 1–4.
23 Henderson to Bonar Law, 17 April 1923; Smith, the chief whip of the Labour parliamentary faction, to Bonar Law, 18 April 1923, *TNA*, PA. Bonar Law Papers. 118/4.
24 William and Zelda Coates, *A History of Anglo-Soviet Relations*, 1: 105–106.

25 Lloyd George to Curzon, 1 May 1923, *DBFP*, First ser., XXV: 86.
26 Amery's diary, 2 May 1923, *TNA*, CU. CAC. AMEL 7/17.
27 Memorandum by Curzon, 2 May 1923, *TNA*, FO 18/59, ff. 151–6; *DBFP*, First ser., XXV: 88–98. For the diplomatic correspondence on the Curzon strong note, see Great Britain. Foreign Office. *Correspondence between His Majesty's Government and the Soviet Government*, 3–14. For the memorandum's initial draft, see Memorandum by Curzon, 2 May 1923 (draft), *TNA*, CUL. Baldwin Papers. F 1. vol. 113.
28 Note by the Soviet Government to the British Government, 7 May 1923, *DVP SSSR*, 6: 279–84; *Izvestiya*, 12 May 1923.
29 Curzon to Hodgson, 8 May 1923, *DBFP*, First ser., XXV: 99–100.
30 Memorandum by the British Government to the Soviet Government, 8 May 1923, *DBFP*, First ser., XXV: 88–98; *AVPRF*, f. 04, op. 4, pap. 23, d. 329, ll. 5–7.
31 Macdonald to Chicherin, 10 May 1923, *DVP SSSR*, 6: 303; Berzin to Litvinov, 11 May 1923, *AVPRF*, f. 04, op. 4, pap. 24, d. 1923, l. 10.
32 Note by the Soviet government to the British government, 11 May 1923, *AVRPF*, f. 04, op. 4, pap. 23, d. 329, ll. 23–33; Note by the Soviet government to the British government, 13 May 1923, *TNA*, FO 418/59, ff. 176–80; ibid., BL. F 112/236; Note by Litvinov to Curzon, 12 May 1923, in Joukoff Eudin, Fisher, *Soviet Russia and the West*, 223–8.
33 D'Abernon, *An Ambassador of Peace*, 2: 172, 216.
34 *Izvestiya*, 12 May 1923.
35 Preston to Hodgson, 13, 15 May 1923, *TNA*, FO 418/59, ff. 194–5; Preston to Curzon, 15 May 1923, *DBFP*, First ser., XXV: 128–30. On the Soviet workers' manifestations under anti-British slogans, see Taigin, *Angliya i SSSR*, 15–24; William and Zelda Coates, *A History of Anglo-Soviet Relations*, 1: 112.
36 Chicherin's speech at the Moscow Soviet plenary session, 12 May 1923, *DVP SSSR*, 6: 306–7. On the international crisis around the German Rhineland, see Salzman, *Great Britain, Germany and the Soviet Union*, 33–44.
37 Vaugham, British Diplomatic Agent in Riga, to Curzon, 6 June 1923, *DBFP*, First ser., XXV: 155–7.
38 *Manchester Guardian*, 7 May 1923. See also Klugman, *History of CPGB*, 1: 148–57.
39 Clippings from British leading newspapers, 13–14 May 1923, *TNA*, PA. LG G/130; William and Zelda Coates, *Anglo-Soviet Relations*, 1: 112; Trukhanovsky, *Vneshniaia politika Anglii*, 117.
40 Klugman, *History of CPGB*, 1: 155–6.
41 *Izvestiya*, 12 May 1923.
42 Krassin to his spouse, Miklashevskaia-Krassina, 12, 18 May 1923, in 'Krassin's Letters to T. V. Miklashevskaia-Krassina', comp. S. S. Khromov, *Voprosy istorii*, no. 10 (2005): 58. See also Krassin's official report to Chicherin, Litvinov and Stalin, 23 May 1923, *RGASPI*, f. 159, op. 2, d. 29, ll. 188–9. On Krassin's contacts with Lloyd George and Macdonald, see Madeira, *Britannia and the Bear*, 117.
43 Meeting of the Cabinet. Conclusion, 15 May 1923, *TNA*, CAB 23/45/27.
44 Note of Curzon's parley with Krassin, 17 May 1923, ibid., FO 418/59, f. 183.
45 Gregory, *On the Edge of Diplomacy*, 143.
46 Note of Curzon's parley with Krassin, 17 May 1923, *TNA*, FO 418/59, ff. 183–7; Note of Krassin's parley with Curzon, 17 May 1923, *AVPRF*, f. 04, op. 4, pap. 23, d. 330, ll. 1–6, 7–11; *RGASPI*, f. 159, op. 2, d. 29, ll. 174–82.
47 Krassin to Chicherin, 22 May 1923, *RGASPI*, f. 159, op. 2, d. 29, l. 184; Klyshko to Chicherin, 23 May 1923, *AVPRF*, f. 04, op. 4, pap. 24, d. 332, ll. 18–32.

48 Gregory to Krassin, 29 May 1923, *DBFP*, First ser., XXV: 137–42.
49 Note by the Soviet government to the British government, 23 May 1923, *DVP SSSR*, 6: 325–7; Krassin to Curzon, 23 May 1923, *TNA*, CAB 24/160/50, ff. 1–3; ibid., FO 418/59, ff. 193–4; Great Britain. Foreign Office, *Correspondence between His Majesty's Government and the Soviet Government*, 3–4.
50 Krassin to Miklashevskaia-Krassina, 24 May 1923, in Khromov, 'Krassin's Letters', 60.
51 Krassin to Chicherin, Litvinov and Stalin, 23 May 1923, *RGASPI*, f. 159, op. 2, d. 29, ll. 185–93.
52 Memorandum by the Foreign Office, 24 May 1923, *BLAAS*. L/PJ/12/119; Amery's diary, 24 May 1923, *TNA*, CU. CAC. AMEL 7/17.
53 See, for example, Besedovsky, *Na putiakh k Termidoru*, 218–20.
54 Hodgson to Curzon, 19 June 1923, *DBFP*, First ser., XXV: 179–80.
55 Note of Krassin's parley with Curzon, 28 May 1923, *AVPRF*, f. 04, op. 4, pap. 23, d. 331, l. 39.
56 Gregory to Krassin, 29 May 1923, *DBFP*, First ser., XXV: 137–42; Note by the British government to the Soviet government, 29 May 1923, *DVP SSSR*, 6: 327–30.
57 Krassin to Miklashevskaia-Krassina, 30 May 1923, in Khromov, 'Krassin's Letters', 60.
58 Litvinov to Berzin, 4 June 1923, *AVPRF*, f. 04, op. 4, pap. 24, d. 333, ll. 11–18.
59 Memorandum by the Soviet government to the British government, 4 June 1923, *DVP SSSR*, 6: 334–8.
60 Minute of the Bolshevik Politburo meeting, 9 June 1923 (decrypt), *BLAAS*. L/PJ/12/119.
61 Note of the parley between Gregory and Krassin, 9 June 1923, *DBFP*, First ser., XXV: 160–1; Hodgson to Curzon, 10 June 1923, *TNA*, FO 418/59, ff. 195–8.
62 Memorandum by Krassin to Curzon, 11 June 1923, Great Britain. Foreign Office, *Correspondence between His Majesty's Government and the Soviet Government*. Russia, no. 3 (1923), 9–13; Memorandum by Curzon to Krassin, 13 June 1923, ibid., 13–14; *DBFP*, First ser., XXV: 172–3; Note by the British government to the Soviet government, 13 June 1923, *DVP SSSR*, 6: 338–9.
63 Karakhan to the Soviet Republic's plenipotentiaries in the oriental countries, 15 June 1923, ibid., 352–3; Chicherin to Curzon, 18 June 1923, ibid., 353–354; Chicherin to Curzon, 19 June 1923 (received), *DBFP*, First ser., XXV: 178–9.
64 Stephen White, *Britain and the Bolshevik Revolution*, 167–8.
65 Kremnev, *Krassin*, 227; Sergeev, *George Nathaniel Curzon*, 255.
66 Chicherin to the Soviet republic's plenipotentiaries in the oriental countries, 4 September 1923, *RGASPI*, f. 159, op. 2, d. 51, ll. 160–1.
67 Quoted in Gromyko, *Istoriia diplomatii*, 3: 327.
68 See, for example, Volkov, *Krakh angliiskoi politiki interventsii*, 316; Vygodsky, *U istokov sovetskoi diplomatii*, 316–17.
69 See, for example, Nicolson, *Curzon*, 356–60; Stephen White, *Britain and the Bolshevik Revolution*, 168; Madeira, *Britannia and the Bear*, 113–20; Quinlan, *The Secret War between the Wars*, 28–30; etc.
70 Fischer, *The Soviets in World Affairs*, 1: 445.
71 See Yu. N Tikhonov, *Afganskaia voina Stalina. Bitva za Tsentral'nuyu Asiiu* (Yausa, Exmo, 2008), 158.
72 Lubov Krassin, *Leonid Krassin*, 219–20.

73 Curzon to Hodgson, 5 July 1923, *DBFP*, First ser., XXV: 190–1; Peters, deputy diplomatic agent in Moscow, to Ovey, the Foreign Office counsellor, 27 July 1923, ibid., 214.; Hodgson to Curzon, 7 November 1923, ibid., 264.
74 Memorandum by the Foreign Office for the Cabinet, 20 September 1923, *BLAAS*. L/PS/10/1108/1, ff. 249–53.
75 Note by Gregory, 10 December 1926, *TNA*, CUL. Baldwin Papers, F 1, vol. 113.
76 Curzon to Crew-Milnes, ambassador to Paris, 13 June 1923, in Ronaldshay, *The Life of Lord Curzon*, 3: 356; Bennett, *British Foreign Policy during the Curzon Period*, 73–4.
77 Quoted in Keeble, *Britain and the Soviet Union*, 93.
78 Carolyn Kitching, *Britain and the Problem of International Disarmament 1919–1934* (London – New York: Routledge, 1999), 20.
79 D'Abernon, *An Ambassador of Peace*, 2: 218; Bennett, *British Foreign Policy during the Curzon Period*, 26.
80 Chicherin to Krassin, 3 June 1923, *AVPRF*, f. 04, op. 4, pap. 23, d. 236, l. 122.
81 Chicherin to Stalin, 8 January 1924, *RGASPI*, f. 159, op. 2, d. 52, ll. 45–6; Phillips, Consul in Harbin, to Macleay, Charge D'Affaires in China, 24 August 1923, *TNA*, FO 228/3364; Macleay to Macdonald, Ambassador in China, 14 June 1924, *TNA*, FO 228/3565.
82 William and Zelda Coates, *A History of Anglo-Soviet Relations*, 1: 127–8; Keeble, *Britain and the Soviet Union*, 93.
83 *Evening Standard*, 3 September 1923.
84 Trotsky, *Moia zhizn'*, 1: 261.
85 Krassin to Miklashevskaia-Krassina, 3 July 1923, in 'L. B. Krassin, Pis'ma zhene i detiam, 1917–1926' (comps) Yu. G. Fel'shtinskii, and G. N. Cherniavskii, *Voprosy istorii*, no. 4 (2002): 119.
86 C. G. Rakovski, *Angliia i SSSR* (Kiev: Gosudarstvennoe izdtel'stvo Ukrauny, 1923), 113–14.
87 Correspondence on Rakovski's appointment as a diplomatic agent in Great Britain, July–August 1923, *AVPRF*, f. 04, op. 4, pap. 23, d. 321, l. 1; Curzon to Hodgson, 1 August 1923, *DBFP*, First ser., XXV: 210–11; Conte, *Christian Rakovski*, 273–6.
88 Peters, Acting Diplomatic Agent in Russia, to Curzon, 6, 10 August 1923, *DBFP*, First ser., XXV: 218–19, 223.
89 Henderson to Baldwin, 16 August 1923, *TNA*, CUL. Baldwin. F 2, vol. 114, ff. 75–6.
90 Correspondence on Rakovski's appointment as a Diplomatic Agent in Great Britain, July–August 1923, *AVPRF*, f. 04, op. 4, pap. 23, dd. 321, 322; Peters to Curzon, 30 August 1923, *TNA*, FO 371/9356; Memorandum by Selby, the Foreign Office Counselor, 15 August 1923, *DBFP*, First ser., XXV: 227–9.
91 Zinoviev's speech at the Bolshevik Central committee's plenary session, 23 September 1923, in Adibekov, *Politburo TsK RKP(b) – VKP(b) i Komintern*, 191–3.
92 Rakovski to Chicherin, 6–7 October 1923, *RGASPI*, f. 159, op. 2, d. 30, l. 3.
93 Pavlovich, *Sovetskaia Rossiia i kapitalisticheskaia Angliia*, 140.
94 *Izvestiya*, 4 November 1923.
95 Ryzhikov, *Sovetsko-angliiskie otnosheniia*, 47–8.
96 Rakovski to Curzon, 16 October 1923, *TNA*, FO 418/60, f. 103.
97 Conte, *Christian Rakovski*, 278–9.
98 Curzon to Hodgson, 19 November 1923, *TNA*, FO 418/60, ff. 100–1.
99 Curzon to Hodgson, 19 November 1923, ibid., FO 371/9356. See also Conte, *Christian Rakovski*, 279–81.

Chapter 10

1. Quoted in *Anglo-sobvetskii dogovor i SSSR* (Molodaia gvardiia, 1925), 51.
2. Salzman, *Great Britain, Germany and the Soviet Union*, 53.
3. Hodgson to Curzon, 28 December 1923, Hodgson to Curzon, 18 January 1924, TNA, FO 418/61, ff. 36–90; ff. 98–100.
4. Pavlovich, 'Russkiy vopros', 48–52.
5. Lyman, *The First Labour Government*, 185.
6. Memorandum by Gregory, 20 January 1924, in DBFP, First ser., XXV: 322–30.
7. Macdonald to Rakovski, 12 January 1924, *TNA*, FO 371/10588. Quoted in Conte, *Christian Rakovski*, 486.
8. See Gorodetsky, *The Precarious Truce*, 11.
9. Memorandum by Lord Stamfordham, 22 January 1924. Quoted in Nicolson, *King George the Fifth*, 384–6.
10. Conte, *Christian Rakovski*, 285.
11. The British government's note to the Soviet government, 1 February 1924, in *Anglo-Soviet Relations*, 59–60; Macdonald to Hodgson, 1 February 1924, *TNA*, FO 418/61, ff. 101–2; The British government's note to the Soviet government, 2 February 1924, AVPRF, f. 69, op. 1, pap. 12, d. 31a, ll. 24–35.
12. Macdonald to Chicherin, 1 February 1924 (privately), RGASPI, f. 159, op. 2, d. 27, ll. 262–3.
13. Chicherin to Macdonald, 3 February 1924. Quoted in Conte, *Christian Rakovski*, 283.
14. Macdonald to Rakovski, 11 February 1924, *TNA*, FO 418/61, ff. 131–3.
15. A political programme of negotiations with England, 6–8 March 1924, *RGASPI*, f. 159, op. 2, d. 27, ll. 267–80.
16. *Izvestiya*, 6 February 1924.
17. Hodgson to Macdonald, 15 February 1924, *DBFP*, First ser., XXV: 354–5.
18. *Izvestiya*, 29 February 1924.
19. Williams, *Trading with the Bolsheviks*, 218–19.
20. Henry Winkler, *Paths Not Taken. British Labor and International Policy in the 1920s* (Chapel Hill – London: University of North Caroline Press, 1994), 69.
21. Lyman, *The First Labour Government*, 187.
22. Memorandum by Field, 26 March 1924, *TNA*, FO 418/61, ff. 206–12.
23. Memorandum by Gregory, 1 April 1924, *DBFP*, First ser., XXV: 366–72
24. Andrew, *The Defence of the Realm. The Authorized History of MI5* (Penguin Books, 2010), 147–8.
25. Shishkin, *Stanovlenie vneshnei politiki*, 191–2.
26. Quoted in L. D. Trotsky, *Zapad i Vostok. Voprosy mirovoi poliytiki i mirovoi revolutsii* (Krasnaiya nov', 1924), 17–18, 20.
27. Proceedings of the Anglo-Soviet conference first plenary meeting, 14 April 1924, *TNA*, T 60/195; *Izvestiya*, 25 March 1924.
28. Diary, 7 June 1924, in Raymond Jones, *Arthur Ponsonby. The Politics of Life* (Christopher Helm Publishers, 1989), 10–11, 147.
29. Arthur Ponsonby (ed.), *The Anglo-Soviet Treaties* (Labour Joint Publications Department, 1924), 2–4.
30. I. I. Radchenko, *Sovrenennaia Angliia i anglo-sovetskii dogovor* (Ekaterinislav: Tipografiia Ekaterininskoi zheleznoi dorogi, 1924), 10.
31. *The Times*, 14 April 1924.

32 Speeches by Rakovski and Churchill, 14 April 1924, *TNA*, FO 418/61, ff. 227–34; *DVP SSSR*, 7: 193–200, 201–4; Proceedings of the Anglo-Soviet conference 1st plenary meeting, 15 April 1924, *TNA*, T 160/195. See also Windrich, *British Labour's Foreign Policy*, 42.
33 Speeches by Rakovski and Macdonald, 14 April 1924, *TNA*, FO 418/61, ff. 227–34; *DVP SSSR*, 7: 193–200, 201–4; Proceedings of the Anglo-Soviet conference first plenary meeting, 15 April 1924, *TNA*, T 160/195. See also Windrich, *British Labor's Foreign Policy*, 42.
34 The memorandum by the Soviet delegation, 20 May 1924, *DVP SSSR*, 7: 287–304.
35 Graubard, *British Labour and the Russian Revolution*, 242–3; Klugman, *History of the CPGB*, 1: 293; Lyman, *The First Labour Government*, 188.
36 Chamberlain to his sister Ida, 9 November 1924, in Self, *The Austen Chamberlain Diary Letters*, 261.
37 Lyman, *The First Labour Government*, 197.
38 Quoted in Lyman, *The First Labour Government*, 199.
39 *Ibid.*, 198.
40 The record of the conversation between Rakovski and Ponsonby, 30 April 1924, *RGASPI*, f. 159, op. 2, d. 30, ll. 89–91; *DVP* SSSR, 7: 221–6; Rakovski to Macdonald, 14 May 1924, ibid., 270–3.
41 Gregory, *On the Edge of Diplomacy*, 149.
42 Hodgson to Macdonald, 2 May 1924, *TNA*, FO 418/61, f. 288.
43 *The Times*, 21 July 1924.
44 Macdonald to Rakovski, 26 July 1924, *TNA*, FO 418/62. Quoted in Conte, *Christian Rakovski*, 287; Nicolson, *King George the Fifth*, 401.
45 Ponsonby to Rakovski, 30 May 1924, *DVP SSSR*, 7: 362–4; Rakovski to Ponsonby, 31 May 1924, ibid., 358–62. See also Jones, *Arthur Ponsonby*, 147.
46 Tomsky to Zinoviev, 9 May 1924, *RGASPI*, f. 17, op. 170, d. 196, l. 40; Tomsky to Stalin, 16 June 1924, ibid., f. 558, op. 11, d. 815, ll. 13–14. Quoted in Khromov, *Leonid Krassin*, 57. See also Lyman, *The First Labor Government*, 198–9.
47 For the Soviet and British approaches, refer to the drafts, 30 July 1924, *TNA*, FO 418/62, ff. 14–20; Soviet draft, 30 July 1924, ibid., ff. 20–9; British draft, 5 July 1924, *DBFP*, First ser., XXV: 516–49; Soviet draft, 12 July 1924, ibid., 549–51; Memorandum by Gregory, 28 July 1924, ibid., 549–51.
48 Minutes of the Cabinet meeting, 22 July 1924, *TNA*, CAB 23/48/18.
49 Memorandum by Ponsonby, 18 July 1924; Minutes of the Cabinet meeting, 30 July 1924, ibid., CAB 23/48/19.
50 Memorandum by Snowden, 30 July 1924, ibid.
51 Jones, *Arthur Ponsonby*, 149.
52 See Owen O'Malley, *The Phantom Caravan* (J. Murray, 1954), 67.
53 The Anglo-Soviet conference eighth plenary session, 4 August 1924, *TNA*, FO 418/62, ff. 30–58; Minutes of the Cabinet meeting, 5 August 1924, ibid., CAB 23/48/22; *DBFP*, First ser., XXV: 573–614. See also Marquand, *Ramsay Macdonald*, 362–3.
54 Jones, *Arthur Ponsonby*, 157.
55 The Anglo-Soviet conference ninth plenary session, 6 August 1924, *TNA*, FO 418/62, ff. 62–78; *DBFP*, First ser., XXV: 614–15; The Anglo-Soviet conference tenth plenary session, 8 August 1924, *TNA*, FO 418/62, ff. 79–81; *DBFP*, First ser., XXV: 616–17. See also Snowden, *An Autobiography*, 682–3; Lyman, *The First Labour Government*, 193–4.

56 *Pravda, Izvestiya*, 10 August 1924; Information by the NKID, 10 August 1924, *TNA*, FO 418/62, f. 99; *DVP SSSR*, 7: 414–15.
57 The Anglo-Soviet conference eleventh plenary session, 12 August 1924, *TNA*, FO 418/62, ff. 81–92; *DBFP*, First ser., XXV: 618–31; Declarations by the Soviet delegation, 12 August 1924, *Izvestiya*, 14 August 1924; *DVP SSSR*, 7: 418–27.
58 Rakovski's, Chicherin's and Kamenev's speeches at the Moscow Soviet plenary meeting, 20 August 1924, *Pravda*, 29 August 1924.
59 Khromov, *Po stranitsam lichnogo arkhiva Stalina*, 216–7.
60 Miliukov, *Rossiya na perelome*, 1: 341; Borman, A. V. Tyrkova-Williams, 210–1.
61 Speech by Lloyd George, 7 August 1924, PD, Fifth ser., CLXXVI: 3031–6; Speech by Asquith, 7 August 1924, *ibid.*, 3175–83; Correspondence. Russia, 1923–39. Pamphlets and brochures on the loan for the USSR, August–September 1924, *TNA*, PA. LG G/130; David Lloyd George, 'A Sham Treaty', *Liberal Magazine*, 3 September 1924, 523–31; Idem., 'Lulling the Middle Class to Sleep', *Daily Chronicle*, 16 August 1924.
62 British federation of industries to Macdonald, 17 September 1924, *AVPRF*, f. 05, op. 4, pap. 1a, d. 4, ll. 62–3.
63 A. A. Ioffe, *Angliya v nashi dni* (Moscow – Leningrad: Gosudarstvennoe zdatel'stvo, 1925), 48, 50.
64 Memorandum by Amery, 18 November 1924, *TNA*, Macdonald Papers. PRO 30/69/105; *The Times*, 27 October 1924.
65 Klugman, *History of the CPGB*, 1: 280–2.
66 Quoted in Lyman, *The First Labour Government*, 237; Jeffrey, *MI6*, 21. See also Diary, 10 October 1924 in Norman and Jeanne Mackenzie, *The Diary of Beatrice Webb*, 4: 210.
67 Snowden, *An Autobiography*, 692–3; Klugman, *History of the CPGB*, 1: 343. For further details of the 'Campbell case', see Thorpe, *The British Communist Party and Moscow*, 78–9; etc.
68 For the recent most comprehensive interpretations of the 'Zinoviev letter', refer to John Ferris and Uri Bar-Joseph, 'Getting Marlowe to Hold His Tongue: The Conservative Party, the Intelligence and the Zinoviev Letter', *Intelligence and Security* 8, no. 4 (1993): 100–33; Winkler, *Path Not Taken*, 158–9; Beckett, *Enemy Within*, 25–6; Stafford, *Churchill and Secret Service*, 144–7; Brook-Shepherd, *Iron Maze*, 306–10; West, Tsarev, *The Crown Jewels*, 33–43; Judd, *The Quest for C.*, 446–8; Gillian Bennett, 'A Most Extraordinary and Mysterious Business', *The Zinoviev Letter of 1924*, FCO History Note, no. 14 (Foreign and Commonwealth Office, 1999); Idem., *Churchill's Man of Mystery: Desmond Morton and the World of Intelligence* (London – New York: Routledge, 2007), 79–85; Jeffrey, *MI6*, 214–22; Smith, *Six*, 291–311; Madeira, *Britannia and the Bear*, 124–30; Carley, *Silent Conflict*, 116–33; Dan Lomas, 'The Zinoviev Letter', *International Affairs* 95, no. 1 (2019): 201–6. The Soviet version may be found in A. A. Zdanovich, 'Chuzhoi sredi svoikh', in *Dvoinoi Agent*, ed. V. G. Orlov (Sovremennik, 1998), 284–323; E. M. Primakov (ed.), *Ocherki istorii vneshnei razvedki* (Mezhdunarodnye otnosheniya, 1997), 2: 107–8; Nezhinsky, *V intresakh naroda*, 180–2.
69 Minute by Austen Chamberlain. Encl. 1. History of the Zinoviev incident, 11 November 1924, *TNA*, CAB 168/87.
70 'Zinoviev Letter', 15 September 1924, *TNA*, KV 2/3331.
71 Minutes by Crowe, 13–14 October 1924, *TNA*, FO 371/10478. On Crowe's contribution to the publication of the letter, see Great Britain. Foreign Office, *Report of the Board of Enquiry Appointed by the Prime Minister to Investigate Certain Statements Affecting Civil Servants*, Cmd. 3037 (HMSO, 1928), 17; Gregory, *On the*

Edge of Diplomacy, 219–22, 255; Strang, *Home and Abroad*, 57–8; Diary, 4 March 1925, in Wilson, *The Political Diaries of C.P. Scott*, 478; Gorodetsky, *The Precarious Truce*, 36; Neilson, Otte, *The Permanent Under-Secretary for Foreign Affairs*, 182. Snowden, *An Autobiography*, 708–9.

72 Crowe to Macdonald, 15 October 1924, *DBFP*, First ser., XXV: 434.
73 William and Zelda Coates, *A History of Anglo-Soviet Relations*, 1: 191; Jeffrey, *MI6*, 222; Andrew, *The Defence of the Realm*, 149.
74 *Daily Mail*, 25 October 1924. See also Macdonald to Rakovski, 24 October 1924, TNA, FO 418/62, ff. 153–5; Great Britain. Foreign Office, *A Selection of Papers Dealing with the Relations between His Majesty's Government and the Soviet Government 1921–1927* (Russia, no. 3 (1927), 28–32; Macdonald to Rakovski, 24 October 1924, DVP SSSR, 7: 510–11.
75 Morrison, *Government and Parliament*, 65.
76 Quoted in Snowden, *An Autobiography*, 712. *An Autobiography*, 711–12; Robert Warth, 'The Mystery of the Zinoviev Letter', *South Atlantic Quarterly* 49, no. 4 (1950): 446.
77 Diary, 29 October 1924, in Norman and Jeanne Mackenzie, *The Diary of Beatrice Webb*, 4: 42–3.
78 Rakovski to Macdonald, 25 October 1924, *TNA*, FO 418/62, ff. 155–6; *DVP SSSR*, 7: 508–10.
79 Rakovski to Macdonald, 27 October 1924, ibid., 7: 513–14.
80 Diary, 31 October 1924, in Middlemas, *Thomas Jones. Whitehall Diary*, 3: 300.
81 *The Times*, 27 October 1924. See also Lyman, *The First Labour Government*, 259.
82 Speech by Lloyd George, 14 October 1924, in Campbell, *Lloyd George*, 106.
83 A secret report by the special agent CX/1174, 25 October 1924, *TNA*, KV/2/3331.
84 Lyman, *The First Labour Government*, 286.
85 A secret report by the special agent CX/1174, 29 October 1924, *TNA*, KV/2/3331; Chicherin to Zinoviev, 1 November 1924, AVPRF, f. 69, op. 8, pap. 15, d. 47, l. 19; Rakovski to the NKID, 18 November 1924 (decrypt), *TNA*, HW 12/65; Minute of the Politburo meeting, 17 November 1924, in D. Yu. Kozlov, 'Podlozhnye dokumenty Kominterna i Politburo TsK VKP(b)'. *Novaia i noveishaia istoriia*, no. 6 (1996): 27.
86 *Izvestiya*, 26, 29, 30 October 1924; *Pravda*, 30 October 1924. See also Extracts from the Soviet press, October 1924, *TNA*, FO 418/62, ff. 191–5.
87 Chicherin to Zinoviev, 25 October 1924, *RGASPI*, f. 159, op. 2, d. 27, l. 340; *Izvestiya*, 28 October 1924.
88 Amery, *My Political Life*, 2: 296.
89 Gregory to Rakovski, 31 October 1924, *TNA*, FO 418/62; Gregory, *On the Edge of Diplomacy*, 227.
90 Rakovski to Chicherin, 3 November 1924, *DVP SSSR*, 7: 530.
91 Minute by the Cabinet, 17 November 1924, *TNA*, CAB 27/254; Report and conclusions by Chamberlain's commission, 19 November 1924, ibid., CAB 23/49/59, CAB 23/49/60.
92 Memorandum by the Foreign Office, 11 November 1924, *TNA*, CAB 24/168/87; ibid., FO 371/10479/8467/108/38; *DBFP*, First ser., XXV: 440–5.
93 Chamberlain to Rakovski, 21 November 1924, *TNA*, FO 518/62, f. 203; Great Britain. Foreign Office, *A Selection of Papers*, 34–5; *DVP SSSR*, 7: 561. See also Lubov Krassin, *Leonid Krassin*, 230–2; Gorodetsky, *The Precarious Truce*, 55–6; Grayson, *Austen Chamberlain*, 255.
94 Minute of the Politburo meeting, 21 November 1924, *RGASPI*, f. 159, op. 2, d. 27, ll. 342–5.

95 Aino Kuusinen, *Before and after Stalin* (Joseph, 1974), 41–2; Cristopher Andrew, 'More on the Zinoviev Letter', *Historical Journal* 22, no. 1 (1979): 211; Andrew, Gordievsky, *KGB*, 67.
96 Peters to Austen Chamberlain, 19 December 1924, *TNA*, FO 418/62. See also Lyman, *The First Labour Government*, 286; Gorodetsky, 'The Formulation of Soviet Foreign Policy', 35–6.
97 All-Russian central council of trade-unions' open letter to the TUC, 14 December 1924, *RGASPI*, f. 17, op. 170, d. 213, ll. 22-5.
98 Rakovski to Austen Chamberlain, 28 November 1924, *Izvestiya*, 29 November 1924 г.; *TNA*, FO 418/62, ff. 203–4; *DVP SSSR*, 7: 556–9.
99 Chicherin to Zinoviev, 15 December 1924, *AVPRF*, f. 69, op. 8, pap. 15, d. 47, l. 28; Rakovski to Austen Chamberlain, 21 December 1924, *DVP SSSR*, 7: 584.
100 Austen Chamberlain to Rakovski, 24 December 1924, ibid., 584; Rakovski to Austen Chamberlain, 2 January 1925, *Anglo-Sovetskie otnosheniya*, 88; A. Chamberlain to Peters, 6 January 1925, *DBFP*, First ser., XXV: 632–4.
101 Krassin to Chicherin, 7 January 1925, *DVP SSSR*, 8: 19–20; Rakovski to Chicherin, 10 January 1925, ibid., 8: 33–8.
102 On Reilly's purported participation in the matter, see, especially, Rhoer, *Master Spy*, 174–6; Kettle, *Sidney Reilly*, 116–30. Other, mostly fantastic interpretations of the 'Zinoviev case' may be found in Sayers and Kahn, *The Great Conspiracy*, 139–40; Ramsden, *The Age of Balfour and Baldwin*, 205; Conte, *Christian Rakovski*, 311; Leonard, *Secret Soldiers of the Revolution*, 75; Hopkirk, *Setting the East Ablaze*, 195; Beckett, *Enemy Within*, 25; etc.
103 *Daily Herald*, 18 May 1925; *Manchester Guardian*, 23 May 1927; *Morning Star*, 12, 19 December 1966; *The Times*, 20, 22 December 1966; *Sunday Times*, 18, 19 December 1966, 1 July 1967. For additional versions, see also Sybil Crowe, 'The Zinoviev Letter, A Reappraisal', *Journal of Contemporary History* 10, no. 3 (1975): 407–8; Corson and Crowley, *The New KGB*, 81–124; etc.
104 See, for example, Gooch, *British Foreign Policy*, 8.
105 Quoted in Warth, 'The Mystery of the Zinoviev Letter', 448.
106 Crowe, 'The Zinoviev Letter', 428–9.
107 See, for example, Fischer, *Stalin and German Communism*, 460; Keeble, *Britain and the Soviet Union*, 95.
108 Report by the secret agent CX/1174, 16 December 1924, *TNA*, KV 2/3331.
109 Analytical note by G. E. Wakefield, an MI5 expert, *TNA*, KV/2/3331. See also, Kuusinen, *Before and after Stalin*, 50–1; Andrew, 'More on the Zinoviev Letter', 211–12; Corson and Crowley, *The New KGB*, 88.
110 Jeffrey, *MI6*, 216–17.
111 Chicherin to Zinoviev, 15 November 1924, *AVPRF*, f. 69, op. 8, pap. 15, d. 47, l. 28.
112 Interview by Marlowe, 3 March 1928, *Observer*, 4 March 1928. See also Warth, 'The Mystery of the Zinoviev Letter', 451–3; Chester, Fay and Young, *The Zinoviev Letter*, 79; Ferris and Bar-Joseph, *Getting Marlowe*, 129–31; Stafford, *Churchill and Secret Service*, 144–5.
113 Bennett, *Churchill's Man of Mystery*, 81–3; Andrew, *The Defence of the Realm*, 148–9; Jeffrey, *MI6*, 218.
114 Orlov, *Dvoinoi agent*, 260. On the fabrication of official documents, see Brook-Sheppard, *Iron Maze*, 308; Smith, *Six*, 309, 311; Zdanovich, 'Chuzhoi sredi svoikh', 315.
115 Brook-Sheppard, *Iron Maze*, 309; Bennett, '*A Most Extraordinary and Mysterious Business*', 89–92; West, Tsarev, *The Crown Jewels*, 41–3.

116 *Morning Post, Daily Chronicle*, 4 November 1924.
117 Intelligence report, 19 November 1924, *TNA*, KV 2/3331. See also Kuusinen, *Before and after Stalin*, 41.
118 West and Tsarev, *The Crown Jewels*, 43.
119 For more information about Stalin's possible involvement in the case, refer to Fischer, *Stalin and the German Communism*, 462–3; Vansittart, *The Mist Procession*, 331; Chester, Fay and Young, *The Zinoviev Letter*, 42; Corson and Crowley, *The New KGB*, 87; Costello, *Mask of Treachery*, 632.
120 See V. A. Golovko et al. (eds), *Mezhdu Moskvoi i Zapadom: Diplomaticheskaia deiatel'nost' C. G. Rakovskogo* (Kharkov: Oko, 1994), 251–7.

Epilogue

1 Neilson, *Britain, Soviet Russia and the Collapse of the Versailles Order*, 3–4.
2 See Hodgson to the Foreign Office, 25 February 1925, *BLAAS*. L/PS/10/1108/1.
3 Roskill, *Hankey*, 2: 383.
4 See, for example, Taigin, *Angliya i SSSR*, 53.
5 Quoted in Solomon Lozovsky, *Anglo-sovetskaiya konferentsiya*, 98.
6 Chamberlain to Rakovski, 1 April 1925, in Lubov Krassin, *Leonid Krassin*, 239.
7 Chamberlain to Graham, British Envoy to Latvia, 26 February 1926. Quoted in Cohrs, *The Unfinished Peace after World War I*, 213–14.

Select bibliography

For reasons of space, this bibliography is restricted to sources and published works cited in the footnotes. All British publishers have London offices and Russian publishers – Moscow offices, unless otherwise stated.

Primary sources

Unpublished

Arkhiv vneshnei politiki Rossiskoi Federatsii, Moscow
British Library, African and Asian Studies, London
British Library, Manuscript Collections, London
Cambridge University Library, Department of Manuscripts, Cambridge
Churchill Archives Centre, Cambridge
Gosudarstvennyi arkhiv Rossiiskoi Federatsii, Moscow
The National Archives, Kew
Oxford University Bodleian Library, Special Collections, Oxford
Parliamentary Archives, House of Lords Record Office, London
Rossiiskii gosudarstvennyi arkhiv ekonomiki, Moscow
Rossiiskii gosudarstvennyi arkhiv sotsial'no-politicheskoi istorii, Moscow
Rossiiskii gosudarstvennyi arkhiv Voenno-Morskogo Flota, St Petersburg
Rossiiskii gosudarstvennyi voennyi arkhiv, Moscow
University of Birmingham, Cadbury Research Library, Special collections, Birmingham

Published

Official documents and correspondence

Adamthwaite, Anthony. (ed.) *The Lost Peace: International Relations in Europe, 1918–1939.* E. Arnold, 1980.
Adibekov, G. M. et al. (eds) *Politburo TsK RCP(b) – VCP(b) i Evropa. Resheniia 'osoboi papki'.* ROSSPEN, 2001.
Adibekov, G. M. et al. (eds, comps) *Politburo TsK RKP(b) – VKP(b) i Komintern. 1919–1943. Dokumenty.* ROSSPEN, 2004.
Angliia i SSSR. Sbornik statei, materialov i dokumentov. Moscow – Leningrad: Moskovskii rabochii, 1927.
Anglo-sovetskie otnosheniia so dnia podpisaniia torgovogo soglasheniia do razryva (1921–1927). Noty i dokumenty. NKID, 1927.

Bourne, Kenneth, and Watt, David. (eds) *British Documents on Foreign Affairs: Reports and Papers from the Foreign Office Confidential Print.* Washington, DC: University Publications of America, 1990-1.

British Labour Delegation to Russia 1920. Report. Office of the Trade Union Congress and Labour Party, 1920.

Bukshpan, A. S. (comp.) *Poslednie dni Bakinskoi kommuny. Po materialam sudebnykh protsessov.* Baku: Gosudarstvennaia tipografiia 'Krasnyi Vostok', 1928.

Burdett, A. L. P. (ed.) *Afghanistan Strategic Intelligence: British Records 1919-1970.* Chippenham: Archive Editions, 2002, vol. 1.

Dmitrishyn, Basil, and Cox, Frederick. (eds) *The Soviet Union and the Middle East: A Documentary Record of Afghanistan, Iran, and Turkey, 1917-1985.* Princeton, NJ: Kingston Press, 1987.

Eleulov, T. E., and Inoiatov, K. S. (eds) *Inostrannaia voennaia interventsiia i grazhdanskaia voina v Srednei Asii i Kazakhstane. Dokumenty i materialy.* Alma-Ata: Izdatel'stvo. AN Kazakhskoi SSR – Nauka, 1963–4, 2 vols.

Gilbert, Martin. (comp., ed.) *Winston S. Churchill: A Companion.* Boston: Houghton Mifflin, 1975, vol. 4; W. Heinemann, 1976, vol. 5.

Gromyko, A. A. (ed.) *Dokumenty vneshnei politiki SSSR.* Gospolitizdat, 1957–63, 7 vols.

Hurewitz, J. C. (ed.) *Diplomacy in the Near and Middle East. A Documentary Record: 1914–1956.* New York: Octagon Books, 1972, vol. 2.

Ivanov, A. A. (comp.) 'Gorskaia kontrrevolutsiia i interventy'. *Krasnyi arkhiv* 68, no. 1 (1935): 125–53.

Jones, David. (comp., ed.) 'Documents on British Relations with Russia 1917–1918. F. N. A. Cromie's Letters'. *Canadian – American Slavic Studies* 7 (1973): 350–75, 498–510; 8 (1974): 544–62.

Joukoff Eudin, Xenia, and Fisher, Harold. (comps, eds) *Soviet Russia and the West, 1920–1927: A Documentary Survey.* Stanford, CA: Stanford University Press, 1957.

Joukoff Eudin, Xenia, and North, Robert. (comps, eds) *Soviet Russia and the East, 1920–1927: A Documentary Survey.* Stanford, CA: Stanford University Press, 1957.

Kim, M. (comp.) 'Iz archiva organizatorov grazhdanskoi voiny i interventsii v Rossii'. *Istoricheskii arkhiv*, no. 6 (1961): 58–117.

Kliuchnikov, Yu. V., and Sabanin, A. V. (comps) *Mezhdunarodnaia politika noveishego vremeni v dogovorakh, notakh i deklaratsiiakh.* Litizdat NKID, 1926–8, pts II–III.

Kvashonkin, A. V. et al. (comps, eds) *Bol'shevistskoe rukovodstvo. Perepiska, 1912–1927.* ROSSPEN, 1996.

Lashkevich, G. N. (ed.) *Gaagskaia konferentsiia 1922 g. Polnyi stenographicheskii otchet (materialy i dokumenty).* NKID, 1922.

Lifshiz, M., and Chagin, P. (eds) *Pamiati 26 (materialy k istorii Bakinskoi kommuny 1918 g).* Gosudarstvennaia tipografiia, 1922.

Lozovsky, Solomon. *Anglo-sovetskaiya konferentsiya professional'nykh soyuzov.* Moscow – Leningrad: Gosudarstvennoe izdatel'stvo, 1925.

Macmanus, Arthur. (comp.) *History of the Zinoviev Letter.* Communist Party of Great Britain, 1925.

Meijer, Jan. (ed.) *The Trotsky Papers, 1917–1922.* The Hague: Mouton, 1964–1971, vols. 1–2.

Minz, I. (comp.) 'Anglichane na Severe (1918–1919)'. *Krasnyi arkhiv* 19, no. 6 (1926): 39–52.

Minz, I. (comp.) *Iaponskaia interventsiia 1918–1922 gg. v. dokumentakh.* Zentrarkhiv, 1934.

Persiz, M. A., and Meier, M. S. (comps) *Persidkii front mirovoi revolutsii. Dokumenty o sovetskom vtorzhenii v Gilian (1919–1921)*. Kvadriga, 2009.
Pervi s'ezd narodov Vostoka. Baku, 1–8 September 1920. Petrograd: Izdatel'stvo Kominterna, 1920.
Pokrovsky, A. S. (comp.) 'K istorii zagovora R. Lokharta (1918)'. *Istoricheskii arkhiv*, no. 4 (1962): 234–7
Ponsonby, Arthur. (ed.) *The Anglo-Soviet Treaties*. Labour Joint Publications Department, 1924.
Riddell, John. (ed.) *To See the Dawn. Baku, 1920 – First Congress of the Peoples of the East*. New York – London, etc.: Pathfinder, 1993.
Sandomirsky, G. B. (ed.) *Genuezskaia konferentsiia 1922 g. Materialy i dokumenty*. NKID, 1922.
Tashliev, S. (ed.) *Turkmenistan v period inostrannoi interventsii i grazhdanskoi voiny. 1918–1920 gg*. Ashgabat: Turkmenskoe gosudarstvennoe izdatel'stvo, 1957.
Tikhonov, Yu. N. (comp.) 'Dokumenty Kominterna o podgotovke vooruzhennogo vosstaniia v Britanskoi Indii v 1921 g.' *Vostochnyi arkhiv*, no. 10 (2003): 35–42.
Tikhonov, Yu. N. (comp.) *Sovetskaia Rossiia v bor'be za 'afganskii koridor' (1919–1925)*. Kvadriga, 2017.
United States Department of State. *Papers Relating to the Foreign Relations of the United States (FRUS). The Paris Peace Conference. 1919*. Washington, DC: Department of State, 1941–2, vols II–III.
Vinogradov, V. K. et al. (comps, eds) *Arkhiv VCheka*. Kuchkovo pole, 2007.
Woodman, E. L. et al. (eds) *Documents on British Foreign Policy, 1919–1939*. HMSO, 1947–1984. First ser., vols I–III, VIII, XI–XII, XVIII–XX, XXIII, XXV.

Parliamentary debates and command papers

Great Britain. Foreign Office. *A Collection of Reports on Bolshevism in Russia*. Russia, no. 1 (1919). Cmd. 8. HMSO, 1919.
Great Britain. Foreign Office. *Agreement between His Britannic Majesty's Government and the Soviet Government of Russia for Exchange of Prisoners*. Russia, no. 1 (1920). Cmd. 587. HMSO, 1920.
Great Britain. Foreign Office. *Trade Agreement between His Britannic Majesty's Government and the Government of the Russian Socialist Federal Soviet Republic*. Cmd. 1207. HMSO, 1921.
Great Britain. Foreign Office. *Correspondence with M. Krassin respecting Russia's Foreign Indebtedness. Accounts and Papers*. Russia, no. 3 (1921). Cmd. 1546. HMSO, 1921.
Great Britain. Foreign Office. *Papers Relating to International Economic Conference. Genoa, April–May 1922*. Cmd. 1667. HMSO, 1922.
Great Britain. Foreign Office. *Correspondence between His Majesty's Government and the Soviet Government Respecting the Murder of Mr. C.F. Davison in January 1920*. Russia, no. 1 (1923). Cmd. 1846. HMSO, 1923.
Great Britain. Foreign Office. *Correspondence between His Majesty's Government and the Soviet Government Respecting the Relations between the Two Governments*. Russia, no. 2 (1923). Cmd. 1869. HMSO, 1923.
Great Britain. Foreign Office. *Further Correspondence between His Majesty's Government and the Soviet Government Respecting the Relations between the Two Governments*. Russia, no. 3 (1923). Cmd. 1874. HMSO, 1923.

Great Britain. Foreign Office. *Further correspondence between His Majesty's Government and the Soviet Government Respecting the Relations between the Two Governments.* Russia, no. 4 (1923). Cmd. 1890. HMSO, 1923.

Great Britain. Foreign Office. *Documents Illustrating the Hostile Activities of the Soviet Government and Third International against Great Britain.* Russia, no. 2 (1927). Cmd. 2874. HMSO, 1927.

Great Britain. Foreign Office. *A Selection of Papers Dealing with the Relations between His Majesty's Government and the Soviet Government, 1921–1927.* Russia, no. 3 (1927). Cmd. 2895. HMSO, 1927.

Great Britain. Foreign Office. *Report of the Board of Enquiry Appointed by the PM to Investigate Certain Statements Affecting Civil Servants.* Cmd. 3037. HMSO, 1928.

Great Britain. War Office. *Army: The Evacuation of North Russia, 1919.* Cmd. 818. HMSO, 1920.

Hansard Parliamentary Debates, 1919–1939. HMSO, 1947, Fifth ser.

Memoirs, diaries, private correspondence and contemporary works

Abrikosov, D. I. *Sud'ba russkogo diplomata.* Russkii Put', 2008.

Agar, Augustus. *Footprints in the Sea.* Evans Brothers, 1959.

Agar, Augustus. *Baltic Episode: A Classic of Secret Service in Russian Waters.* Hodder and Stoughton, 1963.

Amery, Leo. *My Political Life.* Hutchinson, 1953, vol. 2.

Antonelli, Etiene. *Bolshevik Russia.* New York: A. Knopf, 1920.

Aralov, S. I. *Vospominaniia sovetskogo diplomata. 1922–1923.* Mezhdunarodnye otnosheniia, 1960.

Avalov (Bermondt), P. V. *V bor'be s bolshevizmom.* Glückstadt – Hamburg: Izdatel'stvo I. I. Augustina, 1925.

Bailey, Frederick. 'In Russian Turkestan under the Bolsheviks'. *Journal of the Central Asian Society* 8, pt. I (1921): 49–69.

Bailey, Frederick. *Mission to Tashkent.* J. Cape, 1946.

Barmine, Alexandr. *Memoirs of a Secret Diplomat: Twenty-Five Years in the Service of the USSR.* Lovat and Dickson Publishers, 1938.

Barnes, John, and Nicholson, David. (eds) *The Leo Amery Diaries.* Hutchinson, 1980, vol. 1.

Beaverbrook, William. *The Decline and Fall of Lloyd George: And Great Was the Fall Thereof.* W. Collins, 1963.

Begak, R. *Sud nad anglichanami, sdavshimi Baku turkam v 1918 g.* Baku: Azgiz, 1927.

Berberova, N. N. *Zheleznaia zhentschina.* Izdatel'stvo imeni Sabashnikovykh, 2001.

Bertie, Francis. *Za kulisami Antanty. Dnevnik britanskogo posla v Parizhe*, trans. and ed. K. V. Miniar-Beloruchev. Izdatel'stvo Gosudarstvennoi publichnoi istoricheskoi biblioteki, 2014.

Besedovskii, G. Z. *Na puti k termidoru. Iz vospominanii byvshego sovetskogo diplomata.* Paris: Mishen, 1930, 2 vols.

Beveridge, William. *Power and Influence.* Hodder and Stoughton, 1953.

Blacker, Latham. *On Secret Patrol in High Asia.* J. Murray, 1922.

Blacker, Latham. 'Wars and Travels in Turkestan, 1918–1920'. *Journal of the Central Asian Society* 11, pt I (1922): 4–20.

Borman, A. *A. V. Tyrkova-Williams po eio pis'mam i vospominaniiam syna*. Leuven – Washington: A. Rosseels Printing, 1964.
Bothmer, Karl. *S grafom Mirbakhom v Moskve*, trans. Yu. G. Fel'shtinsky. Knigovek, 2010.
Brailsford, Henry. *The Russian Workers' Republic*. G. Allen and Unwin, 1921.
Brun, Alf. *Troublous Times: Experience in Bolshevik Russia and Turkestan*. A. Constable, 1931.
Buchanan, George. *My Mission to Russia and Other Memoirs*. Cassell, 1923, vol. 2.
Buchanan, Meriel. *Petrograd: The City of Trouble 1914–1918*. W. Collins, 1918.
Buchanan, Meriel. *The Dissolution of an Empire*. J. Murray, 1932.
Buikis, I. 'Proschet Lockarta'. In *Osoboe zadanie*, ed. I. E. Polikarpenko, 78–88. Moskovskii rabochii, 1968.
Bullitt, William. *The Bullitt Mission to Russia*. New York: B. Hübsch, 1919.
Buxton, Charles. *In a Russian Village*. Labour Publishing, 1922.
Campbell, John. 'The Campbell Case'. *Labour Monthly* 6, no. 11 (1924): 673–7.
Cecil, Robert. *A Great Experiment: An Autobiography*. J. Cape, 1941.
Cecil, Robert. *All the Way*. Hodder and Stoughton, 1949.
Chaikin, V. *Kazn' 26 bakinskikh komissarov*. I. Grzhebin, 1922.
Chamberlain, Austen. *Down the Years*. Cassell, 1935.
Cherepanov, A. I. *Zapiski voennogo sovetnika v Kitae*. Nauka, 1964.
Chicherin, G. V. *Vneshniaia politika Sovetskoi Rossii za dva goda*. Gosizdat, 1920.
Childs, Windham. *Episodes and Reflections*. Cassell, 1930.
Churchil, Winston. *The World Crisis: The Aftermath*. Thornton Butterworth, 1929.
Churchill, Winston. *Great Contemporaries*. Thornton Butterworth, 1937.
Coates, William. *The Anglo-Russian Treaties*. Anglo-Russian Parliamentary Committee, 1924.
Coates, William. *The 'Zinoviev Letter': The Case for a Full Investigation*. Anglo-Russian Parliamentary Committee, 1928.
Curzon, George. *The Place of India in the Empire*. J. Murray, 1909.
D'Abernon, Edgar. *Ambassador of Peace: Lord D'Abernon's Diary*. Hodder and Stoughton, 1929–1930, 2 vols.
Dalton, Hugh. *Call Back Yesterday: Memoirs 1887–1931*. F. Muller, 1953.
Denikin, A. I. *Ocherki russkoi smuty*. Berlin: Slovo, 1925, vol. 4; Berlin: Mednyi vsadnik, 1926, vol. 5.
Dennis, Alfred. *The Foreign Policy of Soviet Russia*. New York: J. M. Dent and Sons, 1924.
Dillon, Emile. *The Eclipse of Russia*. London – Toronto: J. M. Dent and Sons, 1918.
Dioneo, Yu. *Angliia posle voiny*. Prague: Plamia, 1924.
Dobson, Christopher, and Miller, John. *The Day We Almost Bombed Moscow: The Allied War in Russia, 1918–1920*. Hodder and Stoughton, 1986.
Donohoe, M. *With the Persian Expedition*. E. Arnold, 1919.
Dukes, Paul. *The Story of 'ST 25': Adventures and Romance in the Secret Intelligence Service in Red Russia*. Cassell, 1938.
Dunsterville, Lionel. *The Adventures of the Dunsterforce*. E. Arnold, 1920.
Dunsterville, Lionel. 'Military Mission to North-West Persia, 1918'. *Journal of the Central Asian Society* 8, pt III (1921): 79–98.
Dvadtsat' shest'. 1918–1928. Sbornik poem i stikhov pamiati 26-ti Bakinskikh komissarov. Baku: TsK MOPR ASSR, 1928.
Ellis, Charles. *The Transcaspian Episode, 1918–1919*. Hutchinson, 1963.
Emelianov, A. G. *Persidkii front (1915–1918)*. Berlin: Gamayun, 1923.

Esher, Oliver. (ed.) *Journals and Letters of Reginald, Viscount Esher*. I. Nicholson and Watson, 1938, vol. 4.

Etherton, Percy. *In the Heart of Asia*. A. Constable, 1925.

Fel'shtinskii, Yu. G. (comp.) 'Karl Gelferich. Moia moskovskaia missiia'. *Grani*, no. 155 (1990): 251–303.

Fel'shtinskii, Yu. G., and Cherniavskii, G. N. (comps) 'L. B. Krassin. 'Pis'ma zhene i detiam, 1917–1926'. *Voprosy istorii*, no. 1 (2002): 83–98; no. 3 (2002): 79–104; no. 4 (2002): 98–126.

Gins, G. K. *Siberia, soyuzniki i Kolchak. Povorotnyi moment russkoi istorii. 1918–1920 gg.* Airis-Press, 2013.

Globachev, K. I. 'Pravda o russkoi revolutsii. Vospominaniia byvshego nachal'nika Petrogradskogo okhrannogo otdeleniia'. *Voprosy istorii*, no. 9 (2002): 60–84.

Goldin, V. I. (comp.) *Belyi Sever. 1918–1920 gg.: memuary i dokumenty*. Archangelsk: 'Pravda Severa', 1993, iss. 1–2.

Goltz, Rüdiger. *Meine Sendung in Finnland und im Balticum*. Leipzig: K. Köhler Verlag, 1920.

Goode, William. *Bolshevism at Work*. G. Allen and Unwin, 1920.

Gough, Hugh. *Soldiering On*. A. Barker, 1954.

Gregory, John. *On the Edge of Diplomacy: Rambles and Reflections, 1902–1928*. Hutchinson, 1928.

Gurko-Kriazhin, V. A. 'Angliiskaia interventsiia 1918–1919 gg. v Zakaspii i Zakavkazie'. *Istorik-Marxist*, no. 2 (1926): 115–39.

Hankey, Maurice. *Diplomacy by Conference: Studies in Public Affairs, 1920–46*. E. Benn, 1946.

Harding, Stan. 'The Case of Mrs. Stan Harding'. *Nineteenth Century and After* 92, no. 1 (1922): 1–16.

Harding, Stan. 'The Moscow Trial'. *Nineteenth Century and after* 92, no. 1 (1922): 280–7.

Hardinge, Charles. *Old Diplomacy*. J. Murray, 1947.

Hellferich, Karl, 'Moia moskovskaia missiia'. trans. and.ed. Yu. G. Fel'shtinsky. *Grani* no. 155 (1990): 251–303.

Hill, George. *Go Spy the Land*. Cassell, 1932.

Hoare, Samuel. *The Fourth Seal: The End of Russian Chapter*. W. Heinemann, 1930.

Hodgson, Robert. 'Memoirs of an Official Agent: Trading with Russia, 1921–1923'. *History Today* 6, no. 8 (1954): 522–8.

Hopkirk, Peter. (ed.) *The Spy Who Disappeared: Diary of a Secret Mission to Russian Central Asia in 1918*. V. Gollancz, 1990.

Ioffe, A. A. *Genuezskaia konferentsiia*. Krasnaia nov', 1922.

Ioffe, A. A. *Angliia v nashi dni*. Moscow – Leningrad: Gosudarstvennoe zdatel'stvo, 1925.

Ironside, William. *Archangel 1918–1919*. A. Constable, 1953.

Kaye, Cecil. *Communism in India*. Delhi: Government of India Press, 1926.

Kedrov, M. S. *Pod igom angliikikh gromil*. Moscow – Leningrad: Gosudarstvennoe izdatel'stvo, 1927.

Kedrov, M. S. *Za Sovetskii Sever. Lichnye vospominaniia i materialy o pervykh etapakh grazhdanskoi voiny 1918*. Leningrad: Priboi, 1927.

Kemal', Mustapha. *Put' novoi Turtsii, 1919–1927*, trans. and ed. I. Petrov. Gosudarstvennoe izdatel'stvo – Litizdat NKID, 1929–1934, 4 vols.

Kerensky, A. F. *Rossiia na istoricheskom povorote. Memuary*. Zentrpoligraf, 1993.

Kerzhentsev, V. *Angliia i anglichane. Ocherki sovremennoi Anglii*. Petrograd: Izdatel'stvo Socialist, 1918.

Keynes, John. 'Reconstruction in Europe'. *Manchester Guardian Commercial*, no. 3 (10 June 1922): 132–3.
Khromov, S. S. (comp.) 'L. B. Krassin. Pis'ma k T. V. Miklashevskoi-Krassinoi'. *Voprosy istorii*, no. 10 (2005): 53–74.
Koestenberger, Rudolf. *Mit der Roten Armee durch Russisch Zentralasien*. Graz: Verlag von U. Mosers Buchhandlung, 1925.
Korostovetz, Ivan. *Seed and Harvest*. Faber and Faber, 1931.
Krassin, L. B. *Voprosy vneshnei torgovli*. Gosudarstvennoe izdatel'stvo, 1928.
Krassin, Lubov. *Leonid Krassin: His Life and Work*. Skeffington and Son, 1929.
Kuusinen, Aino. *Before and after Stalin*. Joseph, 1974.
Lansbury, George. *What I Saw in Russia?* L. Parsons, 1920.
Lansbury, George. *My Life*. A. Constable, 1928.
Latsis, M. I. *Dva goda bor'by na vnutrennem fronte*. Gosudarstvennoe izdatel'stvo, 1920.
Lenin, V. I. *Polnoe sobranie sochinenii*. Politizdat, 1970–1982, vols. 35–6; 40–1; 43–5; 50.
Lenin, V. I. *Lenin o vneshnei politike Sovetskogo gosudarstva*. Institut marxisma-leninisma pri TsK KPSS, 1960.
Levidov, M. Yu. *K istorii soyuznoi interventsii v Rossiyu*. Leningrad: Priboi, 1925, vol. 1.
Lifshits, M. I. *Kto vinovat v ubiistve 26-ti?* Tiflis: Zakkniga, 1926.
Lishin, N. N. *Na Kaspiiskom more. God beloi bor'by, 1918–1919*. Prague: Izd.atel'stvo 'Morskogo zhurnala', 1938.
Lloyd George, David. 'A Sham Treaty'. *Liberal Magazine*, no. 3 (1924): 523–31.
Lloyd George, David. *Memoirs of the Peace Conference*. New York: H. Fertig, 1972, vol. 1.
Lloyd George, David. *War Memoirs*. New York: AMS, 1982, vols IV–V.
Lloyd George (Stevenson), Francis. *The Years that Are Past*. Hutchinson, 1967.
Lockhart, Robert Bruce. *Memoirs of a British Agent: Being an Account of the Author's Early Life in Many Lands and of His Official Mission to Moscow in 1918*. London – New York: Putnam, 1932.
Lockhart, Robert Bruce. *Agoniia Rossiiskoi imperii: vospominaniia ofitsera britanskoi razvedki*, trans. V. N. Karpov. Algoritm, 2016.
Lozovsky, A. *Anglo-sovetskaia konferentsiia professional'nykh soyuzov*. Gosudarstvennoe izdatel'stvo, 1925.
Lubimov, N. N., and Erlikh, A. N. *Genuezskaia konferentsiia. Vospominaniia uchastnikov*. Izdatel'stvo Instituta mezhdunarodnykh otnoshenii, 1963.
Macculagh, Francis. *A Prisoner of the Reds: The Story of a British Officer Captured in Siberia*. J. Murray, 1921.
Macdonell, Ronald. *And Nothing Long*. A. Constable, 1938.
Macewen, John. (ed.) *The Riddell Diaries: A Selection. 1908–1923*. Athlone Press, 1986.
Mackenzie, Norman, and Mackenzie, Jeanne. (eds) *The Diary of Beatrice Webb*. Cambridge, MA: HUP, 1984–5, vols 3–4.
Maisky, I. M. *Vneshniaia politika RSFSR, 1917–1922*. Krasnaia nov', 1923.
Maisky, I. M. 'Anglo-Sovetskoe torgovoe soglashenie 1921 goda'. *Voprosy istorii*, no. 5 (1957): 60–77.
Maisky, I. M. *Puteshestvie v proshloe*. Izdatel'stvo AN SSSR, 1960.
Mal'kov, P. D. *Zapiski komendanta Moskovskogo Kremlia*. Molodaia gvardiia, 1959.
Malleson, Wilfrid. 'The British Military Mission to Turkestan, 1918–1920'. *Journal of the Central Asian Society* 9, pt. 2 (1922): 95–110.
Malleson, Wilfrid. 'The Twenty-Six Commissars'. *Fortnightly Review* 40, no. 133 (1933). Available online: http://turkmeny.h1.ru/memuar/m1.html
Malone, Cecil. *The Russian Republic*. G. Allen and Unwin, 1920.

Mannerheim, Karl. *Memoirs*. Vagrius, 2003.
Marchand, Rene. *Allied Agents in Soviet Russia*. People's Russian Information Bureau, 1918.
Martynov, A. *Zagovor britanskikh imperialistov protiv SSSR*. Moscow – Leningrad: Moskovskii rabochii, 1925.
Maugham, William Somerset. *The Summing Up*. W. Heinemann, 1938.
Maynard, Charles. *The Murmansk Venture*. Hodder and Stoughton, 1928.
Mikhailovsky, G. N. *Zapiski. Iz istorii rossiiskogo vneshnepoliticheskogo vedomstva, 1914–1920*. Mezhdunarodnye otnosheniia, 1993, vol. 2.
Middlemas, Keith. (ed.) *Thomas Jones: Whitehall Diary*. OUP, 1969, vol. 1.
Mikoian, A. I. *Dorogoi bor'by*. Gospolitizdat, 1971.
Miliukov, P. N. *Rossiia na perelome*. Paris: Imprimerie d'Art Voltaire, 1927, vol. 1.
Monkhouse, Allan. *Moscow, 1911–1933*. V. Gollancz, 1933.
Nabokov, K. D. *Ispytaniia diplomata*. Stockholm: Severnye ogni, 1923.
Nicolson, Harold. *Some People*. A. Constable, 1927.
Nicolson, Harold. *Peacemaking 1919*. A. Constable, 1944.
Nikiforov, P. M. *Zapiski premiera DVR*. Gospolitizdat, 1974.
Noulens, Joseph. *Mon Ambassade en Russie Sovietique: 1917–1919*. Paris: Plon, 1933, vol. 2.
O'Malley, Owen. *The Phantom Caravan*. J. Murray, 1954.
Orlov, Alexandr. *The March of Time: Reminiscences*. St Ermin's Press, 2004.
Orlov, V. G. *Dvoinoi agent*. Sovremennik, 1998.
Oudendyk, William. *Ways and By-Ways in Diplomacy*. P. Davies, 1939.
Pavlovich, M. *'Russkiy vopros' v angliiskoi vneshnei politike (1922–1924)*. Vsesoyuznaia nauchnaia assotsiatsiia vostokovedov, 1924.
Pavlovich, M. *Sovetskaia Rossiia i kapitalisticheskaia Angliia*. Gosudarstvennoe izdatel'stvo, 1925.
Peters, Yakov. 'Vospominaniia o rabote v VCheka v pervyi god revolutsii'. *Proletarskaia revolutsiia* 33, no. 10 (1924): 5–32.
Petrie, Charles. (ed.) *The Life and Letters of Sir Austen Chamberlain*. Cassell, 1940, vol. 2.
Petrie, David. *Communism in India, 1924–27*. Calcutta: Government of India Press, 1927.
Preobrazhensky, E. A. *Itogi Genuezskoi konferentsii i khoziastvennye perspektivy Evropy*. Gosudarstvennoe izdatel'stvo, 1922.
Pimlott, Ben. (ed.) *The Political Diary of Hugh Dalton*. J. Cape, 1986.
Price, Morton. *The Truth about the Allied Intervention in Russia*. Tipografiia Tovaritschestva Riabushinskogo, 1918.
Price, Morton. *My Reminiscences of the Russian Revolution*. G. Allen and Unwin, 1921.
Radchenko, I. I. *Sovremennaia Angliia i anglo-sovetskii dogovor*. Ekaterinoslav: Tipografiia Ekaterininskoi zheleznoi dorogi, 1924.
Radek, Karl. *Deviat' mesiatsev angliiskogo rabochego pravitel'stva*. Leningrad: Gosudarstvennoe izdatel'stvo, 1925.
Radek, Karl. 'Lord Curzon and the Soviet Union'. *Labour Monthly* VII, no. 5 (1925): 270–4.
Raevsky, A. *Angliiskaia interventsiia i musavatistskoe pravitel'stvo: iz istorii interventsii i kontrrevolutsii v Zakavkazie*. Baku: Gosudarstvennaia tipografiia 'Krasni Vostok', 1927.
Rakovski, C. G. *Angliia i SSSR*. Kiev: Gosudarstvennoe izdtel'stvo Ukrauny, 1923.
Ramsden, John. (ed.) *Real Old Tory Politics: The Political Diaries of Robert Sanders, Lord Bayford, 1910–1935*. Historians' Press, 1984.
Ransome, Arthur. *Six Weeks in Russia in 1919*. G. Allen and Unwin, 1919.
Ransome, Arthur. *The Truth about Russia*. Workers Socialist Federation, 1919.

Raskol'nikov, F. 'Rossiia i Afghanistan. Istoriheskii ocherk'. *Novyi Vostok*, no. 4 (1923): 12–48.
Raskol'nikov, F. *Rasskazy michmana Il'ina*. Goslitizdat, 1936.
Raskol'nikov, F. *Na boevykh postakh*. Voenizdat, 1964.
Ratgauser, I. *Arest i gibel' komissarov Bakinskoi kommuny*. Baku: Otdel TsK i BK Azerbaidzhanskoi KP(b), 1928.
Rawlinson, Alfred. *Adventures in the Near East, 1918–1922*. J. Cape, 1934.
Raymond, Edward. *Uncensored Celebrities*. T. Fisher Unwin, 1918.
Reilly, Bobadila. (ed.) *The Adventures of Sidney Reilly, Britain's Master Spy*. E. Mathew and Marrot, 1931.
Remer, John. 'The Baltic Republics: Some Revelations'. *Nineteenth Century and after* 94, no. 562 (1923): 887–92.
Riddell, George. (ed.) *Lord Riddell's Intimate Diary of the Peace Conference and after, 1918–1923*. V. Gollancz, 1933.
Robien de, Louis. *Journal d'un diplomate en Russie (1917–1918)*. Paris: Michel, 1967.
Ronaldshay, Lawrence. *The Life of Lord Curzon: Being the Authorised Biography of George Nathaniel Marquise Curzon of Kedleston, K. G.* London – New York: E. Benn, 1928, 3 vols.
Rose, Tania. (ed.) *Morton Price: Dispatches from the Revolution: Russia 1916–18*. Pluto Press, 1997.
Roy, Manabendra. *Memoirs*. Bombay: Allied Publishers, 1964.
Russell, Bertrand. *The Practice and Theory of Bolshevism*. G. Allen and Unwin, 1920, pt. 1.
Self, Robert. (ed.) *The Austen Chamberlain Diary Letters: The Correspondence of Sir Austen Chamberlain with His Sisters Hilda and Ida, 1916–1937*. Cambridge: CUP, 1995.
Sforza, Carlo. *Makers of Modern Europe: Portraits and Personal Impressions and Recollections*. Indianapolis: Bobbs – Merrill, 1928.
Shaumian, L. S. *Rasstrel 26 bakinskikh komissarov angliiskimi interventami*. Izdatel'stvo 'Pravda', 1949.
Shaumian, S. S. *Bakinskaia kommuna*. Baku: Gosudarstvennaia tipografiia 'Krasnyi Vostok', 1927.
Shaumian, S. S. *Poslednie dni komissarov bakinskoi kommuny*. Baku: Gosudarstvennaia tipografiia 'Krasnyi Vostok', 1928.
Shumiatskii, B. Z. *Na postu sovetskoi diplomatii*. Leningrad: Priboi, 1927.
Simpson, John. 'Great Britain and the Baltic States'. *Nineteenth Century and after* 94, no. 560 (1923): 614–21.
Snowden, Ethel. *Through Bolshevik Russia*. Cassell, 1920.
Snowden, Philip. *An Autobiography*. I. Nicholson and Watson, 1934, vol. 2.
Solomon, G. A. *Sredi krasnykh vozhdei*. Sovremennik, 1995.
Soutar, Andrew. *With Ironside in North Russia*. London – Melbourne: Hutchinson, 1940.
Stalin, I. V. 'K rasstrelu 26 bakinskikh komissarov'. *Izvetiia* (23 April 1919): 1.
Steed, Henry. *Through Thirty Years, 1892–1922: A Personal Narrative*. London – New York: W. Heinemann – Doubleday, Page and Company, 1924, vol. 2.
Stein, B. E. *Gaagskaia konferentsiia*. Gosudarstvennoe izdatel'stvo, 1922.
Stein, B. E. *Genuezskaia konferentsiia*. Gosudarstvennoe izdatel'stvo, 1922.
Stein, B. E. *Torgovaia politika i torgovye dogovory Sovetskoi Rossii, 1917–1922*. Petrograd: Gosudarstvennoe izdatel'stvo, 1923.
Strang, William. *The Foreign Office*. G. Allen and Unwin, 1955.
Strang, William. *Home and Abroad*. A. Deutsch, 1956.
Taigin, I. *Angliia i SSSR*. Leningrad: Priboi, 1926.

Tallents, Stephen. *Man and Boy*. Faber and Faber, 1943.
Tanin, M. A. *Mezhdunarodnaia politika SSSR (1917–1924)*. Gosudarstvennoe izdatel'stvo, 1925.
Templewood, Samuel. *Nine Troubled Years*. W. Collins, 1954.
Trotsky, L. D. *V plenu u anglichan*. Petrograd: Kniga, 1918.
Trotsky, L. D. *Zapad i Vostok. Voprosy mirovoi politiki i mirovoi revolutsii*. Krasnaia nov', 1924.
Trotsky, L. D. *Moia zhizn'. Opyt avtobiografii*. Berlin: Granit, 1930, 2 vols.
Troianovsky, K. M. *Vostok i Zapad*. Izdatel'stvo VTsIK RSFSR, 1918.
Twaites, Norman. *Velvet and Vinegar*. Grayson and Grayson, 1932.
Vansittart, Robert. *The Mist Procession: The Autobiography of Lord Vansittart*. Hutchinson, 1958.
Walpole, Herbert. (ed.) 'Denis Garstin and the Russian Revolution: A Brief Word in Memory'. *Slavonic and East European Review* 17, no. 51 (1939): 587–605.
Ward, John. *With the 'Die-Hards' in Siberia*. Cassell, 1920.
Watson, Herbert. *An Account of a Mission to the Baltic States in the Year 1919, with a Record of Subsequent Events*. Waverley Press, 1958.
Wells, Herbert. *Russia in the Shadows*. Hodder and Stoughton, 1920.
Williamson, Hudleston. *Farewell to the Don: The Journal of Brigadier H. N. H. Williamson*. W. Collins, 1970.
Wilson, T. (ed.) *The Political Diaries of C. P. Scott, 1911–1928*. Ithaca, NY: Cornell University Press, 1970.
Winnig, August. *Am Ausgang der deutschen Ostpolitik. Persoenliche Erlebnisse und Erinnerungen*. Berlin: Staatspolitischer Verlag, 1921.
Wise, Edwin 'Anglo–Russian Trade and the Trade Agreement'. *Empire Review* 38, no. 272 (1923): 995–1004.
Young, Kenneth. (ed.) *The Diaries of Sir Robert Bruce Lockhart*. Macmillan, 1973, vol. 1.
Zaitsev, I. M. 'Iz nedavnego proshlogo'. *Solovetskie ostrova*, no. 4 (1926): 55–71.
Zalkind, I. A. 'NKID v 1917 godu'. *Mezhdunarodnaia zhizn'*, no. 10 (1927): 15–25.

Contemporary newspapers and journals

Daily Chronicle
Daily Herald
Daily Mail
Daily Mirror
Economicheskaia Zhizn'
Evening Standard
Izvestiya
Liberal Magazine
Manchester Guardian
New York Times
Pravda
The Times
Vestnik NKID
Vostok
Westminster Gazette

Select bibliography 241

Reference editions

Aster, Sidney. (comp., ed.) *British Foreign Policy, 1918-1945: A Guide to Research and Research Materials.* Tunbridge Wells – Wilmington, DE: Costello, Scholarly Resources Inc., 1984.
Davis, Jonathan. (ed.) *Historical Dictionary of the Russian Revolution.* Lanham, ML: Rowman and Littlefield Publishers, 2020.
Gromyko, A. A. (ed.) *Istoriia diplomatii.* Gospolitizdat, 1965. vol. 3.
Hartley, Janet. *Guide to Documents and Manuscripts in the United Kingdom Relating to Russia and the Soviet Union.* Mansell, 1987.
Johnson, Robert. *Soviet Foreign Policy, 1918-1945: A Guide to Research and Research Materials.* Tunbridge Wells – Wilmington, DE: Costello, Scholarly Resources Inc., 1991.
Primakov, E. M. (ed.) *Ocherki istorii rossiiskoi vneshnei razvedki.* Mezhdunarodnye otnosheniia, 1997, vol. 2.
Torkunov, A. V. (ed.) *Izvestnye diplomaty Rossii. Ministry inostrannykh del. XX vek.* Moskovskie uchebniki, 2007.

Secondary sources

Books

Abraham, Richard. *Alexander Kerensky: The First Love of the Revolution.* New York: Columbia University Press, 1987.
Alexander, Ted, and Verizhnikova, Tatiana. *Ransome in Russia: Arthur's Adventures in Eastern Europe.* Fareham: Portchester Publishing, 2003.
Andrew, Christopher. *The Defence of the Realm: The Authorized History of MI5.* Penguin Books, 2010.
Andrew, Christopher, and Gordievsky, Oleg. *KGB: The Inside Story of Its Foreign Operations from Lenin to Gorbachev.* Hodder and Stoughton, 1990.
Ashmore, L. H. *Forgotten Flotilla: British Submarines in Russia 1914–1919.* Portsmouth: Manuscript Press – the Royal Navy Submarine Museum, 2001.
Azimov, G. S. *Bakinskaia kommuna (1917–1918).* Baku: Giandzhlik, 1982.
Babokhodzhaev, A. K. *Proval angliiskoi interventsii v Srednei Azii i na Srednem Vostoke (1918–1924).* Vostochnaia literatura, 1962.
Bainton, Roy. *Honoured by Strangers: The Life of Captain Francis Cromie, CB DSO, 1882-1918.* Shrewsbury: Airlife Publishers Ltd., 2002.
Baron, Nickolas. *The King of Karelia: Colonel P.J. Woods and the British Intervention in North Russia, 1918–1919: A History and Memoir.* F. Boutle Publishers, 2007.
Beckett, Francis. *Enemy within: The Rise and Fall of the British Communist Party.* J. Murray, 1995.
Beesly, Patrick. *Room 40: British Naval Intelligence 1914–18.* Oxford: OUP, 1984.
Beloff, Max. *Imperial Sunset.* Methuen, 1969, vol. 1.
Bennett, Geoffrey. *Cowan's War: The Story of British Naval Operations in the Baltic, 1918-1920.* W. Collins, 1964.
Bennett, Geoffrey. *Freeing the Baltic.* Edinburgh: Birlinn, 2002.

Bennett, George. *British Foreign Policy during the Curzon Period, 1919–24*. St Martin's Press, 1995.

Bennett, Gillian. *A Most Extraordinary and Mysterious Business: The Zinoviev Letter of 1924*. Foreign and Commonwealth Office, 1999.

Bennett, Gillian. *Churchill's Man of Mystery: Desmond Morton and the World of Intelligence*. London – New York: Routledge, 2007.

Bennett, George, and Gibson, Marion. *The Latter Life of Lord Curzon of Kedleston – Aristocrat, Writer, Politian, Statesman: An Experiment in Political Biography*. Lewiston – Queenstown – Lampeter: E. Mellen Press, 2000.

Besugolny, A. Yu. *General Bicherakhov i ego Kavkazskaia armiia: neizvestnye stranitsy istorii grazhdanskoi voiny i interventsii na Kavkaze: 1917–1919*. Zentrpoligraf, 2011.

Blake, Robert. *Unrepentant Tory: The Life and Times of Andrew Bonar Law*. New York: St Martin's Press, 1956.

Blinov, S. I. *Vneshniaia politika Sovetskoi Rossii. Pervyi god proletarskoi diktatury*. Mysl', 1958.

Bond, Brian. *British Military Policy between the Two World Wars*. Oxford: Clarendon Press, 1980.

Boyce, Robert. *The Great Interwar Crisis and the Collapse of Globalization*. Palgrave Macmillan, 2009.

Bradley, John. *Allied Intervention in Russia, 1917–20*. Weidenfeld and Nicholson, 1968.

Brinkley, George. *The Volunteer Army and Allied Intervention in South Russia, 1917–1921*. Notre Dame, IN: University of Notre Dame Press, 1966.

Brogan, Hugh. *The Life of Arthur Ransome*. Pimlico, 1992.

Brook-Shepherd, Gordon. *Iron Maze: The Western Secret Services and the Bolsheviks*. Macmillan, 1998.

Brovkin, V. N. (ed.) *The Bolsheviks in Russian Society: The Revolution and the Civil War*. New Haven – London: YUP, 1997.

Bullock, Ian. *Romancing the Revolution: The Myth of Soviet Democracy and the British Left*. Edmonton: AU Press, 2011.

Burdzhalov, E. *26 bakinskikh komissarov*. Gospolitizdat, 1938.

Bush, Briton. *Britain, India, and the Arabs, 1914–1921*. Berkeley, CA – London: UCP, 1971.

Busch, Briton. *Mudros to Lausanne: Britain's Frontier in West Asia, 1918–1923*. Albany – New York: State University of New York Press, 1976.

Butkovsky, V. L. *Inostrannye konzessii v narodnom khoziaistve SSSR*. Moscow – Leningrad: Gosudarstvennoe izdatel'stvo, 1928.

Bykov, A. V., and Panov, L. S. *Diplomaticheskaia stolitsa Rossii*. Vologda: Ardvisura, 1998.

Bystrova, N. E. *'Russkii vopros' v 1917 – nachale 1920 g.: Sovetskaia Rossiia i velikie derzhavy*. St Petersburg: IRI RAN, 2016.

Callwell, Charles. *Field Marshal Sir Henry Wilson*. Cassell, 1927, vol. II.

Campbell, John. *Lloyd George*. J. Cape, 1977.

Carley, Michail. *Silent Conflict: A Hidden History of Early Soviet-Western Relations*. Lanham, ML: Rowman and Littlefield Publishers, 2014.

Carlton, David. *Churchill and the Soviet Union*. Manchester – New York: MUP, 2000.

Carr, Edward. *The Twenty Years' Crisis, 1919–1939: An Introduction to the Study of International Relations*. Macmillan, 1940.

Chamberlin, William. *The Russian Revolution, 1917–1921*. Macmillan, 1935, 2 vols.

Chambers, Roland. *The Last Englishman: The Double Life of Arthur Ransome*. Faber and Faber, 2009.

Chester, Lewis, Fay, Stephen, and Young, Hugo. *The Zinoviev Letter*. W. Heinemann, 1967.
Chossudovsky, Evgeny. *Chicherin and the Evolution of Soviet Foreign Policy and Diplomacy*. Geneva: Graduate Institute of International Relations, 1973.
Chubarian, A. O. *Brestskii mir. 1918*. Gospolitizdat, 1963.
Clayton, Anthony. *The British Empire as a Superpower, 1919–1939*. Athens: The University Press of Georgia, 1985.
Coates, William, and Coates, Zelda. *Armed Intervention in Russia. 1918–1922*. V. Gollancz, 1935.
Coates, William, and Coates, Zelda. *A History of Anglo-Soviet Relations*. Lawrence and Wishart, The Pilot Press, 1943, vol. 1.
Coates, William, and Coates, Zelda. *Soviets in Central Asia*. Lawrence and Wishart, 1951.
Cohrs, Patrick. *The Unfinished Peace after World War I: America, Britain and Stabilization of Europe, 1919–1932*. Cambridge: CUP, 2008.
Connaughton, Richard. *The War of the Rising Sun and Tumbling Bear: A Military History of the Russo-Japanese War, 1904–1905*. London – New York: Routledge, 1988.
Connell, John. *The 'Office'. A Study of British Foreign Policy and Its Makers, 1919–1951*. A. Wingate, 1958.
Conte, Francis. *Christian Rakovski (1873–1941): A Political Biography*. New York: The Boulder Press, 1989.
Cook, Andrew. *Ace of Spies: The True Story of Sidney Reilly*. Stroud: Tempus, 2004.
Corson, William, and Crowley, Robert. *The New KGB: Engine of Soviet Power*. New York: W. Morrow, 1985.
Corthorn, Paul, and Davis, Jonathan. (eds) *The British Labour Party and the Wider World: Domestic Politics, Internationalism and Foreign Policy*. London – New York: Tauris Academic Studies, 2008.
Costello, John. *Mask of Treachery: Spies, Lies and Betraial*. New York: W. Morrow, 1988.
Cowden, Morton. *Russian Bolshevism and British Labour 1917–1921*. Boulder, CO: East European Monographs, 1984.
Crankshaw, Edward. *Russia and Britain*. W. Collins, 1944.
Crosby, Travis. *The Unknown Lloyd George: A Statesman in Conflict*. I. B. Tauris, 2014.
Crowe, Sibyl, and Corp, Edward. *Our Ablest Public Servant: Sir Eyre Crowe 1864–1925*. Braunton, Dev.: Merlin Books, 1993.
Dallin, Alexander. *Soviet Conduct in World Affairs*. New York: Columbia University Press, 1960.
Darwin, John. *Britain, Egypt and the Middle East Imperial Policy in the Aftermath of War, 1918–22*. Macmillan, 1981.
Das, Durga. *India from Curzon to Nehru and after*. W. Collins, 1969.
Davies, Norman. *White Eagle, Red Star: The Polish–Soviet War, 1919–1920*. Macdonald, 1972.
Davies, R. W. et al. (eds) *The Economic Transformation of the Soviet Union, 1913–1945*. Cambridge: CUP, 1994.
Deacon, Robert. *A History of the Russian Secret Service*. Grafton, 1987.
Debo, Richard. *Revolution and Survival: The Foreign Policy of Soviet Russia 1917–1918*. Liverpool: Liverpool University Press, 1979.
Debo, Richard. *Survival and Consolidation: The Foreign Policy of Soviet Russia, 1918–1921*. Montreal: MacGill University Press, 1992.
Deriabin, A. I. *Grazhdankaia voina v Rossii 1917–1922. Voiska interventov*. AST, 1999.
Dmitriev, G. L. *Indian Revolutionaries in Central Asia*. Calcutta: Greenwich Millennium Press, 2002.

Dockrill, Michael, and Goold, J. *Peace without Promise: Britain and the Peace Conferences, 1919-23*. Hamden, CT: Archon Books, 1981.
Dugdale, Blanche. *Arthur James Balfour*. Hutchinson, 1936, vol. 2.
Dumova, N. G., and Trukhanovsky, V. G. *Churchill i Miliukov protiv Sovetskoi Rossii*. Nauka, 1989.
Dutton, David. *Austen Chamberlain: Gentleman in Politics*. Bolton: R. Anderson, 1985.
Eaden, James, and Renton, David. *The Communist Party of Great Britain since 1920*. Palgrave, 2002.
Fel'shtinsky, Yu. G. *Krushenie mirovoi revolutsii, Brestskii mir: October 1917 – November 1918*. Terra, 1992.
Ferguson, Harry. *Operation Kronstadt*. Hutchinson, 2008.
Ferris, John. *Men, Money, and Diplomacy: The Evolution of British Strategic Policy, 1919-26*. Ithaca, NY: Cornell University Press, 1989.
Figes, Orlando. *A People's Tragedy: The Russian Revolution 1891-1924*. Pimlico, 1997.
Fink, Caroline. *The Genoa Conference: European Diplomacy, 1921-1922*. Chapel Hill – London: University of North Carolina Press, 1993.
Fischer, Louis. *The Soviets in World Affairs: A History of the Relations between the Soviet Union and the Rest of the World. 1917-1929*. Princeton, NJ: PUP, 1951, 2 vols.
Fischer, Ruth. *Stalin and German Communism: A Study in the Origins of the State Party*. London – Oxford: G. Cumberlege, OUP, 1948.
Fisher, John. *Curzon and the British Imperialism in the Middle East, 1916-1923*. F. Cass, 1999.
Fleming, Denna. *The Cold War and Its Origins, 1917-1960*. G. Allen and Unwin, 1961, vol. 1.
Foglesong, David. *America's Secret War against Bolshevism: U.S. Intervention in the Russian Civil War, 1917-1920*. Chapel Hill – London: University of North Carolina Press, 1995.
Fomin, A. M. *Voina s prodolzheniem. Velikobritaniia i Frantsiia v bor'be za 'Osmanskoe nasledstvo'. 1918-1923*. Russkii fond sodeistviia obrazovaniyu i nauke – Universitet D. Pozharskogo, 2010.
French, David. *The Strategy of the Lloyd George Coalition, 1916-1918*. Oxford: Clarendon Press, 1995.
Friedman, Isaia. *British Miscalculations: The Rise of Muslim Nationalism, 1918-1925*. New Brunswick – London: Transaction Publishers, 2012.
Gardner, Lois. *Safe for Democracy: The Anglo-American Response to Revolution, 1913-1923*. New York – Oxford: OUP, 1987.
Gasparian, A. S. *Operatsiia 'Trest'. Sovetskaia razvedka protiv russkoi emigratsii. 1921-1937*. Veche, 2008.
Genis, V. L. *Krasnaia Persia: Bol'sheviki v Giliane. 1920-1921. Dokumental'naia khronika*. Zentr strategicheskikh i politicheskikh issledovanii, 2000.
Genis, V. L. *Vice-Consul Vvedenskii. Sluzhba v Persii i Bukharskom khanstve (1906-1920 gg.)*. Izdatel'stvo sotsial'no-politicheskaia mysl', 2003.
Gilbert, Martin. *Churchill: A Life*. Minerva, 1992.
Gilmor, David. *Curzon*. J. Murray, 1994.
Gilmor, David. *Curzon: Imperial Statesman*. Penguin Books, 2003.
Girault, Rene, and Frank, Robert. *Histoire des relations internationals contemporaines*. Paris: Masson, 1988, vol. 2.
Goekay, Buelent. *A Clash of Empires: Turkey between Russian Bolshevism and British Imperialism, 1918-1923*. London – New York: Tauris Academic Studies, 1997.
Goldin, V. I. et al. (eds) *Russkii Sever v istoricheskom prostranstve rossiiskoi grazhdanskoi voiny*. Arkhangelsk: Solty, 2005.

Goldstein, Erik. *Winning the Peace: British Diplomatic Strategy, Peace Planning, and the Paris Peace Conference, 1916-1920*. Oxford: Clarendon Press, 1991.
Golovko, V. A. et al. (eds) *Mezhdu Moskvoi i Zapadom: Diplomaticheskaia deiatel'nost' C. G. Rakovskogo*. Khar'kov: Oko, 1994.
Gorodetsky, Gabriel. *The Precarious Truce. Anglo-Soviet Relations, 1924-1927*. Cambridge: CUP, 1977.
Graham, Malbone. *The League of Nations and the Recognition of States*. Berkeley, CA: UCP, 1933-41, vol. 3, nos. 1-4.
Graubard, Stephen. *British Labour and the Russian Revolution, 1917-1924*. Cambridge, MA: HUP, 1956.
Grayson, Richard. *Austen Chamberlain and the Commitment to Europe: British Foreign Policy, 1924-29*. F. Cass, 1997.
Haithcox, John. *Communism and Nationalism in India, M. N. Roy and Comintern Policy 1920-1939*. Princeton, NJ: PUP, 1971.
Harrison, Robert. *Britain in the Middle East, 1619-1971*. Bloombsbury Academic Publishing, 2016.
Haslam, Jonahtan. *Russia's Cold War. From the October Revolution to the Fall of the Wall*. New Haven – London: YUP, 2011.
Haslam, Jonahtan. *Near and Distant Neighbours: A New History of Soviet Intelligence*. New York: Farrar, Straus and Giroux, 2015.
Headlam-Morley, John. *Studies in Diplomatic History*. Methuen, 1930.
Heywood, Anthony. *Modernising Lenin's Russia. Economic Reconstruction, Foreign Trade and the Railways*. Cambridge: CUP, 1999.
Hinkkanen-Lievonen, Merja-Liisa. *British Trade and Enterprise in the Baltic States, 1919-1925*. Helsinki: SHS, 1984.
Hopkirk, Peter. *Setting the East Ablaze: On Secret Service in Bolshevik Asia*. J. Murray, 1984.
Hopkirk, Peter. *On Secret Service East of Constantinople: The Plot to Bring Down the British Empire*. J. Murray, 1994.
Hovi, Olaf. *The Baltic Area in British Policy, 1918-1921*. Helsinki: SHS, 1980. 2 vols.
Hudson, Miles. *Intervention in Russia, 1918-1920: A Cautionary Tale*. Barnsley: L. Cooper, 2004.
Hughes, Michael. *Inside the Enigma: British Officials in Russia, 1900-39*. London – Rio Grande: The Hambledon Press, 1997.
Ignatiev, A. V. *Russko-angliiskie otnosheniia nakanune Oktiabr'skoi revoliutsii (February –October 1917 g.)*. Nauka, 1966.
Imam, Zafar. *Colonialism in East–West Relations: A Study of Soviet Policy towards India and Anglo-Soviet Relations, 1917-1947*. New Delhi: Patriot Publishers, 1987.
Ioffe, Ya. A. *Organisatsiia interventsii i blokady Sovetskoi respubliki, 1918-1920. Ocherk*. Moscow – Leningrad: Voenizdat, 1930.
Isakov, P. S. *Kaspii. 1920*. Gospolitizdat, 1973.
Ivanov, Yu. V. *Ocherki istorii rossisko- (sovetsko-) pol'skikh otnoshenii v dokumentakh. 1914-1945 gg*. Mezhdunarodnye otnosheniia, 2014.
Ivanovich, V. *Sovetskii Soyuz i Angliia v Pribaltike*. Moscow – Leningrad: Moskovskii rabochii, 1927.
Jackson, Robert. *At War with the Bolsheviks: The Allied Intervention into Russia 1917-20*. T. Stacey, 1972.
Jacobson, Jon. *When the Soviet Union Entered World Politics*. Berkeley, CA: UCP, 1994.
Jeffrey, Keith. *MI6: The History of the Secret Intelligence Service, 1909-1949*. Bloomsbury Academic Publishing, 2010.

Johnson, Robert. *Spying for Empire: The Great Game in Central and South Asia, 1757–1947*. Greenhill Books, 2006.

Jones, Bill. *The Russia Complex: The British Labour Party and the Soviet Union*. Manchester: Manchester University Press, 1977.

Jones, Raymond. *Arthur Ponsonby: The Politics of Life*. Christopher Helm Publishers, 1989.

Judd, Alan. *The Quest for C. Sir Mansfield Cumming and the Founding of the British Secret Service*. HarperCollins Publishers, 1999.

Judd, Denis. *Balfour and the British Empire: A Study in Imperial Evolution 1874–1932*. Macmillan, 1968.

Judd, Denis. *The Life and Times of George V*. Weidenfeld and Nicolson, 1973.

Kadishev, A. B. *Interventsiia i grazhdanskaia voina v Zakavkazie*. Voenizdat, 1960.

Kapitonova, N. K., and Romanova, E. V. *Istoriia vneshnei politiki Velikobritanii*. Mezhdunarodnye otnosheniia, 2016.

Karpova, R. F. *Krassin – sovetkii diplomat*. Sotsial'no-ekonomicheskoe izdatel'stvo, 1962.

Kapur, Harish. *Soviet Russia and Asia. 1917–1927: A Study of Soviet Police towards Turkey, Iran and Afghanistan*. London – Geneva: Graduate Institute of International Studies, 1966.

Kazemzadeh, Firuz. *The Struggle for Transcaucasia (1917–1921)*. Anglo-Caspian Press, 2008.

Keeble, Curtis. *Britain and the Soviet Union, 1917–1989*. Macmillan, 1990.

Kennan, George. *Russia and the West under Lenin and Stalin*. Boston – Toronto: Little, Brown and Co., 1961.

Kennan, George. *Soviet-American Relations, 1917–1920*. New York: Athenaeum, 1967, 2 vols.

Kettle, Michael. *Sidney Reilly: The True Story*. Corgi Books, 1983.

Kettle, Michael. *Russia and the Allies. 1917–1920*. A. Deutsch, 1981, vol. 1; London – New York: Routledge, 1988, vol. 2; Routledge, 1992, vol. 3.

Khariukov, L. N. *Anglo-russkoe sopernichestvo v Zentral'noi Asii i ismailism*. Izdatel'stvo Moskovskogo gosudarstvennogo universiteta, 1995.

Kheifez, A. I. *Sovetskaia Rossiia i sopredel'nye strany Vostoka. 1921–1927*. Nauka, 1968.

Khromov, S. S. *Leonid Krassin. Neizvestnye stranitsy biografii. 1920–1926 gg*. Institut rossiiskoi istorii RAN, 2001.

Khromov, S. S. *Po stranitsam arkhiva Stalina*. Izdatel'stvo Moskovskogo gosudarstvennogo universiteta, 2009.

Kinvig, Clifford. *Churchill's Crusade: The British Invasion of Russia, 1918–1920*. Continuum, 2006.

Kirby, David. *The Baltic World, 1772–1993: Europe's Northern Periphery in an Age of Change*. London – New York: Longman, 1995.

Kitching, Carolyn. *Britain and the Problem of International Disarmament, 1919–1934*. London – New York: Routledge, 1999.

Klugmann, James. *History of the Communist Party*. Laurence and Wishart, 1968, vol. 1.

Kocho-Williams, Alastair. *Russian and Soviet Diplomacy, 1900–1939*. Palgrave Macmillan, 2012.

Kondratiev, N. D. *Tovaritsch Peterson*. Riga: Latviiskoe gosudarstvennoe izdatel'stvo, 1959.

Kononova, M. M. *Russkie diplomaticheskie predstaviteli v emigratsii (1917–1925 gg.)*. Institut vseobtschei istorii RAN, 2004.

Kozlov, D. Yu. *Britanskie podvodnye lodki v Baltiiskom more. 1914–1918 gody*. St Petersburg: Izdatel'stvo LeKo, 2006.

Kravchenko, V. F. *Pod imenem Shmidkhena*. Sovetskaia Rossiia, 1970.

Kremnev, B. G. *Krassin*. Molodaia gvardiia, 1968.
Lannik, L. V. *Posle Rossiiskoi imperii: germanskaiya okkupatsiya 1918 g.* St Petersburg: Eurasia, 2020.
Laqueur, Walter. *The Fate of the Revolution: Interpretations of the Soviet History from 1917 to the Present*. New York: C. Scribner's Sons, 1987.
Lasarev, M. S. *Imperialism i kurdskii vopros (1917–1923)*. Nauka, 1989.
Latyshev, A. G. *Rassekrechenni Lenin*. Izdatel'stvo Mart, 1996.
Legget, George. *The Cheka: Lenin's Political Police: The All-Russian Extraordinary Commission for Combatting Counter-Revolution and Sabotage (December 1917 to February 1922)* Oxford: Clarendon Press, 1981.
Lenczowski, George. *Russia and the West in Iran, 1918–1948: A Study in Big-Power Rivalry*. Ithaca, NY: Cornell University Press, 1949.
Lentin, Anthony. *Lloyd George and the Lost Peace: From Versailles to Hitler, 1919–1940*. Palgrave, 2001.
Leonard, Raymond. *Secret Soldiers of the Revolution: Soviet Military Intelligence, 1918–1933*. Westport, CT – London: Greenwood Press, 1999.
Lifshits, L. M., *Geroicheskii podvig bakinskikh bolshevikov*. Baku: Azerneshr, 1964.
Lockhart, Robin. *Ace of Spies*. Hodder and Stoughton, 1967.
Louis, William. *British Strategy in the Far East, 1919–1939*. Oxford: Clarendon Press, 1971.
Lowe, Cedric, and Dockrill, Michael. *The Mirage of Power: British Foreign Policy, 1902–1922*. Routledge and Kegan Paul, 1972, vols. 2–3.
Lyman, Richard. *The First Labour Government*. Chapman and Hall, 1957.
Macdonald, Deborah, and Dronfield, Jeremy. *A Very Dangerous Woman: The Lives, Loves and Lies of Russia's Most Seductive Spy*. Oneworld, 2016.
Mackay, Ruddock. *Balfour: Intellectual Statesman*. Oxford – New York: OUP, 1985.
Mackenzie, David. *From Messianism to Collapse: Soviet Foreign Policy. 1917–1991*. Fort Worth – London: Harcourt Brace College Publishers, 1994.
Macmeekin, Sean. *History's Greatest Heist: The Looting of Russia by the Bolsheviks*. New Haven, CT: YUP, 2009.
Macmeekin, Sean. *The Ottoman Endgame: War, Revolution and the Making of the Modern Middle East, 1908–1923*. G. Allen and Unwin, 2015.
Macmillan, Margaret. *Peacemakers: The Paris Conference of 1919 and Its Attempt to End War*. J. Murray, 2001.
Madeira, Victor. *Britannia and the Bear: The Anglo-Russian Intelligence Wars 1917–1929*. Woodbridge, Suffolk: The Boydell Press, 2014.
Magadeev, I. E. *V teni Pervoi mirovoi voiny. Dilemmy evropeiskoi bezopasnosti v 1920-e gody*. Aspect Press, 2021.
Maisel, Ephraim. *The Foreign Office and Foreign Policy, 1919–1926*. Brighton: Sussex Academic Press, 1994.
Malia, Martin. *Russia under Western Eyes: From the Bronze Horseman to Lenin Mausoleum*. Cambridge, MA – London: The Belknap Press – HUP, 1999.
Marks, Sally. *The Ebbing of European Ascendancy: An International History of the World, 1914–1945*. E. Arnold, 2002.
Marquand, David. *Ramsay Macdonald*. J. Cape, 1977.
Mawdsley, Evan. *The Russian Civil War*. Edinburgh: Birlinn, 2017.
Medlicott, William. *British Foreign Policy since Versailles, 1919–1963*. Methuen, 1968.
Meyer, Karl, and Brysac, Sharon. *Tournament of Shadows: The Great Game and the Race for Empire in Asia*. Abacus, 2001.
Mil'stein, N. I. *Iz istorii Turkestanskoi Cheka*. Tashkent: Nauka UzSSR, 1965.

Milton, George. *Russian Roulette: How British Spies Defeated Lenin*. Scepter, 2013.
Minz, I. I. *Angliiskaia interventsiia i severnaia kontrrevolutsiia*. Moscow – Leningrad: Gosudarstvennoe sotsial'no-ekonomicheskoe izdatel'stvo, 1931.
Miroshnikov, L. I. *Angliiskaia expansiia v Irane (1914–1920)*. Vostochnaia literatura, 1961.
Moffat, Ian. *The Allied Intervention in Russia, 1918–1920: The Diplomacy of Chaos*. Houndsmills, Basingstoke, Hampshire: Palgrave Macmillan, 2015.
Monroe, Elizabeth. *Britain's Moment in the Middle East (1914–1971)*. Baltimore, ML: The Johns Hopkins University Press, 1981.
Morgan, Kennth. *Lloyd George*. Weidenfeld and Nicolson, 1974.
Morgan, Kenneth. *Consensus and Disunity: The Lloyd George Coalition Government, 1918–1922*. Oxford: Clarendon Press, 1979.
Morgan, Kenneth. *Bolshevism and the British Left*. Lawrence and Wishart, 2006, pt I.
Mowat, C. L. (ed.) *The New Cambridge Modern History*. Cambridge: CUP, 1968, vol. XII.
Mowat, Robert. *A History of European Diplomacy 1914–1925*. E. Arnold, 1927.
Naylor, Richard. *A Man and an Intrusion: Sir Maurice Hankey, the Cabinet Secretariat and the Custody of Cabinet Secrecy*. Cambridge: CUP, 1984.
Neilson, Keith. *Britain, Soviet Russia and the Collapse of the Versailles Order, 1919–1939*. Cambridge: CUP, 2006.
Neilson, Keith, and Otte, T. G. *The Permanent Under-Secretary for Foreign Affairs, 1854–1946*. London – New York: Routledge, 2012.
Newman, Paul. *Britain and the Baltic*. Methuen, 1930.
Nezhinskii, L. N. *V interesakh naroda ili vopreki im? Sovetskaia mezhddunarodnaia politika v 1917–1933*. Nauka, 2004.
Nicolson, Harold. *Curzon: The Last Phase, 1919–1925: A Study in Post-War Diplomacy*. A. Constable, 1937.
Nicolson, Harold. *King George the Fifth: His Life and Reign*. A. Constable, 1953.
Nikonova, S. V. *Antisovetskaia vneshniaia politika angliiskikh konsevatorov, 1924–1927*. Izdadel'stvo AN SSSR, 1963.
Northedge, Frederick. *The Troubled Giant: Britain among the Great Powers, 1916–1939*. New York – Washington: F. Praeger, 1966.
Northedge, Frederick, and Wells, Audrey. *Britain and the Soviet Communism: The Impact of Revolution*. Macmillan, 1982.
O'Brien, Terence. *Milner. Viscount Milner of St James's and Cape Town. 1854–1925*. A. Constable, 1979.
Occleshaw, Michael. *The Romanov Conspiracies: The Romanovs and the House of Windsor*. Chapmans, 1993.
Occleshaw, Michael. *Dances in Deep Shadows: The Clandestine War in Russia, 1914–20*. New York: Carrol and Graf Publishers, 2006.
O'Connor, Timothy. *Georgii Chicherin i sovetskaia vneshniaia politika 1918–1930*. Progress, 1991.
O'Connor, Timothy. *The Engineer of Revolution: L. B. Krassin and the Bolsheviks, 1870–1926*. Boulder, CO: Westview Press, 1992.
Orde, Anne. *British Policy and European Reconstruction after the First World War*. Cambridge, MA: HUP, 2002.
Owen, Frank. *Tempestuous Journey: Lloyd George, His Life and Times*. Hutchinson, 1954.
Page Arnot, Robert. *The Impact of the Russian Revolution in Britain*. Lawrence and Wishart, 1967.
Page, Stanley. *The Formation of the Baltic States: A Study of the Effects of Great Power Politics upon the Emergence of Lithuania, Latvia, and Estonia*. Cambridge, MA: HUP, 1959.

Panin, S. B. *Sovetskaia Rossiia i Afghanistan, 1919–1929 gg.* Moscow – Irkutsk: Irkustkii gosudarstvennyi pedagogicheskii universitet, 1998.

Pares, Bernard. *The Fall of the Russian Monarchy: A Study of the Evidence.* J. Cape, 1939.

Park, Alexander. *Bolshevism in Turkestan, 1917–27.* New York: Columbia University Press, 1957.

Pearce, Brian. *How Haig Saved Lenin.* Houndmills – London: Macmillan, 1987.

Persiz, M. A. *Revoliutsionery Indii v Strane Sovetov. U istokov indiiskogo kommunisticheskogo dvizheniia.* Nauka, 1973.

Persiz, M. A. *Zastenchivaia interventsiia.* Muravei-Gaid, 1999.

Phillips, Hugh. *Between the Revolution and the West: A Political Biography of Maxim Litvinov.* Boulder, CO – Oxford: Westview Press, 1992.

Phillips, Timothy. *The Secret Twenties: British Intelligence, the Russians and the Jazz Age.* Granta Books, 2018.

Pipes, Richard. *Russia under the Bolshevik Regime, 1919–1924.* Harvill Press, 1997.

Plotke, A. J. *Imperial Spies Invade Russia: The British Intelligence Interventions, 1918.* Westport, CT: Greenwood Press, 1993.

Popplewell, Richard. *Intelligence and Imperial Defence: British Intelligence and the Defence of the Indian Empire, 1904–1924.* F. Cass, 1995.

Quinlan, Kevin. *The Secret War between the Wars: MI5 in the 1920's and 1930's.* Woolbridge, Suffolk: The Boydell Press, 2014.

Ramsden, John. *The Age of Balfour and Baldwin, 1902–1940.* Longman, 1978.

Rat'kovsky, I. S. *Krasnyi terror i deiatel'nost' VCheka v 1918 g.* St Petersburg: Izdatel'stvo Sankt-Peterburgskogo gosudarstvennogo universiteta, 2006.

Read, Anthony. *The World on Fire: 1919 and the Battle with Bolshevism.* J. Cape, 2008.

Reynolds, Michael. *Shattering Empires: The Clash and the Collapse of the Ottoman and Russian Empires, 1908–1918.* Cambridge: CUP, 2011.

Rhoer van der, Edward. *Master Spy: A True Story of Allied Espionage in Bolshevik Russia.* New York: C. Scribner's Sons, 1981.

Rodgers, Hugh. *Search for Security: A Study in Baltic Diplomacy, 1920–1934.* Hamden, Conn.: Archon Books, 1975.

Rose, Inbal. *Conservatism and Foreign Policy during the Lloyd George Coalition, 1918–1922.* F. Cass, 1999.

Rose, Kenneth. *King George V.* Weidenfeld and Nicolson, 1983.

Roskill, Stanley. *Hankey, Man of Secrets.* W. Collins, 1972, vol. 2.

Rothstein, A. *Kogda Angliia vtorglas' v Sovetskuyu Rossiyu.* Progress, 1982.

Rowland, Peter. *David Lloyd George: A Biography.* New York: Macmillan, 1975.

Ryzhikov, V. A. *Sovetsko-angliiskie otnosheniia: osnovnye etapy istorii.* Mezhdunarodnye otnosheniia, 1987.

Sabahi, Houshang. *British Policy in Persia 1918–1925.* Macmillan, 1990.

Salzmann, Stephanie. *Great Britain, Germany, and the Soviet Union: Rapallo and after, 1922–1934.* Woodbridge, Suffolk: The Boydell Press, 2003.

Samra, Chattar. *India and Anglo-Soviet Relations, 1917–1947.* Bombay, etc.: Asia Publishing House, 1959.

Sargent, Michael. *British Military Involvement in Transcaspia (1918–1919).* Camberley: Conflict Studies Research Centre, 2004.

Sayers, Michael, and Kahn, Albert. *The Great Conspiracy against Russia.* Boston: Little Brown and Company, 1946.

Semianychev, A. K. *Volzhsko-Kaspiiskaia flotillia v bor'be za Kaspii. 1918–1920 gg.* Voenmorizdat, 1952.

Sergeev, E. Yu. *George Nathaniel Curzon – poslednii rytsar' Britanskoi imperii*. Tovaritschestvo nauchnykh izdanii KMK, 2015.

Sergeev, Evgeny. *The Great Game 1856–1907: Russo-British Relations in Central and East Asia*. Washington, DC: Woodrow Wilson Center Press – Baltimore, MD: The Johns Hopkins University Press, 2013.

Service, Robert. *Spies and Commissars: Bolshevik Russia and the West*. Basingstoke – Oxford: Macmillan, 2011.

Sharp, Alan. *The Versailles Settlement: Peacemaking in Paris, 1919*. Basingstoke – London: Macmillan, 1991.

Sheinis, Z. S. *Maxim Maximovich Litvinov: revolutsioner, diplomat, chelovek*. Gospolitizdat, 1989.

Shishkin, V. A. *Sovetskoe gosudarstvo i strany Zapada v 1917–1932*. Leningrad: Nauka, 1969.

Shishkin, V. A. *Stanovlenie vneshnei politiki poslerevoliutsionnoi Rossii (1917–1930-e gody) i kapitalisticheskii mir: ot revoliutsionnogo 'zapadnichestva' k 'natsional-bol'shevismu'*. St Petersburg: D. Bulavin, 2002.

Silverlight, John. *The Victor's Dilemma: Allied Intervention in the Russian Civil War*. Barrie and Jenkins, 1970.

Sladkovsky, M. I. *Kitai i Angliia*. Nauka, 1980.

Smele, Jonathan. *The 'Russian' Civil Wars, 1916–1926: Ten Years That Shook the World*. Hurst and Company, 2015.

Smith, Michael. *Six: The Real James Bonds, 1909–1939*. Biteback Publishing, 2010.

Smolin, A. V. *Beloe dvizhenie na severo-zapade Rossii (1918–1920 gg.)*. St Petersburg: D. Bulavin, 1999.

Somin, Ilia. *Stillborn Crusade: The Tragic Failure of Western Intervention in the Russian Civil War, 1918–1920*. New Brunswick – London: Transaction Publishers, 1996.

Sorokin, G. Z. *Pervyi s'ezd narodov Vostoka*. Vostochnaia literatura, 1961.

Spector, Ivar. *The Soviet Union and the Muslim World, 1917–58*. Washington: Washington University Press, 1959.

Stafford, David. *Churchill and Secret Service*. J. Murray, 1997.

Stein, B. E. *Vneshniia politika SSSR, 1917–1923*. Gospolitizdat, 1945.

Stein, B. E. *'Russkii vopros' na Parizhskoi mirnoi konferetsii*. Gospolitizdat, 1949.

Steinberg, E. L. *Istoriia britanskoi agressii na Srednem Vostoke*. Voenizdat, 1951.

Steiner, Zara. *The Lights That Failed: European International History, 1919–1933*. Oxford: OUP, 2005.

Stevenson, David. *The First World War and International Politics*. Oxford: OUP, 1988.

Stewart, Alan. *Persian Expedition: The Australians in Dunsterforce, 1918*. Loftus, NSW: Australian Military History Publications, 2006.

Strakhovsky, Leonid. *Intervention at Archangel: The Story of Allied Intervention and Russian Counter-Revolution in North Russia 1918–1920*. London – Oxford – Princeton, NJ: H. Milford – PUP, 1944.

Sudeikin, A. G. *Kolonial'naia politika leiboristskoi partii Anglii mezhdu dvumia mirovymi voinami*. Nauka, 1976.

Suny, Ronald. *The Baku Commune, 1917–1918: Class and Nationality in the Russian Revolution*. Princeton, NJ: PUP, 1972.

Swain, Geoffrey. *The Origins of the Russian Civil War*. London – New York: Longman, 1996.

Swain, Geoffrey. *A Short History of the Russian Revolution*, London: I.B. Tauris, 2017.

Swinson, Arthur. *Beyond the Frontiers: The Biography of Colonel F. M. Bailey, Explorer and Special Agent*. Hutchinson, 1971.

Ter Minassian, Taline. *Reginald Teague-Jones. Au service secret de l'Empire brinannique.* Paris: Grasset, 2012.
Thompson, William. *The Good Old Cause: British Communism 1920–1991.* Pluto Press, 1992.
Thorpe, Andrew. *The British Communist Party and Moscow. 1920–43.* Manchester – New York: Manchester University Press, 2000.
Tikhonov, Yu. N. *Afganskaia voina Stalina. Bitva za Tsentral'nuyu Asiiu.* Yausa, Exmo, 2008.
Timoshkov, S. P. *Bor'ba s angliiskoi interventsii v Turkestane.* Voenizdat, 1941.
Trukhanovsky, V. G. *Vneshniaia politika Anglii na pervom etape obtschego krizisa kapitalisma (1918–1939 gg.).* Mezhdunarodnye otsheniia, 1962.
Trukhanovsky, V. G. *Winston Churchill.* Progress Publishers, 1978.
Ulam, Adam. *Expansion and Coexistence: The History of Soviet Foreign Policy, 1917–1967.* New York – Washington: F. Praeger, 1968.
Uldricks, Teddy. *Diplomacy and Ideology: The Origins of Soviet Foreign Relations. 1917–1930.* London – Beverley Hills: Sage Publications, 1979.
Ullman, Richard. *Anglo-Soviet Relations, 1917–1921.* Princeton, NJ: PUP, 1961–1972, 3 vols.
Ulunian, Ar. A. *Turkestanskii platsdarm. 1917–1922: Britanskoe razvedyvatel'noe soobtschestvo i britanskoe pravitel'stvo.* LENAND, 2019.
Vares, P., and Osipova, O. *Pokhitschenie Evropy, ili Baltiiskii vopros v mezhdunarodnykh otnosheniiakh XX veka.* Tallinn: Estonskaia entsiklopediia, 1992.
Vinogradov, K. B. *David Lloyd George.* Nauka, 1970.
Volkov, F. D. *Krakh angliiskoi politiki intervetsii i diplomaticheskoi isoliatsii Sovetskogo gosudarstva (1917–1924).* Gospolitizdat, 1954.
Volkov, F. D. *Anglo-Sovetskie otnosheniia 1924–1929 gg.* Gospolitizdat, 1958.
Volkov, F. D. *Tainy Whitehall i Downing Street.* Mysl', 1980.
Volodarsky, Boris. *Stalin's Agent: The Life and Death of Aleksander Orlov.* Oxford: OUP, 2015.
Volodarsky, M. I. *Sovety i ikh yuzhnye sosedi Iran i Afghanistan (1917–1933).* London: Overseas Publications Interchange Ltd., 1985.
Vygodsky, S. Ia. *U istokov sovetskoi diplomatii.* Gospolitizdat, 1965.
Wade, Rex. *The Russian Search for Peace: February – October 1917.* Stanford, CA: Stanford University Press, 1969.
Ward, A., and Gooch, G. (eds) *The Cambridge History of British Foreign Policy, 1783–1919.* Cambridge: CUP, 1923, vol. 3.
Ward, Stephen. *James Ramsay Macdonald: Low Born among the High Brows.* New York, etc.: P. Lang, 1990.
Warth, Robert. *The Allies and the Russian Revolution.* Durham, NC: Duke University Press, 1954.
Watt, Donald. *Personalities and Policies: Studies in the Formation of British Foreign Policy in the Twentieth Century.* Longmans, 1965.
West, Nigel. *MI6: British Intelligence Service Operations.* Weidenfeld and Nicolson, 1983.
West, Nigel. *MASK: MI5's Penetration of the Communist Party of Great Britain.* London – New York: Routledge, 2005.
West, Nigel, and Tsarev, Oleg. *The Crown Jewels: The British Secrets at the Heart of the KGB Archives.* New York: HarperCollins Publishers, 1998.
Wheeler-Bennett, John. *Brest-Litovsk: The Forgotten Peace. March 1918.* Macmillan, 1939.
White, Christine. *British and American Commercial Relations with Soviet Russia, 1918–1924.* Chapell Hill – London: The University of North Carolina Press, 1992.
White, Stephen. *Britain and the Bolshevik Revolution: A Study in the Politics of Diplomacy, 1920–1924.* Macmillan, 1979.

White, Stephen. *The Origins of Detente: The Genoa Conference and Soviet-Western Relations, 1921-1922*. Cambridge: CUP, 1985.
Williams, Andrew. *Trading with the Bolsheviks: The Politics of East-West Trade, 1920-1939*. Manchester: Manchester University Press, 1992.
Williams, Ann. *Britain and France in the Middle East and North Africa (1914-1967)*. Hutchinson, 1968.
Windrich, Elaine. *British Labour's Foreign Policy*. Stanford: Stanford University Press, 1952.
Winegard, Timothy. *The First Oil War*. Toronto – Buffalo: University of Toronto Press, 2016.
Winkler, Henry. *Paths Not Taken: British Labor and International Policy in the 1920s*. Chapel Hill – London: University of North Carolina Press, 1994.
Winkler, Henry. *British Labor Seeks a Foreign Policy, 1900-1940*. Chapel Hill – London: University of North Carolina Press, 2005.
Yakushin, E., and Polunin, S. *Angliiskaia interventsiia v 1918-1920 gg*. Moscow – Leningrad: Gosudarstvennoe izdatel'stvo, 1928.
Young, George. *Stanley Baldwin*. R. Hart-Davis, 1952.
Zarnitskii, S. V., and Sergeev, A. N. *Chicherin*. Molodaia gvardiia, 1968.
Zubachevsky, V. A. *Politika Rossii v otnoshenii vostochnoi chasti Evropy (1917-1923 gg.): geopoliticheskii aspect*. Omsk: Izdatel'stvo Omskogo gosudarstvennogo pedagogicheskogo universiteta, 2005.

Articles and contributions to collective works

Alston, Charlotte. 'International Intervention in Russia's Civil War: Policies, Experiencies, and Justifications'. In *Russian International Relations in War and Revolution, 1914-22*, ed. David Schimmelpenninck van der Oye et al., 273-99. Bloomington, IN: Slavica Publishers, 2021, bk 2.
Anderson, Edgar. 'The British Policy toward the Baltic States 1918-1920'. *Journal of Central European Affairs* 19, no. 3 (1959): 276-89.
Andrew, Christopher. 'The British Secret Service and the Anglo-Soviet Relations in the 1920's'. *Historical Journal* 20, no. 3 (1977): 673-706.
Andrew, Christopher. 'More on the Zinoviev Letter'. *Historical Journal* 22, no. 1 (1979): 211-14.
Arkhipova, E. V. 'Britanskii sled na Yuzhnom Kavkaze (1918-1919 gg.)'. *Novaia i noveishaia istoriia*, no. 3 (2016): 216-23.
Bondarevskaia, L. G. 'Anglo-iranskoe soglashenie 1919 g.' In *Problemy britanskoi istorii*, ed. V. G. Trukhanovsky, 81-94. Nauka, 1987.
Carr, Edward. 'The Zinoviev Letter'. *Historical Journal* 22, no. 1 (1979): 209-10.
Chossudovsky, Evgeny. 'Genoa Revisited: Russia and Coexistence'. *Foreign Affairs* 50, no. 3 (1972): 554-77.
Coolidge, A. C. 'Russia after Genoa and the Hague'. In *The Soviet Union, 1922-1962. A Foreign Affairs Reader*, ed. Philip Mosely, 3-24. New York – London: F. Praeger, 1963.
Cross, Anthony. 'A Corner of a Foreign Field: The British Embassy in St Petersburg 1863-1918'. *Slavonic and East European Review* 88, nos. 1-2 (2010): 328-58.
Crowe, Sybil. 'The Zinoviev Letter': A Reappraisal'. *Journal of Contemporary History* 10, no. 3 (1975): 407-32.
Damie, V. V. 'Mandiama Prativadi Bkhaiankara Tirumala Achariia: ot bol'shevisma k anarkhismu'. *Novoe literaturnoe obozrenie*, no. 5 (2017): 199-213.
Davidson, A. B. 'Obraz Britanii v Rossii XIX i XX stoletii'. *Novaia i noveishaia istoriia*, no. 5 (2005): 51-64.

Debo, Richard. 'Lockhart Plot or Dzerzhinskii Plot?' *Journal of Modern History* 47, no. 3 (1971): 413-39.
Debo, Richard. 'Litvinov and Kamenev – Ambassadors Extraordinary: The Problem of Soviet Representation Abroad'. *Slavic Review* 34, no. 3 (1975): 463-82.
Debo, Richard. 'Lloyd George and the Copenhagen Conference of 1919-1920: The Initiation of Anglo-Soviet Negotiations'. *Historical Journal* 24, no. 2 (1981): 429-41.
Demidov, S. V. 'Vneshniaia politika i diplomatiia Velikobritanii mezhdu dvumia mirovymi voinami'. In *Ocherki istorii Velikobritanii XVII – XX vv.*, ed. A. V. Nikitin, 158-207. Prometei, 2002.
Dilks, David. 'The British Foreign Office between the Wars'. In *Shadow and Substance in British Foreign Policy, 1895-1939: Memorial Essays Honoring C. J. Lowe*, ed. Brian Mackercher and David Moss, 181-204. Edmonton: University of Alberta Press, 1984.
Elcock, H. 'Britain and the Russo-Polish Frontier, 1919-1921'. *Historical Journal* 12, no. 1 (1969): 137-54.
Ferris, John. 'Far Too Dangerous a Gamble?' British Intelligence and Policy during the Chanak Crisis, September-October 1922'. In *Power and Stability: British Foreign Policy, 1865-1965*, ed. Erik Goldstein and Brian Mackercher, 139-84. F. Cass, 2003.
Ferris, John, and Bar-Joseph, Uri. 'Getting Marlowe to Hold His Tongue: The Conservative Party, the Intelligence and the Zinoviev Letter'. *Intelligence and National Security* 8, no. 4 (1993): 100-33.
Fink, Caroline. 'The NEP in Foreign Policy: The Genoa Conference and the Treaty of Rapallo'. In *Soviet Foreign Policy, 1917-1991. A Retrospective*, ed. Gabriel Gorodetsky, 11-20. F. Cass, 1994.
Fisher, John. '"On the Glacis of India": Lord Curzon and British Policy in the Caucasus, 1919'. *Diplomacy and Statecraft* 8, no. 2 (1997): 50-82.
Fisher, John. 'Interdepartmental Committee on Eastern Unrest and British Responses to Bolshevik and Other Intrigues against the Empire during the 1920s'. *Journal of Asian History* 34, no. 1 (2000): 1-34.
Foglesong, David. 'Xenophon Kalamatiano: An American Spy in Revolutionary Russia'. *Intelligence and National Security* 6, no. 1 (1991): 154-95.
Fomin, A. M. 'Derzhavy Ententy i Blizhnii Vostok v 1918-1923 gg.' *Novaia i noveishaia istoriia*, no. 4 (2010): 77-103.
Fomin, A. M. 'Voenno-politicheskie tseli Velikobritanii na zavershayutschem etape Pervoi mirovoi voiny'. *Novaia i noveishaia istoriia*, no. 3 (2012): 72-91.
Fuller, Howard. 'Great Britain and Russia's Civil War: The Necessity for a Definite and Coherent Policy'. *Journal of Slavic Military Studies* 32, no. 4 (2019): 553-9.
Glenny, Michael. 'The Anglo-Soviet Trade Agreement, March 1921'. *Journal of Contemporary History* 2, no. 2 (1970): 63-82.
Goldstein, Erik. 'The British Official Mind and the Lausanne Conference, 1922-23'. In *Power and Stability: British Foreign Policy, 1865-1965*, ed. Erik Goldstein and Brian Mackercher, 185-206. F. Cass, 2003.
Gorodetsky, Gabriel. 'The Other "Zinoviev Letters": New Light on the Mismanagement of the Affair'. *Slavic and Soviet Series* 1, no. 3 (1976): 135-47.
Grant, Natalie 'The "Zinoviev Letter" Case'. *Soviet Studies* 19, no. 2 (1967): 264-77.
Guard, J. 'The Royal Navy in the Caspian Sea 1918-1920' – Access available http://www.gwpda.org/naval/caspian.htm
Gurovich, P. V. 'Pervaia delegatsiia tred-unionov i leiboristskoi partii v Sovetskoi Rossii'. *Novaia i noveishaia istoriia*, no. 4 (1973): 71-7.

Gusterin, P. V. 'Politika Sovetskogo gosudarstva na musul'manskom Vostoke v 1917–1921 gg.' *Voprosy istorii*, no. 1 (2010): 92–100.

Haslam, Jonahtan. 'Litvinov, Stalin and the Road Not Taken'. In *Reexamining the Soviet Experience: Essays in Honor of Alexander Dallin*, ed. David Holloway and Norman Naimark, 55–62. Boulder, CO – Oxford: Westview Press, 1996.

Heywood, Anthony. 'Russian and Soviet Trade, 1914–28: Rethinking the Initial Impact of the Bolshevik Revolution'. In *Russian International Relations in War and Revolution, 1914–22*, ed. David Schimmelpenninck van der Oye et al., 395–414. Bloomington, Ind.: Slavica Publishers, 2021, bk 2.

Hughes, Michael. 'The Virtues of Specialization: British and American Diplomatic Reporting in Russia, 1921–39'. *Diplomacy and Statecraft* 11, no. 2 (2000): 79–104.

Hughes, Michael. 'From the February Revolution to the Treaty of Brest-Litovsk'. In *Russian International Relations in War and Revolution, 1914–22*, ed. David Schimmelpenninck van der Oye et al., 3–35. Bloomington, Ind.: Slavica Publishers, 2021, bk 2.

Ignatiev, A. V. '1917 god – politika Vremennogo pravitel'stva'. In *Ocherki istorii MID Rossii*, ed. A. V. Torkunov, 7–32. Mezhdunarodnye otnosheniia, 2002, vol. 2.

Ivanov, A. A. 'Russkaia revoliutsiia i konflikt v britanskom razvedyvatel'nom soobtschestve v 1917–1918 gg.' *Voprosy istorii*, no. 10 (2012): 150–6.

Ivanov, A. A. 'Britanskie spetssluzhby i diskussii vokrug sozdaniia antibol'shevistskoi koalitsii v 1918–1919 godakh'. *Novaia i noveishaia istoriia*, no. 3 (2019): 118–28.

Jeffrey, Keith, and Sharp, Alan. 'Lord Curzon and Secret Intelligence'. In *Intelligence and International Relations, 1900–1945*, ed. Christopher Andrew and John Noakes, 103–26. Exeter: University of Exeter Press, 1987.

Johnson, Gaynor. 'Preparing for Office: Lord Curzon as Acting Foreign Secretary, January – October 1919'. In *The Foreign Office and British Diplomacy in the Twentieth Century*, ed. Gaynor Johnson, 53–73. London – New York: Routledge, 2005.

Katouzian, H. 'The Campaign against the Anglo–Iranian Agreement of 1919'. *British Journal of Middle Eastern Studies* 25, no. 1 (1998): 5–46.

Kolonitsky, B. I. 'Britanskie missii i A. F. Kerensky (March–October 1917 goda)'. In *Rossiia v XIX–XX vv.*, ed. A. A. Fursenko, 67–76. St Petersburg: D. Bulavin, 1998.

Kozlov, V. P. 'Podlozhnye dokumenty Kominterna i Politburo TsK VKP(b)'. *Novaia i noveishaia istoriia*, no. 6 (1996): 23–44.

Kravchenko, V. F. 'Pervye shagi VCheka (novoe o zagovore Lockharta)'. *Sovetskoe gosudarstvo i pravo*, no. 3 (1967): 96–102.

Lavrov, S. V. 'Bor'ba v politicheskikh krugakh Velikobritanii vokrug anglo-sovetskikh peregovorov 1920–1921 gg.' *Voprosy istorii*, no. 6 (1977): 59–80.

Lavrov, S. V. 'Politika Anglii na Kavkaze i v Srednei Asii v 1917–1921 gg.' *Voprosy istorii*, no. 5 (1979): 78–92.

Lemon, Edward. 'Dunsterforce or Dunsterfarce? Re-Evaluating the British Mission to Baku, 1918'. *First World War Studies* 6, no. 2 (2015): 133–49.

Lim, Preston. 'Upon the Altar of British Prestige: A Re-Evaluation of Dunsterforce's Exploits and Legacy'. *Caucasus Survey* 5, no. 2 (2017): 103–20.

Listikov, S. V. 'Velikie derzhavy i "russkii vopros": resheniia Versal'skoi mirnoi konferentsii 1919–1920 godov i ikh posledstviia'. *Rossiiskaia istoriia*, no 5 (2011): 15–29.

Listikov, S. V. 'Missiia Williama Bullita v Sovetskuyu Rossiiu, 1919 g.' In *Amerikanskii ezhegodnik*, ed. V. V. Sogrin, 211–28. Ves' Mir, 2013.

Lobanov-Rostovsky, A. 'Anglo–Russian Relations through the Centuries'. *Russian Review* 12, no. 2 (1948): 41–52.

Lomas, Dan. 'The Zinoviev Letter'. *International Affairs* 95, no. 1 (2019): 201–6.

Long, John. 'Plot and Counterplot in Revolutionary Russia: Chronicling the Bruce Lockhart Conspiracy'. *Intelligence and National Security* 10, no. 1 (1995): 122–43.

Long, John. 'Searching for Sidney Reilly: The Lockhart Plot in Revolutionary Russia, 1918'. *Europe – Asia Studies* 47, no. 7 (1995): 1225–41.

Macfarlane, L. J. '"Hands off Russia": British Labour and the Russo-Polish War, 1920'. *Past and Present*, no. 38 (1968): 126–52.

Mackercher, Brian. 'Old Diplomacy and New: The Foreign Office and Foreign Policy, 1919–1939'. In *Diplomacy and World Power: Studies in British Foreign Policy, 1890–1950*, ed. Michael Dockrill and Brian Mackercher, 79–114. Cambridge: CUP, 1996.

Madeira, Victor. 'Moscow's Interwar Infiltration of British Intelligence 1919–1929'. *Historical Journal* 46, no. 4 (2003): 915–33.

Madeira, Victor. '"Because I Do Not Trust Him, We Are Friends": Signals Intelligence and the Reluctant Anglo–Soviet Embrace 1917–24'. *Intelligence and National Security* 19, no. 1 (2004): 29–51.

Martin, Thomas. 'The Urquhart Concession and Anglo-Soviet Relations, 1921–1922'. *Jaerbuecher fuer Geschichte Osteuropas* 20, no. 4 (1972): 551–70.

Morris, L. P. 'British Secret Missions in Turkestan, 1918–1919'. *Journal of Contemporary History* 12, no. 2 (1977): 363–79.

Neilson, Keith. 'Wishful Thinking: The Foreign Office and Russia, 1907–1917'. In *Shadow and Substance in British Foreign Policy, 1895–1939: Memorial Essays Honoring C.J. Lowe*, ed. Brian Mackercher and David Moss, 151–80. Edmonton: University of Alberta Press, 1984.

Neilson, Keith. 'Anglo-Russian Relations in the First World War'. In *Russian International Relations in War and Revolution, 1914–22*, ed. David Schimmelpenninck van der Oye et al., 147–70. Bloomington, Ind.: Slavica Publishers, 2021, bk 1.

Norris, D. 'Caspian Naval Expedition'. *Journal of the Central Asian Society* 10, pt. 1 (1923): 3–15.

Pearce, Brian. 'The 26 Commissars: On the Fate of the 26 Commissars'. In *Papers of the Sixth and Seventh International Conferences of the Study Group on the Russian Revolution*, 54–66, 83–95. Leeds: Leeds University Press, 1981.

Pipes, Richard. 'Unpublished Lenin'. In *The Bolsheviks in Russian* Society. *The Revolution and the Civil Wars*, ed. V. N. Brovkin, 201–11. New Haven – London: YUP, 1997.

Prokopov, A. Yu. 'Evropeiskoe napravlenie britanskoi vneshnei politiki v 1920-kh gg.' *Vestnik MGIMO-Universiteta*, no. 2 (2012): 112–19.

Sakhnovsky, E. V. 'Missiia Somerset Maughama v Rossiyu v 1917 g.' *Novaia i noveishaia istoriia*, no. 7 (1987): 173–86.

Scheffer, Peter. 'Maxim Litvinov: An Intimate Study'. *Current History* 34, no. 4 (1931): 670–7.

Sergeev, Evgeny. 'Great Britain and the Baltic States, 1918–22'. In *From Versailles to Munich: Twenty Years of Forgotten Wars*, ed. David Artico and Brunello Mantelli, 17–36. Wroclaw: UTET SpA, 2010.

Sergeev, Evgeny. 'Parizhskaia mirnaia konferentsiia v kontekste sovetsko-britanskikh otnoshenii, 1919–1920 gg.' In *Evropeiskie sravnitel'no-istoricheskie issledovaniia*, ed. A. A. Ulunian and E. Yu. Sergeev, 51–75. Institut vseobtschei istorii RAN, 2017.

Sergeev, E. Yu. 'Sovetsko-britanskie otnosheniia na rubezhe 1917–1918 gg.' *Vestnik Moskovskogo universiteta* 1, ser. 25, no. 1 (2018): 42–71.

Sergeev, E. Yu. 'Britaniia i nachalo interventsii v Rossii v pervoi polovine 1918 g.' *Rossiskaia istoriia*, no. 1 (2019): 43–59.

Sergeev, E. Yu. 'Russian Military Intelligence in the Coalition War, 1914–1918'. In *Russian International Relations in War and Revolution, 1914–22*, ed. David Schimmelpenninck van der Oye et al., 299–316. Bloomington, Ind.: Slavica Publishers, 2021, bk 1.

Sharp, Alan. 'Adapting to a New World? British Foreign Policy in the 1920's'. *Contemporary British History* 18, no. 3 (2004): 74–86.
Shubin, A. V. 'Bakinskaia kommuna i vozniknovenie Azerbaijanskoi respubliki: perekrestie faktorov'. In *Evropeiskie sravnitel'no-istoricheskie issledovaniia*, ed A. A. Ulunian and E. Yu. Sergeev, 4: 9–44. Institut vseobstchei istorii RAN, 2014.
Shubin, A. V. 'Latyshskie strelki mezhdu Rodinoi i revoliutsiei'. In *Rossiia i Latviia v potoke istorii: vtoraia polovina XIX – pervaia polovina XX v*, ed. E. L. Nazarova, 165–81. Institut vseobstchei istorii RAN, 2015.
Simonenko, R. G. 'Genuezskaia konferentsiia, Sovetskaia Rossiia i angliiskaia diplomatiia'. *Novaia i noveishaia istoriia*, no. 3 (1982): 92–110.
Smele, Jonathan. 'Mania grandiose and "The Turning Point in World History": Kerensky in London in 1918'. *Revolutionary Russia* 20, no. 2 (2007): 1–34.
Sokolov, A. S., and Golitsyn, Yu. P. 'Problema dorevoliutsionnogo dolga v sovetsko-britanskikh otnosheniyakh v 1920e gg.'. *Istoriya* 7, no. 2 (2016) – Access available http://www.history.jes.su
Soloviev, O. F. 'Iz istorii bor'by sovetskogo pravitel'stva za mirnoe sosustchestvovanie s Angliei'. *Voprosy istorii*, no. 12 (1965): 54–64.
Steiner, Zara. 'British Power and Stability: The Historical Record'. In *Power and Stability: British Foreign Policy, 1865–1965*, ed. Erik Goldstein and Brian Mackercher, 23–44. F. Cass, 2003.
Susloparova, E. A. 'George Lansbury (1859–1940). Stranitsy politicheskoi biografii lidera britanskikh leiboristov'. *Novaia i noveishaia istoriia*, no. 2 (2014): 179–97.
Swain, Geoffrey. '"An Interesting and Plausible Proposal": Bruce Lockhart, Sidney Reilly and the Latvian Riflemen, Russia 1918'. *Intelligence and National Security* 14, no. 3 (1999): 81–102.
Sweet, David. 'The Baltic in British Diplomacy before the World War First'. *Historical Journal* 13, no. 3 (1970): 451–90.
Ter Minassian, Taline. 'Some Fresh News about the 26 Commissars: Reginald Teague-Jones and the Transcaspian Episode'. *Asian Affairs* 45, no. 1 (2014): 65–78.
Ter Minassian, Taline. 'From the Transcaspian to the Caucasus: Reginald Teague-Jones's Secret War (1918–21)'. In *Russian International Relations in War and Revolution, 1914–22*, ed. David Schimmelpenninck van der Oye et al., 359–75. Bloomington, IN: Slavica Publishers, 2021, bk 2.
Tod, J. K. 'The Malleson Mission to Transcaspia in 1918'. *Journal of the Royal Central Asian Society* 27, no. 1 (1940): 15–40.
Tomaselli, P. 'C's Moscow's Station – The Anglo-Russian Trade Mission as Cover for SIS in the Early 1920s'. *Intelligence and National Security* 17, no. 3 (2002): 173–80.
Warman, R. 'The Erosion of Foreign Office Influence in the Making of Foreign Policy, 1916–1918'. *Historical Journal* 15, no. 1 (1972): 133–59.
Warth, Robert. 'The Mystery of the Zinoviev Letter'. *South Atlantic Quarterly* 49, no. 4 (1950): 441–53.
Waugh, Daniel. 'Britain Confronts the Bolsheviks in Central Asia: Great Game Myths and Local Realities'. In *Russian International Relations in War and Revolution, 1914–22*, ed. David Schimmelpenninck van der Oye et al., 341–58. Bloomington, Ind.: Slavica Publishers, 2021, bk 2.
Wheatcroft, S. G. 'Population Loses, 1914–22'. In *The Economic Transformation of the Soviet Union, 1913–1945*, ed. R. W. Davies et al., 57–80. Cambridge: CUP, 1994.
White, Christine. '"Riches Have Wings": The Use of Russian Gold in Soviet Foreign Trade, 1918–1922'. In *Contact or Isolation? Soviet-Western Relations in the Interwar Period*, ed.

John Hidden and Alexander Loit, 117–36. Uppsala: Stockholm University Centre for Baltic Studies, 1989.
White, Christine. 'The Gateway to Russia. The Baltic States as a Conduit for British and American Trade with Soviet Russia, 1918-1924'. In *Emancipation and Interdependence: The Baltic States as New Entities in the International Economy. 1918-1940*, ed. Anders Johansson et al., 41–62. Uppsala: Stockholm University Centre for Baltic Studies, 1994.
White, Stephen. 'British Labour and the Russian Revolution: The Labour Delegation to Russia, 1920'. In *Contact or Isolation? Soviet-Western Relations in the Interwar Period*, ed. John Hidden and Alexander Loit, 231–48. Uppsala: Stockholm University Centre for Baltic Studies, 1989.
Williams, A. 'The Genoa Conference of 1922: Lloyd George and the Politics of Recognition'. In *Genoa, Rapallo, and European Reconstruction in 1922*, ed. Caroline Fink et al., 29–47. Washington, DC – Cambridge: German Historical Institute – CUP, 1991.
Winegard, Timothy. 'Dunsterforce: A Case Study of Coalition Warfare in the Middle East, 1918-1919'. *Canadian Army Journal* 8, no. 3 (2005): 93–109.
Zdanovich, A. A. 'Latyshskoe delo. Nuansy raskrytiia zagovora poslov'. *Voenno-istoricheskii zhurnal*, no. 3 (2004): 23–32.

Unpublished dissertations and theses

Balbirnie, Steven. 'British Imperialism in the Arctic: The British Occupation of Archangel and Murmansk, 1918-1919'. PhD diss., University College Dublin, 2016.
Jeffrey, Keith. 'The Military Defence of the British Empire 1918-1922'. PhD diss., University of Cambridge, 1978.
Kopisto, Leo. 'The British Intervention in South Russia 1918-1920'. PhD diss., Academic Dissertation, University of Helsinki, 2011.
Long, John. 'Civil War and Intervention in North Russia, 1918-1920'. PhD diss., Columbia University, New York, 1972.
Madeira, Victor. 'British Official and Intelligence Responses to Soviet Subversion against the United Kingdom, 1917-1929'. PhD diss., University of Cambridge, 2008.
Mikhailov, V. V. 'Vostochnyi vopros i positsii Velikobritanii i Rossii v Pervoi mirovoi voine'. Avtoref. diss. kandidata istoricheskikh nauk, Sankt-Peterburgskii gosudarstvennṣ universitet, St Petersburg, 2010.
Mironiuk, S. A., Interventsiia v Rossiu v politicheskikh diskussiakh praviatshchikh krugov Velikobritanii (1917-1919 gg.)'. Avtoref. diss. kandidata istoricheskikh nauk, Rossiiskii gosudarstvennyi universitet druzhby narodov, 2021.
Morse, William. 'Leonid Borisovich Krasin: Soviet Diplomat, 1918-1926'. PhD diss., University of Wisconsin, Madison, 1971.
Shevchenko, D. V. 'Basmacheskoe dvizhenie. Politicheskie process i vooruzhennaia bor'ba v Srednei Asii. 1917-1931 gg.' Avtoref. diss. kandidadta istoricheskikh nauk, Irkutskii gosudarstvennyi pedagogicheskii universitet, Irkutsk, 2006.
Vasilenkova, O. V. 'Anglo-sovetskie otnosheniia v 1918-1921 gg.' Avtoref. diss. kandidata istoricheskikh nauk, Vladimirskii gosudarstvennyi pedagogicheskii universitet, Vladimir, 2007.
Yusupov, A. F. 'Anglo-Sovetskie ekonomicheski otnosheniia v 1921-1924 gg.' Avtoref. diss. kand. istoricheskikh nauk, Leningradskii gosudarstvennyi universitet, Leningrad, 1982.

Index

Aberdeen 18, 49
Admiralty 8, 15, 33, 43, 90–1, 135, 141
Afghanistan 53–4, 56, 58, 66–8, 110, 116–18, 126, 136, 139, 142, 146, 168
Africa 56, 109
Agar, Augustus 91
Agdzhagum desert 64
Ahmad, Shah 114
Aland Island 99
Alexander-Sinclair, Edwin 90
Alexeev, Michail 25
Algeria 112
Ali Fuad, Cebesoi 135
Allied: conferences (see Entente conferences); intervention (see Entente intervention); military plans (see Entente military plans); Supreme War Council (ASWC) 32, 34, 36
Allies (see Entente)
All-Russian: Central executive committee 18, 32, 41, 46, 91; Central congress of trade unions 163; congress of political propagandists (second) 126; congress of Soviets, second 8; fourth 20; sixth 52, 75; eighth 106; (National) Constituent Assembly 8, 10–11, 17, 46, 52, 79; Cooperative Society (ARCOS) 99–100
Amanullah, Emir 116–17, 126
'ambassadors plot' (see 'Lockhart plot')
America (see United States)
American Relief Administration (ARA) 50, 124
Amery, Leo 6, 20, 141
Amritsar 117
Anatolia 110, 112
Andrei Pervozvannyi 91
Anglo-Afghan: treaty of 1921 126; war of 1919 116–17
Anglo-Indian troops (riflemen) 56
Anglo-Persian agreement of 1919 114

Anglo-Russian convention of 1907 5, 168
Anglo-Russian Oil Company 134
Anglo-Russian trade chamber 149
Anglo-Soviet trade agreement of 1921 107, 136, 144
Ankara (Angora) 112, 134, 145
anti-Bolshevik resistance 10–11, 15, 19, 30, 33, 37, 39, 41, 43, 47, 71, 85, 123
Arab: people 58; territories 54
Argentina 165
Arkhangelsk 11, 21, 25–6, 28, 34–7, 44, 76, 82, 84, 93; province 24, 34; railroad 30; Soviet 24, 36
Armed Forces of Southern Russia (AFSR) 80–1
Armenia 65, 121
Armenians 58, 60, 111
Armour, Henry 45
Armstrong 105
Army of God 69; of Islam 61; of Liberty 78
Asahi 31
Aseev, Nikolai 53
Ashgabat: 38, 62, 64, 113; government 61–2, 64–5, 113
Asia: 5, 21, 31, 53, 61, 68, 72, 106–7, 109–10, 114, 118, 121, 144; Central 54, 61, 66, 75, 79, 123, 135, 168, 170
Asquith, Herbert 157
Association of British creditors of Russia 141
Astoria 49
Astrakhan 59, 63
Atlantic ocean 135
Australia 31
Austria 92, 101, 124, 150
Austria-Hungary 15
Austrian contingents 13; front 7
Aysors 58
Azerbaijan 55, 65, 111, 115, 121
Azerbaijans 111
Azov Sea 81

Baghdad 58
Bailey, Frederick 56, 68; intelligence mission to Soviet Turkestan 66–8
Bairam-Ali 66
Baker, Newton 37
Baku 37, 55, 59–63, 111–12, 115, 121, 143
Baku–Batum railroad 71, 111, 116
Baku commissars 62, 142; execution of twenty-six 53–5
Baku: Commune (SNK) 55–6, 59, 65; oil fields 116; Soviet 59–60
Baldwin, Francis 147; Stanley 40, 129, 144, 162–3
Balfour, Arthur 6, 12, 18, 45, 64–5, 72–3, 87, 89–90, 92, 95, 168
Baltic: area 89, 110, 153; League 90–4; problem 89–93; provinces 43; Sea 18, 27, 33, 79, 84, 90, 92, 135; states 84, 89–90; theatre of the First World War 25
Bank of England 113, 155
Baratov, Nikolai 58
Barkatullah, Mohammed 67, 118
Barter, Charles 12
Batum (Batumi) 55, 93, 111
Beatty, David 98, 115
Beau Rivage
Becos 157
Bedford 12
Bednyi, Demian 139
Belarus (Belorussia) 15, 91, 94, 96, 140
Belgium 95, 147
Belomor-Onega Republic (see Russian Northern Federation)
Belomor region 34
Belyi Sea 37
Benares 119
Bengal province 69
Berberova, Nina 19
Bergen 49
Berlin 7, 9, 18, 25, 35, 56, 67, 69, 101, 142
Bermondt-Avalov, Pavel 92–3
Berthelot, Henri 27
Bertie, Francis 12, 17, 29
Berzin, Edward 44, 46; Janis 125–6, 141, 144
Bessarabia 13, 18, 142, 156
Bialystok 94, 101
Bicherakhov, Lasar 58–60, 63, 110–11

Bilduri 93
Birkinhead, Lord 73
Birmingham 104, 143
Bismarck, Otto 19, 72
Black Sea 27, 56, 61, 81, 84, 93, 111–12, 135; Federation 81; Straits (see also Bosporus and Dardanelles) 135–7, 142, 153, 157
Blacker, Latham 66–7
Blagoveshchensk 140
Board of Trade 29–30, 54, 98, 130, 144
Boil, George 28
Bokhara: Emir of 67; Emirate of 54, 62, 66, 110, 117
Bokharian People's Republic 119
Bolshevik: annulment of foreign debts 25; concept of international relations 9; dictatorship 1; geopolitical interests 110; government (see Council of People's Commissars); Higher Military Council 20; local Soviets 34, 39; party 5, 32–3, 55, 77; party Politburo 107, 134, 139, 145, 154, 157, 162–3; propaganda in the UK 104–5; smuggling diamonds and jewelleries to the UK 103–4; Supreme revolutionary tribunal 50
Bolshevism 58, 73–4, 90, 105, 107, 112, 139, 167
Bombay 69, 118
Bonar Law, Andrew 95, 99, 106, 135, 141, 144
Bonch-Bruevich, Vladimir 42
Borden, Robert 75–6
Bosporus 6, 135
Botha, Louis 75
Brailsford, Henry 150
Bravin, Nikolai 67, 117
Brazil
Brest peace treaty 5, 21, 23, 31, 33, 38–9, 53–5, 58–9, 71, 89, 131
Brest-Litovsk (Brest) 94; negotiations in 11–12, 15–16, 18–20
Bright, John 161
Britain (see also British Empire, British Isles, Great Britain, United Kingdom) 1–2, 5, 10, 12, 15, 17, 22, 24, 29, 32, 35, 37, 43, 50, 54, 72, 79–80, 82, 86, 89–90, 97, 103,

106, 109, 111, 115, 121, 123, 125, 127, 129, 137, 152, 154, 167–70; aid to White armies 80; Anti-Famine relief committee 124–5; Cabinet (see British government); chemical weapons 82; Committee to help fight famine in Russia 124; Committees of action 143; Conservative (Unionist) party (see also Tories) 151, 164; Empire (see Britain); expenditure on intervention in Russia 84; Federation of industries 157; Friends' emergency and war victims committee 125; government 5–6, 8, 10, 24, 28–9, 40, 49–50, 55, 62, 69, 81, 95, 102, 115, 121, 131, 141, 149, 162–3, 167–70; Government School of Codes and Ciphers (GC&CS) 134; House of Commons (see Parliament); House of Lords (see Parliament); Imperial conference of 1921 139; Imperial (General) Staff 56, 61, 75, 115; Imperial war relief fund 125; intervention 'by agreement' 23–38, 66; Independent Labour party (ILP) 97; Labor party (LP) 5, 17, 95, 97, 102, 141, 143, 150–1, 153; Liberal party 6, 151, 157, 161–2, 164; Mediterranean Fleet squadron 94, 135; military counter-intelligence (MI5) 2, 9, 78, 100, 103, 105, 159, 164–5; military intelligence (MI6) 7, 9, 39–40, 42, 48, 51, 67, 135, 140, 149, 161, 163–5; military mission to Poland in 1920 102; national archives 2; Naval Staff 115; North Atlantic Squadron 25; Parliament (see also House of Commons and House of Lords, Westminster) 67, 79–80, 85, 107–8, 141, 157–9, 162–3; Raj (see India); recognition of Soviet Russia (USSR) 18–19, 151–66, 168; Royal Air Forces 116; Royal Navy 108; Save the children fund 125; Social Democratic Federation of 104; Society for cultural relations with the USSR 150; Society of the friends of the USSR 150; submarines 18, 33; Trade Chamber 158; trawlers 140–1; troops evacuation from Russia 84, 87, 112–13
British Agent 50
Briusov, Valerii 150
Brock, Osmond 135
Bronsky, Mikhail 30
Brussels 125
Buchanan, George 6–8, 10–11, 14, 25, 52
Buchanan, Meriel 45
Budkievicz, Konstantin 140
Bukharin, Nikolai 134
Bulak-Balakhovich, Stanislav 105
Bulgaria 75, 81
Bullitt, William, diplomatic mission to Soviet Russia 78–9
Butyrka prison 140

C. (see Smith-Cumming, Mansfield)
Calcutta 119
Campbell, John (case) 157–8
Canada 28; General Staff 75
Cannes 127, conference 128
Canterbury 125, 140
Caporetto 7
Cardiff 161
Carson, Edward 14
Caspian: Military Flotilla (Red) 60, 93, 114; Naval Flotilla (White) 113, 115
Caspian Sea 56, 58, 61–2, 81, 110–11, 113
Caucasus 13, 55, 81, 84, 110, 116, 135; front 53
Cave, George 17
Caxton-Hall 14
Cecil, Robert 10–11, 15, 17, 21, 26, 29, 33, 52, 54, 72–3
Cecil-Milner memorandum 13
Central Asian railroad 61–2
Central Caspian dictatorship (government) 60–1, 63, 110, 113
Central executive committee of Siberian Soviets 30–1
Central powers (empires) 7, 10, 12, 15, 18, 21, 32, 38–41, 43
Central Rada 30
Central Union of Russian consumer societies 86
Ceylon 118

Chaikin, Vadim 64–5
Chaikovsky, Nikolai 37, 85
Chalon 101
Chamberlain, Austen 47, 72–4, 95, 104, 125, 130, 154, 162–3
Chamberlain, Hilda 47
Chanak crisis 134
Chandpur 119
Chechnya 116
Cheka (VCheka, OGPU) 31, 38–40, 43, 45–51, 64, 67, 103, 140, 154, 165
Chelmsford, Frederick 56, 61, 65, 113, 117
Chelyabinsk 34
Chesham House 17
Chicherin, Georgy 16, 18, 21, 26, 30, 34–5, 38, 47, 52, 54, 64–5, 75, 77, 85–6, 95–7, 100, 103, 107, 110–11, 116, 120, 124–5, 127–33, 135–7, 139, 142–5, 149–50, 153, 157, 162–3
China 54, 119–20, 146–7
Chinese (Eastern) Turkestan 119–20, 168
Chinese; military volunteers 47; revolution of 1925–7 120
Chita 69
Churchill, Winston 5–6, 10, 12, 18, 27–8, 47, 72–4, 77–8, 80, 82, 84–8, 90–5, 98, 103–7, 111–12, 129, 133, 137, 168
Cieplak, Jan 140
Clarke, William 30
Clemenceau, George 13, 76, 85
Clive, Robert 92
Cohran 26
Cold War 2; mythology 23
Committee for the Salvation of Motherland and Revolution 8
Committee of Imperial Defense (CID) 98
Committee of India independence 67
Compiegne armistice 23, 69, 71, 76
complot of ambassadors (see Lockhart plot)
Communist International (Comintern) 97–8, 110, 115–17, 126, 135, 139, 142–3, 146, 149, 154, 156, 161–2, 164, 168–9; Central Asian bureau 118; letter to British Communists (see 'Zinoviev letter')
Communist International of trade unions (Red Profintern) 97, 169
Communist party of Great Britain (CPGB) 102–3, 105, 119, 121, 154, 163–6

Communist university for the toilers of the East 116, 119
Constantinople 54, 110, 126, 135, 137
Copenhagen 85
Cossacks: of the Don 10, 58; Kuban 10, 58; Orenburg 66–7; Terek 58
Council of People's commissars (SNK) (see also Bolshevik government) 5, 8–10, 17–18, 20–21, 25–7, 30, 32, 35, 38, 40, 42, 53, 65, 68, 100, 103, 107, 125–7, 131–2, 134, 141–4, 146–7, 161–2, 167–70
Cowan, Walter 91
Cox, Percy 114
Crew-Milnes, Robert 147
Crimea (Crimean Peninsula) 13, 33, 93–6, 100, 105
Crimean-Cossack Federation (see Black Sea Federation)
Cromie, Francis 8, 33, 38, 40, 42, 44–5, 51; murder of 47–50, 72
Crowe, Eire 136, 144, 159–60, 165
Curzon, George 5, 14, 18, 54, 72, 82–3, 85, 90–2, 95, 98–9, 104–7, 111–16, 124–9, 133–47, 149, 168
'Curzon line' 94, 96, 101, 105
Curzon ultimatum: 138, 140–6; protests against 143
Czechoslovak: legion 30, 32–3, 38, 80; national committee 34
Czechoslovakia 96, 124

D'Abernon, Edgar 102
Daily Chronicle 165
Daily Express 72
Daily Herald 17, 103–4, 127, 161, 164
Daily Mail 78–9, 104, 160–1, 165
Daily Telegraph 7, 12, 80, 134
Dandy 143
Dardanelles 75, 135
Davidson, George 164
Davison, Charles 140, 144–5
Dawes plan 151
Declaration of Fourteen Points 14
Delhi 55, 67–9, 119
Denikin, Anton 78, 80–1, 84, 86, 93–4, 113, 124
Dickens, Charles 16
Dobbs, Henry 126

Don region 10, 81
Donbass 28
Druzhkin, Sergei 63
Dunsterforce (see also Hush Hush brigade) 58-61
Dunsterville, Lionel 37-8, 56-7, 68, 110; mission to Persia 56-62
Dushak 113
Dutch Red Cross 76
Dutov, Aleksander 67
Dyer, Reginald 117
Dzerzhinsky, Felix 31-2, 41-2, 44, 47-8, 51, 142, 162, 165
'Dzerzhinsky plot' (see 'Lockhart plot')
Dzungar republic 120

East: Far 30-3, 37, 69, 75, 109, 120, 14, 147, 170; Galicia 142; Middle 13, 53-4, 56, 58, 61, 66, 106, 109, 111, 113-14, 116-18, 137-8, 145, 147, 168; Near 53, 109, 112, 116, 127, 134, 137-8; Prussia 92
Eastern; Anatolia 53; Committee 54, 58, 113; front 6, 9, 11, 27, 31-2
Egypt 53, 124, 142
Eichhorn, Hermann von 37
Ekaterinburg 44
Ekaterinodar 76, 81
Ekonomicheskaia Zhizn 105
Engelgardt (Bredis) 44
England (see United Kingdom)
English club 46
Entente 5, 11, 15, 19, 23, 29, 32, 38, 56, 58, 71, 77, 81, 95, 107, 123, 125, 132, 137, 167-70; aid to White armies 80, 92; conferences 7, 31; cooperation with Soviet Russia 20-1, 26-7; diplomatic corps evacuation from Russia 20; diplomatic missions in Russia 32-4, 39; governments 13, 52, 83, 87, 102, 111; intervention against Russia 1, 8, 24, 30, 34, 39, 45, 50, 54, 69, 77, 154, 157, 167; (Inter-Allied) commission on the Baltic problem 91, 94; military plans 8; strategic position 6; Supreme economic council 86, 124-5, 127; Supreme (military) council 75, 85; troops evacuation from Russia 84
Enver, Pasha 120-1

Enzeli 58-60, 93, 111, 114-15
Esher, Reginald 79, 87
Estonia 83, 90, 93
Etherton, Percy 66-7, 120
Europe 9, 11-12, 23, 39, 56, 72, 75-6, 78, 83, 88, 93-4, 100, 104, 106-7, 121, 124, 148, 152, 167
Evening Standard 134, 147

fatwa 112
Far East Democratic Republic 120
Ferghana valley 56
Fersman, Alexander 150
Figaro 41, 51
Finland 20, 25-6, 72, 79, 83, 93, 95
Finnish Gulf 33, 91
Finns 92
First Latvian light artillery battalion 44
First Light cruiser squadron 90-1
First World War 1, 5, 9, 14, 19, 24, 27, 38, 49, 53-4, 66, 90, 97, 168
Flanders 66
Foch, Ferdinand 78, 95
Foreign Office 6, 9, 11, 14-15, 17, 19, 24, 35, 45, 49, 54, 63, 66, 77, 79, 81, 89, 95, 108, 112-13, 115, 125-6, 129, 136-7, 141, 144-7, 149-52, 154, 159-65
France (see also Third republic): 11-12, 28-9, 35, 37, 40, 43, 72, 86, 90, 97, 100, 108, 111-12, 124-5, 129, 137, 147, 154; military mission to Russia 20
Francis, David 36, 40
Fride, Alexander 43, 50
Frunze, Mikhail 113
Funtikov, Feodor 61-2, 113

Gallipoli 66
Gandhi, Mahatma 68, 119
Ganges 126
Gaudiz, Semion 63
Gavriil 91
Geneva: 135, 153; protocol 151, 156
Genoa conference; preparations 127-30; sessions 130-3, 167
George V 6, 45, 95, 100, 105-6, 130, 153, 156, 162
Georgians 111

Germany 6–7, 9–11, 15, 20, 27, 31, 40, 46–7, 52–3, 75–6, 78, 83, 91, 96–7, 101, 120, 124, 130, 140, 147, 165; armed intervention in Russia 11, 20, 30, 32; General Staff of 26; naval blockade of 6; submarines 6; subsides for the Bolsheviks 17; troops 6, 13, 24–6, 28, 33, 42, 56, 89
Gibraltar 113
Gillian (republic) 114
Gladstone, William 161
Glasgow 72
Glory 26
Gorky, Maxim 10, 124, 168
Gorsk republic 110
Gough, Hugh 91
Grabski, Vladislav 96
Grant, Hamilton 55
Great Britain (see Britain)
Great Game 53, 117, 121, 167
Great Turan 13
Great War (see First World War)
Greco-Catholic hierarchy 140
Greco-Turkish war 119, 134
Greece 112, 136
'Greens' 95
Gregorian calendar 2
Gregory, John 141, 144–5, 147, 150, 152, 156–7, 159–60
Grenard, Joseph Fernand 37, 45, 50
Grodno 94
Guomindang party 119
Gypsies 81

Habibullah, Emir 116
The Hague: 133; conference in 133–4, 167
Haller, Stanislav 96
Hamadan 58–9
Hampshire infantry regiment 62
'Hands off Russia' committees 72, 102, 104, 127, 143
Hankey, Maurice 73, 98, 102, 130
Harbin 31
Harding, Stan 140, 144–5
Headlam-Morley, James 12
Helfferich, Karl 37, 43
Helsinki (Helsingfors) 8, 25, 93
Henderson, Arthur 141, 150
Hill, George 9, 27–8, 42, 46

Hindustan (see India)
Hoare, Samuel 27
Hodgson, Robert 65, 108, 140–4, 168
Hollman, Herbert 82
Hollywood 50
Home Office 16, 159
Hong Kong 37, 119
Hopkirk, Peter 62, 68
Horne, Robert 98, 106–7, 127, 129, 133
House of Commons (see Britain, Parliament)
House of Lords (see Britain, Parliament)
Hughes, William 73, 75
Huns 101
Hungary 96, 110
Hush-Hush brigade (see Dunsterforce)

Ili, protocol of 120
Incitement to mutiny act of 1797 159
India (see also, British Raj, Hindustan) 5, 21, 53–4, 58, 61, 66–9, 117–20, 139, 142, 167; Bolshevik plans for insurrection in 68, 109, 118; Chelmsford–Montagu reforms in 68–9; Communist party of 119; North-West Frontier Province of 67, 115; Provisional government of 67, 119
India Office 54, 61, 63, 69, 113, 119, 164
Indian Army Main Staff 56
Indian Ocean 117
Indo-British society 69
Inkpin, Albert 161, 164
Intergovernmental commission for famine rescue 124
International famine relief committee 124
Ioffe, Adolf 35, 120
Iran (see Persia)
Iraq 58, 112, 115–16, 121, 135
Ireland 127
Irish: crisis 106; liberation (national) movement 104, 141
Irkutsk 31, 37
Ironside, William 30, 77
Islam 111, 118, 129
Islam and Bolshevism 118
Italy 6, 11, 37, 86, 96, 101, 112, 129; army 7
Ivami 31
Izvestiia 29, 39, 48, 65, 142, 153–4, 162

Jacobins 49
Jalalabad 116
Jallianwala Bagh massacre 117
Japan 37, 53-4, 68, 78, 121; intervention in Russia 20, 31-2, 35-6
Jarvis, T. 63
Jelgava 91
Jews 81
jihad 56
Journal of the Central Asian Society 66
Judas Iscariot 161

Kaakha 62
Kabul 69, 109, 116-18, 139, 142, 145-6
Kaiser (see William II)
Kalamatiano, Xenophon 45, 49-50
Kaledin, Alexei 10-11
Kamchatka republic 33
Kamenev, Lev 49, 97, 100, 129, 151, 155-7; mission to Britain in 1918 17-18; 1920 100-5
Kanegisser, Leonid 46
Karakhan, Lev, Deputy People's commissar 16, 54, 65, 115-16, 135; plenipotentiary to China 145, 147
Karakorum desert 119
Karelia 25, 34
Kashgar 66-7, 118; republic 120
Kazan 38
Kazvin 59
Kedrov, Mikhail 35-8
Kem 36, 46
Kemal, Mustapha 112, 119, 134-5
Kemp, Thomas 25-6, 34
Kerensky, Alexander 6-8, 10, 12, 35, 42, 75
Kerr, Philip 18, 36, 78
Keyes, Terence 10
Keynes, John 29, 131-3
Khabarovsk 140
Kharkov 82, 143
Khaybar Pass 119
Khiva Khanate 54, 62, 66, 110, 117, 125
Khorasan province 61
Kiev 19, 24, 30, 32
Kinmochu, Shionji 76
Kipling, Rudyard 56
Kizyl-Arvat 64
Klyshko, Nikolai 125, 141
Knox, Alfred 12, 79-80

Kola Peninsula 34
Kolchak, Alexander 75, 78-80, 83, 124
Kolomiitsev, Ivan 67
Korea 140
Kornev (Black) 165
Kornilov, Lavr 6, 25, 80
Kotlas 25
Krasnaia Gazeta 46
Krasnovodsk 60, 62-4, 113
Krassin, Leonid 9, 29, 84, 98-107, 125-9, 132-4, 142-5, 153-4, 157
Krassina, Lubov 145
Kremlin (see Council of People's Commissars)
Krestinsky, Nikolai 133
Kronstadt 33, 91
Kropotkin, Petr 97
Krupp, Friedrich
Kuban region 81, 110-11
Kuchik Khan, Mirza 56, 114
Kudashev, Nikolai
kuli 27
Kuelmann, Richard 35
Kuldja 120
Kurdistan 54, 112
Kurds 58
Kyshtym area 29

Lansbury, George 12, 103, 157
Lansdowne, Henry 6-7
Lansing, Robert 31
Lasi 10
Latsis, Martin 39, 41
Latvia 43, 83, 90, 93, 96, 165
Latvian: Club 44; National committee 44; rifle division 45-6; riflemen 27, 33, 36, 43, 45; troops 92
Lausanne conference 134-8, 142-3
League of Nations 78-9, 93, 95-6, 124-5, 135, 156; General Assembly 131, 151
Leeds Convention of 1917 5
Leeper, Reginald 17-18
Lemnos 81
Lena area 29
Lena Goldfields Company 125-6, 134
Lenin, Vladimir 5, 7-10, 15-17, 20, 24-5, 27, 32-4, 36, 41-3, 46, 51-2, 54, 60, 68, 75, 77-8, 83, 91, 93,

96, 98, 101, 106, 109–10, 115–16, 118, 120–1, 123, 129–30, 148, 151; death of 153, 168
Liepaja 90
Lieven, Anatoly 92
Lindley, Francis 14, 19, 25, 36
Lithuania 6, 83, 90–1, 94, 96
Little Entente 93
Litvinov, Maxim, plenipotentiary to Britain 15–16, 21; deputy People's commissar 49, 54, 77, 85–7, 100, 103, 126, 128, 141, 155, 168
Litvinov–O'Grady agreement 85–6, 99, 140
Liverpool 143
Lloyd George, David 5–7, 12–15, 18–19, 28, 30–1, 35–6, 40, 54, 71–6, 78–9, 82–7, 89, 94–6, 98–103, 105–7, 111–12, 114–15, 125–33, 138, 141, 151, 157, 161
Lloyd-Graeme, Philip 130, 134, 144
Lockhart, Robert Bruce 13–14, 19, 22, 31; diplomatic mission to Soviet Russia 14–15, 17–18, 20–1, 27–9, 32, 34–8; 'plot' (see also 'ambassadors plot', 'Dzerzhinsky plot') 38–52
London 1–2, 8, 10–11, 14–15, 17–19, 21, 23–4, 28–31, 35–6, 38–9, 45, 47, 50, 53, 55, 60–1, 64, 66–9, 75, 80, 84, 86–8, 90, 93–5, 98, 105, 117, 119, 121, 130–2, 13, 141–5, 149–50, 154, 164, 168, 170; Guildhall 84
Long, Walter 90, 95
Lord Astor 141
Low, Ivy 16
Lozovsky, Solomon 169
Lubyanka prison 49, 140

Macartney, George 66
Macdonald, James Ramsay 5, 142, 150–61, 168–9
Macdonell, Ronald 60
Macdonough, George 73
Mackinder, Halford 81
Macmanus, Arthur 161, 164
Macneill, Ronald 140–1, 144
Main committee on economic concessions 156
Maisky, Ivan 109

Makhachkala (Petrovsk) 110
Maklakov, Vasiliy 17
Malleson, Wilfrid 38, 56–7, 61, 65, 67–9; intelligence mission to Persia 61–3, 112–13
Mal'kov, Petr 41
Malta 81
Manchester 104
Manchester Guardian 6, 30, 114, 133, 161; *Commercial* 133
Manchuria 140
Manifest of the peoples of the East 121
Mannerheim, Karl 25
Marchand, Réne 41
Marchlevski, Julian 96
Marconi 105
Marlow, Thomas 165
Marne, battle on 102
Marr, Nikolai 150
Marx, Karl 161
Mary (see Merv)
Mashhad 61–3, 67–8, 112
Masterton-Smith, James 125
Maugham, William Somerset 7, 32
Maximalists (see Bolsheviks)
Maynard, Charles 37, 77
Mediterranean Sea 135
Memel (Klaipeda) 142
Merv (Mary) 62, 66, 113
Mesopotamia 56 (see Iraq)
Mexico 68
Meynell, Francis 103
Middlesex Royal regiment 37
Midland Bank 157
Miliukov, Pavel 89, 118
Miller, Evgeny 82
Millerand, Alexander 95
Milner, Alfred 12, 14–15, 24, 27, 29, 35, 72
Mirbach-Harff, Wilhelm von 33, 36–7, 43
Mittel Europa 13
Moffat, Jay 101
Molotov-Ribbentrop pact 22
Monsoon islands 6
Montagu, Edwin 73, 75, 95
Morel, Edmund 157
Morning Post 7, 69, 147, 165
Moscow 2, 8–10, 22, 27, 29–32, 35–6, 38–40, 43, 50, 56, 62, 66, 68, 71, 77–9, 82, 84–8, 94, 97–8, 101, 103–5, 111–12,

114–15, 117–18, 120, 127, 130–2, 134, 140–5, 148, 150, 155–7, 164, 167, 170; military district 46; municipal conference 33; People's Bank 16; province executive committees 83; Soviet 46
Mosul 135
Mudanya 134
Mudros armistice 110
Murmansk 11, 25, 28, 30–1, 34, 36–7, 40, 44, 84, 93, 140; railroad 27, 30, 36; Soviet 24–6, 31, 34, 36
Murphy, George 97
Mussolini, Benito 135

Nabokov, Konstantin 7, 17, 85
Nagorno-Karabakh 65
Nansen, Fridtjof 124
National Liberation Federation 156
National Minority Movement 97, 157
Natsarenus, Sergei 34, 36
Netherlands 47
Neva 46
New Hampshire regiment 37
New York 125
New York Times 12
Newcastle 143
Nicholas II 8, 31, 142
Nile 126
Nineteenth Punjab infantry regiment 62
Nizhny Novgorod 97
NKID (see People's Commissariat for foreign affairs)
North Persian Force 61
Northern Dvina-river 37; front 82
Northern province 82
Nottingham 17, 143
Noulens, Joseph 7–8, 23, 25, 32, 34, 36, 40
Novgorod 33
Novocherkassk 10, 25
Novorossiisk 71–2, 81, 93
Nuorteva, Santori 146

Odessa 33, 39, 84
Ogorodnikov, Feodor 35
OGPU (see Cheka, VCheka)
O'Grady, James 85–6, 168
Oleg 91
Olonetsk province 24

O'Malley, Edward 141
Omsk 34, 76, 80
Onega 37
Orient (see also East) 11, 56, 109, 117; First congress of the peoples of 65, 115, 121
Orlando, Vittorio 76
Orlov, Alexandr 165
Ottoman empire (see also Turkey) 53–4, 69, 76, 110, 112, 116–17, 121, 124, 134–5, 138, 146; troops 6, 13, 29, 59, 63, 113

Pacific region 120
Padererewski, Ignatius 85
Pahlavi, Reza Khan
Palestine 115
Pamiat' Azova 91
Pamir 139
pan-Arabism 110
pan-Turkism 110
Paris 7, 10–11, 15, 28, 39, 41, 47, 51, 75, 78–9, 84, 86, 92, 124; Council of Ten 76, 84; peace conference 71–86, 91, 93–4, 109, 111, 115, 130, 167
Patek, Stanislav 94
Pates, Konstantin 93
Pavlovich, Mikhail 110
Peking 31, 146, 169
Penza 34
People's commissariat; for foreign affairs (NKID) 9, 14, 29, 31, 33–4, 36, 38, 49, 52, 68, 75, 77, 100, 105, 117–18, 125–6, 135, 140–4, 146, 156–60; for nationalities 31, 54, 118; of trade and industry 30; for war and naval affairs 42
People's Socialist Revolutionary party 37
Persia (Iran) 53–4, 58–9, 61–2, 66–7, 99, 110–11, 113–15, 117, 121, 136, 142, 168
Persian Cossack brigade 114
Persian Gulf 119
Persian Red Army 114
Persian Soviet Socialist Republic 56
Peshawar 119
Peters, Yakov 41, 44, 49–51
Petliura, Simon 94

Pettit, William 78
Petrograd (St Petersburg) 1, 6–11, 13–14, 17–21, 24, 27, 33, 35–6, 38–9, 41, 43–7, 51, 53, 62, 78–9, 84, 92, 97, 140, 145; military district 46; Smolensk cemetery 48; Soviet 48
Petrograd Pravda 49
Petropavlovsk 91
Pickwick 16
Pilsudki, Joseph 93, 95–6, 101, 140
Poincaré, Raymond 135
Pokrovsky, Ivan 165
Poland 6, 10, 72, 79, 81, 85, 90, 93, 95–6, 101–2, 108, 110, 124, 130, 165; Greater, plans of 93–4, 140
Polish: problem 100, 103; Provisional revolutionary committee 96, 101; troops 95, 102
Pollitt, Harry 158–9
Pollock, Francis 84
Ponsonby, Arthur 150, 155–60
Poole, Dewitt Clinton 45
Poole, Frederick 25–6, 34–5, 37
Poti 56
POWs (prisoners-of-war): Austrian 27–8, 56, 61–2, 66–7; Czech 32–3, 66; German 11, 56, 61–2, 66–7; Hungarian 27, 34, 56; Russian 27, 84–5, 123–4; Slovak 32–3
Pratap, Maharana 118
Pravda 39, 48
Preston, Thomas 143
Price, Morton 24, 30, 71
Prinkipo (Principe Islands) conference 76, 85
Prussian militarism 28
Przemysl 94
Pskov 33
Poincaré, Raymond 41
Punjab province 69
Purcell, Albert 157
Pushkin, Alexander 19

Quadruple Alliance: 6, 32, 58, 75; peace talks with 5, 11
Queen's Hall 161

Radcliffe, Percy 102
Radek, Karl 36, 49, 142, 162

Rakovski, Christian 148–51, 153–62, 165, 168
Ransome, Arthur 36, 142
Rapallo agreement 131
Rasht 56, 114
Raskol'nikov, Feodor, Commander of the Caspian Military Flotilla 115; plenipotentiary to Afghanistan 126, 139
Rava-Russkaya 94
Ravnina 113
Red Army 27–8, 44, 49, 77–8, 81–2, 92, 94–6, 100–2, 105, 111, 117, 120–1, 156
Red Caucasian army 59
Red Cross: British 125; Danish 85; Dutch 76; International 85, 124
Red guards 8–9, 17, 19, 25, 27, 30, 33, 35, 41, 61–2, 66, 82
'Red letter' (see 'Zinoviev letter')
Red Profintern (see Communist International of trade unions)
Red terror 41, 46, 51–2
Reilly, Sidney 39–40, 42, 44–51, 164
Reuter, Ernst
Revel (Tallinn) 35, 85, 89–90, 95
Reza Khan Pahlavi 114
Riddell, George 86
Riga 6, 89–90, 92–3, 124, 164–5
Romania 31, 75, 81, 85, 96, 130
Romanian troops 18, 156
Rome 13, 47, 153
Romanov, Mikhail 31
Roosevelt, Theodore 28
Rostov-on-the Don 33, 81
Rothstein, Theodore 49, 126
Round Table 6
Roy, Manabendra 68, 119
Royal Central Asian Society 68
Royal Geographical Society 66
Rumbold, Horatio 102
Ruhr crisis 141
Russell, Bertrand 97
Russia (see also Soviet Union, USSR): 1, 5, 8–9, 11–13, 20, 22–3, 27–9, 31–2, 38, 42–3, 45, 50, 54, 64, 68–9, 72–3, 79, 82–3, 86–7, 89–91, 96–7, 103, 106, 111, 121, 123, 135, 138, 146, 149, 154–6, 167–70; Baltic Sea Fleet

8, 11, 33, 41, 91; Bank of payments 115; Black Sea Fleet 11, 28; bureau in Petrograd 27; capital removal in 1918 22; Caucasian army 58; Civil War 2, 23, 30, 132, 140, 167; Committee 15, 21, 26, 29; Constitutional Democratic Party 17; diplomatic and economic blockade of 11, 86, 97; famine of 1920-2 124–5; front (see Eastern front); General Staff 27; gold reserve 106; Karelian Federation 25–6; Main Staff 43; Muslim Communist party 116; Naval General Staff 6, 49; North-West Army 92; Northern Federation 24; Orthodox Church 46, 103, 140; problem (question) 10, 14, 52, 77, 79, 82–3, 85, 103, 127, 132–3, 141, 167; Provisional government 5, 7–8, 24, 30, 93, 152; revolution of 1917 2; South-Eastern Union of 10; Soviet Socialist Federation (see Russia); 'spheres of responsibility' in 12–13; White armies 77
Russian-British relations scholarship of 1–2
Russkii Island 80
Russo-British convention of 1917 38
Russo-Japanese War 40
Russo-Turkish alliance 136–7
Rybinsk 33

Sabir 48
Sablin, Evgeny 80
Said Alim Khan 120
Samara 30
Samarkand 119
Sanders, Robert 96
San-Remo 112
Saracens 101
Saratov 97
Save the children of Central Europe fund 124
Savinkov, Boris 42, 44, 48, 105
Sazonov, Sergei 83
Scandinavian countries 123
Scotland Yard (Special Branch) 17, 98, 104, 156, 165
Scott, Charles 6, 31, 98
Sea of Marmara 76

Second Reich (see Germany)
Second World War 117, 137
Semenov, Grigory 31
Seton-Watson, Robert 12
Sevastopol 33, 72
Shakhovskoi, Dmitry 10
Shanghai 119
Shanghai Life 119
Shaumian, Stepan 55, 59–61, 63–9
Shaw, Bernard 150
Shtekel'man (Shtegel'man) 48
Shuckburgh, John 66
Siberia 21, 23, 29, 31–2, 37, 119, 123; Provisional government of 31
Silbert, William 82
Simla 62, 64, 67
Skoropadsky, Petr 24
Slavo-British legion 35
Smith, A. 49
Smith, Arthur 141
Smith-Cumming, Mansfield (C.) 40, 42, 46
Smolny Institute (Smolny) 9, 41
Smuts, Jan 12, 14, 31
SNK (see Council of People's commissars)
Snowden, Ethel 97
Snowden, Philip 5, 155
Socialist revolutionaries (party) 32, 37, 42, 46–7, 49, 61, 64
Sokol'nikov, Grigory 20, 29, 32
South Africans 60
Soviet-Afghan treaty of 1921
Soviet-British conference of 1924 155–8
Soviet-British trade talks of 1920–21 98–100
Soviet-British treaties of 1924 158
Soviet-Persian treaty of 1921
Soviet-Polish War 89, 94–6, 99, 100–3, 118
Spa: conference 95; declaration 96
Sprogis (Shmidkhen) 44
Srinagar 66
Stalin, Joseph 31, 54, 60, 65, 96, 110, 129, 139, 147–8, 156, 162, 165, 169
Steamship and Trading Corporation 165
Stefanovich, Georgy 66
Steffens, Louis 78
Stockholm 45, 92
Suffolk 32
Sun Yisian 119, 147
Suritz, Jakov 117

Svalbard Island 95
Sverdlov, Jakov 32
Sweden 92
Sydenham, Lord 69
Sykes-Picot agreement 54

Tabriz 59
Taganrog 81
Tallents, Stephen 91
Talleyrand, Charles Maurice 19
Tarsier, Mohammed 126
Tashkent 62, 65-8, 109, 116-18, 143; training center 69, 119
Teague-Jones, Reginald 62-5
Tehran 58, 112, 114, 126, 142, 145-6
Tejend-river 68
Ten-Year Rule 147
Terek-river 110
Teretschenko, Mikhail 7
Thames 149, 155
The Hague: 133; conference in 133-4, 167
The Times 9, 16, 25, 79, 104-5, 111, 118, 134, 147
The Truth About the Russian Revolution 71
Third republic (see France)
Thomas, Albert 28
Thomson, Basil 17, 71-2, 98
Thomson, William 61
Thurn, Donald im 165
Tibet 53-4
Tiflis (Tbilisi) 55, 58, 72, 154
Tikhon, Patriarch 46, 125, 140
The Times 9, 16, 25, 79, 104-5, 111, 118, 134, 147
To All Honest Citizens 124
To All the Laboring Class Moslems of Russia and the Orient 53
Tokyo 31
Tolstoi, Alexei 150
Tolstoism 9
Tomsk 31
Tomsky, Mikhail 163
Torretta, Pietro de la 36
Tours 101
Toynbee, Arnold 12, 115
Trade Union Congress (TUC) 65, 79, 97; national united council 143, 151; delegation visits to Soviet Russia in 1920 97; 1924 163

Trafalgar Square 143
Transcaspian government (see Ashgabat government)
Transcaspian province (Transcaspia) 38, 61, 113; executive committee of 61
Transcaucasia 20, 29, 37, 54-5, 59-60, 71, 79, 109-14, 136, 170
Transcaucasian Democratic Federation 55-6
Trans-Siberian railroad 11, 30, 32, 34
Treasury 17, 29, 45, 82, 85, 96, 111, 113
Treaty: of Riga 103, 107, 124; Sevres 112, 135; Unkiar Skelessi 136
Trevelyan, George 150
Troianovsky, Konstantin 68
Trotsky, Lev, People's commissar for foreign affairs 9-12, 15, 17, 19-21, 25; military and naval affairs 22, 24-9, 32, 34-8, 42, 47, 49, 52, 54, 77, 91, 95, 97, 100-1, 109-10, 115-19, 130, 142, 145, 148, 154, 156, 168
Tsar (see Nicholas II)
Tsaritsyn (Volgograd) 82, 113
Tuba-Karakhan Bay, battle in 113
Tukhachevsky, Mikhail 96
Turkestan 54, 61, 71-2, 110, 113, 118, 139; front 120; military district's counter-intelligence department 67; Red army 62, 113; Soviet Republic 65, 67, 112
Turkey (see also Ottoman empire) 99; Great National Assembly of 112
Turkish Communist party 135
Turkish Oil Company 112
Turkman 63
Turks 102
Turner, Benjamin 97

Ufa 49
Ukraine 10, 13, 15, 21, 24, 30, 50, 81, 91, 94, 96, 110, 123
Ukrainian People's Republic (see Ukraine)
Union for Protection of Motherland and Freedom 42
Unionists (see Britain, Conservative Party)
United States of America 37, 43, 50, 53, 68, 72, 77, 88, 90, 108, 112, 121, 124-5, 129, 154; Library of Congress 3;

Senate military committee 37; siding with the Entente 6, 11–12, 31; troops on the Russian territory 36
Ural-Kuznetsk republic 33
Urals (Ural region) 33, 37, 113, 118
Uritsky, Moses 41, 46
Urquhart, Leslie 29, 125–7, 134, 156–7
Uruguay 165
USSR (see Russia)

Vacetis, Joachim 27
Verkhoturie 49
Versailles: international (world) order (see also Versailles-Washington international system) 1, 82, 89, 110, 133, 151; treaty 92, 94
Veselago, Georgy 24
Vienna 18, 102
Villa: Alberti 130; Raggi 131
Vilna 94
Vimiera 100
Vistula, battle on 101–2, 104
Vladivostok 21, 29–32, 36–7, 40, 69, 80, 84, 140
Volga-river region 20, 51, 63, 82, 97, 113, 125
Volodarsky, Vladimir 46
Vologda 20, 24–5, 30, 36, 40
Vostok 110

'wait-and-see policy' 11
Wakhan Mountain Corridor 139
War Office 6, 8, 15, 24, 38, 45, 54, 58, 61, 71–2, 82, 91, 102, 111–13, 159
Wardrope, Robert 45
Warsaw 93–4, 100–3, 105
Washington 10, 13, 16, 47, 84; naval conference 127
Webb, Beatrice 11, 16, 18, 150; Sidney 150
Wedgwood, Josiah 66, 125
Weihaiwei 119
Weimar republic (see Germany)

Weinstein, Grigory 141–2, 144, 146
Wells, Herbert 150, 168
Western front 6, 27–8, 32, 39
Westminster (see British Parliament)
Whirlwinds Hostile 50
White Finnish troops 26
White guards 49, 140
White Russians 23, 93, 145, 162, 164–5
Whitechapel 103
Whitehall (see British government)
William II (see also Kaiser) 7, 35
Wilson, Henry 71, 73, 82, 84–5, 115
Wilson, Woodrow 6, 14, 31, 36, 74, 76, 79
Wise, Edward 86, 127
Workers' international famine relief committee 125
Workers' Weekly 157
World 140
Worowski, Waclaw 137, 142
Worthington-Evans, Laming 130
Wrangel, Petr 93–4, 98–9, 105

Xinjiang 120

Younger, Lord 164
York 140
Yorkshire infantry regiment 62
Young, Douglas 25
Yudenich, Nikolai 91–4
Yuon, Konstantin 150
Yuriev, Alexei 26

Z. (air) squadron 81
Zakrevskaiya, Maria (Mura) 44, 50
Zalkind, Ivan, special mission to Britain in 1918 18
Zinoviev, Gregory 9, 48–9, 77, 79, 118, 121, 129, 143, 145, 149, 156, 159–65, 168
'Zinoviev letter' (see also Comintern letter, Red letter) 159–66, 168–9

www.ingramcontent.com/pod-product-compliance
Lightning Source LLC
Chambersburg PA
CBHW052215300426
44115CB00011B/1695